Methods in Mind

Cognitive Neuroscience
Michael S. Gazzaniga, editor

Gary Lynch, *Synapses, Circuits and the Beginning of Memory*

Barry E. Stein and M. Alex Meredith, *The Merging of the Senses*

Richard B. Ivry and Lynn C. Robertson, *The Two Sides of Perception*

Steven J. Luck, *An Introduction to the Event-Related Potential Technique*

Roberto Cabeza and Alan Kingstone, eds., *Handbook of Functional Neuroimaging of Cognition*

Carl Senior, Tamara Russell, and Michael S. Gazzaniga, eds., *Methods in Mind*

Methods in Mind

edited by Carl Senior, Tamara Russell, and Michael S. Gazzaniga

The MIT Press
Cambridge, Massachusetts
London, England

MIT Press books may be purchased at special quantity discounts for business or sales promotional use. For information, please email special_sales@mitpress.mit. edu or write to Special Sales Department, The MIT Press, 55 Hayward Street, Cambridge, MA 02142.

This book was set in Sabon by SNP Best-set Typesetter Ltd., Hong Kong and was printed and bound in the United States of America.

Library of Congress Cataloging-in-Publication Data

Methods in mind / edited by Carl Senior, Tamara Russell, and Michael S. Gazzaniga.
    p. cm.—(Cognitive neuroscience)
ISBN 10: 0-262-19541-0   ISBN 13: 978-0-262-19541-6 (hbk. : alk. paper)
1. Cognitive neuroscience. 2. Magnetic brain stimulation. 3. Neuropharmacology. 4. Developmental psychology. I. Senior, Carl. II. Russell, Tamara. III. Gazzaniga, Michael S. IV. Series.

QP360.5.M48 2006
612.8′233—dc22

                                                              2005056124

10 9 8 7 6 5 4 3 2 1

Contents

Preface: Cognitive Neuroscience: The Evolution of a Discipline

Many years have passed since Phineas Gage lost his frontal lobes and gained his unusual kind of fame. Thanks in no small part to this man's unfortunate accident, we now have an unparalleled understanding of the role of the frontal lobes specifically and cortical function in general. Our insatiable thirst for knowledge about cognitive behavior has driven the development of increasingly sophisticated tools to study human cognition; as investigative methods have developed and cognitive processes have been explicated, cognitive neuroscience has flourished and evolved.

In the "early days," studies linking brain activity to a particular behavioral response filled the pages of many respectable journals. Examination of the hemodynamic response to motion perception, to tool naming, and so on, aided by evidence from comparative studies, laid the crucial foundation for the application of the tools that were to come.

Scientific findings are strengthened when evidence from comparative approaches or techniques converges. In the case of cognitive neuroscience, empirical support and convergent evidence have come not only from studies of nonhuman primates but also from further afield. Indeed, the gradual convergence of other approaches under the rubric of cognitive neuroscience continues to this day. The book you now hold in your hands contains chapters written by leading authorities in the field who were given the express mandate to describe how their respective techniques could be integrated with a range of other tools neuroscientists have at their disposal.

Thus Peter Bandettini (chapter 9) describes the possible routes we can take to link together the hemodynamic response with other measurable indices such as the galvanic skin response (GSR). This symbiotic relationship is elaborated by Nasir Naqvi and Antoine Bechara (chapter 5), who explore how the GSR can be used to address higher cognitive functions such as decision making. Krish Singh (chapter 12) details alternative uses of the fMRI signal to constrain magnetoencephalography, thereby allowing us to better understand spatial, temporal, and frequency information mediating neural activity. Gina Rippon (chapter 10) highlights the potential benefit of using electroencephalography (EEG) to guide application of transcranial magnetic stimulation (TMS), enabling us to create a virtual lesion not only at a particular cortical site but also at a specific frequency. Lauren Stewart and Vincent Walsh (chapter 1) elaborate on other applications of the TMS technique.

Given the gathering consensus in the neuroscience community that differences in the frequency of neuronal oscillations are the "cognitive footprint" of a particular task, selective disruption at a given frequency will allow us to test the necessity of a cortical network at two distinct levels of analysis. The importance of modeling and interrogating cortical networks is driven home by Glyn Humphreys, Dietmar Heinke, and Eun Young Yoon (chapter 4).

We would be seriously remiss if we were to neglect the equally crucial role of innovation in the evolution of cognitive neuroscience. Indeed, in the last decade or so there has been a veritable explosion of innovation. A working knowledge of other techniques and what they can bring to the neuroscience debate will fuel this innovation. Phillip Shaw and Anthony David (chapter 2) draw together clinical psychiatry, psychology, and neurology in their discussion of cognitive neuropsychiatry. Elisabeth Murray and Mark Baxter (chapter 3) and Robert Wurtz and Marc Sommer (chapter 6) remind us to appreciate the full importance of the study of nonhuman primates and how they can inform the study of human cognition.

The continued evolution of cognitive neuroscience is also driven by innovative applications of particular techniques. To ensure that such applications be made transparent, the contributors to this volume were given a second mandate, to report on innovation in their respective specialist fields.

As John Henderson (chapter 8) makes clear, the study of eye movements can do much to help us understand how visual attention drives what enters our complex cognitive system. Venkata Mattay, Andreas Meyer-Lindenberg, and Daniel Weinberger (chapter 11) report on the successful convergence of neuroimaging and genetic analysis, and discuss the creative potential of this fairly novel technique. Stephen Hall and Peyman Adjamian (chapter 13) examine the chemical underpinnings of cognitive processes.

Many of these new neuroscience approaches clearly require, and have only been made possible in latter years by, a dramatic increase in computing power. With this in mind, Jack Van Horn and colleagues (chapter 7) describe how distributed or Grid computing allows us to analyze massive data sets in cyberspace.

Clearly, the future of cognitive neuroscience looks exciting. We hope this book lets you see the potential of convergent technologies and share in this excitement. We are grateful to Barbara Murphy and Kate Blakinger of MIT Press for their tireless efforts (and for putting up with an endless barrage of emails).

Methods in Mind

1 Transcranial Magnetic Stimulation in Human Cognition

Lauren Stewart and Vincent Walsh

Why Have So Many Different Techniques?

The many different ways one can now investigate human brain function allow one to take snapshots of structure and function from different perspectives. The particular snapshot one sees is determined by the temporal and spatial resolution of the technique being used and by whether one is recording activity from the brain or trying to interfere with or stimulate the brain to change stimulus processing or behavioral responses. The relative spatial and temporal resolutions of various neuroimaging and recording techniques at one's disposal are vast. But the claimed resolution of a technique is only a partial guide to its utility. One might consider that the higher the spatial resolution, the more precise and therefore fundamental is a measure. One might also think that sampling brain activity at millisecond resolution is self-evidently better than doing so in longer time windows. A consequence of thinking in this way is that one expects the results obtained using different techniques to converge on explanations of sensory and cognitive function, and that there is, in some sense, a hierarchy of explanation dependent on spatial and temporal specificity. If we examine this somewhat optimistic and simplistic view, it is easily found wanting, at least at our current state of knowledge of cognitive architecture and neural functions. The correct level at which to examine brain function depends on what one wants to know, and what one wants to know depends on what is already believed. Richard Feynman made this point with disarming honesty; theories, he explained, differ in two ways: first, either you like them or you don't (a good way to choose between most things); and second, different theories make you look for different things when making predictions. In the context of cognitive neuroscience, we can translate this to mean, for example, that if one believes that single-unit responses are evidence of mechanisms, then one will tend to make predictions that posit other localized mechanisms. At a different level of neural recording, if one believes that cognitive functions are widely distributed and can only be examined in terms of brain activation across different brain sites simultaneously, then one will embark on whole-brain imaging and find distributed networks of task-related activity. The two different approaches *can* yield evidence that is convergent, but there is no reason to believe they actually will. And if there is such a reason, we have to ask why have both approaches in our armory? Comparing the findings from imaging and lesion studies can also yield converging findings but the differences may be important. In the number domain, for example, brain-imaging studies consistently show that both the right and left parietal cortices are activated in numerical tasks, whereas neuropsychological deficits tend to follow only left-hemisphere damage. This is an example of nonconverging evidence, most often treated as a problem to be solved—but there is no law to state that measuring behavior in a brain-damaged subject should be directly comparable to measuring brain activity in a healthy undergraduate; indeed, by insisting on convergence, we may discard valuable knowledge from the differences. The same is true in the temporal domain: the millisecond resolution of transcranial magnetic stimulation is clearly an important addition to the portfolio of human lesion analysis because patients undergo brain reorganization and often have multiple deficits. Even so, it would be naive to think that short-term lesions are always more informative than long-term lesions, or that reorganization is always an impediment to understanding. The two lesion methods can be expected to yield informatively different findings. Some techniques that the cognitive neuroscientist has at his or her disposal record brain activity, whereas others depend on interfering with it or using the consequences of damage to study function. These different techniques differ not merely in space and time but also in how they can be used to make inferences about the brain. Take, for example, functional, magnetic resonance imaging (fMRI), in which one obtains differential activation maps of brain areas in two or more tasks. Do these activation maps signal that these brain areas are necessary or sufficient for the particular task for which they are found? Of course, the answer is no. The activations observed may reflect what the brain may be expecting or planning to do next with the stimulus delivered. Thus, if subjects are asked to identify or discriminate the sound of a musical instrument, a tool, or a door slamming shut, activation in auditory cortex will be accompanied by activation in the visual cortex. This need not signify the importance of the visual cortex in auditory discriminations; rather, it may signify that visual and auditory cortices work in concert to make predictions about the world—and, indeed, subjects are faster to detect or identify visual objects if they have been primed by the sound of that object. The simple point is that unless you understand the initial brain state perfectly (you don't), and unless you understand the cognitive architecture of the tasks being used perfectly (you don't, or you wouldn't be doing an experiment), the strongest statement you can make about data from human brain imaging studies is that activity is correlated with the particular tasks demands used. The issue is not trivial, even with such a fundamental feature of human sensory processing as color, small differences in stimulation and response parameters have shown that many different areas outside the striate cortex may respond to color stimuli, although it is not clear that any of them are more critical for color perception than any of the others. One of the uses of transcranial magnetic stimulation (TMS) is to test whether the activations in imaging studies indicate that an area is necessary for a task or activated for some other reason (what is meant by "necessary" is discussed below). Using TMS to test the claims of brain-imaging studies is open to question, however, and it would be misleading to suggest that TMS always establishes a causal relationship between focal activity and task performance or that brain-imaging results always need to be tested by a lesion method. And, in the absence of imaging, we may not know at which sites TMS may be having its main effects on a task because an effect may sometimes be due to secondary activation of cortex at a site connected to that directly stimulated.

We may seem to be giving a negative message: faster or smaller spatial sampling isn't always better; brain activations may be misleading; TMS effects may be due to secondary activations; techniques shouldn't necessarily give converging evidence. In the face of claims based on spatial and temporal resolution, however, it seems necessary to establish why we have so many different techniques, how they do and do not lead in the same direction. Each of these different techniques can best be thought of as inhabiting a distinct problem space. We may expect differences in the results obtained when questions are posed from within these different problem spaces. Our goal in this chapter is to show that TMS occupies one of these problem spaces uniquely and, as such, can address questions within sensory, motor, and cognitive neuroscience that can be addressed in no other way. This situation is not unique to TMS, of course, but in considering why we have so many different techniques for investigating the brain, we can answer the question of why we use any one technique in particular.

Principles

Transcranial magnetic stimulation is based on Faraday's principle of electromagnetic induction. A brief current pulse flowing through a coil of wire will generate a magnetic field. The rate of change of this field determines the induction of a secondary current in any nearby conducting body. In TMS, a current is passed through the stimulating coil held close to a subject's head over the brain region one wishes to stimulate; in this form of induction, the nearby secondary conductor happens to be the human brain—one is stimulating neurons, just as one might stimulate a secondary coil. Figure 1.1 shows a schematic diagram of a typical TMS machine used in cognitive neuroscience experiments. The sequence of events in applying TMS is shown in figure 1.2. The current is discharged into a circular or figure-of-eight coil, which produces the TMS pulse of up to 2 tesla. This pulse has a short rise time of between 100 and 200 μsec and a typical duration of less than one millisecond. The induction of an electric field in the neural tissue causes neural activity, which operates as the "lesion" induced by TMS. This process has been described as "creating virtual patients," "inducing virtual lesions," or the "induction of neural noise." Of the two pulse types used in TMS, monophasic and biphasic, the latter is important in repetitive TMS (rTMS) because of energy efficiency, but in a virtual lesion paradigm, the two types have similar behavioral effects (see Barker, 1999; Walsh and Pascual-Leone, 2003). What is important here is how to think of the effects of TMS.

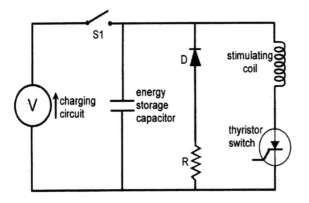

Figure 1.1
Schematic diagram of a standard (single-pulse) magnetic nerve stimulator. (From Barker, 1999, with permission)

The behavioral consequences of TMS-induced neural activity depend on the context and the region over which TMS is applied. Some apparently productive or generative effects of TMS can be seen when stimulation is applied over the primary visual or motor cortex. When applied over primary motor cortex, TMS can produce muscular activity such as an observable twitch. Systematic movement of the coil from the midline in a lateral direction results in a change in the affected muscle group, from the shoulder, to the wrist, the hand, the fingers, and, most laterally, the face, in accordance with the somatotopic representation of body parts in the motor cortex. Similarly, when applied over visual cortex, TMS generates phosphenes—brief flashes of light perceived by the subject in the absence of any external visual stimulus. Small movements of the coil result in a change in the spatial location at which the phosphene appears in the visual field, in accordance with the retinotopic organization of primary visual cortex. These TMS effects can be used to study excitatory and inhibitory pathways, especially in the motor cortex (e.g., Mills, 1999). More commonly, in cognitive neuroscience experiments, TMS is applied as a subject performs a sensory, motoric, or cognitive task of interest. In this context, the induced neural activity over a cortical area that is known to be involved in the task can be described as constituting "neural noise," which interferes with the coordinated neural processing required for the task and results in a decrement in task performance (increased reaction times, error rates, shifts in a psychometric function). Used in this way, TMS simulates the effect of a lesion in neuropsychological patients, with the important difference that the interference is transient and spatially specific.

Why?

The virtual lesion metaphor for TMS emphasizes its utility in revealing causal connections between the brain and behavior. Although "real" neuropsychology also permits causal inferences to be drawn, it is constrained by several inherent limitations to which TMS is not subject. First, it must deal with neuropsychological patients whose lesions are rarely focal, and whose behavioral deficits, likewise, rarely occur in isolation. In contrast, TMS can be targeted at specific cortical areas and can be used in several tasks to test for specific behavioral deficits. Second, neuropsychology must deal with patients whose damaged brains may have reorganized and, depending on the length of time between the injury and the testing, may have adopted compensatory neural and cognitive strategies. The study

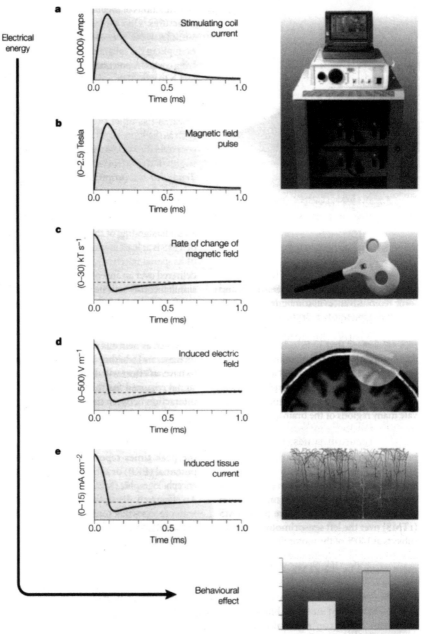

Figure 1.2

Sequence of events in TMS. An electrical current of up to 8 kA is generated by a capacitor and discharged into a circular or figure of eight–shaped coil, which in turn produces a magnetic pulse of up to 2 T. The pulse has a rise time of approximately 200 μsec and a duration of 1 msec and due to its intensity and brevity changes at a rapid rate. The changing magnetic field generates an electric field resulting in neural of neuropsychological patients thus may reveal more about the abnormal than the normal brain. In contrast, the effects of TMS are too brief for functional reorganization to occur. Third, neuropsychological researchers must compare their patients' performance in the presence of lesion effects to that of a control group of neurologically normal subjects without such effects. In contrast, subjects in TMS studies can act as their own controls, performing a task with and without stimulation.

Although TMS allows researchers to test anatomical hypotheses that may arise from neuroimaging studies (is the activation in area X necessary for task performance, or is it merely incidental or secondary to activation in another area?), TMS also has many other applications. It can provide a measure of the excitability of different cortical areas; it can probe the time course of an area's involvement in a task; it can chart relative changes in brain function with development, learning, or relearning (such as after a stroke); and, finally, it can reveal dynamic functional interactions within the brain.

Perhaps here we should state what is meant by testing whether a brain region is "necessary" for performing a task. If one considers the neural activity induced by TMS as highly unlikely to be organized in the pattern necessary for the brain area being stimulated to make its normal contribution to a task, one can consider such induced activity to act as "neural noise." By analogy, say visual white noise is added to a display during a visual identification task. With a little noise added, the subject may not immediately make misidentifications but may take longer to identify the target. As the noise level is increased, the time required to identify the target also increases. Only when the noise level is substantially increased are subjects likely to start making errors. In other words, introducing noise to a signal is more likely to slow down correct performance than to force errors. Can a reaction time deficit without an error deficit be considered as evidence that the stimulated area is "necessary" to perform the task ("necessary" meaning "necessary for *normal performance*")? If it can, and if the induced neural noise slows down performance, then we can consider it to have induced an abnormal performance and thus to have demonstrated that the stimulated area is necessary for normal performance.

Figure 1.2
(continued)
activity or changes in resting potentials. The net change in charge density in the cortex is zero. Although the pulse shown here is a monophasic pulse, in repetitive TMS (*rTMS*) studies, the waveform will be a train of sinewave pulses that allow repeated stimulation. (Adapted from Walsh and Cowey, 2000)

How, When, and Where to Stimulate

There are several decisions to be made when designing a TMS experiment. Because TMS in its disruptive or virtual lesion mode is the most common application of TMS in cognitive neuroscience, it is on this mode that we will concentrate. The first decision is likely to concern the choice of dependent variable. TMS can slow manual or saccadic reaction times, can increase error rates, and, in the case of speech production, can cause a distortion or cessation of the output. On the other hand, TMS can also cause a change in bias in a task, making signal detection analysis appropriate in some cases. It is impossible to know, a priori, which dependent variable to use; the only guidance one can suggest is to pay attention to previous TMS experiments and to pilot experiments extensively. With this in mind, it is worth noting that a failure to obtain an effect in a TMS experiment may be due to an incorrect choice of task or dependent variable rather than a true null result.

All TMS experiments must have a neuroanatomical hypothesis. Although they may also include a temporal hypothesis or a hypothesis about functional connectivity, the most basic issue they must test is whether stimulation over area X will affect function Y. It is therefore necessary to ascertain where on the subject's scalp one should place the TMS coil. There are several ways this can be done. One way is to use the electroencephalography (EEG) coordinates and to stimulate at the 10–20 EEG electrode sites (see Rippon, chapter 10, this volume). Although this has been successful in many TMS experiments, one would not of course expect a direct correspondence between EEG electrode sites and underlying brain anatomy. A more precise method is to obtain a functional magnetic resonance imaging (fMRI) scan of the brain of a subject and to mark the scalp with landmarks that will be visible on the scan. This allows a degree of coregistration between coil placement and brain anatomy, which can be improved if one uses available TMS fMRI coregistration software that tracks the location of the coil relative to the subject's head. This method guarantees accurate stimulation of the cortical surface. Accuracy can be enhanced by using prespecified fMRI coordinates with the same subjects in the TMS and fMRI experiments.

On the other hand, these anatomical methods may not be necessary. If one can define an area by its function, one can accurately stimulate a region. This was first shown by Ashbridge, Walsh, and Cowey (1997), who devised a hunting procedure to locate the region on the scalp most likely to be involved in conjunction visual search. Stewart et al. (1999) developed the method of moving phosphenes to identify human V5 (now a standard procedure). The use of functional localization however, demands that one knows a good deal about what one is looking for and where to find it. Once a stimulation site is chosen, questions arise as to how wide and how deep the current will spread. Using PET, Paus and colleagues (Paus et al. 1997, 1998; Paus and Wolforth, 1998; Paus, 1999) showed that TMS has a primary effect roughly below the center of a figure-of-eight coil and secondary effects at anatomically connected sites. Similarly, using EEG, Ilmoniemi et al. (1997) showed that stimulation over visual or motor cortex elicits EEG responses around the site of stimulation within a few milliseconds of TMS, followed by responses from a secondary area of activity in the homotopic region of the contralateral hemisphere. Regarding the depth of stimulation, models of the TMS electric field at different depths from the coil suggest that the area of stimulation has an egg-shaped profile and progressively shrinks with distance from the coil (Barker, 1999).

The more relevant issue for cognitive neuroscience, however, is functional rather than physiological focality. Although we will never know in a TMS experiment exactly where the current ceases, either in depth or breadth, we can define the functional region—the functional specificity—of a TMS pulse. For example, consider a TMS experiment that induces a phosphene by stimulating over the occipital cortex. If one moves the coil slightly and a phosphene is now produced, say 2 degrees of visual angle away, we can infer that the stimulation has a functional range of 2 degrees in the cortex. What has been called "leaky current," then, namely, lateral spread beyond target of stimulation, is rarely a problem in TMS experiments (for a particularly good example of dissociating anatomically adjacent sites, see Rushworth, Ellison, and Walsh, 2001). The second type of spread one needs to consider is connectional spread. If one stimulates the parietal cortex, it is highly likely that there will be secondary stimulation of an area connected to the parietal cortex, for example, the frontal eye field (FEF) or extrastriate cortex. Where connectional spread is being studied, the secondary activations are not an impediment to the experiment; rather, they are a good guide as to which site to choose for a control site.

The next decision after where to stimulate is when—and how long—to stimulate (see figure 1.3). The commonest type of TMS experiment uses stimulation online to disrupt neural processing during task performance. A single TMS pulse lasts for approximately one millisecond and its neural effects typically for only a few milliseconds. Except when one is attempting to affect a process within a short time window or when one has an idea of the time course of the area of interest in the task being used, it will often be sufficient to use a train of pulses. Since there are limits to the number

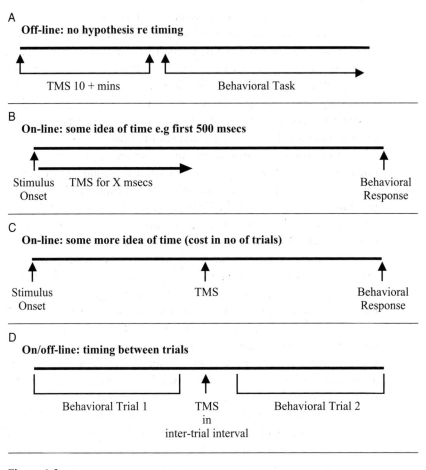

A

Off-line: no hypothesis re timing

TMS 10 + mins   Behavioral Task

B

On-line: some idea of time e.g first 500 msecs

Stimulus   TMS for X msecs   Behavioral
Onset   Response

C

On-line: some more idea of time (cost in no of trials)

Stimulus   TMS   Behavioral
Onset   Response

D

On/off-line: timing between trials

Behavioral Trial 1   TMS   Behavioral Trial 2
                            in
                  inter-trial interval

Figure 1.3
Different temporal uses of TMS.

of pulses and the length of a train of pulses (for safety and practical reasons—for example, overheating of coils), the interval between task onset and response should be short, typically, less than a second. Using a train of pulses over the entire period between task onset and response processing in the targeted area, one will, in theory, disrupt normal processing throughout the stimulation period. If there is a TMS effect, such as an increase in reaction times (RTs), one can then use repetitive TMS (rTMS) to narrow down the time window of investigation as shown in figure 1.3.

An alternative type of TMS experiment uses stimulation off-line, applying TMS for several minutes before a task; any TMS effect is interpreted to be due to the residual physiological changes caused by stimulation. For example, Chen et al. (1997) have shown that low-frequency TMS (1–3 Hz) decreases cortical excitability. On the other hand, the effects of off-line stimulation are, by definition, more indirect; as Pascual-Leone et al. (1999) have shown, these effects vary as a function of the stimulation parameters used and the cortical areas stimulated.

Another way TMS can be used, one that may be of particular interest to cognitive neuroscientists, is to stimulate during the intertrial interval in a block of tasks. This mode of stimulation is especially useful in the context of priming experiments, where the performance on a given trial may be influenced by the content of a prior trial. When applied between trials, TMS can disrupt the processes of short-term memory or consolidation (Campana, Cowey, and Walsh, 2002).

After deciding where, when, and how long to stimulate, one must also decide how much stimulation to give with each pulse and how often to apply these pulses. Safety guidelines provide some constraints. There is a trade-off between intensity, duration, and frequency. Intensity guidelines recommend applying stimulation at a fixed percentage of a subject's motor threshold, that is, the amount of TMS required to elicit a motor-evoked potential (MEP) of at least $50\,\mu V$ on 50 percent of trials). In this way, the level of stimulation is presumed to be calibrated to an individual's cortical excitability, although previous studies (Stewart, Walsh and Rothwell, 2001) have shown a lack of correlation between the level of excitability in different cortical areas. When rTMS is used, 10–15 Hz has become the typical rate at which stimulation is delivered over 500 msec.

It is important to control for the nonspecific effects of TMS, such as arousal caused by the auditory click produced on pulse discharge or the involuntary muscle twitches that can be produced by TMS. A control site presumed not to be involved in the experimental task should therefore be stimulated to ensure that any changes in performance can be compared with TMS over the site being studied. A control task, to which the area being studied does not contribute, should also be given to subjects under the same stimulation conditions. This will allow experimenters to conclude that area A is important for task X, but not for task Y, and that area B is not important for task X. The use of a task control and a site control should be considered a prerequisite for a good behavioral TMS experiment.

Innovation

To illustrate the innovative uses of TMS we have selected experiments that deploy TMS to explore psychological models, to make spatial predictions about a brain area, to make timing predictions about an area, and to elucidate the temporal interactions between two or more areas. These experiments have been chosen because their generic methodology can, in principle, be transferred to the study of any cognitive system.

The first TMS experiments to explore a psychological model were carried out by Amassian et al. (1989, 1993), who used TMS in the virtual lesion mode to probe the cortical basis of visual masking. In their first experiment, Amassian and colleagues presented subjects with small, low-contrast trigrams and required them to identify each of the three letters. Using a round coil approximately 2 cm above the inion, they delivered TMS pulses once every trial at a trigram-TMS onset asynchrony of between 0 and 200 msec. They demonstrated that, when delivered between 80 and 100 msec after the onset of the visual stimulus, TMS abolished the ability to identify the letters (figure 1.4). They further demonstrated the retinotopic specificity of the effect by moving the coil first to the left and then to the right, disrupting the report of letters on the right, then left of a horizontal trigram, and by moving the coil first upward and then downward, disrupting the report of lower, then upper letters of a vertical trigram. They extended the experiment to a classic masking paradigm, reasoning that it should be possible to demonstrate that, when the subjects were presented with competing inputs, disruption of one of those inputs should enhance the processing of the other. When subjects were presented with a trigram followed 100 msec later by a masking trigram, the presentation of this second trigram reduced their ability to report the letters in the first. By applying TMS over the occipital cortex after the presentation of the second

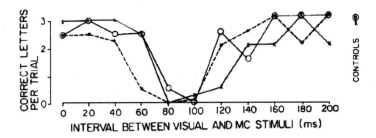

Figure 1.4
Visual suppression of trigrams by TMS. The proportion of correct identifications of three briefly flashed dark letters on a bright background is plotted as a function of the delay between stimulus onset and the application of TMS over occipital visual cortex. The magnetic stimulation was delivered with a round coil. (From Amassian et al., 1989, with permission)

trigram, however, Amassian and colleagues were able to reinstate the subjects' trigram report performance (figure 1.5): TMS had masked the mask. This is a remarkable example of how TMS can be used within the context of a psychological model with a specific temporal hypothesis.

Following the success of Amassian and colleagues in probing the neurochronometry of one psychological task, Ashbridge, Walsh, and Cowey (1997) used TMS to test the role of the posterior parietal cortex (PPC) in visual search. Lying on the dorsolateral surface of the cortex, posterior parietal cortex is easily accessible to TMS. To model the effects of lesions to this region, they stimulated the PPC while subjects carried out feature and conjunction visual search tasks (figure 1.6). Patients with PPC lesions are impaired on conjunction but not on feature tasks, a finding that underpins the view that the posterior parietal cortex is important for visual feature binding. Although Ashbridge, Walsh, and Cowey sought to replicate this finding, their experiment also gave rise to different findings. When they applied single-pulse TMS on each trial at a search array–TMS asynchrony of between 0 and 200 msec, subjects showed two patterns of effects: there was no effect on the simple feature trials, but an increase in reaction times on the conjunction trials. When subjects were reporting the target was

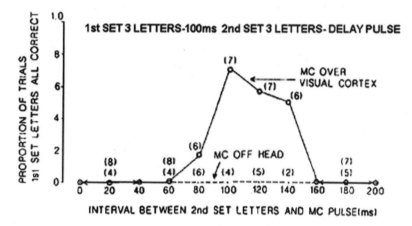

Figure 1.5
Masking of the first trigram produced by the presentation of a second trigram can be unmasked when the second trigram is suppressed by TMS. The proportion of trials in which the subjects correctly reported all the letters of the first trigram is presented as a function of the delay between the presentation of the second trigram and the TMS pulse. In parentheses are the numbers of trials with TMS (top) and with sham TMS (bottom). (From Amassian et al., 1993, with permission)

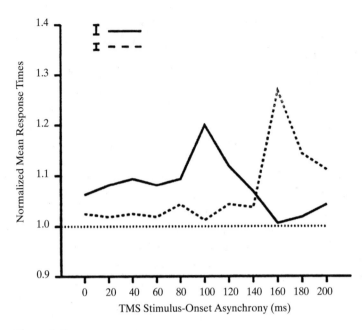

Figure 1.6
Effects of TMS, applied over the right posterior parietal cortex of naive subjects on a conjunction visual search task (with 8 stimuli in the array). Data are normalized to the reaction time on trials when search was performed without TMS. There is a clear effect of TMS on trials both when the target was present with the pulse delivered 100 msec after stimulus onset and when the target was absent with the pulse delivered 160 msec after target onset. Solid line indicates target present; broken line, target absent. Vertical bars represent ±1 standard error. (From Walsh, Ashbridge, and Cowey, 1998, with permission)

present, TMS had its maximal effect when applied around 100 msec after array onset, but when they were reporting that the target was absent, the maximal effect of TMS was around 160 msec after array onset. On the one hand, their findings replicated the neuropsychological patient data—PPC damage impairs conjunction but not feature search. On the other, they went beyond these data in two important respects. They found, first, that the PPC is important for target-absent responses, a finding that speaks against the PPC's importance for feature binding because on target-absent trials there is, of course, no target to be bound. Second, they found that the contribution of the PPC in conjunction search occupies different time windows on target-present and target-absent trials—indeed, these time windows were locked to subjects' reaction times, suggesting that the role of posterior parietal cortex is tied to response programming rather than any visual process such as binding (see also Ellison, Rushworth and Walsh, 2003; Rosenthal et al., forthcoming).

Amassian et al. (1989, 1993) and Ashbridge, Walsh, and Cowey (1997) used single-pulse TMS because they had specific temporal hypotheses. But unless one knows exactly when one wants to stimulate, single-pulse TMS can be very time consuming and difficult to achieve; indeed, in the absence of a temporal hypothesis, repetitive TMS can be used to good effect. Typically, TMS is applied for 500 msec at the onset of a task. As figure 1.4 shows, it can be used to define a time window for further exploration. There are now many examples of using rTMS to disrupt cognitive functions. Pascual-Leone, Gates, and Dhuna (1991) induced speech arrest by stimulating over the left frontal lobe of a population of subjects awaiting surgery for epilepsy. Pascual-Leone, Grafman, and Hallett (1994) induced extinction effects by stimulating over the parietal lobe; their work has been extended by Fierro et al. (2000) using 1 Hz off-line stimulation, and by Bjoertomt, Cowey, and Walsh (2002) and Oliveri et al. (1999a). Oliveri and colleagues, for example, delivered single-pulse TMS to the right posterior parietal cortex between 20 and 40 msec after bimanual stimulation of the fingers, which interfered with both ipsilateral and contralateral tactile detection, whereas delivering TMS over the same site 50 msec before the application of the right tactile stimulation led to an increase in sensitivity to the ipsilateral tactile stimuli. This can be interpreted as evidence that right-hemisphere stimulation can cause a disinhibition of the left hemisphere and result in improved performance (see also Walsh et al., 1998; Hilgetag, Theoret and Pascual-Leone, 2001; Rushworth, Ellison, and Walsh, 2001; Oliveri and Calvo, 2003).

Few studies have capitalized on the ability of transcranial magnetic stimulation to interfere with speech; indeed, the use of TMS to investigate language functions remains relatively unexplored territory. Among those few studies, however, Epstein et al. (1999), Bartres-Faz et al. (1999), and Stewart et al. (2001) have all induced speech arrest in nonneurological populations. Although the Epstein study suggested that the effect was due to interference with the motor cortex, the Bartres-Faz and Stewart studies clearly showed that motor effects could be dissociated from the effects of stimulating speech-related regions in the frontal lobe. Bartres-Faz et al., 1999, and Stewart et al., 2001, locate the critical area for TMS stimulation to disrupt speech to be over the middle frontal gyrus, dorsal to the inferior frontal gyrus, and are thus in agreement with lesion studies (Rostomily et al., 1991), human electrical stimulation studies (Penfield and Roberts, 1959; Ojemann and Mateer, 1979; Ojemann, 1983), and PET studies (Ingvar,

1983). On the basis of findings in brain-imaging studies, Stewart et al. (2000) tested the hypothesis that Brodmann area (BA) 37 is important for object naming and phonological retrieval. Repetitive TMS was applied over the posterior region of BA 37 of the right and left hemispheres and over the vertex. Stimulation of BA 37 impaired performance on picture naming but not on word reading, nonword reading, or color naming. Thus, with respect to object encoding and naming, the posterior region of BA 37 would seem to be important for recognition. Topper et al. (1998) applied single-pulse TMS over Wernicke's area prior to picture presentation and, some-what paradoxically, found that this improved the speed of picture naming. The effect was specific to task and area; they concluded that TMS "is able to facilitate lexical processes due to a general pre-activation of language-related neuronal networks when delivered over Wernicke's area" (Topper et al., 1998: 372). While these effects are intriguing, they raise the general question of why TMS should have facilitatory effects within a system, a question we will return to later.

TMS has been used to study awareness by stimulating the brains of both neuropsychological patients and nonneuropsychological subjects alike with two coils to selectively produce and interfere with perception. To examine the role of the visual cortex in awareness in a totally retinally blind subject who had suffered damage to the optic nerves but had an intact visual cortex, in a blindsight subject with a hemianopia caused by damage to striate cortex, and in normally sighted individuals, Cowey and Walsh (2000) induced phosphenes with TMS. They easily elicited vivid phosphenes from the blind and the normally sighted subjects when they applied TMS over the occipital pole and moving phosphenes when they applied TMS over MT/V5. In contrast, despite extensive and intensive stimulation of an intact MT/V5 in the damaged hemisphere of the hemianopic subject, they were unable to elicit any phosphenes. Thus the experience of motion seems to depend on an intact striate cortex. Pascual-Leone and Walsh (2001) reasoned that, if V1 was important for visual awareness of motion, it should be possible to show that V1 stimulation can disrupt perceptions caused by activity in MT/V5. They stimulated MT/V5 to produce a perception of motion and followed this with subthreshold stimulation over V1. If the V1 stimulation was between approximately 10 and 40 msec after the MT/V5 stimulation the perception of the moving phosphene induced by TMS over MT/V5 was degraded or abolished (figure 1.7), consistent with the hypothesis that awareness is medi-ated by backprojections from extrastriate to striate cortex (see also Silvanto et al., 2005). Silvanto, Lavie, and Walsh (2005) extended this work to show

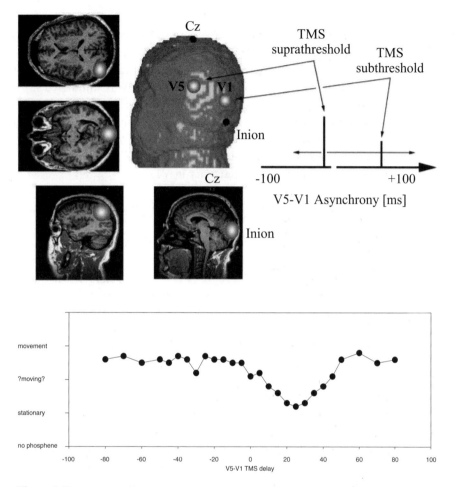

Figure 1.7
V5-V1 backprojections and the perception of motion. The brain MRI image from
one of the study subjects displays a representative example of the site of stimulation for induction of stationary (V1) and moving phosphenes (MT/V5). The location on the subject's scalp of the center of the intersection of the wings in the Figure
of eight–shaped TMS coil is projected perpendicularly to the scalp surface, onto
the subject's brain as reconstructed from an anatomical MRI. (*Bottom*) Mean
responses of all subjects (*n* = 8) to combined stimulation of V5 and V1. The V5-
V1-TMS asynchrony is displayed on the *x*-axis: negative values indicate that V1
received TMS prior to V5, and positive values indicate that V1 was stimulated after
V5. The subjects made one of four judgments about the phosphene elicited by V5
TMS: (1) present and moving; (2) present but subject uncertain whether moving;
(3) present but stationary; or (4) absent (no phosphene observed). TMS over V1
between 10 and 30 msec after TMS over V5 affected the perception of the
phosphene. (Adapted from Pascual-Leone and Walsh, 2001)

that not only is V1 important in the circuitry of awareness but that the level of activity in V1 determines awareness. Silvanto and colleagues applied subthreshold stimulation over MT/V5, followed by either supra- or subthreshold stimulation over V1. When MT/V5 was stimulated subthreshold, subjects had no perception of motion; when V1 was stimulated suprathreshold, they perceived a small, stationary phosphene. When the MT/V5 subthreshold stimulation was followed by a V1 suprathreshold pulse, subjects perceived a moving phosphene that was larger than the one they perceived with V1 stimulation alone. In other words, the activity in MT/V5 became accessible due to the level of activity in V1.

Plasticity, Rehabilitation, and Transcranial Magnetic Stimulation

Of the many ways in which TMS is used, the aim of using it to aid recovery of perceptual, motoric, or cognitive functions in neuropsychological patients or following trauma represents one of the greatest challenges. There are now many examples of how TMS can be used to understand or promote rehabilitation. For example, recent efforts have focused on the effects of TMS on somatosensory areas to investigate whether, when stimulated, one hemisphere can significantly affect ipsilateral or contralateral sensory perception during unimanual or bimanual detection tasks. TMS has already proved useful in charting recovery of function (Brasil-Neto et al., 1992, 1993; Kew et al., 1994), learning-related changes (Butefisch et al., 2000; Classen et al., 1998), long-term changes in blind subjects (Pascual-Leone and Torres, 1993), as well as changes during skill acquisition (Pascual-Leone et al., 1995b) and skill deployment (Pascual-Leone et al., 1993a). Remarkable though many of these findings are, developing TMS as a treatment in rehabilitation has proven difficult, although there are indications that TMS may be useful in the treatment of depression (e.g., George et al., 1996), and significant effort is now directed at the use of TMS in recovery from stroke. TMS can, of course, be used to mimic neglect or extinction; in several studies, there has been a facilitatory effect on perception in the visual field or hand ipsilateral to the site of TMS (Seyal et al., 1995; Oliveri et al., 1999b; Hilgetag et al., 2001; Rushworth, Ellison, and Walsh, 2001). This raises the possibility that by disrupting one hemisphere, one might be able to "disinhibit" (without confusing this term with simple neural disinhibition) the unstimulated, competing hemisphere. Although progress in TMS rehabilitation has been comprehensively and critically assessed by Rossi and Rossini (2004), it is worth detailing one specific example.

Oliveri et al. (1999b) sought to test whether single- and paired-pulse TMS of an intact hemisphere in brain-damaged patients could modulate extinction. Testing 28 patients with right ($n = 14$) or left ($n = 14$) brain lesions, they delivered single-pulse TMS to frontal and parietal scalp sites of the intact hemisphere 40 msec after applying a unimanual or bimanual electric digit stimulus. In patients with right hemispheric damage, left frontal TMS significantly reduced the rate of contralateral extinctions compared with controls, whereas left parietal TMS did not significantly affect the number of extinctions as compared with baseline. Patients with left hemispheric damage did not show equivalent results: TMS to their intact, right hemisphere did not alter their recognition of bimanual stimuli. These results suggest that extinctions produced by right hemisphere damage may be dependent on a breakdown in the balance of hemispheric rivalry in directing spatial attention to the contralateral hemispace, so that the unaffected hemisphere generates an unopposed orienting response ipsilateral to the lesioned hemisphere. TMS to the left frontal cortex in patients with right-hemisphere damage and contralesional extinction ameliorates their deficit. Brighina et al. (2003) have also showed convincingly that stimulation of the unaffected hemisphere in patients with neglect can diminish their symptoms. Clearly, there is a basis here for further therapeutic exploration (see Rossi and Rossini, 2004).

Safety and TMS

TMS must, of course, be used responsibly. If one applies exclusion criteria to the selection of TMS subjects (Wassermann, 1998), single-pulse TMS carries virtually no risk and repetitive TMS as typically used in cognitive neuroscience experiments falls well within the safety guidelines. Nevertheless, one should be aware of the risks, however small. Because TMS produces an auditory click, which can cause discomfort and temporary elevation in auditory thresholds (Pascual-Leone et al., 1993b), ear plugs should be used in all experiments. Some TMS subjects may experience headaches or discomfort from the facial or neck muscle twitches common when more anterior sites are stimulated. Such subjects are, of course, under no obligation to continue; it is worth remembering that uncomfortable or worried subjects are not likely to produce good data. The most serious theoretical concern is the possibility of spread of activity or even of seizure. Although there are a few cases of TMS-induced seizures, none occurred when the simulation parameters have been within the Wassermann guidelines (Wassermann, 1998). Provided reasonable caution is exercised and the Wassermann paper is consulted, one can therefore have confidence in these guidelines.

Integration

Thus, as we noted at the outset, there are two ways of looking at why we might use the many different techniques available to the cognitive neuroscientist: (1) in the hope that they might lead to converging conclusions and (2) to take advantage of the different kinds of answers the different techniques provide and the different kinds of questions they cause us to ask (see Walsh and Butler, 1996). Consistent with both of these views is the attraction of integrating TMS with other techniques, in particular, with PET, fMRI, and EEG (Paus et al., 1997, 1998; Paus and Wolforth, 1998; Paus, 1999; Ilmoniemi et al., 1997). Bohning et al. (1999) have successfully combined TMS and fMRI to directly measure the neurophysiological consequences of magnetic stimulation. Although there are now several examples of such a combination, none to date has successfully addressed behavior, which remains an avenue to be explored in future research. Using sub- and suprathreshold 4 Hz repetitive TMS over M1/S, Bestmann et al. (2003) investigated changes in brain activity. They observed changes in BOLD activation in the areas under the coil and in the supplementary motor area (SMA) in seven out of eight subjects. Although subthreshold TMS did not produce changes in the BOLD signal under the coil, it did produce secondary BOLD changes in SMA. Bestmann and colleagues concluded that BOLD changes correlated with suprathreshold TMS are predominantly caused by reafferent input to the motor cortex following TMS-induced hand movements. Siebner et al. (1998) compared the changes in regional cerebral blood flow (rCBF) induced by 2 Hz rTMS over the motor cortex, sufficient to cause an arm movement, with those caused by the actual movement of the arm. The correspondence was striking; both conditions activated area 4 ipsilateral to the movement and the voluntary movement also activated area 6 of SMA.

Conclusion

Instruments and techniques are only as good as the people using them: a finely tuned sports car is dangerous, and a Stradivarius violin squeals horribly in the wrong hands. In this chapter, we have tried to explain what one needs—and how one needs to think about lesion methodology—to carry out experiments using TMS. We have also suggested that, when different techniques give different results, one might have an interesting finding, rather than simply a failure to confirm or to find converging evidence. Althouh much remains to be done in integrating TMS with EEG and fMRI and in using TMS to investigate reorganization in neuropsychological patients, nevertheless, the core contribution of TMS to cognitive neuroscience lies, not in serving as an adjunct to other techniques, but in interfering with cortical functions in precise time windows to parse the organization of behavior. To date, many TMS studies have sought to replicate the effects observed in neuropsychological patients or to confirm the findings of fMRI experiments. The new challenge will be to ask what can TMS interference with behavior show that cannot be found by other means.

References

Amassian, V. E., Cracco, R. Q., Maccabee, P. J., Cracco, J. B., Rudell, A. P., and Eberle, L. (1989). Suppression of visual perception by magnetic coil stimulation of human occipital cortex. *Electroencephalography and Clinical Neurophysiology*, 74, 458–462.

Amassian, V. E., Cracco, R. Q., Maccabee, P. J., Cracco, J. B., Rudell, A. P., and Eberle, L. (1993). Unmasking human visual perception with the magnetic coil and its relationship to hemispheric asymmetry. *Brain Research*, 605, 312–316.

Ashbridge, E., Walsh, V., and Cowey, A. (1997). Temporal aspects of visual search studied by transcranial magnetic stimulation. *Neuropsychologia*, 35, 1121–1131.

Barker, A. T. (1999). The history and basic principles of magnetic nerve stimulation. *Electroencephalography and Clinical Neurophysiology*, Suppl. 51, 3–21.

Bartres-Faz, D., Pujol, J., Deus, J., Tormos, J. M., Keenan, J. P., and Pascual-Leone, A. (1999). Identification of the brain areas from which TMS induces speech arrest in normal subjects. *NeuroImage*, 9, S1051.

Bestmann, S., Baudewig, J., Siebner, H., Rothwell, J. C., and Frahm, J. (2003). Is functional magnetic resonance imaging capable of mapping transcranial magnetic cortex stimulation? In W. Paulus, F. Tergau, M. A. Nitsche, J. C. Rothwell, U. Ziemann, and M. Hallett (Eds.), *Transcranial magnetic stimulation and transcranial direct current stimulation*, 55–62. Supplement to *Clinical neurophysiology*, vol. 56. Amsterdam: Elsevier Science.

Bjoertomt, O., Cowey, A., and Walsh, V. (2002) Spatial neglect in near and far space investigated by repetitive transcranial magnetic stimulation. *Brain*, 125, 2012–2022.

Bohning, D. E., Shastri, A., Blumenthal, K. M., Nahas, Z., Lorberbaum, J., Roberts, D., Teneback, C., Vincent, D. J., and George, M. S. (1999). A combined TMS/fMRI study of intensity-dependent TMS over motor cortex. *Biological Psychiatry*, 45, 385–394.

Brasil-Neto, J. P., Cohen, L. G., Pascual-Leone, A., Jabir, F. K., Wall, R. T., and Hallett, M. (1992). Rapid reversible modulation of human motor outputs after transient deafferentation of the forearm: A study with transcranial magnetic stimulation. *Neurology, 42*(7), 1302–1306.

Brasil-Neto, J. P., Valls-Sole, J., Pascual-Leone, A., Cammarota, A., Amassian, V. E., Cracco, R., Maccabee, P., Cracco, J., Hallett, M., and Cohen, L. G. (1993). Rapid modulation of human cortical motor outputs following ischaemic nerve block. *Brain, 116*(pt. 3), 511–525.

Brighina, F., Bisiach, E., Oliveri, M., Piazza, A., La Bua, V., Dancele, O., Fierro, B. (2003). 1 Hz repetitive transcranial magnetic stimulation of the unaffected hemisphere amelirates antralesicral viscespatial neglect in humans. *Neuroscience letters, 336*(2), 131–133.

Butefisch, C. M., Davis, B. C., Wise, S. P., Sawaki, L., Kopylev, L., Classen, J., and Cohen, L. G. (2000). Mechanisms of use-dependent plasticity in the human motor cortex. *Proceedings of the National Academy of Sciences, USA, 97*(7), 3661–3665.

Campana, G., Cowey, A., and Walsh, V. (2002). Priming of motion perception and area V5/MT: A test of perceptual memory. *Cerebral Cortex, 12*(6), 663–669.

Chen, R., Classen, J., Gerloff, C., Celnik, P., Wassermann, E. M., Hallett, M., and Cohen, L. G. (1997), Depression of motor cortex excitability by low-frequency transcranial magnetic stimulation. *Neurology, 48*(5), 1398–1403.

Classen, J., Liepert, J., Wise, S. P., Hallett, M., and Cohen, L. G. (1998). Rapid plasticity of human cortical movement representation induced by practice. *Journal of Neurophysiology, 79*(2), 1117–1123.

Cowey, A., and Walsh, V. (2000). Magnetically induced phosphenes in sighted, blind and blindsighted observers. *NeuroReport, 11*(14), 3269–3273.

Ellison, A., Rushworth, M., and Walsh, V. (2003). The parietal cortex in visual search: A visuomotor hypothesis. *Clinical Neurophysiology, 56*(4), 321–330.

Epstein, C. M., Lah, J. J., Meador, K., Weissman, J. D., Gaitan, L. E., and Dihenia, B. (1996). Optimum stimulus parameters for lateralized suppression of speech with magnetic brain stimulation. *Neurology, 47*(6), 1590–1593.

Epstein, C. M., Meador, K. J., Loring, D. W., Wright, R. J., Weissman, J. D., Sheppard, S., Lah, J. J., Puhalovich, F., Gaitan, L., and Davey, K. R. (1999). Localization and characterization of speech arrest during transcranial magnetic stimulation. *Clinical Neurophysiology, 110*(6), 1073–1079.

Fierro, B., Brighina, F., Oliveri, M., Piazza, A., La Bua, V., Buffa, D., and Bisiach, E. (2000). Contralateral neglect induced by right posterior parietal rTMS in healthy subjects. *NeuroReport, 11*(7), 1519–1521.

George, M. S., Wassermann, E. M., Williams, W. A., Callahan, A., Ketter, T. A., Basser, P., Hallett, M., and Post, R. M. (1995). Daily repetitive transcranial magnetic stimulation (rTMS) improves mood in depression. *NeuroReport, 6*(14), 1853–1856.

George, M. S., Wassermann, E. M., Williams, W. A., Steppel, J., Pascual-Leone, A., Basser, P., Hallett, M., and Post, R. M. (1996). Changes in mood and hormone levels after rapid-rate transcranial magnetic stimulation (rTMS) of the prefrontal cortex. *Journal of Neuropsychiatry and Clinical Neurosciences*, 8(2), 172–180.

Hilgetag, C. C., Theoret, H., and Pascual-Leone, A. (2001). Enhanced visual spatial attention ipsilateral to rTMS-induced "virtual lesions" of human parietal cortex. *Nature Neuroscience*, 4(9), 953–957.

Ilmoniemi, R. J., Virtanen, J., Ruohonen, J., Karhu, J., Aronen, H. J., Naatanen, R., and Katila, T. (1997). Neuronal responses to magnetic stimulation reveal cortical reactivity and connectivity. *NeuroReport*, 8(16), 3537–3540.

Ingvar, D. (1983) Serial aspects of language and speech relative to prefrontal cortical activity. *Human Neurobiology*, 2(3), 177–189.

Kew, J. J., Ridding, M. C., Rothwell, J. C., Passingham, R. E., Leigh, P. N., Sooriakumaran, S., Frackowiak, R. S., and Brooks, D. J. (1994). Reorganization of cortical blood flow and transcranial magnetic stimulation maps in human subjects after upper limb amputation. *Journal of Neurophysiology*, 72(5), 2517–2524.

Mills, K. R. (1999). *Magnetic stimulation of the human nervous system.* Oxford: Oxford University Press.

Ojemann, G. (1983). Brain organization for language from the perspective of electrical stimulation mapping. *Behavioral and Brain Sciences*, 6, 189–230.

Ojemann, G., and Mateer, C. (1979). Human language cortex: Localization of memory, syntax and sequential motor-phoneme identification systems. *Science*, 205(4413), 1401–1403.

Oliveri, C., and Calvo, M. (2003). Increased visual central excitability in Ecstasy users: A transcranial magnetic stimulation study. *Journal of Neurology, Neurosurgery and Psychiatry*, 34(11), 2653–2658.

Oliveri, M., Rossini, P. M., Pasqualetti, P., Traversa, R., Cicinelli, P., Palmieri, M. G., Tomaiuolo, F., and Caltagirone, C. (1999a). Interhemispheric asymmetries in the perception of unimanual and bimanual cutaneous stimuli: A study using transcranial magnetic stimulation. *Brain*, 122(96), 1721–1729.

Oliveri, M., Rossini, P. M., Traversa, R., Cicinelli, P., Filippi, M. M., Pasqualetti, P., Tomaiuolo, F., and Caltagirone, C. (1999b). Left frontal transcranial magnetic stimulation reduces contralesional extinction in patients with unilateral right brain damage. *Brain*, 122(96), 1731–1739.

Pascual-Leone, A., Cammarota, A., Wassermann, E. M., Brasil-Neto, J. P., Cohen, L. G., and Hallett, M. (1993a). Modulation of motor cortical outputs to the reading hand of braille readers. *Annals of Neurology*, 34(1), 33–37.

Pascual-Leone, A., Gates, J. R., and Dhuna, A. (1991). Induction of speech arrest and counting errors with rapid-rate transcranial magnetic stimulation. *Neurology*, 41(5), 697–702.

Pascual-Leone, A., Gomez-Tortosa, E., Grafman, J., Alway, D., Nichelli, P., and Hallett, M. (1994). Induction of visual extinction by rapid-rate transcranial magnetic stimulation of parietal lobe. *Neurology, 44*(3, pt. 1), 494–498.

Pascual-Leone, A., Grafman, J., and Hallett, M. (1994). Modulation of cortical motor output maps during development of implicit and explicit knowledge. *Science, 263*(5151), 1287–1289.

Pascual-Leone, A., Houser, C. M., Reese, K., Shotland, L. I., Grafman, J., Sato, S., Valls-Sole, J., Brasil-Neto, J. P., Wassermann, E. M., Cohen, L. G., et al. (1993b). Safety of rapid-rate transcranial magnetic stimulation in normal volunteers. *Electroencephalography and Clinical Neurophysiology, 89*(2), 120–130.

Pascual-Leone, A., Nguyet, D., Cohen, L. G., Brasil-Neto, J. P., Cammarota, A., and Hallett, M. (1995a). Modulation of muscle responses evoked by transcranial magnetic stimulation during the acquisition of new fine motor skills. *Journal Neurophysiology, 74*(3), 1037–1045.

Pascual-Leone, A., Tarazona, F., Keenan, J. P., Tormos, J. M., Hamilton, R., and Catala, M. D. (1999). Transcranial magnetic stimulation and neuroplasticity. *Neuropsychologia, 37*(2), 207–217.

Pascual-Leone, A., and Torres, F. (1993). Plasticity of the sensorimotor cortex representation of the reading finger in braille readers. *Brain, 116*(1), 39–52.

Pascual-Leone, A., and Walsh, V. (2001). Fast backprojections from the motion area to the primary visual area necessary for visual awareness. *Science, 292*(5516), 510–512.

Pascual-Leone, A., Wassermann, E. M., Sadato, N., and Hallett, M. (1995b). The role of reading activity on the modulation of motor cortical outputs to the reading hand in braille readers. *Annals of Neurology, 38*(6), 910–915.

Paus, T. (1999). Imaging the brain before, during, and after transcranial magnetic stimulation. *Neuropsychologia, 37*(2), 219–224.

Paus, T., Jech, R., Thompson, C. J., Comeau, R., Peters, T., and Evans, A. C. (1997). Transcranial magnetic stimulation during positron-emission tomography: A new method for studying connectivity of the human cerebral cortex. *Journal of Neuroscience, 17*(9), 3178–3184.

Paus, T., Jech, R., Thompson, C. J., Comeau, R., Peters, T., and Evans, A. C. (1998). Dose-dependent reduction of cerebral blood flow during rapid-rate transcranial magnetic stimulation of the human sensorimotor cortex. *Journal of Neurophysiology, 79*(2), 1102–1107.

Paus, T., and Wolforth, M. (1998). Transcranial magnetic stimulation during PET: Reaching and verifying the target site. *Human Brain Mapping, 6*(5–6), 399–402.

Penfield, W., and Roberts, L. (1959). *Speech and brain mechanisms.* Princeton, NJ: Princeton University Press.

Rossi, S., and Rossini, P. M. (2004). TMS in cognitive plasticity and the potential for rehabilitation. *Trends in Cognitive Sciences, 8*(6), 273–279. Review.

Rostomily, R. C., Berger, M. S., Ojemann, G., and Lettich, E. (1991). Postoperative deficits and functional recovery following removal of tumours involving the dormant hemisphere. *Journal of Neurosurgery*, 75(1), 62–68.

Rushworth, M. F. S., Ellison, A., and Walsh, V. (2001). Complementary localization and lateralization of orienting and motor attention. *Nature Neuroscience*, 4(9), 656–661.

Sadato, N., Pascual-Leone, A., Grafman, J., Ibanez, V., Deiber, M. P., Dold, G., and Hallett, M. (1996). Activation of primary visual cortex by braille reading in blind subjects. *Nature*, 380(6574), 526–528.

Siebner, H. R., Willoch, F., Peller, M., Auer, C., Boecker, H., Conrad, B., and Bartenstein, P. (1998). Imaging brain activation induced by long trains of repetitive transcranial magnetic stimulation. *NeuroReport*, 9(5), 943–948.

Silvanto, J., Cowey, A., Lavie, N., and Walsh, V. (2005). Striate cortex (V1) activity gates awareness of motion. *Nature Neuroscience*, 8(2), 143–144.

Silvanto, J., Lavie, N., and Walsh, V. (2005). Double dissociation of V1 and V5/MT activity in visual awareness. *Cerebral Cortex*, 15, 1736–1741.

Stewart, L. M., Battelli, L., Walsh, V., and Cowey, A. (1999). Motion perception and perceptual learning studied by magnetic stimulation. *Electroencephalography and Clinical Neurophysiology*, 51, 334–350.

Stewart, L. M., Frith, U., Meyer, B. U., and Rothwell, J. (2000). *Left Posterior BA 37 is involved in object recognition: A TMS Study. Neuropsychologia*, 39(1), 1–6.

Stewart, L., Walsh, V., Frith, U., and Rothwell, J. C. (2001). TMS produces two dissociable types of speech disruption. *NeuroImage*, 13(3), 472–478.

Stewart, L., Walsh, V., and Rothwell, J. (2001). Motor and phosphene thresholds: A transcranial magnetic stimulation correlation study. *Neuropsychologia*, 39(4), 415–419.

Topper, R., Mottaghy, F. M., Brugmann, M., Noth, J., and Huber, W. (1998). Facilitation of picture naming by focal transcranial magnetic stimulation of Wernicke's area. *Experimental Brain Research*, 121(4), 371–378.

Walsh, V., Ashbridge, E., and Cowey, A. (1998). Cortical plasticity in perceptual learning demonstrated by transcranial magnetic stimulation. *Neuropsychologia*, 36(4), 363–367.

Walsh, V., and Butler, S. R. (1996). Different ways of looking at seeing. *Behavioural Brain Research*, 76(1–2), 1–3.

Walsh, V., and Cowey, A. (1998). Magnetic stimulation studies of visual cognition. *Trends in Cognitive Sciences*, 2(3), 103–110.

Walsh, V., and Cowey, A. (2000). Transcranial magnetic stimulation and cognitive neuroscience. *Nature Reviews Neuroscience*, 1(1), 73–79. Review.

Walsh, V., Ellison, A., Ashbridge, E., and Cowey, A. (1999). The role of the parietal cortex in visual attention—Hemispheric asymmetries and the effects of learning: A magnetic stimulation study. *Neuropsychologia, 37*(2), 245–251.

Walsh, V., Ellison, A., Battelli, L., and Cowey, A. (1998). Task-specific impairments and enhancements induced by magnetic stimulation of human visual area V5. *Proceedings of the Royal Society, London, B265*(1395), 537–543.

Walsh, V., and Pascual-Leone, A. (2003). *Magnetic stimulation and cognition.* Cambridge, MA: MIT Press.

Wassermann, E. M. (1998). Risk and safety of repetitive transcranial magnetic stimulation: Report and suggested guidelines from the International Workshop on the Safety of Repetitive Transcranial Magnetic Stimulation, June 5–7, 1996. *Electroencephalography and Clinical Neurophysiology, 108*(1), 1–16.

2   The Cognitive Neuropsychiatric Approach

Philip Shaw and Anthony S. David

Many core clinical symptoms in psychiatry are readily conceptualized as the product of dysfunction in normal cognitive processes. Despite the intuitive appeal of this approach, only recently has there been a systematic attempt to account for clinical psychopathologies in terms of deficits to the mechanisms mediating basic cognitive processes, such as attention, perception, and memory. The term *cognitive neuropsychiatry* (CNP) has been coined to capture the key components of this approach, which emphasizes links with the basic neurosciences—and which makes particular use of advances in functional neuroimaging—in its attempt to delineate the psycho neural substrates for clinical symptoms (David and Halligan, 2000; Halligan and David, 2001). This chapter will review the origins of CNP in cognitive psychology and clinical psychiatry, illustrating how the interaction of these disciplines has improved our understanding of core psychiatric symptoms.

Principles

The cognitive neuropsychiatric approach reflects the principles of CNP's parent disciplines (figure 2.1) and rests in part on a range of available models of abnormal cognitive phenomena, and of "normal" cognitive processes inferred from them, often developing and refining the models. Its experimental techniques in turn rest largely on single case studies in which individual patients with particular psychopathologies are studied extensively to characterize the precise nature of their respective deficits. The study of series of individual patients with distinctly different psychopathological conditions reveals patterns of association and dissociation between particular cognitive functions (Caramazza, 1986). Within the CNP approach, double or complementary dissociations, which arise when one patient has an intact performance on cognitive task A but is impaired on cognitive task

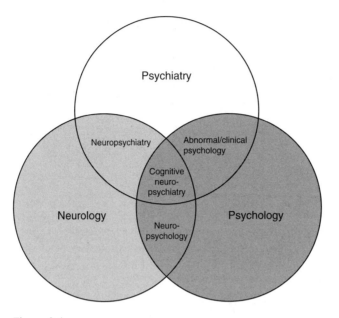

Figure 2.1
Venn diagram illustrating the intellectual and clinical "territory" occupied by cognitive neuropsychiatry.

B, whereas a second patient with a corollary symptom profile shows the reverse pattern of cognitive skills, are held to be particularly important (Teuber, 1955; Shallice, 1998). Indeed, such dissociations are held to imply the functional independence of the systems mediating the two cognitive skills, which illustrates how an analysis of patterns of deficits in clinical populations can inform models of cognitive function in healthy subjects. One could even argue that demonstrating complementary cognitive dissociations between groups of subjects with differing psychopathologies might prove to be a powerful way of avoiding false positives (see Robertson et al., 1993).

Detailed analysis at the level of the single patient serves to highlight important individual differences that might otherwise be disregarded when data from multiple subjects are pooled together. Group studies of patient populations defined by objective criteria (such as the presence of a psychiatric symptom) are also used to test the validity of models derived from single case studies and to develop models that have more general applicability.

In cognitive neuropsychiatry, the level of analysis is that of the clinical symptom (or, occasionally, group of symptoms) rather than that of diagnostic categories, as is the case in most branches of clinical psychiatric research. CNP thus circumvents the problem posed by most psychiatric diagnoses, which represent the victory of pragmatism over theory and bear little relationship to current models of psychological processes.

Delusions, Hallucinations, and Thought Disorder

Cognitive neuropsychiatry has given rise to novel ways of addressing psychotic phenomena in particular. Several symptoms lie at the core of psychotic disorders: delusions, hallucinations, and disorganized speech (reflecting "thought disorder"). Delusions evade easy definition, but are generally considered to be a species of erroneous beliefs held with startling conviction (for a discussion of the difficulties in attaining a comprehensive definition, see Gilleen and David, 2005). Within CNP, they can be understood as the product of a dysfunction in the normal stages of belief formation. One set of abnormal beliefs—delusional misidentification—demonstrates the strengths of the detailed case study approach. In the Capgras delusion, patients believe that a familiar person has been replaced by an almost identical other. Ellis and Young (1990) propose that this delusion arises from a deficit in face processing, specifically, from a deficit in attaching relevant affective information stored about an individual to the process of recognizing that person's identity. Thus patients with Capgras syndrome fail to show the normal electrophysiological (and, by inference, affective) response to pictures of individuals they explicitly recognize. By contrast prosopagnosic patients, who have the converse pattern of deficits, may show normal skin conductance responses to pictures of familiar people but are unable to explicitly recognize or name them. This double dissociation of two sets of patients (Capgras patients intact in overt, but impaired in covert, face recognition; prosospagnosic patients showing the reverse deficits) provides evidence for the existence of two independent routes by which faces are processed. A mere loss of affective information about a familiar face might lead someone to be puzzled, but does not itself explain the typically bizarre and elaborate explanation that patients with Capgras delusions provide for their experiences. A consideration of deficits in more general processes of reasoning and memory is needed to provide explanations for the bizarre and affectively negative tone that characterizes many delusions (Gilleen and David, 2005).

In this vein, a CNP approach to more common delusions (on persecutory, nihilistic, or grandiose themes) has focused on possible deficits in normal processes of reasoning.

Several studies (see Garety et al., 2001; Freeman et al., 2004) have found that deluded patients have faulty reasoning: they tend to jump to conclusions and change their minds readily in the face of contradictory evidence. Their findings suggest a "data-collecting bias" that may contribute to the formation and maintenance of delusions. In a different reasoning paradigm, Kemp et al. (1997) instructed deluded patients to choose between logically fallacious and valid responses on tests requiring judgments of conditionality, syllogism, and probability. The deluded patients were slightly more prone than healthy controls to endorse fallacious responses, especially when emotive themes were involved. The reasoning differences were, however, subtle and clearly impairments in other basic cognitive mechanisms need to be examined.

Impairments in attention—particularly in the processes underlying selective attention—may shape delusions. Deluded patients appear to attend selectively to self-referential or threatening information in their environment (Fear, Sharp, and Healey, 1996), a finding that can also be demonstrated psychophysiologically by tracking eye movement in patients as they scan the environment (Phillips and David, 1998). Patients with paranoid delusions respond quickly to threatening elements in ambiguous pictures, but actually spend less time than healthy controls in appraising such threatening elements (Phillips, Senior, and David, 2000). Other data suggested that they may search for threatening stimuli in nonthreatening areas of the stimuli, looking for threat in inappropriate places. This selective focus on threat-related material is reflected in a preferential recall of threatening episodes (Kaney et al., 1992). It is clear how selective attention to threat in the environment, and enhanced recall of such negative percepts, could provide fertile ground for the growth of paranoid beliefs. And, finally, physiological "dissociations" may promote aberrant cognitive processing of potential threat in people with schizophrenia. Williams et al. (2004) showed a lack of the normal correlation between skin conductance responses and amygdala activation on fMRI.

Others have formulated delusions as the direct product of abnormal attribution styles, claiming that there is no need to invoke additional perceptual and attentional biases. Freeman et al. (2004) have described a tendency of deluded patients to blame other people when things go wrong, which they term a *personalizing attribution style*. Blackwood et al. (2000, 2003, 2004) have used fMRI to delineate the neural basis of such attributional styles. They found that deluded patients show underactivation of a region of the brain held to mediate self-monitoring (the anterior cingulate gyrus) when they evaluated negative personal statements, which they interpret as reflecting a lack of self-reflection in the persecutory delusional state.

Emotion has a clear impact on belief formation, which may exist in an exaggerated form in the formation of delusions. Rossell, Shapleske, and David (1998) demonstrated that the criteria for what qualifies as a truth statement may be relaxed when the topic is related to a deluded person's preoccupations. David and Howard (1994) demonstrated that highly emotive delusional memories are rated by patients as more perceptually rich than fantasies and even memories of actual real events. This "abnormal memory" can be related to dysfunction in the mechanism of emotional memory formation, in which the amygdala plays a central role. Elaborating on this finding, Gibbs and David (2003) suggest that abnormal emotional enhancement of memory (consolidation) may occur in delusions, in part due to pathology of the amygdala (a pathology well established in psychotic disorders). This predicts that patients with mood-congruent delusions, which are shaped by the patients' underlying affective disorders, may demonstrate more severe functional and perhaps structural pathology of the amygdala.

A recent theory emphasizes deficits in central processes that govern social cognitive reasoning, such as reasoning about the mental states of others in order to explain and predict their behavior. Deluded patients were found to be impaired in a task that required reasoning about the belief states of others, specifically, a second-order theory of mind (ToM) task that required reasoning about the belief one person holds about the belief of another—"He thinks that she thinks . . ." (Corcoran, Mercer, and Frith, 1995; Frith and Corcoran, 1996). There is also a decrease in the normative tendency among deluded patients to attribute social meaning to the movements of two cartoon shapes in the Heider and Simmel paradigm (see Blakemore et al., 2003). Much of the circuitry implicated in processes of self-monitoring and source memory is also involved in TOM reasoning—particularly the medial prefrontal cortex (and anterior portions of the anterior cingulate gyrus) and perhaps mesial and polar temporal regions (Frith and Frith, 2003). An fMRI study (Russell et al., 2000) has also shown reduced left prefrontal cortical activation during tasks of ToM reasoning in patients with schizophrenia. There is some debate over whether deficits in ToM reasoning are a characteristic of the psychotic state and not a trait feature: studies are inconsistent as to whether theory of mind deficits are found among deluded patients in remission (see Drury, Robinson, and Birchwood, 1998; Herold et al., 2002). The finding of ToM deficits in first-degree relatives of patients with schizophrenia is evidence in favor of the concept of a trait—a core deficit in mentalizing—although the empirical findings of such deficits are mixed (see Herold et al., 2002; Kelemen et al., 2004).

The cognitive neuropsychiatric study of delusions thus demonstrates two of the cardinal features of the CNP approach. First, adopting classical neuropsychological methods, it explores delusion-like phenomena in people with demonstrable organic brain lesions to inform models of the "functional" psychoses. Second, it frames psychotic symptoms in terms of dysfunction in normal cognitive processes, thus allowing them to be linked to neural systems that can then be studied using functional neuroimaging techniques.

A similar mix of methods can be seen in the CNP analysis of hallucinations. Auditory verbal hallucinations have drawn particular interest, in part because they represent the most common form of hallucinations encountered by psychiatrists. According to the current main theories, hallucinations have several common features: (1) mental contents are translated into auditory verbal form—"voices"; (2) the sense of ownership of this internal "speech" is somehow lost (David, 2004); and (3) elaborate systems of beliefs are developed about the origin of the "voices". Given the pervasive tendency for the source of the speech to assume a hostile, alien character, the process behind the third feature clearly does not occur at random.

Earlier neuropsychological models were based on the premise that hallucinations are the product of abnormal activation of auditory sensory mechanisms intimately linked with the generation of internal speech (or its proximate sources). This premise derives some support from functional neuroimaging studies (Woodruff et al., 1997; Shergill et al., 2000), which show that activation in the frontotemporal regions ceases when hallucinations do. More recently, Shergill et al. (2004) showed that, several seconds before the onset of hallucinations, activation occurs in cortical regions held to be important in generating inner speech (the inferior frontal cortex and middle temporal gyri), and that, once the hallucinations start, activation switches to the bilateral temporal gyri and the left insula—areas implicated in the perception of auditory verbal material. Structural neuroimaging studies report subtle structural cortical anomalies in some of the same regions. For example, using automated voxel-based morphometry techniques, Shapleske et al. (2002) found a reduction in the gray matter in the left insula and adjacent temporal cortex of hallucinators.

More recent cognitive models of hallucination (see Bentall, Baker, and Havers, 1991) argue for a primary deficit in memory, specifically, for difficulties in reconstructing and integrating sensory, semantic, and source components of a memory. In this framework, hallucinations arise when an auditory memory of a negative thought about the self is recalled as originating from another source and is experienced as an alien hallucination. Paradigms that systematically manipulate the source of memories do not, however, find consistent evidence for a specific deficit in correctly recalling acts as being generated by the self, or they attribute the effects of such a deficit to more general cognitive impairment (see Morrison and Haddock, 1997; Brebion et al., 2000). Most mnemonic impairments are more global in hallucinators than in nonhallucinators, or they are not confined to psychotic hallucinators (Keefe et al., 1999; Brebion et al., 2002). Nevertheless, distinguishing between erroneous and reduced memory does appear to be related positively to symptoms such as delusions and hallucinations, and may be related negatively to deficit symptoms (Brebion et al., 2000).

A more compelling case can be made for models that posit defective self-monitoring as the primary deficit in hallucinations and other psychotic phenomena, a case most clearly made by Frith and colleagues (Frith, 1992; Frith, Blakemore, and Wolpert, 2000; David, 2004) over several years, with several recent proposed refinements. All intentions to act (including the formulation of a speech act) are held to produce an efferent copy that is then fed forward to a comparator, where intended and actual actions are compared. A completed speech act that arrives in the comparator in the absence of an efferent copy is experienced as originating from an external source. If the efferent copy arose at the level of the formulation of a thought, its absence could be experienced as the delusion of an inserted alien thought (a Schneiderian first-rank symptom). If the efferent copy arose at the level of preparing a motor speech act, its absence could be experienced as an auditory verbal hallucination. Johns et al. (2001) have demonstrated that hallucinators tend to misattribute their own voice, fed back to them immediately in a slightly distorted form, to an external speaker.

Functional imaging of this paradigm reveals aberrant activation in temporal, parahippocampal, and cerebellar areas (Fu and McGuire, 2003). Recent electrophysiological studies using event-related potentials (ERPs; Ford et al., 2001, 2002) have also elegantly demonstrated a failure to mark self-generated speech as distinct from the speech of others in hallucinators.

High-end technological approaches are not the only contributors to the evaluation of cognitive models of hallucinations. Single case studies still play an important role. For example, the case for auditory verbal hallucinations as a form of inner speech or phonological short-term memory has been weakened substantially by the finding that a female patient with severe hallucinations still had normal phonological memory function. Despite almost constant auditory verbal hallucinations, this patient demonstrated word length and phonological superiority effects associated with an intact phonological buffer (David and Lucas, 1993). This finding was replicated in a group study by Evans, McGuire, and David (2000), whose hallucinator subjects demonstrated intact phonological memory and intact performance on a battery of tests designed to assess auditory imagery.

Cognitive models of semantic networks operationalized as nodes connected by links of differing weights have been used to study thought disorder, reflected in the disorganized speech often found in psychotic patients. Thus Goldberg and Weinberger (2000) argue that there may be reduced semantic priming in thought-disordered patients. They found that patients with thought disorder displayed lack of priming for highly associated within-category words, suggesting that they could not access them in a timely and semantically relevant manner. This deficit, which occurred in the face of generally intact vocabulary skills, suggests in turn that there is a primary anomaly in the organization of semantic entities. Such an abnormal conceptual framework with weakened or aberrant semantic links between conceptual "nodes" could lead to speech output characterized by bizarre and tenuous connections. Kuperberg, McGuire, and David (2000) demonstrated such weakened semantic links by showing that thought-disordered patients did not dismiss sentences whose endings violated normal semantic rules; this deficit was closely linked to the presence and severity of thought disorder. In more recent work, Kuperberg and colleagues (Sitnikova et al., 2002) have provided electophysiological evidence that thought-disordered patients show abnormal processing of sentences manipulated to assess the degree to which the patients process irrelevant semantic aspects of words. And, finally, an in-depth cognitive neuropsychological case series has produced a pleasing convergence with these more experimental approaches. Seven patients with severe thought disorder were contrasted with healthy controls on an extensive aphasia battery that revealed particular deficits best characterized as an expressive semantic abnormality with preserved naming (Oh, McCarthy, and McKenna, 2002).

Limitations

The limitations of the cognitive neuropsychiatric approach are to some extent those of CNP's parent disciplines. On the one hand, reliance on detailed case studies and double dissociations has been criticized (see

Van Order, Pennington, and Stone, 2001). Particular criticism has been made of the tendency to impute the existence of independent isolable cognitive subsystems or modules from such dissociations, and many argue (see Plaut, 2003) that cognitive functions are better modeled using a more distributed, nonmodular framework. In this vein, Plaut (1995) found that apparent double dissociations can arise when a "lesion" is made to a distributed neural network, although Bullinaria (2003) has disputed this finding. As critics of the CNP approach, see it, double dissociation does not entail functional independence of two cognitive modules. Others have pointed out that there are many implicit assumptions underlying such neural networks—such as the presence of "hidden units"—which may covertly introduce analogues of a modular architecture.

Cognitive models have often been characterized as "box and arrow" models, which are hard to falsify because extra boxes pop up to explain unexpected findings, and the contents of the arrows is never specified. Undoubtedly, there is a need to have tightly constrained models that generate clear, testable hypotheses. On the other hand, the literature is replete with studies that accept the null hypothesis: many of these have been listed above.

Within cognitive psychology, some have criticized the adoption of group studies of clinical populations, arguing that this approach obscures vital individual variations associated with differing patterns of brain dysfunction (see McCloskey, 1993). Indeed the "ultras" among these critics emphasize the importance of findings from single-case series—and even discount evidence from group studies. By far most cognitive psychologists, however, hold to the complementarity of single-case and group studies.

Another problem especially relevant to cognitive neuropsychiatry, but not unique to it, is the assumption of normality prior to the disorder or lesion in question. For example, a stroke patient with prosopagnosia is assumed to have had normal face recognition prior to the patient's stroke. However, the clear evidence of premorbid cognitive deficits, neurodevelopmental origins, and possible long-protracted onset in the major psychiatric disorders makes such assumptions less secure.

Integration

Intuitively, links with functional neuroimaging would seem to hold particular promise: the level of spatial resolution attainable is ideally suited for explaining brain activation patterns framed in neurocognitive terms. In practice, however, the relationship between functional neuroimaging techniques and neuropsychological methods in general and CNP in particular is a matter of debate. Some have argued that functional neuroimaging has a rather severely limited role insofar as evidence from this modality cannot be used to falsify a cognitive model (see Coltheart, 2003). The recent explosion of interest in functional neuroimaging may also outstrip advances made in basic cognitive psychology. This could lead to conceptually confused interpretations as poorly elaborated basic cognitive models are forced onto increasingly sophisticated brain activation maps.

A more optimistic and perhaps pragmatic approach reflects on the progress already made in mapping cognitive modules defined in neuropsychological models onto brain structures (see Shallice, 2003). Those who hold this view stress that it need not entail a simple direct correspondence between cognitive modules or separable subsystems and individual anatomical regions. Indeed, a cognitive level of analysis may not necessarily map neatly onto the brain. However, there is increasing evidence of patterns of dissociation of brain activation while performing different cognitive tasks thought to rely on separable systems or cognitive modules. Shallice (2003) has given an elegant analysis of how fMRI studies demonstrate dissociations in activation patterns found to arise in the encoding and retrieval of episodic memory. Similarly, there is clear evidence of a dissociation of activation of the amygdala and hippocampus during the encoding of affectively neutral and arousing memories (Dolcos, LaBar, and Cabeza, 2004). As mentioned earlier, an understanding of the normal processes of encoding and retrieving emotional memories may explain some core symptoms in the formation of delusions. Overall, such findings give strong support to the promise of linking psychiatric symptoms with dysfunction of cognitive systems that can be conceptually defined and functionally localized.

Efforts to determine the genetic basis of psychiatric disorders have yielded some remarkable taxonomic results. A syndromic approach has proved a useful starting point, but it is unlikely that the genome will adhere closely to this taxonomy. Many have advocated the use of endophenotypes, constructs that serve as an index of predisposition to a disorder or symptom, identify more elementary and specific processes along pathogenic pathways, are stable and not illness dependent, and present in unaffected relatives (Gottesman and Gould, 2003). Cognitive endophenotypes are particularly promising candidates. For example, Glahn et al. (2003) have proposed deficits in working memory as an endophenotype for schizophrenia. These deficits in working memory show a clear effect of genotype in schizophrenia, illustrating how a cognitive deficit may relate closely to the neurobiology of mental disorders. It is likely that syndromes—which are clinically useful—will increasingly be studied in terms of the cognitive mechanism underlying the cardinal symptoms of each disorder.

A final potential benefit of cognitive neuropsychiatry relates to the therapeutic implications of the CNP approach. Techniques that alter basic cognitive processes are widely applied in many psychiatric disorders; a greater understanding of the cognitive basis of distressing symptoms may lead to more theoretically driven and targeted development of novel neurocognitive therapies for psychiatric disorders. That techniques bolstering reality testing and verification may reduce delusions is thus theoretically as well as practically important (Jolley and Garety, 2004). One hitherto untested target is insight or awareness of illness. There appears to be an inverse relationship between insight and mood, such that low mood invariably accompanies gains in insight, and vice versa (Mintz et al., 2003). Targeting one of these variables specifically, by cognitive means, might tease out the direction of causality.

Conclusion

In applying the tools of cognitive psychology to psychopathology, cognitive neuropsychiatry provides a level of analysis ideally suited to bridge different research approaches—informing the interpretation of neuroimaging studies and providing cognitive endophenotypes for genetic studies. Its research potential is matched by its therapeutic promise in guiding novel cognitive therapies to remove the very symptoms it seeks to explain.

References

Bentall, R. P., Baker, G. A., and Havers, S. (1991). Reality monitoring and psychotic hallucinations. *British Journal of Clinical Psychology*, *30*(pt 3), 213–222.

Blackwood, N. J., Bentall, R. P., Ffytche, D. H., Simmons, A., Murray, R. M., and Howard, R. J. (2003). Self-responsibility and the self-serving bias: An fMRI investigation of causal attributions. *Neuroimage*, *20*(2), 1076–1085.

Blackwood, N. J., Bentall, R. P., Ffytche, D. H., Simmons, J., Murray, R. M., and Howard, R. J. (2004). Persecutory delusions and the determination of self-relevance: An fMRI investigation. *Psychological Medicine*, *34*(4), 591–596.

Blackwood, N. J., Howard, R. J., Ffytche, D. H., Simmons, A., Bentall, R. P., and Murray, R. M. (2000). Imaging attentional and attributional bias: An fMRI approach to the paranoid delusion. *Psychological Medicine*, *30*(4), 873–883.

Blakemore, S. J., Sarfati, Y., Bazin, N., and Decety, J. (2003). The detection of intentional contingencies in simple animations in patients with delusions of persecution. *Psychological Medicine*, *33*(8), 1433–1441.

Brebion, G., Amador, X., Smith, M. J., Malaspina, D., Sharif, Z., and Gorman, J. M. (2000). Positive symptomatology and source-monitoring failure in schizophrenia: An analysis of symptom-specific effects. *Psychiatry Research*, *95*(2), 119–131.

Brebion, G., Gorman, J. M., Amador, X., Malaspina, D., and Sharif, Z. (2002). Source monitoring impairments in schizophrenia: Characterisation and associations with positive and negative symptomatology. *Psychiatry Research*, *112*(1), 27–39.

Bullinaria, J. A. (2003). Dissociation in connectionist systems. *Cortex*, *39*(1), 142–144.

Caramazza, A. (1986). On drawing inferences about the structure of normal cognitive systems from the analysis of patterns of impaired performance: The case for single-patient studies. *Brain and Cognition*, *5*(1), 41–66.

Coltheart, M. (2003). *Cognitive neuropsychology. Stevens' Handbook of experimental psychology* (3rd ed.), vol. 4. H. Pashler, S. Yantis, D. Mĕdin, R. Gallistel and J. Wixted (eds.) New York: Wiley.

Corcoran, R., Mercer, G., and Frith, C. D. (1995). Schizophrenia, symptomatology and social inference: Investigating "theory of mind" in people with schizophrenia. *Schizophrenia Research*, *17*(1), 5–13.

David, A. S. (2004). The cognitive neuropsychiatry of auditory verbal hallucinations: An overview. *Cognitive Neuropsychiatry*, *9*(1–2), 107–123.

David, A. S., and Halligan, P. W. (2000). Cognitive neuropsychiatry: Potential for progress. *Journal of Neuropsychiatry and Clinical Neurosciences*, *12*(4), 506–510.

David, A. S., and Howard, R. (1994). An experimental phenomenological approach to delusional memory in schizophrenia and late paraphrenia. *Psychological Medicine*, *24*(2), 515–524.

David, A. S., and Lucas, P. A. (1993). Auditory verbal hallucinations and the phonological loop: A cognitive neuropsychological study. *British Journal of Clinical Psychology*, *32*(4), 431–441.

Dolcos, F., LaBar, K. S., and Cabeza, R. (2004). Interaction between the amygdala and the medial temporal lobe memory system predicts better memory for emotional events. *Neuron*, *42*(5), 855–863.

Drury, V. M., Robinson, E. J., and Birchwood, M. (1998). "Theory of mind" skills during an acute episode of psychosis and following recovery. *Psychological Medicine*, *28*(5), 1101–1112.

Ellis, H. D., and Young, A. W. (1990). Accounting for delusional misidentifications. *British Journal of Psychiatry*, *157*, 239–248.

Evans, C. L., McGuire, P. K., and David, A. S. (2000). Is auditory imagery defective in patients with auditory hallucinations? *Psychological Medicine*, *30*(1), 137–148.

Fear, C., Sharp, H., and Healey, D. (1996). Cognitive processes in delusional disorders. *British Journal of Psychiatry, 168*(1), 61–67.

Ford, J. M., Mathalon, D. H., Heinks, T., Kalba, S., Faustman, W. O., and Roth, W. T. (2001). Neurophysiological evidence of corollary discharge dysfunction in schizophrenia. *American Journal of Psychiatry, 158*(12), 2069–2071.

Ford, J. M., Mathalon, D. H., Whitfield, S., Faustman, W. O., and Roth, W. T. (2002). Reduced communication between frontal and temporal lobes during talking in schizophrenia. *Biological Psychiatry, 51*(6), 485–492.

Freeman, D., Garety, P. A., Fowler, D., Kuipers, E., Bebbington, P., and Dunn, G. (2004). Why do people with delusions fail to choose more realistic explanations for their experiences? An empirical investigation. *Journal of Consulting and Clinical Psychology, 72*(4), 671–680.

Frith, C. (1992). *The cognitive neuropsychology of schizophrenia*. Hove, England: Psychology Press.

Frith, C. D., Blakemore, S. J., and Wolpert, D. M. (2000). Abnormalities in the awareness and control of action. *Philosophical Transactions of the Royal Society, London, B355*(1404), 1771–1788.

Frith, C. D., and Corcoran, R. (1996). Exploring "theory of mind" in people with schizophrenia. *Psychological Medicine, 26*(3), 521–530.

Frith, U., and Frith, C. D. (2003). Development and neurophysiology of mentalizing. *Philosophical Transactions of the Royal Society, London, B358*(1431), 459–473.

Fu, C. H. Y., and McGuire, P. K. (2003). Hearing voices or hearing the self in disguise? Revealing the neural correlates of auditory hallucinations in schizophrenia. In T. Kircher and A. David (Eds.), *The self in neuroscience and psychiatry*, 425–435. New York: Cambridge University Press.

Garety, P. A., Kuipers, E., Fowler, D., Freeman, D., and Bebbington, P. (2001). A cognitive model of the positive symptoms of psychosis. *Psychological Medicine, 31*(2), 189–195.

Gibbs, A. A., and David, A. S. (2003). Delusion formation and insight in the context of affective disturbance. *Epidemiologia e Psichiatria Sociale, 12*(3), 167–174.

Gilleen, J., and David, A. (2005). The cognitive neuropsychiatry of delusions: From psychopathology to neuropsychology and back again. *Psychological Medicine, 35*, 5–12.

Glahn, D. C., Therman, S., Manninen, M., Huttunen, M., Kaprio, J., Lohnqvist, J., and Cannon, T. D. (2003). Spatial working memory as an endophenotype for schizophrenia. *Biological Psychiatry, 53*(7), 624–626.

Goldberg, T. E., Egan, M. F., Gscheidle, T., Coppola, R., Weickert, T., Kolachana, B. S., Goldman, D., and Weinberger, D. R. (2003). Executive subprocesses in working memory: relationship to catechol-O-methyltransferase Val158Met genotype and schizophrenia. *Archives of General Psychiatry, 60*(9), 889–896.

Goldberg, T. E., and Weinberger, D. R. (2000). Thought disorder in schizophrenia: A reappraisal of older formulations and an overview of some recent studies. *Cognitive Neuropsychiatry*, 5(1), 1–19.

Gottesman, II, and Gould, T. D. (2003). The endophenotype concept in psychiatry: Etymology and strategic intentions. *American Journal of Psychiatry*, 160(4), 636–645.

Halligan, P. W., and David, A. S. (2001). Cognitive neuropsychiatry: Towards a scientific psychopathology. *Nature Reviews Neuroscience*, 2(3), 209–215.

Herold, R., Tenyi, T., Lenard, K., and Trixler, M. (2002). Theory of mind deficit in people with schizophrenia during remission. *Psychological Medicine*, 32(6), 1125–1129.

Johns, L. C., Rossell, S., Frith, C., Ahmad, F., Helmsley, D., Kuipers, E., and McGuire, P. K. (2001). Verbal self-monitoring and auditory verbal hallucinations in patients with schizophrenia. *Psychological Medicine*, 31(4), 705–715.

Jolley, S., and Garety, P. (2004). *Insight and psychosis: Awareness of illness in schizophrenia and related disorders* (2nd ed). Oxford: Oxford University Press.

Kaney, S., Wolfenden, M., Dewey, M. E., and Bentall, R. P. (1992). Persecutory delusions and recall of threatening propositions. *British Journal of Clinical Psychology*, 31(pt 1), 85–87.

Keefe, R. S. E., Arnold, M. C., Bayen, W. J., and Harvey, P. D. (1999). Source monitoring deficits in patients with schizophrenia: A multinomial modelling analysis. *Psychological Medicine*, 29(4), 903–914.

Kelemen, O., Kéri, S., Must, A., Benedek, G., and Janka, Z. (2004). No evidence for impaired "theory of mind" in unaffected first-degree relatives of schizophrenia patients. *Acta Psychiatrica Scandinavica*, 110(2), 146–149.

Kemp, R., Chua, S., McKenna, P., and David, A. S. (1997). Reasoning and delusions. *British Journal of Psychiatry*, 170(111), 398–405.

Kuperberg, G. R., McGuire, P. K., and David, A. S. (2000). Sensitivity to linguistic anomalies in spoken sentences: A case study approach to understanding thought disorder in schizophrenia. *Psychological Medicine*, 30(2), 345–357.

McCloskey, M. (1993). Theory and evidence in cognitive neuropsychology. *Journal of Experimental Psychology: Learning, Memory, and Cognition*, 19, 718–734.

Mintz, A. R., Dobson, K. S., and Romney, D. M. (2003). Insight in schizophrenia: A meta-analysis. *Schizophrenia Research*, 61, 75–88.

Morrison, A. P., and Haddock, G. (1997). Cognitive factors in source monitoring and auditory hallucinations. *Psychological Medicine*, 27(3), 669–679.

Oh, T. M., McCarthy, R. A., and McKenna, P. J. (2002). Is there a schizophasia? A study applying the single case approach to formal thought disorder in schizophrenia. *Neurocase*, 8(3), 233–244.

Phillips, M. L., and David, A. S. (1998). Abnormal visual scan paths: A psychophysiological marker of delusions in schizophrenia. *Schizophrenia Research*, 29(3), 235–245.

Phillips, M. L., Senior, C., and David, A. S. (2000). Perception of threat in schizophrenics with persecutory delusions: An investigation using visual scan paths. *Psychological Medicine*, 30(1), 157–167.

Plaut, D. C. (1995). Double dissociation without modularity: Evidence from connectionist neuropsychology. *Journal of Clinical and Experimental Neuropsychology*, 17(2), 291–321.

Plaut, D. C. (2003). Interpreting double dissociations in connectionist networks. *Cortex*, 39(1), 138–141.

Robertson, L. C., Knight, R. T., Rafal, R., and Shimamura, A. P. (1993). Cognitive neuropsychology is more than single-case studies. *Journal of Experimental Psychology: Learning, Memory, and Cognition*, 19(3), 710–717.

Rossell, S. L., Shapleske, J., and David, A. S. (1998). Sentence verification and delusions: A content-specific deficit. *Psychological Medicine*, 28(5), 1189–1198.

Russell, T. A., Rubia, K., Bullmore, E. T., Soni, W., Suckling, J., Brammer, M. J., Simmons, A., Williams, S. C. R., and Sharma, T. (2000). Exploring the social brain in schizophrenia: Left prefrontal underactivation during mental state attribution. *American Journal of Psychiatry*, 157(12), 2040–2042.

Shallice, T. (1998). *From neuropsychology to mental structure*. Cambridge: Cambridge University Press.

Shallice, T. (2003). Functional imaging and neuropsychology findings: How can they be linked? *Neuroimage*, 20(suppl 1) S146–S154.

Shapleske, J., Rossell, S. L., Woodruff, P. W. R., Suckling, J., and Bullmore, E. (2002). A computational morphometric MRI study of schizophrenia: Effects of hallucinations. *Cerebral Cortex*, 12(12), 1331–1341.

Shergill, S. S., Brammer, M. J., Amaro, E., Williams, S. C. [R.], Murray, R. M., and McGuire, P. K. (2004). Temporal course of auditory hallucinations. *British Journal of Psychiatry*, 185, 516–517.

Shergill, S. S., Brammer, M. J., Williams, S. C. R., Murray, R. M., and McGuire, P. K. (2000). Mapping auditory hallucinations in schizophrenia using functional magnetic resonance imaging. *Archives of General Psychiatry*, 57(11), 1033–1038.

Sitnikova, T., Salisbury, D. F., Kuperberg, G., and Holcomb, P. J. (2002). Electrophysiological insights into language processing in schizophrenia. *Psychophysiology*, 39(6), 851–860.

Teuber, H. L. (1955). Physiological psychology. *Annual Review of Pscyhology*, 6, 267–296.

Van Order, G. C., Pennington, B. F., and Stone, G. O. (2001). What do double dissocations prove? *Cogntive Science*, 25, 111–172.

Williams, L. M., Das, P., Harris, A. W. F., Liddell, B. J., Brammer, M. J., Skerrett, D., Phillips, M. L., David, A. S., Peduto, A., and Gordon, E. (2004). Dysregulation of arousal and amygdala-prefrontal systems in paranoid schizophrenia. *American Journal of Psychiatry*, *161*(3), 480–489.

Woodruff, P. W., Wright, I. C., Bullmore, E. T., Brammer, M., Howard, R. J., Williams, S. C. R., Shapleske, J., Rossell, S., David, A. S., McGuire, P. K., and Murray, R. M. (1997). Auditory hallucinations and the temporal cortical response to speech in schizophrenia: A functional magnetic resonance imaging study. *American Journal of Psychiatry*, *154*(12), 1676–1682.

3 Cognitive Neuroscience and Nonhuman Primates: Lesion Studies

Elisabeth A. Murray and Mark G. Baxter

From the battlefields of antiquity to the present, military medicine found that damage to different parts of the brain caused different deficits. Injury to the left brain produced paralysis of the right limbs, and injury to the right brain, paralysis on the left; injury to the back brain produced blindness, whereas extensive excisions of the front brain had scarcely any effect at all. In the fourth and fifth centuries B.C.E., for example, Hippocratic physicians observed that damage to one side of the brain caused motor disabilities on the opposite side of the body (Lassek, 1954). And, during World War I, military doctors noticed that bullets lodged in the back of the brain disrupted sight in discrete portions of the visual scene.

Inevitably, physicians and surgeons attempted to replicate the deficits observed in military medicine and clinical neurology in nonhuman animals—to "create a patient," as one practitioner so famously declared. Although condemned by antivivisectionists of the time as inapplicable to humans, such animal research of the late nineteenth century established the principles of cortical organization for all mammals, including our species. Needless to add, the field of cognitive neuroscience faces a ferocious attack from contemporary antivivisectionists, and so it is particularly appropriate to consider its place in modern neuroscience at this pivotal juncture.

If we are to understand how the brain carries out its myriad cognitive functions—processing sights, sounds, and bodily sensations, thinking, feeling, learning, attending, and guiding action, among others—the problem before us is one of reverse engineering (Pinker, 1997). This is because the brain, an amazing computational device (or collection of devices), already exists, and its computations have been shaped by evolution. In taking apart the brain to see "how the mind works," lesion studies in nonhuman animals represent an essential part of the armamentarium of reverse engineering.

The relationship between brain bits and their cognitive functions is difficult to pin down in humans. This is because accidental brain damage—

whether caused by injury, stroke, tumors, or disease—typically involves an array of brain structures and produces an array of cognitive disabilities. Occasionally, however, circumstances arise that reveal the relationship between regions of the human brain and their cognitive functions in an individual. Two celebrated cases are Phineas Gage, who exhibited marked changes in personality as a consequence of frontal lobe damage (Damasio et al., 1994), and H.M., who developed severe and persistent anterograde amnesia after bilateral surgical removal of the medial aspect of the temporal lobes (Scoville and Milner, 1957). In the case of Phineas Gage, a construction foreman, an accidental blast sent a tamping iron through his frontal lobes. After the accident, he began to exhibit socially inappropriate behavior, including use of profane language; once highly reliable, he became irresponsible. In the case of H.M., although the surgical excision intended to reduce the frequency and severity of his epileptic seizures did indeed produce the desired effect—alleviation of the seizures—it also had the unintended effect of producing a selective impairment in his ability to retain new information for more than a few minutes. In both these cases, and in other instances of brain damage, the effects were at once profound yet strikingly selective; that is, the mental faculties (e.g., general intelligence, speech) outside the specific area of change were otherwise remarkably intact. For this reason, lesion studies constitute a highly relevant and essential source of information for modern cognitive neuroscience.

The specific contribution of experimental lesion studies in animals is the ability to make anatomically circumscribed lesions and to exert a high degree of control over the protocols used to assess cognitive function both before and after the lesion is induced. Today, most neuropsychological studies in nonhuman primates are carried out in three species of macaques—the rhesus monkey (*Macaca mulatta*), the cynomolgus monkey (*Macaca fascicularis*), and the Japanese macaque (*Macaca fuscata*)—and in one species of New World primate, the common marmoset (*Callithrix jacchus*; e.g., Dias, Robbins, and Roberts, 1996; Ridley, Baker, and Weight, 1980).

Although recently developed techniques such as fMRI can point to structures involved in a cognitive function, experimental lesion studies are still the only way to determine if a given brain structure is necessary for a given function. Consequently, findings from lesion studies complement those from physiological studies employing neuronal recording or functional imaging techniques. The reverse is also true; because physiological measures such as fMRI can reflect activity in the whole brain, whereas lesion studies necessarily focus on a specific structure or set of structures, functional imaging in humans may inform the work in nonhuman primates. Or, in the words of Gerhardt von Bonin (1960: vii), musing about the promise of the then newly developed electrophysiological and cellular physiological methods: "Much of this is all to the good, but the older approach should not be completely forgotten when one gets dazzled by the modern treatment of the subject."

Both the experimental lesion method itself and the behavioral tasks used to assess cognition are critical elements of cognitive neuroscience research. Lesion methods and behavioral tasks have not been static. Recent research has used sophisticated methods to produce lesions of particular neurochemical systems or gene products within the brain; when used in conjunction with behavioral designs of increasing complexity, these new approaches permit finer-grained determinations of the cognitive processes affected by the lesion. This chapter will review how behavioral techniques have changed over the years, the types of experimental lesion techniques available (e.g., induction of excitotoxic lesions and of immunotoxic lesions with agents such as 192 IgG-saporin), the limitations of lesion studies, how specific lesion techniques might be improved (e.g., induction of reversible lesions with antisense or other receptor-specific manipulations), and how lesion techniques might be applied in the future to enhance our understanding of monkey and human cognition.

Development

The systematic use of selective cerebral lesions and disconnections in animals to study cerebral localization of function has a long history, one dating from the early nineteenth century and the work of Marie-Jean-Pierre Flourens, Hermann Munk, Sir David Ferrier, Gustav Fritsch, and Eduard Hitzig, among others. To learn about the work of these early investigators, the reader is directed to a translation of selected works by these authors (von Bonin, 1960). In addition, Gross (1998) documents the history of research investigations into the neural substrates of visual memory, with an emphasis on work in nonhuman primates.

This section focuses on relatively recent developments in lesion techniques applied to nonhuman primates. In our view, the critical developments arising from roughly the 1980s onward fall into two main categories: (1) conceptual developments in the behavioral assessments of cognitive function; and (2) technical developments allowing greater accuracy and precision in the placement of lesions.

Advances in Behavioral Testing

Early work in monkey neuropsychology relied on only a few behavioral tests, of which discrimination learning, delayed response, and their variants figured prominently. Indeed, a popular handbook of standard methods used to investigate behavior in nonhuman primates (Schrier, Harlow, and Stollnitz, 1965) outlines techniques of discrimination learning, oddity, delayed response, and delayed alternation. Subsequently, researchers gradually migrated from what might be called a "selection mode," in which they chose from the handful of available tasks, to an "instructed mode," in which they designed tasks to test specific hypotheses. For example, although retention of discrimination problems was once the standard task used to measure memory in monkeys (e.g., Orbach, Milner, and Rasmussen, 1960), the use of the delayed matching- and nonmatching-to-sample tasks, in which memory was taxed by requiring monkeys to remember objects over increasingly longer delay intervals or to remember lists of items (Mishkin and Delacour, 1975; Gaffan, 1974), and in which new objects were used on every trial, provided a breakthrough in understanding the contribution of medial temporal lobe structures to stimulus memory (for review, see Murray, 1996). In the following paragraphs, we provide three additional examples of lesion studies in monkeys that represent the conceptual development in behavioral assessment alluded to earlier—that is, the shift away from the use of standard, "off-the-shelf" tasks toward the design and use of theoretically motivated tasks designed to test specific hypotheses. We hope these examples, which necessarily involve relatively specific descriptions of behavioral tasks, will provide the reader with a sense not only of the challenges confronting experimenters but also of the thrill of tackling tough issues in cognitive neuroscience.

One underrepresented topic of study in monkey neuropsychology is the use of strategies and rules. To investigate the neural substrates for the acquisition and performance of strategies, Gaffan et al. (2002) designed a "strategy task" in which two different classes of objects needed to be treated differently. Specifically, on each trial the monkey was offered a choice between two objects, one from each class. Rewards could be obtained in one of two ways: first, "persistent" responses to the first class of object across trials, which resulted in reward after four consecutive "persistent" responses, and second, a "sporadic" response to the second class, which resulted in reward only when a "persistent" reward had been earned previously. Repeated responses to the "sporadic" class of object did not give reward until another reward had been earned for touching the "persistent" class of objects. Monkeys learned to apply a strategy that resulted in the most efficient delivery of rewards under this schedule (four "persistent" object choices followed by a single "sporadic" object choice). Using this task, together with a crossed-lesion design, Gaffan and his colleagues were able to demonstrate that inferior temporal cortex and frontal cortex need to interact to support performance on the task and therefore, presumably, to implement strategies. Furthermore, although the monkeys with the crossed disconnection surgery could not apply the preoperatively learned strategy, they could perform other visual tasks, demonstrating that their deficit was not due to altered visual perceptual abilities. Although there have been other forays into the neural basis of rule learning and implementation in monkeys, this is certainly one of the more creative ones.

In another example of the instructed mode, using tasks that evaluate the candidate operating characteristics of episodic memory, Rapp, Kansky, and Eichenbaum (1996) have investigated the specific information-processing functions that enable episodic memory in humans. One such task is transitive inference, which requires the ability to derive inferences from information stored in memory. Monkeys are first trained on a series of over-lapping discrimination problems (e.g., A+ vs. B−, B+ vs. C−, C+ vs. D−, and D+ vs. E−). After learning these individual problems, they are given a test of transitive inference, which involves presentation of a choice between B and D, two items that have never been paired with each other. In this example, because the relationships between the items can be organized hier-archically as A > B > C > D > E, the choice consistent with this hierarchy would be B over D, a tendency indeed displayed by intact monkeys. A related task employs paired-associate learning in which visual cues instruct visual choices. Monkeys first learn conditional problems of the structure "If A, choose B and not Y; if X, choose Y and not B." A new set of over-lapping problems is then given: "If B, choose C and not Z; if Y, choose Z and not C." On probe trials meant to test the contents of memory, the monkeys are presented with a cue from the first set of problems, A, and with choices from the second set of problems, C versus Z. Here, as in the transitive inference task, a monkey is required to make an inference, but one based on stimulus-stimulus association rather than ordinal position. Recently, Buckmaster et al. (2004) found that monkeys with entorhinal cortex lesions were impaired on both of these tests. Because of the exten-sive interconnections between the entorhinal cortex and hippocampus, and because the tasks required flexible use of stored information, these researchers interpreted their findings as support for the idea that the hip-pocampal formation enables episodic memory in nonhuman animals.

Finally, some authors have designed tasks based on predictions derived from computational modeling. For example, Bussey and his colleagues (Bussey and Saksida, 2002; Bussey, Saksida, and Murray, 2002) proposed that perirhinal cortex, a region in the medial temporal lobe, contained visual representations of complex conjunctions of features. They further proposed that various effects of perirhinal cortex damage could be accounted for by the nature of the visual representations stored in perirhinal cortex. To test this notion, they designed tasks that required the representation of complex conjunction of features for their solution. In one study, objects were constructed to contain overlapping elements and these were presented for discrimination. The objects were made by placing two different complex grayscale pictures (A and B) side by side, thereby creating a compound object AB. Monkeys were required to discriminate these compound objects (e.g., AB+ vs. AD− and CD+ vs. BC− and other trial configurations involving the same objects). As predicted by the model, monkeys with perirhinal cortex lesions were found to be impaired on this task. In contrast, object pairs that did not involve overlapping elements (e.g., MN+ vs. OP− and WX+ vs. YZ−) could be discriminated at a normal rate by monkeys with perirhinal cortex damage, indicating a specificity of the impairment for discrimination problems that required resolution of overlapping features. Additional tests of this idea involved complex objects created through stimulus morphing. This work showed that not only are monkeys with perirhinal cortex lesions impaired in processing these kinds of complex stimuli (Bussey, Saksida, and Murray, 2003), but humans with damage to perirhinal cortex damage are impaired as well (Lee et al., 2005). Tests designed for monkeys were thus used to assess cognitive abilities in humans, leading to new insights in brain function.

Advances in Lesion Methodology

The standard, aspirative lesion technique, in large part set and disseminated by Karl Pribram (e.g., Pribram et al., 1952), employs the use of small-gauge aspirative suckers that permitted precise removal of brain tissue, combined with use of electrocautery to control loss of blood. The systematic manner in which gray matter is removed just below the pia mater, the method of reconstructing brain lesions by performing histological processing of brain tissue and microscopic examination of the lesion boundaries, and the identification of patterns of thalamic degeneration all can be traced to Pribram.

Another standard practice in lesion studies is transection of discrete white matter bundles such as the corpus callosum (Sperry, Stamm, and

Miner, 1956), the fornix (e.g., Gaffan et al., 1984), white matter of the temporal stem (Cirillo, Horel, and George, 1989) and uncinate fascicle (Eacott and Gaffan, 1992). Fornix transection has the advantage, over direct hippocampal damage, of being reproducible. Even more important, the procedure can be carried out in an operation that inflicts negligible damage to extrahippocampal structures. Weighing against these advantages of fornix transection is the growing realization that the effects of fornix transection and hippocampal removal can differ (e.g., Whishaw and Jarrard, 1995).

Another useful method is the cooling of brain tissue (e.g., Horel et al., 1987). By blocking nerve conduction, cooling produces an acute dysfunction of the cooled tissue. Because it can be rapidly applied and reversed and, more important, because it apparently produces no permanent damage to the cooled tissue, cooling can be used repeatedly, across days and across months, within subjects. Researchers can measure cognitive abilities under the influence of cooling and in a control (warm) condition within a single test session. Disadvantages of this method are that it is difficult to specify the amount of tissue affected by the cooling and that cooling may not yield the same behavioral effects as a chronic lesion.

Current state-of-the-art procedures include use of MRI-guided stereotaxic procedures combined with the injection of excitotoxins to achieve a selective lesion. Before the advent of magnetic resonance imaging, it had been difficult to localize brain structures—especially deep structures—with sufficient accuracy to employ stereotaxic approaches. This is because there is extensive interanimal variability, even within a given species of nonhuman primate, in the locations of structures relative to a landmark like the external auditory meatus (location of ear bar 0 of a stereotaxic apparatus). For example, as shown in figure 3.1, the distance in the anteroposterior (AP) plane from the middle of the amygdala to ear bar 0 in a set of rhesus monkeys ranges from about 16 to 24 mm (coauthor Murray, unpublished data). These data are comparable to those reported by Aggleton and Passingham (1981), who found, in a group of 35 rhesus monkeys, that the distance in the AP plane from the middle of the mammillary bodies to the external auditory meatus (ear bar 0) ranged roughly from 12 to 19 mm. In a traditional stereotaxic surgical approach based on a standard atlas, the locations of brain structures appear as a fixed distance from ear bar 0.

Thus the kind of variability shown in figure 3.1 makes it unlikely that stereotaxic coordinates of the amygdala or the mamillary bodies, as determined from a "standard" brain, would target either of these structures with a high degree of accuracy. To circumvent this problem, Aggleton and Passingham (1981) used x-radiographs to find bony landmarks in the skull

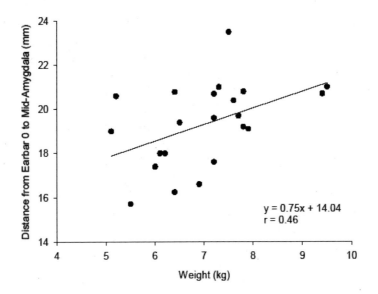

Figure 3.1
Distance between the middle of the amygdala and the external auditory meatus (location of ear bar 0), plotted as a function of body weight, in rhesus monkeys. Data are from 22 hemispheres, half left and half right, in 18 rhesus monkeys.

that were located close to the targeted structure, thereby providing better reliability in their stereotaxic approach. Now, however, MRI is used to obtain a brain atlas of each monkey. Consequently, stereotaxic coordinates are simply tailored to the individual monkey brain and accuracy is as good as the resolution obtained from the scanner times the margin of error in the stereotaxic approach. Standard methods have been described by several groups (e.g., Saunders, Aigner, and Frank, 1990; Alvarez-Royo et al., 1991; Hampton et al., 2004), and figure 3.2 shows the kinds of images enabling one such approach (see plate 1).

One additional advantage of MRI is that the location and extent of an aspirative lesion can be assessed in vivo, allowing publication of data while the animals are undergoing additional behavioral testing. Interestingly, extended periods of behavioral evaluation could translate to within-subject data on a greater number of tasks, which could then lead to more powerful analyses of cognitive functions (e.g., correlational analyses) within lesion groups. Furthermore, excitotoxic lesions may also be assessed by MRI (Málková et al., 2001), a method that will undoubtedly become more useful as investigators gain additional information in this area. Figure 3.3 provides examples of postoperative structural magnetic resonance images

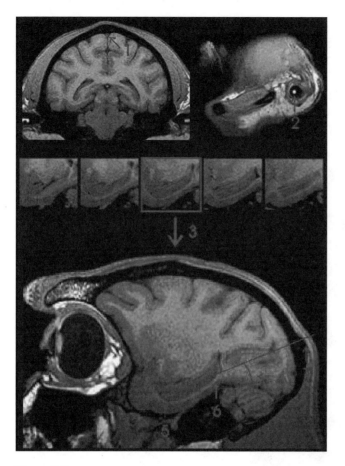

Figure 3.2
T1-weighted MR images obtained from a young adult rhesus monkey. Images show
the brain in the coronal plane (top left) and several parasagittal planes (all others).
The arrows and numerals highlight landmarks used to plan MRI-guided longitudi-
nal surgical approaches to the hippocampus. (Reprinted from Hampton et al., 2004)
See plate 1 for color version.

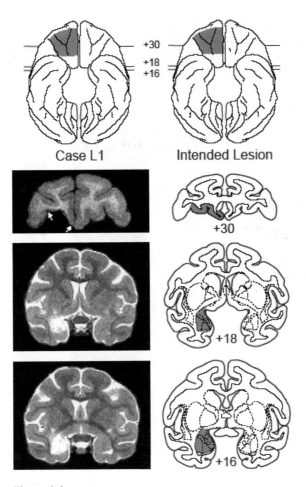

Figure 3.3
Schematic diagram showing the location and extent of the intended lesion (right column) on both the ventral view of a macaque brain (top) and coronal sections (bottom). The intended lesion (shaded area) includes both the orbital prefrontal cortex and the amygdala in the left hemisphere. A reconstruction of the orbital prefrontal cortex lesion (shaded region, top) and MR images through the lesion (bottom) from one case are shown in the left column. The orbital prefrontal cortex lesion (marked by the white arrows) was assessed with T1-weighted MR images (e.g., level +30) and the amygdala lesion was assessed with T2-weighted MR images (levels +18 and +16) obtained within 7–10 days of surgery. The white region ("hypersignal") in the MR images at levels +18 and +16 reveals local edema consequent to injections of ibotenic acid into the amygdala. Numerals indicate distance from the interaural plane (0). (Adapted from Izquierdo and Murray, 2004)

illustrating both an aspirative lesion of the orbital prefrontal cortex (level +30) and an excitotoxic lesion of the amygdala (levels +18 and +16). Because the lesion in this monkey was made only in the left hemisphere, the intact right hemisphere is available for comparison with the left. Figure 3.4 shows photomicrographs of Nissl-stained brain sections (taken from another operated monkey in the same study that sustained the same lesion) after traditional histological processing of the brain. A comparison of the two figures reveals that MRI can provide an accurate indication of the extent of a lesion.

Principles

Examination of the cognitive abilities of brain-damaged subjects, whether the damage occurred by accident (as in the case of human neurological patients) or design (as in the case of experimental lesion studies), provides unique insights into the organization of function within the brain. Only lesion analyses can establish the extent to which a particular structure is necessary for a particular function. Structure, in this case, could include particular molecules such as ion channels or neurotransmitter receptors, as well as neuronal fiber tracts, in addition to particular populations of neurons.

The logic of lesion studies is clearly and elegantly laid out by Olton (1991), who summarizes three basic patterns of results from which inferences can be drawn about brain function based on results of lesion studies: (1) no dissociation; (2) single dissociation, and (3) double dissociation. The most powerful designs compare two or more lesion groups on two or more tasks. When there is no dissociation and a single lesion impairs two (or more) tasks, it can be inferred that the tasks have at least one function in common that is required for their correct performance, and this function is disrupted by the lesion in question. Interpretation of similar effects of two or more lesions on a single task is much less straightforward: it cannot be inferred that the structures are involved in a single common function of the task. In a single dissociation, one lesion impairs performance on both task A and task B, whereas the second lesion impairs performance on task B only. This implies, as with no dissociation, that the two tasks share at least one function that is disrupted by the first lesion. Furthermore, task B requires some function that task A does not, which requires the structure damaged by the second kind of lesion. This, in turn, implies a sequential organization of processing. In a double dissociation, one lesion impairs task A but not task B, whereas the second lesion impairs task B but not task A.

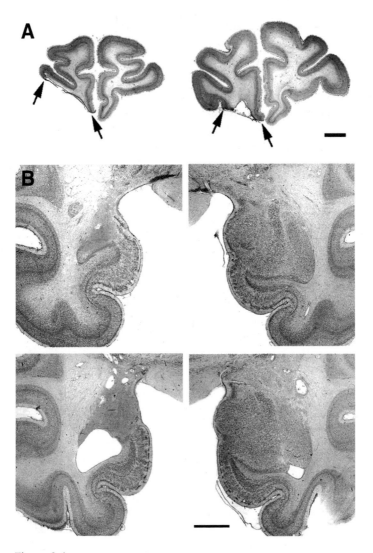

Figure 3.4
Photomicrographs of Nissl-stained coronal sections through the lesion in a monkey that sustained an aspirative removal of the left orbital prefrontal cortex (A) and an excitotoxic lesion of the left amygdala (B). The extent of the lesion in this case can be judged by comparing the left (operated on) and right (intact) hemispheres. The boundaries of the orbital prefrontal cortex lesion are marked by the black arrows. Note the massive cell loss and gliosis in the region of the left amygdala. Scale bar: 7 mm (A) and 3 mm (B). Compare and contrast with figure 3.3. (Adapted from Izquierdo and Murray, 2004)

This implies that each task engages a unique function that is not required for the other task, and that these unique functions require activity in the structure whose damage results in impairment in the particular task.

Lesion methods may also be used to examine the extent to which structures functionally interact in the performance of a task. This approach employs crossed unilateral lesions of different brain structures in each hemisphere, and was first described by Ettlinger (1959). For example, consider a task in which lesions of both structures X and Y impair performance to similar degrees. This does not necessarily imply that X and Y are contributing to task in the same way, or that the contributions of structures X and Y to task performance depend on each other. If, however, intrahemispheric interaction between structures X and Y is required for efficient task performance, then a lesion of structure X in one hemisphere and structure Y in the other hemisphere should produce a comparable impairment to bilateral lesions of either structure X or Y. Aside from providing information about the circuits involved in task performance, this procedure also has the advantage that unilateral lesions of individual structures are often without effect; if such effects occur, they tend to be mild. For instance, bilateral amygdala aspiration lesions produce a syndrome of bizarre behavioral effects including hyperorality and emotional changes (Weiskrantz, 1956; Meunier et al., 1999), which could complicate the interpretation of cognitive deficits after such lesions. Bilateral amygdala aspiration, or crossed unilateral aspiration lesions of amygdala and auditory association cortex, was shown to impair visual discrimination learning for auditory secondary reinforcement (Gaffan and Harrison, 1987). But because only bilateral amygdala aspiration lesions produced overt changes in emotional reactivity, the learning impairment could not be attributed to any global changes in behavior consequent to the lesion. As it happens, the learning impairment in discrimination learning for auditory secondary reinforcement was likely the result of disconnection of inferotemporal cortex rather than damage to the cell bodies of the amygdala itself, which was only discovered when neurotoxic amygdala lesions were applied to this problem (see Málková et al., 1997; Baxter, Hadfield, and Murray, 1999).

As Olton (1991) notes, it is desirable to go beyond "impairment" and "no impairment" in terms of the description of the results of lesion studies. Because there are differing degrees of impairment on many tasks, consideration of the level of impairment (mild to severe) is an important characteristic of the description of results. Moreover, apparently intact performance on one measure may belie differences in strategies used to solve the task. As an example, aged rhesus monkeys show normal signatures of transitive inference learning when their discrimination performance is tested, but reaction time differences between different types of transitive inference probes are not seen, suggesting that the monkeys are using a different cognitive strategy to support their discrimination performance (Rapp, Kansky, and Eichenbaum, 1996). Furthermore, there are more complex aspects of neural organization in which lesions may act in unexpected ways, revealing synergistic or competitive effects on behavior (e.g., Kim and Baxter, 2001). Thus the interpretation of lesion effects may sometimes be complex or controversial; in these circumstances, converging evidence from other experimental approaches becomes important in understanding the nature and organization of the particular cognitive processes being studied.

Another critical aspect of lesion studies is the use of parametric manipulations of task difficulty (Olton, 1991; Olton and Shapiro, 1992). It is difficult to draw conclusions about the extent to which a structure is *not* involved in a task on the basis of dissociations alone. What is really required are parametric manipulations of task difficulty. Difficulty in this sense may be along any one of several different perceptual dimensions, including (for visual sensory stimuli) contrast, brightness, rotation, degradation with white noise, or, in the case of memory, the amount of time over which stimulus material is retained. In the absence of such manipulations, conclusions about the extent to which particular brain structures or psychological functions are required for performance of a task are limited by the constraints of a particular testing situation. For example, a lesion that is without effect on a visual recognition memory task where the delay between sample and choice never exceeds 30 seconds may nevertheless have an effect on visual recognition memory where delays are extended. On the other hand, if the particular structure is not involved in visual recognition memory at all, lesions of that structure should never produce an effect regardless of how difficult the task is made. For example, conjoint neurotoxic lesions of the amygdala and hippocampus in monkeys fail to impair visual recognition as tested in a delayed nonmatching-to-sample procedure, even when the delay between sample and choice is extended to as long as 40 minutes and performance of control monkeys is nearly at chance (Murray and Mishkin, 1998).

An underlying assumption of work with nonhuman primates is that identical cognitive tasks administered to monkeys and humans will be tapping the same cognitive function. The situation is not quite so simple, however. Use of the identical task in humans and monkeys is no assurance that the task is measuring the same cognitive function in both. For example, acquisition of concurrent visual discrimination problems administered with 24-hour intertrial intervals is unaffected by medial temporal lobe (MTL) lesions in monkeys, and therefore thought to be a test of habit formation (Mishkin and Petri, 1984). Interestingly, humans with medial temporal lobe lesions, unlike their monkey counterparts, fail this test (Hood, Postle, and Corkin, 1999; see also Aggleton, Shaw, and Gaffan, 1992). At this time, it is not evident which cognitive functions in humans make this task dependent on the MTL, although it has been conjectured that humans try to impose declarative, language-based solutions unavailable to monkeys. Thus it appears that identifying behavioral homologies between monkeys and humans requires more than presentation with the same or similar task requirements (Roberts, 1996). A related point is that comparisons between monkeys and humans are facilitated when the questions are asked the same way—for example, when nonverbalizable stimuli and forced-choice responses are used in human studies (Weiskrantz, 1977), as they typically are in monkey studies.

In experimental neuropsychological studies that have examined the neural substrates of memory, two main approaches can be identified. One approach, which might be called the "ablation-correlation approach," holds that if damage to a given set of brain structures in humans produces an impairment of a specific type, say, in declarative memory, then any deficits caused by similar damage in nonhuman animals can be classed as "declarative" (Squire, 1992). The "attribute approach," by contrast, seeks to identify characteristics or properties of declarative memory that might be common to monkeys and humans (e.g., Eichenbaum, 1997; for review, see Wise and Murray, 1999). The latter approach can be broadened to include a systematic examination of manipulations (including lesions and pharmacological modulations) of the same brain structures in monkeys and humans using the same or similar tasks. If task performance is affected by manipulations of the same neural networks in monkeys and humans, then it seems highly likely that there is behavioral homology. This approach has been used successfully to delineate the cognitive functions of prefrontal corticostriatal circuits (e.g., Roberts, 1996).

We make no attempt here to argue the merits of one approach over another. The approach taken in any given study is dictated to a large extent by the goal of the study. If the goal is to create an animal model of a particular syndrome, which can then be further studied to characterize the neurobiological correlates of a clinical syndrome or to design and evaluate potential therapeutic interventions, then the "ablation correlation" approach might be justified. On the other hand, if the overarching goal is to analyze the cognitive function of a specific brain region, then the "attribute approach" is warranted. The types of task used to evaluate cognitive functions and the way in which they are selected (see "Development") interact with the approach being employed.

Several animal models have been developed in nonhuman primates to examine the relationship between brain damage and cognitive function. For example, lesions within the medial temporal lobe are thought to model global anterograde amnesia (Mishkin, 1978; Zola-Morgan, 1984); brain lesions produced by ischemic episodes have been used to model the effects of posterior cerebral artery occlusion in humans (Bachevalier and Mishkin, 1989; Zola-Morgan et al., 1992). Other models used in nonhuman primates to assess the relationship between brain damage and cognitive function include basal forebrain damage to model Alzheimer's disease (Aigner et al., 1991; Voytko et al., 1994); exposure to the deadly neurotoxin MPTP to model Parkinson's disease (e.g., Belluzi et al., 1994); simian immunodeficiency virus (SIV) infection to model the cognitive impairments observed in HIV-infected humans (Murray et al., 1992). Also, to the extent that there are neurobiological changes in aging even in the absence of frank cell loss (Morrison and Hof, 1997), effects of lesions in young monkeys provide a neuropsychological framework for interpreting cognitive impairments in aged monkeys and linking them to biological changes in the aged brain (e.g., Baxter, 2001a).

Innovation

In recent years, techniques have been developed to induce lesions in specific neurotransmitter systems or specific receptor subtypes. Some systems can be targeted by metabolic toxins that are taken up through neurotransmitter transporters and then kill the neuron through the generation of free radicals. For example, one can selectively remove the influence of the neurotransmitters dopamine or serotonin by injecting 6-hydroxydopamine (6-OHDA) or 5,7-dihydroxytryptamine, respectively, into a cortical field or nucleus. A related agent, ethylcholine mustard aziridinium ion (AF64A), has been developed for lesions of the cholinergic system, although its selectivity for cholinergic neurons is not clear (e.g., Schliebs et al., 1996). These methods often require adjunct treatment with drugs to prevent uptake into unintended targets. Thus, if a selective dopaminergic lesion is desired, norepinephrine and serotonin uptake must be blocked to protect terminals from 6-OHDA (Roberts et al., 1994).

More recent approaches have involved the use of toxins bound to proteins that permit the targeting of specific cell populations based on their expression of cell surface receptors. Two general strategies are (1) to use an antibody against a particular receptor to target cells expressing that receptor; and (2) to use a peptide receptor ligand to target cells that express receptors binding that peptide. For example, the immunotoxin 192 IgG-saporin is composed of a monoclonal antibody to the low-affinity nerve growth factor (p75) receptor, which is expressed on the surface of basal forebrain cholinergic neurons as well as cerebellar Purkinje cells (Pioro and Cuello, 1990a, 1990b), covalently bound to a molecule of saporin, a ribosome-inactivating protein. When injected into the cerebral ventricles, this toxin produces an efficient lesion of p75 receptor–bearing cells (Wiley, Oeltmann, and Lappi, 1991; Heckers et al., 1994). Selective lesions of particular cell populations can be made by injecting the toxin into specific nuclei, for example, within the basal forebrain of rats (Heckers et al., 1994; Baxter et al., 1995), marmosets (Ridley et al., 1999), or macaques (Easton et al., 2002), or into cortical regions innervated by cholinergic axons, which also express the p75 receptor (Holley et al., 1994; Bucci, Holland, and Gallagher, 1998; Turchi, Saunders, and Mishkin, 2005). An example of the second toxin strategy is the use of a molecule of substance P conjugated to saporin, which produces selective lesions of substance P receptor–bearing neurons (Wiley and Lappi, 1997; Mantyh et al., 1997), although as far as we are aware this latter lesion strategy has not yet been applied in monkeys.

It is also possible to design DNA constructs that interfere with the expression of particular membrane receptor molecules, a strategy recently applied in a behavioral context in nonhuman primates by Liu et al. (2004). The DNA constructs targeting either NMDA receptor subunit 2B (NR2B) or dopamine D2 receptors were injected either separately or in combination into the entorhinal and perirhinal (i.e., "rhinal") cortex of monkeys that had been trained on a visual discrimination task in which visual cues indicated how many trials they had to complete before reward was delivered. Once the cues were learned, monkeys displayed a pattern of performing fewer errors as they got closer to reward delivery. Injection of D2-interfering constructs, like aspiration lesions of rhinal cortex, produced a disruption in the relationship between error rate and distance from reward. Unlike the behavior of monkeys receiving aspiration lesions, however, that of the injected monkeys returned to its preinjection state after a variable period of time (11–19 weeks). Presumably, as the effect of the DNA construct wore off and D2 expression returned to normal, rhinal cortex function was reinstated. The advantages of this technique include its reversibility, long-lasting action, and lack of tolerance (as might occur in pharmacological approaches). Developments in related technologies, such as RNA interference, promise rapid progress in these types of approaches in the coming years.

Limitations

The main limitation of the standard, aspirative lesion technique is that it can interrupt fibers of passage. This is nowhere better demonstrated than by a consideration of the work on the neural substrates of visual recognition in monkeys, in which the initial conclusion that combined damage to the amygdala and hippocampus was required to produce severe impairments (Mishkin, 1978) took roughly 20 years to overturn (Murray and Mishkin, 1998). It is now widely appreciated that, within the medial temporal lobe, damage to the entorhinal and perirhinal cortex (regions immediately subjacent to the amygdala and hippocampus) is both necessary and sufficient to yield severe impairments in visual recognition memory as measured by delayed nonmatching-to-sample. This amazing reversal was precipitated by the inadvertent transection of temporal cortical efferent fibers passing near the amygdala, and probably the hippocampus as well (Horel, 1978; Murray, 1992), which occurs during aspiration removal of these structures. Although aspirative lesions of the cortical surface are less likely to be subject to this problem of interpretation, the use of excitotoxins, which largely spare axons passing near or through the site of cell loss, is clearly the preferred method.

On the interpretation of lesion effects is also limited on several other levels. On a purely methodological level, it is essential to verify that the lesion is actually doing what the experimenter thinks it is doing; generally, this involves careful histological evaluation to confirm that the lesion is confined to the intended structure. If it is not, operated control groups should be included to evaluate the effects of damage outside the region of interest. In addition, verification includes confirmation of neurochemical selectivity in the case of more refined techniques that seek to damage a particular cell population. For example, infusions of 192 IgG-saporin directly into brain tissue may damage noncholinergic neurons if the dose and infusion parameters have not been piloted carefully (for a discussion of methodological issues, see Baxter, 2001b).

On a more psychological level, a criticism commonly levied against lesion studies is that, because they are examining the function of a damaged system, they cannot be used to make inferences about functions of the intact brain. This is a legitimate criticism, but it must be remembered that the goal of a lesion study is to ascertain whether a particular brain structure is essential for a particular psychological function. This cannot be determined without damaging the structure in question to determine whether the function of interest is affected by such damage. A lesion may fail to have an effect because the extent of damage to the structure is not sufficient to produce impairment, a concern that can be addressed at least in part by parametric variations of lesion size.

Both questions, whether and to what extent a particular brain structure is essential, can be considered with respect to human clinical conditions that the lesions might be modeling. If a particular disease state produces a 70 percent depletion of a particular neurotransmitter in a certain cortical area, which is thought to be associated with a particular cognitive impairment, the finding that 80 percent experimental depletion of that neurotransmitter fails to produce cognitive impairment suggests that particular neurochemical deficit is not sufficient to produce the cognitive dysfunction in question.

There are also questions of recovery of function. A permanent lesion may have limited effects on a particular behavior because the effect of the lesion diminishes with time, perhaps because the functions of the damaged area can be taken over by other parts of the brain, or perhaps because different strategies can be developed to solve the tasks that are being examined (e.g., Lomber, 1999). Presumably, transient lesions or pharmacological disruptions are less susceptible to these kinds of concerns because there is not sufficient opportunity for compensatory brain mechanisms to engage or for alternative behavioral strategies to develop. These are important considerations in the interpretation of data from lesion experiments. Once again, it is probably worth noting that in many clinical conditions, damage is permanent rather than transient. Thus permanent (as opposed to transient) lesions may represent better models of clinical brain damage. On the other hand, transient lesion methods have a number of advantages, including the possibility of repeated within-subject comparisons, as well as greater temporal control over the induction of the lesion, such that particular phases of processing in a task might be examined—for example, acquisition versus consolidation in a memory task.

Integration

We have argued that experimental lesion studies in nonhuman primates can make unique contributions to cognitive neuroscience, and that technical and methodological advances in lesion production and behavioral testing have increased their utility. Although we have commented on the usefulness of making discrete lesions (anatomically and neurochemically) in nonhuman primates as a supplement to the testing of human patients with brain damage that occurs through injury or disease, we have not remarked on the relative merits of lesion studies in nonhuman primates compared with the use of transcranial magnetic stimulation (TMS) in humans. TMS permits the transient disruption (or augmentation) of neural activity within a cortical area affected by the TMS probe. Obviously, the collection of data from such temporary lesions on processing in the human brain is highly desirable (see, for example, Stewart and Walsh, chapter 1, this volume). Nonetheless, it is fairly clear that such a technique cannot, at present, replace lesion studies in nonhuman primates. First, TMS is limited to brain structures that can be accessed through the skull, which excludes all sub-cortical structures as well as most of the orbital prefrontal cortex and ventromedial temporal cortex. Second, the spatial extent of tissue that can be affected by the TMS probe is limited. Third, as already mentioned, TMS is susceptible to the same problems with interpretation as other transient lesion methods: the disruption of neural activity in a limited area of neocortex for hundreds of milliseconds is not similar to the damage that occurs in chronic neurological conditions. Nevertheless, the ability to approach some kinds of experimental questions with TMS in humans, rather than with lesions in monkeys, opens the door to replacing some kinds of experiments using monkeys with experiments using human volunteers instead.

With regard to the integration and combination of lesion studies with other experimental modalities, there are at present few studies in nonhuman primates in which lesions have been combined with a physiological measure of brain function, such as immediate early gene expression or unit recording, although this approach has been used productively in rats (e.g., Vann et al., 2000; Schoenbaum et al., 2003). One could imagine, however, that combining the use of selective cerebral lesions or disconnections with these or other physiological measures such as fMRI in awake behaving monkeys, together with sophisticated behavioral measures, might lead to greater understanding of how brain structures interact in cognition. Although converging evidence derived from different techniques provides the strongest evidence for brain-behavior relationships, as an essential element in the armamentarium of reverse engineering, experimental lesion studies remain a valuable tool in cognitive neuroscience.

Acknowledgments

We thank Peter Rapp, Steve Wise, and Ben Basile for helpful comments on an earlier version of this manuscript, and Ping-yu Chen for help with the figures. This work is supported by the Intramural Research Program of the National Institute of Mental Health, National Institutes of Health (E.A.M.), and by the Wellcome Trust (M.G.B.).

References

Aggleton, J. P., and Passingham, R. E. (1981). Stereotaxic surgery under X-ray guidance in the rhesus monkey, with special reference to the amygdala. *Experimental Brain Research*, *44*, 271–276.

Aggleton, J. P., Shaw, C., and Gaffan, E. A. (1992). The performance of postencephalitic amnesic subjects on two behavioural tests of memory: Concurrent discrimination learning and delayed matching-to-sample. *Cortex*, *28*, 359–372.

Aigner, T. G., Mitchell, S. J., Aggleton, J. P., DeLong, M. R., Struble, R. G., Price, D. L., Wenk, G. L., Pettigrew, K. D., and Mishkin, M. (1991). Transient impairment of recognition memory following ibotenic-acid lesions of the basal forebrain in macaques. *Experimental Brain Research*, *86*, 18–26.

Alvarez-Royo, P., Clower, R. P., Zola-Morgan, S., and Squire, L. R. (1991). Stereotaxic lesions of the hippocampus in monkeys: Determination of surgical coordinates and analysis of lesions using magnetic resonance imaging. *Journal of Neuroscience Methods*, *38*, 223–232.

Bachevalier, J., and Mishkin, M. (1989). Mnemonic and neuropathological effects of occluding the posterior cerebral artery in *Macaca mulatta*. *Neuropsychologia*, *27*, 83–105.

Baxter, M. G. (2001a). Cognitive aging in nonhuman primates. In P. Hof and C. Mobbs (Eds.), *Functional neurobiology of aging*, 407–419. San Diego: Academic Press.

Baxter, M. G. (2001b). Effects of selective immunotoxic lesions on learning and memory. In W. A. Hall (Ed.), *Immunotoxin methods and protocols*, 249–265. Methods in Molecular Biology, vol. 166. Totowa, NJ: Humana Press.

Baxter, M. G., Bucci, D. J., Gorman, L. K., Wiley, R. G., and Gallagher, M. (1995). Selective immunotoxic lesions of basal forebrain cholinergic cells: Effects on learning and memory in rats. *Behavioral Neuroscience*, *109*, 714–722.

Baxter, M. G., Hadfield, W. S., and Murray, E. A. (1999). Rhinal cortex lesions produce mild deficits in visual discrimination learning for an auditory secondary reinforcer in rhesus monkeys. *Behavioral Neuroscience*, *113*, 243–252.

Belluzzi, J. D., Domino, E. F., May, J. M., Bankiewicz, K. S., and McAfee, D. A. (1994). N-0923, a selective dopamine D2 receptor agonist, is efficacious in rat and monkey models of Parkinson's disease. *Movement Disorders*, *9*, 147–154.

Bucci, D. J., Holland, P. C., and Gallagher, M. (1998). Removal of cholinergic input to rat posterior parietal cortex disrupts incremental processing of conditioned stimuli. *Journal of Neuroscience*, *18*, 8038–8046.

Buckmaster, C. A., Eichenbaum, H., Amaral, D. G., Suzuki, W. A., and Rapp, P. R. (2004). Entorhinal cortex lesions disrupt the relational organization of memory in monkeys. *Journal of Neuroscience*, *24*, 9811–9825.

Bussey, T. J., and Saksida, L. M. (2002). The organization of visual object representations: A connectionist model of the effects of lesions in perirhinal cortex. *European Journal of Neuroscience*, *15*, 355–364.

Bussey, T. J., Saksida, L. M., and Murray, E. A. (2002). Perirhinal cortex resolves feature ambiguity in complex visual discriminations. *European Journal of Neuroscience*, *15*, 365–374.

Bussey, T. J., Saksida, L. M., and Murray, E. A. (2003). Impairments in visual discrimination after perirhinal cortex lesions: Testing "declarative" vs. "perceptual-mnemonic" views of perirhinal cortex function. *European Journal of Neuroscience*, *17*, 649–660.

Cirillo, R. A., Horel, J. A., and George, P. J. (1989). Lesions of the anterior temporal stem and the performance of delayed match-to-sample and visual discriminations in monkeys. *Behavioural Brain Research*, *34*, 55–69.

Damasio, H., Grabowski, T., Frank, R., Galaburda, A. M., and Damasio, A. R. (1994). The return of Phineas Gage: Clues about the brain from the skull of a famous patient. *Science*, *264*, 1102–1105.

Dias, R., Robbins, T. W., and Roberts, A. C. (1996). Dissociations in prefrontal cortex of affective and attentional shifts. *Nature*, *380*, 69–72.

Eacott, M. J., and Gaffan, D. (1992). Inferotemporal-frontal disconnection: The uncinate fascicle and visual associative learning in monkeys. *European Journal of Neuroscience*, *4*, 1320–1332.

Easton, A., Ridley, R. M., Baker, H. F., and Gaffan, D. (2002). Unilateral lesions of the cholinergic basal forebrain and fornix in one hemisphere and inferior temporal cortex in the opposite hemisphere produce severe learning impairments in rhesus monkeys. *Cerebral Cortex*, *12*, 729–736.

Eichenbaum, H. (1997). Declarative memory: Insights from cognitive neurobiology. *Annual Review of Psychology*, *48*, 547–572.

Ettlinger, G. (1959). Visual discrimination following successive temporal ablations in monkeys. *Brain*, *82*, 232–250.

Gaffan, D. (1974). Recognition impaired and association intact in the memory of monkeys after transection of the fornix. *Journal of Comparative and Physiological Psychology*, *86*, 1100–1109.

Gaffan, D., Easton, A., and Parker, A. (2002). Interaction of inferior temporal cortex with frontal cortex and basal forebrain: Double dissociation in strategy implementation and associative learning. *Journal of Neuroscience, 22,* 7288–7296.

Gaffan, D., and Harrison, S. (1987). Amygdalectomy and disconnection in visual learning for auditory secondary reinforcement by monkeys. *Journal of Neuroscience, 7,* 2285–2292.

Gaffan, D., Saunders, R. C., Gaffan, E. A., Harrison, S., Shields, C., and Owen, M. J. (1984). Effects of fornix transection upon associative memory in monkeys: Role of the hippocampus in learned action. *Quarterly Journal of Experimental Psychology, 36B,* 173–221.

Gross, C. G. (1998). *Brain, vision, memory: Tales in the history of neuroscience.* Cambridge, MA: MIT Press.

Hampton, R. R., Buckmaster, C. A., Anuszkiewicz-Lundgren, D., and Murray, E. A. (2004). Method for making selective lesions of the hippocampus in macaque monkeys using NMDA and a longitudinal surgical approach. *Hippocampus, 14,* 9–18.

Heckers, S., Ohtake, T., Wiley, R. G., Lappi, D. A., Geula, C., and Mesulam, M. M. (1994). Complete and selective cholinergic denervation of rat neocortex and hippocampus but not amygdala by an immunotoxin against the p75 NGF receptor. *Journal of Neuroscience, 14,* 1271–1289.

Holley, L. A., Wiley, R. G., Lappi, D. A., and Sarter, M. (1994). Cortical cholinergic deafferentation following the intracortical infusion of 192 IgG-saporin: A quantitative histochemical study. *Brain Research, 663,* 277–286.

Hood, K. L., Postle, B. R., and Corkin, S. (1999). An evaluation of the concurrent discrimination task as a measure of habit learning: Performance of amnesic subjects. *Neuropsychologia, 37,* 1375–1386.

Horel, J. A. (1978). The neuroanatomy of amnesia: A critique of the hippocampal memory hypothesis. *Brain, 101,* 403–445.

Horel, J. A., Pytko-Joiner, D. E., Voytko, M. L., and Salsbury, K. (1987). The performance of visual tasks while segments of the inferotemporal cortex are suppressed by cold. *Behavioural Brain Research, 23,* 29–42.

Izquierdo, A., and Murray, E. A. (2004). Combined unilateral lesions of the amygdala and orbital prefrontal cortex impair affective processing in rhesus monkeys. *Journal of Neurophysiology, 91,* 2023–2039.

Kim, J. J., and Baxter, M. G. (2001). Multiple brain-memory systems: The whole does not equal the sum of its parts. *Trends in Neurosciences, 24,* 324–330.

Lassek, A. M. (1954). *The pyramidal tract: Its status in medicine.* Springfield, IL: Charles C. Thomas.

Lee, A. C. H., Bussey, T. J., Murray, E. A., Saksida, L. M., Epstein, R. A., Kapur, N., Hodges, J. R., and Graham, K. S. (2005). Perceptual deficits in amnesia: Challenging the medial temporal lobe "mnemonic" view. *Neuropsychologia, 43,* 1–11.

Liu, Z., Richmond, B. J., Murray, E. A., Saunders, R. C., Steenrod, S., Stubblefield, B. K., Montague, D. M., and Ginns, E. I. (2004). DNA targeting of rhinal cortex D2 receptor protein reversibly blocks learning of cues that predict reward. *Proceedings of the National Academy of Sciences, USA, 101*, 12336–12341.

Lomber, S. G. (1999). The advantages and limitations of permanent or reversible deactivation techniques in the assessment of neural function. *Journal of Neuroscience Methods, 86*, 109–117.

Málková, L., Gaffan, D., and Murray, E. A. (1997). Excitotoxic lesions of the amygdala fail to produce impairment in visual learning for auditory secondary reinforcement but interfere with reinforce devaluation effects in rhesus monkeys. *Journal of Neuroscience, 17*, 6011–6020.

Málková, L., Lex, C. K., Mishkin, M., and Saunders, R. C. (2001). MRI-based evaluation of locus and extent of neurotoxic lesions in monkeys. *Hippocampus, 11*, 361–370.

Mantyh, P. W., Rogers, S. D., Honore, P., Allen, B. J., Ghilardi, J. R., Li, J., Daughters, R. S., Lappi, D. A., Wiley, R. G., and Simone, D. A. (1997). Inhibition of hyperalgesia by ablation of lamina I spinal neurons expressing the substance P receptor. *Science, 278*, 275–279.

Meunier, M., Bachevalier, J., Murray, E. A., Málková, L., and Mishkin, M. (1999). Effects of aspiration versus neurotoxic lesions of the amygdala on emotional responses in monkeys. *European Journal of Neuroscience, 11*, 4403–4418.

Mishkin, M. (1978). Memory in monkeys severely impaired by combined but not by separate removal of amygdala and hippocampus. *Nature, 273*, 297–298.

Mishkin, M., and Delacour, J. (1975). An analysis of short-term visual memory in the monkey. *Journal of Experimental Psychology: Animal Behavior Processes, 1*, 326–334.

Mishkin, M., and Petri, H. L. (1984). Memories and habits: Some implications for the analysis of learning and retention. In L. R. Squire and N. Butters (Eds.), *Neuropsychology of memory*, 287–296. New York: Guilford Press.

Morrison, J. H., and Hof, P. R. (1997). Life and death of neurons in the aging brain. *Science, 278*, 412–419.

Murray, E. A. (1992). Medial temporal lobe structures contributing to recognition memory in the monkey: The amygdaloid complex versus the rhinal cortex. In J. P. Aggleton (Ed.), *The amygdala: Neurobiological aspects of emotion, memory and mental dysfunction*, 453–470. New York: Wiley-Liss.

Murray, E. A. (1996). What have ablation studies told us about the neural substrates of stimulus memory? *Seminars in the Neurosciences, 8*, 13–22.

Murray, E. A., and Mishkin, M. (1998). Object recognition and location memory in monkeys with excitotoxic lesions of the amygdala and hippocampus. *Journal of Neuroscience, 18*, 6568–6582.

Murray, E. A., Rausch, D. M., Lendvay, J., Sharer, L. R., and Eiden, L. E. (1992). Cognitive and motor impairments associated with SIV infection in rhesus monkeys. *Science*, *255*, 1246–1249.

Olton, D. S. (1991). Experimental strategies to identify the neurobiological bases of memory: Lesions. In J. L. Martinez and R. P. Kesner (Eds.), *Learning and memory: A biological view* (2nd ed.), 441–466. San Diego, CA: Academic Press.

Olton, D. S., and Shapiro, M. (1992). Mnemonic dissociations: The power of parameters. *Journal of Cognitive Neuroscience*, *4*, 200–207.

Orbach, J., Milner, B., and Rasmussen, T. (1960). Learning and retention in monkeys after amygdala-hippocampus resection. *Archives of Neurology*, *3*, 230–251.

Pinker, S. (1997). *How the mind works*. New York: Norton.

Pioro, E. P., and Cuello, A. C.(1990a). Distribution of nerve growth factor receptor-like immunoreactivity in the adult rat central nervous system: Effect of colchicine and correlation with the cholinergic system. 1. Forebrain. *Neuroscience*, *34*, 57–87.

Pioro, E. P., and Cuello, A. C. (1990b). Distribution of nerve growth factor receptor-like immunoreactivity in the adult rat central nervous system: Effect of colchicine and correlation with the cholinergic system. 2. Brainstem, cerebellum, and spinal cord. *Neuroscience*, *34*, 89–110.

Pribram, K. H., Mishkin, M., Rosvold, H. E., and Kaplan, S. J. (1952). Effects on delayed response performance of lesions of dorsolateral and ventromedial frontal cortex of baboons. *Journal of Comparative and Physiological Psychology*, *45*, 155–159.

Rapp, P. R., Kansky, M. T., and Eichenbaum, H. (1996). Learning and memory for hierarchical relationships in the monkey: Effects of aging. *Behavioral Neuroscience*, *110*, 887–897.

Ridley, R. M., Baker, H. F., and Weight, M. L. (1980). Amphetamine disrupts successive but not simultaneous visual discrimination in the monkey. *Psychopharmacology*, *67*, 241–244.

Ridley, R. M., Barefoot, H. C., Maclean, C. J., Pugh, P., and Baker, H. F. (1999). Different effects on learning ability after injection of the cholinergic immunotoxin ME20.4IgG-saporin into the diagonal band of Broca, basal nucleus of Meynert, or both in monkeys. *Behavioral Neuroscience*, *113*, 303–315.

Roberts, A. C. (1996). Comparison of cognitive function in human and non-human primates. *Cognitive Brain Research*, *3*, 319–327.

Roberts, A. C., De Salvia, M. A., Wilkinson, L. S., Collins, P., Muir, J. L., Everitt, B. J., and Robbins, T. W. (1994). 6-Hydroxydopamine lesions of the prefrontal cortex in monkeys enhance performance on an analog of the Wisconsin card sort test: Possible interactions with subcortical dopamine. *Journal of Neuroscience*, *14*, 2531–2544.

Saunders, R. C., Aigner, T. G., and Frank, J. A. (1990). Magnetic resonance imaging of the rhesus monkey brain: use for stereotactic neurosurgery. *Experimental Brain Research*, *81*, 443–446.

Schoenbaum, G., Setlow, B., Saddoris, M. P., and Gallagher, M. (2003). Encoding predicted outcome and acquired value in orbitofrontal cortex during cue sampling depends upon input from the basolateral amygdala. *Neuron*, *39*, 855–867.

Schliebs, R., Rossner, S., and Bigl, V. (1996). Immunolesion by 192IgG-saporin of rat basal forebrain cholinergic system: A useful tool to produce cortical cholinergic dysfunction. *Progress in Brain Research*, *109*, 253–264.

Schrier, A. M., Harlow, H. F., and Stollnitz, F. (Eds.) (1965). *Behavior of nonhuman primates*. Vol. 1. New York: Academic Press.

Scoville, W. B., and Milner, B. (1957). Loss of recent memory after bilateral hippocampal lesions. *Journal of Neurology, Neurosurgery, and Psychiatry*, *20*, 11–21.

Sperry, R. W., Stamm, J. M., and Miner, N. (1956). Relearning tests for interocular transfer following division of optic chiasma and corpus callosum in cats. *Journal of Comparative and Physiological Psychology*, *49*, 529–533.

Squire, L. R. (1992). Memory and the hippocampus: A synthesis from findings with rats, monkeys, and humans. *Psychological Review*, *99*, 195–231.

Turchi, J., Saunders, R. C., and Mishkin, M. (2005). Effects of cholinergic deafferentation of the rhinal cortex on visual recognition memory in monkeys. *Proceedings of the National Academy of Sciences, USA*, *102*, 2158–2161.

Vann, S. D., Brown, M. W., Erichsen, J. T., and Aggleton, J. P. (2000). Fos imaging reveals differential patterns of hippocampal and parahippocampal subfield activation in rats in response to different spatial memory tests. *Journal of Neuroscience*, *20*, 2711–2718.

von Bonin, G. (1960). *The Cerebral Cortex*, Springfield, IL: Charles C Thomas.

Voytko, M. L., Olton, D. S., Richardson, R. T., Gorman, L. K., Tobin, J. R., and Price, D. L. (1994). Basal forebrain lesions in monkeys disrupt attention but not learning and memory. *Journal of Neuroscience*, *14*, 167–186.

Weiskrantz, L. (1956). Behavioral changes associated with ablation of the amygdaloid complex in monkeys. *Journal of Comparative and Physiological Psychology*, *49*, 381–391.

Weiskrantz, L. (1977). Trying to bridge some neuropsychological gaps between monkey and man. *British Journal of Psychology*, *68*, 431–445.

Whishaw, I. Q., and Jarrard, L. E. (1995). Similarities vs. differences in place learning and circadian activity in rats after fimbria-fornix section or ibotenate removal of hippocampal cells. *Hippocampus*, *5*, 595–604.

Wiley, R. G., and Lappi, D. A. (1997). Destruction of neurokinin-1 receptor expressing cells in vitro and in vivo using substance P-saporin in rats. *Neuroscience Letters*, *230*, 97–100.

Wiley, R. G., Oeltmann, T. N., and Lappi, D. A. (1991). Immunolesioning: Selective destruction of neurons using immunotoxin to rat NGF receptor. *Brain Research*, 562, 149–153.

Wise, S. P., and Murray, E. A. (1999). Role of the hippocampal system in conditional motor learning: Mapping antecedents to action. *Hippocampus*, 9, 101–117.

Zola-Morgan, S. (1984). Toward an animal model of human amnesia: Some critical issues. In L. R. Squire and N. Butters (Eds.), *Neuropsychology of memory*, 316–329. New York: Guilford Press.

Zola-Morgan, S., Squire, L. R., Rempel, N. L., Clower, R. P., and Amaral, D. G. (1992). Enduring memory impairment in monkeys after ischemic damage to the hippocampus. *Journal of Neuroscience*, 12, 2582–2596.

4 Cognitive Neuropsychology and Computational Modeling: The Contribution of Computational Neuroscience to Understanding the Mind

Glyn W. Humphreys, Dietmar G. Heinke, and Eun Young Yoon

Computational neuroscience attempts to use explicit, biologically inspired, computational models to simulate, predict, and explain human performance. This chapter will review research using this approach to model neuropsychological impairments, particularly those of visual object recognition and attention. We argue that computational studies are able to go beyond more traditional "box and arrows" models of cognition, particularly when impairments result from interactions between different components within a given cognitive system. Such studies provide an important means of helping understand how mental function arises from complex neural networks.

Development

Cognitive neuropsychological research is concerned with understanding the cognitive impairments suffered by patients after brain lesions, and with using data from such impairments to inform us about the processes that contribute to performance in normal (intact) participants (Coltheart, 1984). Neuropsychological studies can generate striking, and sometimes counter-intuitive, dissociations between processes, adding to those gained from behavioral and imaging procedures carried out with normal individuals. For example, it remains the case that some of the strongest evidence that constrains our understanding of the processes involved in normal reading comes from the study of acquired dyslexia. Here there is a double dissociation between phonological dyslexia (which entails impaired reading of nonwords along with spared reading of irregular words) and surface dyslexia (which can entail spared reading of nonwords along with impaired reading of irregular words; see Beauvois and Derouesné, 1979; Funnell, 1983; Shallice, Warrington, and McCarthy, 1983). This double dissociation has proved difficult to account for using "single route" models, especially when there are phonological dyslexic patients who seem to show poor comprehension for the irregular words they are able to name, arguing against spared word reading based on access to semantic knowledge (see Funnell, 1983; Plaut et al., 1996). On the other hand, the neuropsychological data are consistent with a "dual route" account which distinguishes between a lexical, knowledge-based reading process and a nonlexical, rule-based process, with each syndrome being linked to damage to one of the two routes: phonological dyslexia, to damage to the nonlexical route; surface dyslexia, to damage to the lexical process (see Coltheart et al., 1993).

Principles

These examples of dyslexia also illustrate two of the fundamental assumptions typically made in cognitive neuropsychology modeling that have aided interpretation of results (see Caramazza, 1986). One assumption is *modularity*, which holds that a task such as reading can be broken down into a set of component processes (e.g., access to the visual lexicon, access to semantic knowledge, the application of nonlexical spelling-sound rules, etc.), and that damage to any of these component processes will lead to an individual having a reduced version of the normal system. Thus, in phonological dyslexia, we witness the operation of a lexical reading route without a contribution to pronunciation from spelling-sound rules, whereas surface dyslexia performance is based on output from the spelling-sound rules without a contribution from the lexical reading route. Inferences can then be made about the nature of the impaired component processes, revealed in the difference between the dyslexic patient's performance and that of normal participants. For example, we may assume that visual lexical access is frequency sensitive, given that surface dyslexics may be more likely to read high- than low-frequency irregular words, in cases where lexical representations for high-frequency words are spared (Bub, Cancelliere, and Kertesz, 1985). A second assumption typically made is that of *transparency*, which holds that the symptoms that characterize a given neuropsychological disorder are telling either about the underlying component process that has been damaged, or about the spared normal process being used. For instance, we use this assumption when we infer that the regularization errors made by surface dyslexics when naming irregular words are indicative of the nonlexical rules that determine reading when the lexical route is damaged.

It can also be argued that the idea of modular cognitive systems was greatly encouraged by the adoption of "box and arrow" theories developed in the 1970s and 1980s. Using these models, a given ability would be conceptualized as representations constructed or accessed at particular stages of processing, along with the processing "routes" that transform input from one stage to the next (see, for example, figure 4.1). Neuropsychological syndromes can be mapped onto such models by positing that a given representation or processing route has been damaged in a particular patient. What was especially noteworthy in the development of these models in the seventies and eighties was the attempt to provide a detailed account of the nature of the representations and processing routes involved. This distinguished the emerging work on cognitive neuropsychology from the conceptually similar, but much more simplified, frameworks put forward by the "diagram makers" at the very start of modern-day neuropsychology (e.g., Lichtheim, 1885). To this day, cognitive neuropsychological theories of performance, based on these articulated "box and arrow" frameworks, remain a powerful influence on neuroscientific thinking.

Limitations

Nevertheless, there are important limitations to such theories, and to their ability to account for neuropsychological impairments where performance appears to emerge from interactions between separable components in the processing system or where a given behavior may be caused by adaptation or a strategy adopted post lesion. In the next section, we discuss two such impairments that have been the focus of study in our laboratory: optic aphasia (see Freund, 1889; Lhermitte and Beauvois, 1973) and visual apraxia (see De Renzi, Faglioni, and Sorgato, 1982).

Optic Aphasia and Visual Apraxia

The term *optic aphasia* is used to describe a selective, modality-specific impairment in naming visually presented objects. Naming in other modalities (e.g., in response to touch, or to a definition) may be relatively intact. In contrast to their poor visual naming, optic aphasic patients can very often perform a gesture to show how an object would be used. Although this good ability to gesture has frequently been interpreted as evidence for the patient being able to access "semantic" knowledge about objects, so that the problem is one of name retrieval, in at least three studies that have closely examined the semantic knowledge available to such patients, performance has been found to be impaired. Thus Riddoch and Humphreys (1987) presented their male patient, J.B., with sets of three objects and

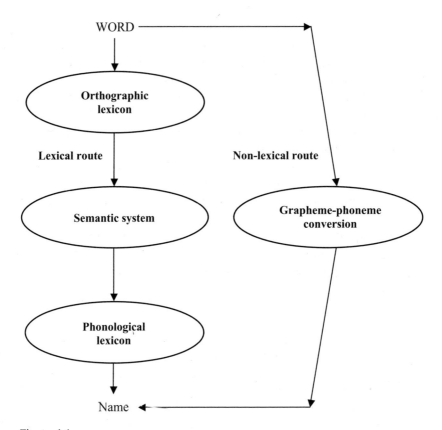

Figure 4.1
"Dual route" model for naming English words. In this model, there are distinct "lexical" and "nonlexical" routes for translating from spelling to sounds, each composed of a variety of processes (e.g., orthographic lexicon, semantic system, phonological lexicon, within the lexical route). The assumption of modularity holds that one representation can be damaged without affecting the performance of independent representations. Thus damage to a nonlexical route should not affect the operation of the lexical route.

asked him to choose which two would be used together (e.g., hammer, nail, wrench). J.B. performed poorly at this task when the objects were visually presented. This was not due to a lack of semantic knowledge per se: J.B. was at ceiling when he was given the names of the objects and asked to make the same choice (see also Hillis and Caramazza, 1995; Yoon, Humphreys, and Riddoch, 2005). Such results suggest that there was a modality-specific problem in accessing semantics. Despite this, J.B. was good at gesturing to visually presented objects. How could this be, given that access to semantic knowledge was impaired? There are at least two ways to think of this, and one way violates the idea that symptoms are transparent. One account, that does fit the "classical" modular framework for cognition (object naming in this instance), assumes that there exist separate "routes" from visually presented objects to action. A "semantic" route would involve access to semantic knowledge from vision—much as one would need to access semantic knowledge to access action from an object's name. Alongside, a second, "direct" route is assumed, based on associations between the visual representation of an object and an action (see, for example, figure 4.2; Humphreys and Riddoch, 2003). In optic aphasia, the direct route may continue to operate even if there is a modality-specific problem in accessing semantic knowledge, with the result that gesturing is relatively spared. Alternatively, though, the gestures made by optic aphasic patients may reflect an adaptation on the part of the patient, using information (and strategies) that are not normally involved when one acts with objects. Hillis and Caramazza (1995), for example, proposed that such gestures may be derived from partial semantic knowledge that the patient still can access, coupled to a visual problem-solving strategy based on explicitly working out how an object might be used, given its visual properties (see also Hodges et al., 2000). If the latter holds, then the gestures made by such patients are not "transparent," and do not inform us about the processes normally involved in retrieving actions to objects.

Take now the impairment visual apraxia, which is difficult to explain in terms of standard modular theories. The term *visual apraxia* is used to describe a selective, modality-specific impairment in acting with visually presented objects, despite having intact recognition and, in some cases, spared object naming (De Renzi, Faglioni, and Sorgato, 1982; Pilgrim and Humphreys, 1991; Riddoch, Humphreys, and Price, 1989). The impairment is again modality specific since the same patient may make a correct gesture when given the names of objects. But this impairment can now be conceptualized in terms of a modular account of how one recognizes and acts with objects, based on a "dual route" account of action (figure 4.2). For example,

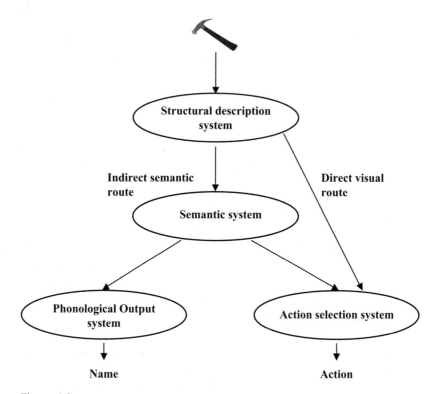

Figure 4.2
"Dual route" model of action retrieval from visually presented objects, separating a direct visual and an indirect (semantically) mediated route to action. The model also proposes that access to object names from vision is semantically mediated (after Riddoch, Humphreys, and Price, 1989).

given that object recognition and naming can be spared, we would assume that the semantic route would be operating, and that the problem lies within the direct route to action from vision. If, however, the semantic route is operating, then it is not clear why this route could not serve to enable the patient to make gestures when objects are presented visually—much as we would assume that the continued existence of the lexical route for reading enables phonological dyslexic individuals still to read words. Thus simple reduction of a proposed normal system fails to account for the data.

Innovation

These problems in the standard assumptions underlying much of cognitive neuropsychology can be addressed, however, once we begin to develop working computational models of performance—particularly, we believe, where the models incorporate some aspects of biological neural systems. Our own work on this topic has focused on the use of artificial neural networks that capture some of the dynamic properties of real neural systems—where whole system performance emerges from local interactions between large numbers of processing units (see McClelland and Rumelhart, 1986; Rumelhart and McClelland, 1986). Due to this interactivity, there can be emergent effects on performance that would not be predicted using a standard, modular "box and arrow" framework, even if there is some degree of functional specialization within a given system. Furthermore, within a dynamic model, the effects of a brain lesion may not be simply to reduce the normal system but to change the nature of the interactions between component processes. This turns out to be important to account for some neuropsychological impairments such as visual apraxia.

To provide a framework for understanding both intact and impaired abilities both to name and to retrieve actions associated with objects, we developed the "Naming and Action Model" (NAM). (Yoon, Heinke, and Humphreys, 2002). Having a quasi-modular structure composed of input (perceptual), semantic, and output (name and action response) units, the NAM is arranged in an architecture that conforms to a "dual route" model of name and action retrieval from objects (see, for example, figure 4.3). Input to the NAM, provided by objects, conforms to a description sensitive to the presence of object features (the number of straight and curved lines, the length and width of the object) in relation to the viewpoint. At a semantic level, units correspond to the specific item and to its superordinate category. At an output level, different sets of units serve to categorize the object either in terms of its name (hammer vs. pen) or the action typically performed (e.g., hitting vs. writing). Input is also provided by words, through an orthographic perceptual recognition system. For both words and objects as input, both names and actions can be accessed via the semantic system (the semantically mediated route to naming and to action); there are also different "direct" routes, from words to names (see Funnell, 1983) and from structural descriptions for objects through to action. At each level, a winner-take-all selection process operates, with the network "relaxing" over time, to achieve activation for the output units corresponding to a particular name or category of action. This winner-take-all selection process is based on activation values being passed continuously between local processing units. Thus, even though the NAM has structural modularity, outputs from the models are contingent on interactions between modules.

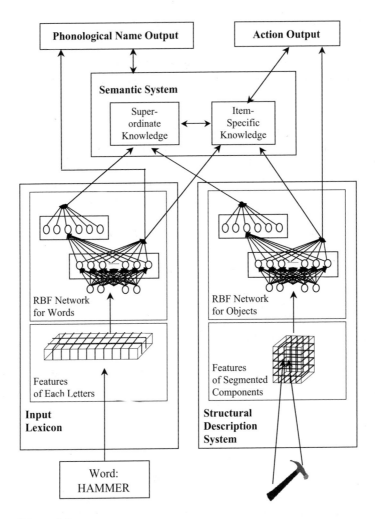

Figure 4.3
Architecture of the Naming and Action Model (NAM; after Yoon, Heinke, and Humphreys, 2002), with inputs provided either by structural descriptions of objects or words. The mapping from each form of structural description into the semantic system was based on a radial basis function network.

Consider how actions are selected in NAM. Activation of the action classification units is determined by joint activity coming from both the semantic and direct routes to action. Rapid activation, coming through the direct connections from the structural description system to the action system, "push" activity states in the action units toward a "basin of attraction," which constitutes a steady state of activity at this level. This activation then converges with activity arising out of the semantic units, to generate selection of the appropriate action to an object.

Now consider the effects of damaging the connections from the structural descriptions to the action units, so that relatively "noisy" activity is transmitted along the "direct" route. Instead of pushing output activity toward a basin of attraction, this noise can move activity away, disrupting activation at an output stage. This disruption, it is important to note, can occur even if the semantic route to action is operating normally, and even if this semantic activity is sufficient to generate the correct output response in the absence of any "direct" input—as would be the case if participants were required to make actions to words in the absence of any object.

Figure 4.4 shows that symptoms of either optic aphasia or visual apraxia emerge in the NAM, according whether a lesion is applied to the direct route for action (simulating visual apraxia—lesion V-A), or from

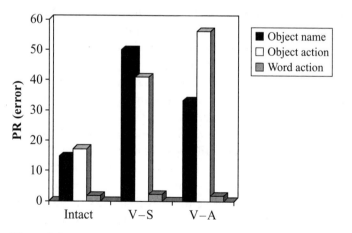

Figure 4.4

Data on action classification to objects and words, along with name retrieval to objects following simulated damage to the direct visual (V-A) and indirect semantic routes to action (V-S), in the Naming and Action Model (NAM; after Yoon, Heinke, and Humphreys, 2002). There is better action retrieval to objects after the V-S lesion than the V-A lesion, but better visual access to object names after the V-A than the V-S lesion. In both cases, action retrieval to words is spared.

visual input into the semantic system (simulating optic aphasia—lesion V-S). When there is impaired access to semantics (lesion V-S), there is impaired visual object naming relative to when there is damage to a direct visual route to action (lesion V-A), whereas the opposite pattern occurs when the task requires action retrieval (performance is worse after lesion V-A than after lesion V-S). Visual apraxia emerges from damage to the direct route here because noisy outputs from this route effectively disrupt the activity coming from the semantic routes. Due to the interactivity in the system, there is not merely loss of the direct route, but also a change in the way that semantic activity influences action selection. On the other hand, when no activity is generated in the damaged visual route (e.g., when the task is simply to retrieve an action given the name of an object), activation from the semantic route is sufficient to allow action selection to be successful. That is, there is action retrieval from a name but not from an object. This is precisely the pattern of performance that violates the assumption of modularity typically made in cognitive neuropsychology. The NAM also simulates optic aphasia, following damage to input coming into the semantic system from vision (lesion V-S). This simulated lesion leads to problems in semantic access from vision, a pattern consistent with the neuropsychological data (Hillis and Caramazza, 1995; Riddoch and Humphreys, 1987). Despite this, actions can be accessed more accurately than names from objects due to the continued operation of the direct route to action. In this case, the direct route provides an early "push" toward correct categorization in the action system, so that noise within the semantic route to action is not too disruptive for performance.

A model such as the NAM can of course prove only that a system with its architecture and processing dynamics can generate the two contrasting patterns of performance characteristic of optic aphasia and visual apraxia. The question remains whether observations such as the good gesturing in optic aphasia reflect the operation of a preserved direct route to action (as suggested by the NAM), or whether they reflect a strategic adaptation on the part of patients, who use visual problem solving combined with partial semantic knowledge to act with objects (is there a "nontransparent" pattern of performance?). This question might be answered by looking in greater detail at patient performance—for example, by measuring the time taken by a patient to retrieve and enact a gesture, compared with normal participants. Here one might expect any strategic, problem-solving process to be relatively slow. Such predictions are not straightforward, however. Thus, although the NAM can select an appropriate action to an object after lesioning visual access to semantics, the latency of action retrieval is slowed (see Yoon, Heinke, and Humphreys, 2002; figure 4.5). The NAM also predicts that the latency of action retrieval will be disrupted in optic aphasics. Another way to distinguish between these accounts needs to be found. One way is to look for converging evidence coming from normal participants. For example, it seems unlikely that normal participants would have to use explicit problem-solving strategies to make gestures to objects, given that their ability to act on the basis of semantic knowledge is intact. These results are consistent with NAM rather than with the suggestion that performance is nontransparent, reflecting strategic adaptation on the part of optic aphasic patients. Perhaps an even more important point is that having an explicit model of performance enables normal as well as abnormal performance to be simulated, so that convergent predictions can be assessed and notions about transparency tested.

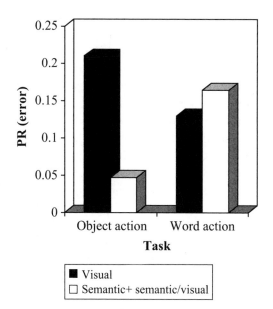

Figure 4.5
Data on action classification and naming to a deadline in the Naming and Action Model (NAM; after Yoon, Heinke, and Humphreys, 2002), showing the proportion of error responses (pr) when retrieving actions to visually presented objects or to words. Relative to when actions were retrieved to words, there were more visual errors when retrieving actions to objects, and fewer semantic + semantic/visual errors (semantic and semantic + visual errors are classed together here because the two error types are difficult to distinguish).

Integration

One complaint sometimes made by nonneuropsychologists about using neu-ropsychological data for building and testing theories is that, in some areas, there seem to be a bewildering number of dissociations—often between single patients—making it appear as if any arbitrary pattern of deficit could arise following a brain lesion. In such cases, it is tempting to think that dif-ferent deficits stem from idiosyncratic learning experiences or from the prior interests of the patient, and thus are not informative about the general cog-nitive architecture of the mind. A particular example here comes from the disorder of unilateral visual neglect, where patients fail to respond to stimuli presented on the contralesionsal side of space following their brain injury (e.g., Heilman, Watson and Valenstein, 1985).

Humphreys and Riddoch (1994, 1995) examined a male patient, J.R., who had sustained bilateral damage to his parietal cortex as well as his right cerebellum, following multiple strokes. In an initial test, J.R. was asked to read words and nonwords positioned randomly on a page. J.R.'s pattern of performance is illustrated in figure 4.6. What was interesting was that, when J.R. misidentified a particular stimulus, the errors were more pronounced at the left ends of the strings. Also, these misidentification errors were more pronounced on nonwords than on words (i.e., they appeared to be affected by top-down knowledge). In contrast, he made com-plete omissions of some stimuli that fell on the right side of the page, omis-sions not affected by the lexical status of the letter string. These apparently opposite forms of neglect occurred not only when J.R. was asked to read, but also when he was asked to name pictures on a page: he continued to make right-side omissions, typically misidentifying the rightmost features of the objects pictured, and neglecting the leftmost features. Thus, when identifying single items, J.R. seemed not to "weight" the left-side features strongly, whereas he appeared not to "weight" the right side of space strongly when scanning multiple objects pictured on a page. These two deficits may stem, respectively, from the right- and left-parietal lesions in J.R.'s case. To make sure that omissions were not being made simply because the stimuli fell into a blind area of field, we conducted a further study where, using the same stimuli, we tried to bias J.R. to code visual ele-ments as a single object or as multiple, separate objects. We presented him with words and nonwords in large print, so that they spanned the width of an A4 page. We then asked him either to read the whole stimulus or to read out the letters making up the stimulus. When asked to read the whole word, J.R. made left-side errors, typically misidentifying the letters present (e.g.,

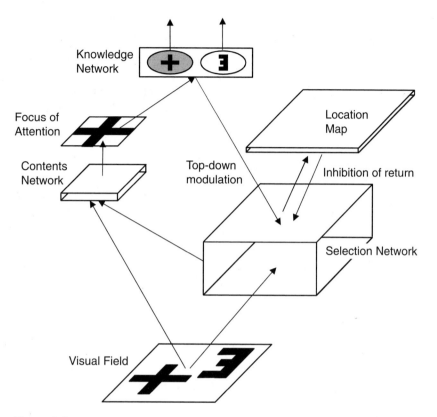

Figure 4.6
Architecture of the Selective Attention for Identification Model (SAIM; after Heinke and Humphreys, 2003).

"LIGHT" as "might"). In contrast, when required to identify each letter in turn, he made right-side omissions (e.g., "LIGHT" as "l," "i," "g," "h"). In this instance, when reading individual letters he omitted letters on the right he had previously read when processing the whole stimulus, whereas he correctly identified letters on the left he had previously misidentified. These results indicate that the spatial positions of the elements in the world are less crucial than the way that the elements are represented for the task at hand. There appear to be separate spatial representations of parts within objects and of the relations between independent objects. These different spatial representations are separately affected in patient J.R., namely, there is left neglect of within-object space, and right neglect of between-object space. Humphreys and Riddoch (1994, 1995) termed these spatial representations *within-* and *between-object* codes, respectively. How are we to understand the relations between these codes? We believe that capturing such patterns of results within an explicit model of performance can greatly help us conceptualize how different disorders can emerge, perhaps after lesions to different loci in a processing system.

The "Selective Attention for Identification Model" (SAIM; Heinke and Humphreys, 2003) provides an example of this because it generates an explicit account of how within- and between-object neglect can emerge in a framework in which the two codes are used for specific computational purposes. Like the NAM, the SAIM is a quasi-modular model, with interactions within and across the several modules of its structure generating dynamic and interactive performance (see figure 4.6); its aim is to achieve translation-invariant object recognition. It does this by mapping input from any lateral position on the retina into a "focus of attention" (FOA) that has a fixed size based on one object. Recognition units, at the higher end of SAIM ("template units" in the "Knowledge network") then respond to the presence of active pixels at particular locations in the FOA, but since these pixels are activated from across the retina, the recognition process is translation invariant. Activation in the FOA is itself controlled by two networks: the "Contents network" and the "Selection network." The contents network can be thought of as a connection matrix specifying all possible relationships between locations on the retina and locations in the FOA. A high level of activation in one unit in the contents network instantiates a particular correspondence between a given retinal location, and a given location in the FOA. The role of the selection network in the model is to gate activity in the contents network, enabling activity to be passed on from some but not other units in the contents network. This "selects" which mapping is implemented from the retina to the FOA. Through bottom-up activation in the contents and selection networks, a given stimulus will be mapped through to the FOA. In addition to this bottom-up form of operation, however, activation can also be conveyed in a top-down manner, from the knowledge network down to the selection network—essentially biasing activity in the selection network to favor known over unknown stimuli. Finally, once a stimulus has been selected in the focus of attention and identified in the knowledge network, the SAIM utilizes a form of "inhibition of return" (Posner and Cohen, 1984) to allow new (unselected) stimuli to be identified. In this process, the representations of an identified stimulus are inhibited, including the positions where the stimulus fell in a "map of locations" (see figure 4.6). This in turn allows previously unselected items to then win the competition for selection, so that the SAIM's "attention" moves from one object to the next.

The heart of the SAIM's ability to select between multiple inputs is the selection network, which identifies one object at a time. This network is shown in simplified form in figure 4.7, where we depict a one-dimensional input from the retina being mapped, through the selection network, onto a one-dimensional representation of units in the focus of attention. Within the selection network, each unit along a row corresponds to a different (but neighboring) location in the visual field, and the units along one row all map onto a single location in the FOA; units along a row compete to control the mapping from the visual field onto one position in the FOA. In contrast, each unit along a column of the selection network corresponds to a different location in the FOA, and the units along a column all correspond to a single location in the visual field; units along a column compete to control the mapping from one position in the visual field onto the FOA. These competitive interactions are based on inhibitory connections between neighboring units along each column and row. In addition, units in the selection network are mutually excitatory if they support mappings from locally neighboring units in the visual field onto locally neighboring units in the FOA, illustrated in figure 4.6 by excitatory connections between units that lie along the diagonals of the selection network. These local connections, then, can be thought of as embodying various constraints about how spatial mapping should operate—for example, that one unit in the visual field should not map onto more than one location in the FOA, and that neighboring units in the field should map onto neighboring units in the FOA.

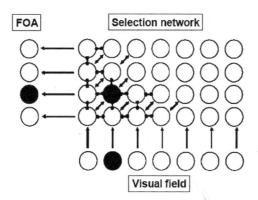

Figure 4.7
Illustration of the Selection network in SAIM. Input from the visual field is depicted by the bottom row of units; the focus of attention (FOA) is depicted by the vertical row of units on the left. Double-headed arrow indicates an excitatory connection; bar between solid dots, an inhibitory connection.

When two objects are presented on the SAIM's retina, local units support one another, but more distant units are not mutually supportive and instead set up competition to control the mapping from different parts of the field onto the focus of attention. Objects may "win" this competition either by having stronger bottom-up activation (e.g., if one object is larger than others), by having more elements packed around their center of gravity (since such units form mutually supportive alliances), or by receiving stronger top-down support from the knowledge network (based either on an expectation formed before stimuli are presented or based on partial activation of the knowledge network before selection has been completed).

These points are illustrated in figure 4.8, where we show the activity in the SAIM when two objects are presented (in this case a "+" and a "2"). Figure 4.8 presents activity at different time intervals in the focus of attention, as well as the activity that builds up (and is inhibited after recognition) in the knowledge network. In this simulation, the "+" is first selected in the FOA, and activation in its template increases to threshold level—the "+" is both attended and recognized. In this example, the "+" is attended first because it enjoys greater bottom-up support from the pixels surrounding its center of gravity. Following this, representations for the "+" are inhibited. When processing continues, there is then a competitive advantage for the "2" over the "+," so that the "2" then comes to be attended and identified. The stimuli are processed in parallel, but there is selection of one object at a time for the response.

Within the framework presented by the SAIM, unilateral neglect can come about by lesioning the selection network. Heinke and Humphreys (2003) examined two different forms of lesioning. One form, which they termed a *vertical lesion*, affected units responding to input coming from one side of the visual field (e.g., all the units on the left side of the connection matrix presented in figure 4.7). This meant that activity in these units suffered a competitive advantage relative to units in the selection network responding to input present in the opposite (ipsilesional) side of the visual field. When two objects were presented, the ipsilesional object was typically attended first, even if the bottom-up input based on the shape alone would favor the stimulus presented in the contralesional field. Figure 4.9a illustrates performance of the model after a "vertical lesion" affecting the left side of the selection network. Although SAIM normally has a bottom-up preference for the "+" over the "2" (figure 4.8), after lesioning, the model selects the "2" first if this item falls in the ipsilesional field and the "+" in the contralesional field. Furthermore, even after selecting the "2," the model has difficulty in selecting the "+," in part because any spatial distortion in

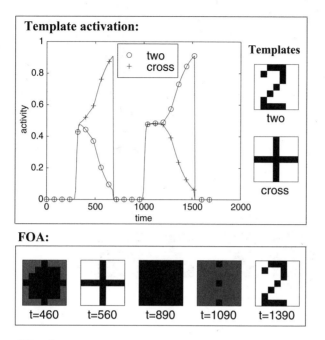

First item: $RT_{temp} = 670$

Second item: $RT_{temp} = 1510$

Figure 4.8
Activity in SAIM when two stimuli (a + and a "2") are presented. There is sequential identification of the items, with a bottom-up advantage for the + (which is selected first, followed by the "2", after there is inhibition of return for the "+").

(a)

Template activation:

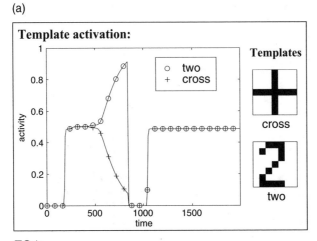

Templates

cross

two

FOA:

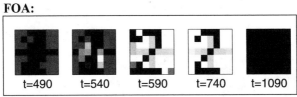

t=490   t=540   t=590   t=740   t=1090

Stimulus:

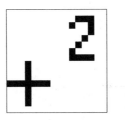

$RT_{foa} = 533$
$RT_{temp} = 830$

(b)

FOA: 857 FOA: 776 FOA: 630 FOA: 555 FOA: 507 FOA: 476 FOA: 453 FOA: 436 FOA: 422 FOA: 412
T: 820   T: 730   T: 680   T: 650   T: 620   T: 600   T: 580   T: 570   T: 560   T: 550

Example stimuli position in the field:

mapping the "2" onto the focus of attention tends to make it difficult to inhibit the stimulus, and in part because the competitive advantage for the "+" is difficult to suppress. Hence only the "2" is attended in this example. And since SAIM selects and identifies the contralesional "+" when it is the only object present (figure 4.9b), this does not represent simply a neglect of the contralesional part of the visual field. There is a relative neglect of the more contralesional of two separate objects: there is neglect between separate objects.

A different pattern of impairment was evident, however, when a "horizontal" lesion was induced, for example, affecting the units in the topmost rows on the selection network. Units in each row of the selection network map are projected from across the visual field, but they map onto one unit in the FOA. Thus a horizontal lesion affects the mapping onto one part of the FOA and does so in a translation-invariant manner. In figure 4.10, the SAIM is presented with two stimuli after a "horizontal lesion" has been induced in order to disrupt access into the left side of the FOA, resulting in a form of sequential neglect for the left parts of both stimuli, which affects even stimuli in the ipsilesional visual field (although, in this case, the model is able to map both stimuli onto the FOA, in every case, there is poor representation of the leftmost pixel; see Gainotti et al., 1986). Thus a horizontal lesion generates a form of "within-object neglect."

These simulations demonstrate that the SAIM can produce the dissociating pattern of deficits found in neglect patients, a pattern that emerges as a natural consequence of the way that stimuli are mapped onto an FOA to achieve translation-invariant object recognition. They suggest that dissociations between within- and between-object neglect are not arbitrary, but rather can be expected as a function of the particular brain lesion affecting a patient. Indeed, by combining the horizontal and vertical lesions in a single simulation, Heinke and Humphreys (2003) were able to demonstrate that there could be left neglect of within-object representations, along with right neglect of between-object representations, in a single simulation—the pattern observed in patient J.R. (Humphreys and Riddoch, 1994, 1995).

Figure 4.9
(a) Activity in SAIM after a "vertical" lesion has affected the left side of the selection network, when two stimuli are presented. (b) Activity in the SAIM following the same lesion as in (a) when a single stimulus is presented in different positions of the field. In this last case, the "+" is always attended, although the time to be attended (time FOA) amd to be identified (time template) varies across the field (slower on the left).

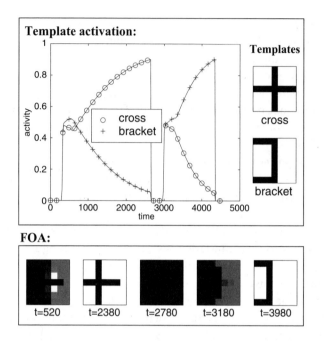

Figure 4.10
Example of "within object" neglect following a "horizontal" lesion of the selection network of the Selection Attention for Identification Model (SAIM). Both stimuli are attended, but the leftmost pixels are excluded from the focus of attention.

Bringing order out of the seeming chaos of empirical results, the SAIM shows how explicit computational models can capture rich patterns of data, although, as we have noted with the simulations of the NAM, the fact that a model can simulate a set of results does not of course prove that the model is correct. Nevertheless, it should be noted that the dissociations between within-object and between-object neglect are not at all easy to simulate in other models that do not employ SAIM's architecture.

Due to its use of top-down activity, SAIM is also able to simulate results showing that there is reduced neglect of known versus unknown objects (Humphreys and Riddoch, 1994, 1995). In figure 4.11a, we provide an illustration of the SAIM's performance when it is given separate templates for each of two letters ("I" and "T") and it is lesioned to produce left-side neglect. When presented with two stimuli, there is neglect of the leftmost object. In this case, the "T" was selected first, and then reselected as this letter continued to win the competition for selection over the "I." In figure 4.11b, we demonstrate performance in the model when a third template is added, corresponding to the word "IT." Now the model is able to recover both of the letters present, even though it still has templates for each individual letter, and thus could be biased to identity the "T" and not the whole word. Top-down activation, from the word template, helps to bias attention to cover both of the letters present, so that both can be attended. In this case, though there is a deficit at a stage that produces input into the knowledge network, interactivity between the knowledge and selection networks affects activity at the earlier stage. Because the model has structural modularity, a lesion can be selectively induced within the selection network, but its operation is nonmodular and interactive. We suggest that this property of neural network–like models is useful for capturing some of the complexity of neuropsychological data.

Although we have presented a case for using biologically inspired models to simulate both normal and neuropsychological data, other kinds of models can also play a useful part in improving our understanding of neurological impairments. As one example, the formal mathematical model of attention provided by Claus Bundesen's theory of visual attention (TVA) proposes that visual selection is based on parallel competition between stimuli to map onto templates, which, once represented in visual short-term memory (VSTM), are made available for report. This competition is said to be influenced by a number of parameters including the strength of the sensory signal, the speed of processing, the attentional weight that may be applied to stimuli as a function of their relevance to the task, and the

(a)

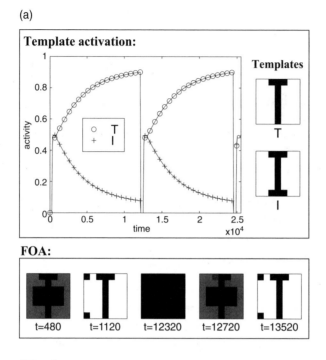

Figure 4.11
(*a*) Activity in SAIM after a "vertical" lesion when the model has separate templates for the two letters presented. (*b*) Activity in the SAIM when subject to the same lesion as in (*a*), but there is now an added template that incorporates both letters.

(b)

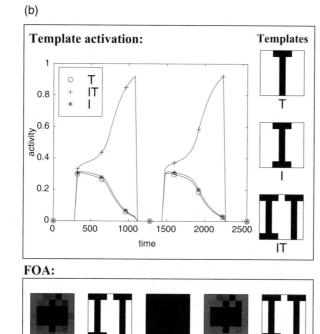

FOA:

Stimulus:

Figure 4.11
(continued)

capacity of VSTM. Duncan et al. (1999, 2003) and Habekost and Bundesen (2003) have applied fits of the parameters in TVA to the performance of brain-lesioned patients when asked to report either all or a subset of letters present in multiletter displays (on whole- and partial-report tasks; see Sperling, 1960, 1967). The parameters were specific to whether stimuli appeared in the ipsi- or contralesional fields. Duncan et al. (1999), found that patients with unilateral parietal damage had altered parameters for the rate of stimulus encoding and for VSTM capacity for stimuli in both visual fields, not just for items appearing on the contralesional side. This may in part explain reports of patients showing not only contralesional neglect but also neglect of ipsilesional items when their attention is drawn to the contralesional side (e.g., Robertson, 1989). Further insights using this approach have been gained into understanding the neuropsychological disorder of "simultanagnosia," in which patients seem impaired at responding when multiple stimuli are presented simultaneously to them (e.g., Kinsbourne and Warrington, 1962). The factors that generate this disorder remain poorly understood, with arguments ranging from impaired integration of information in VSTM (Coslett and Saffran, 1991) to impaired application of an attentional spotlight to space (Treisman, 1998). Analyzing whole- and partial-report performance in terms of Bundesen's theory of visual attention, Duncan et al. (2003) showed that the major parameter change was in the "rate of processing" parameter, and suggested that drastic slowing of processing would lead to many of the phenomena associated with simultanagosia, in which only the most dominant visual elements are reported.

The approach taken in applying TVA to neuropsychological data is both like and unlike that taken in modeling performance with artificial neural networks. In both approaches, experimenters take a well-specified model that provides a fit to normal data, and then use parameter changes after a brain lesion to account for a disorder. With TVA, they use the data to derive the parameters (and the parameter change, when present). In neural network modeling, they typically change the parameters (e.g., adding noise to an activation function or removing units) and then assess the effects on output. The artificial neural network approach offers the possibility of emergent behaviors not specified in the original parameter setting, which may be linked to human disorders, although there is the inherent problem of finding the appropriate parameter change, a problem by-passed in mathematical modeling.

We argue that artificial neural network models such as the NAM and the SAIM, where both the representations and the parameters are set by the experimenters, help us understand disorders that are difficult to account for in terms of standard "box and arrow" models, where strict modularity is assumed. One of the attractions of neural network modeling is that networks can learn the internal representations required to transform a given input into an output. Especially where learning takes place within a quasi-regular environment, and there is some systematicity in the relations between inputs and output, models that incorporate learning can generate interesting emergent properties, which can in turn provide insights into neuropsychological disorders. One example here would be the model of word naming designed by Plaut et al. (1996). In one version of this model input was provided by units representing orthographic properties of stimuli. A second input corresponded to a semantic representation of a word. The contribution of the semantic input was fixed over time, but that of the orthographic input varied and was subject to learning, in which the connections between the orthographic and phonological units were altered using a form of backpropagation (Hinton, 1989). Relative to when learning took place without the semantic input, Plaut and colleagues found that, in the "dual route" version, the "route" mapping orthography onto phonology became more specialized for regular spelling-sound correspondences, with the naming of irregular word more dependent on the semantic route. Lesioning the semantic route then gave rise to a strong pattern of surface dyslexia, in which both regular words and nonwords were produced correctly (where the nonwords had highly regular spelling-sound correspondences), whereas irregular words were selectively impaired. This simulates patterns of "pure" surface dyslexic reading (Shallice, Warrington, and McCarthy, 1983) that have been difficult to simulate in "single route" models incorporating only a single pathway between orthography and phonology (e.g., Patterson, Seidenberg, and McClelland, 1989). For Plaut et al. (1996), there was a division of labor between the semantic and orthographic routes for reading as learning took place, so that a more "regularized" representation was developed than when a single route was used. Clearly, it is of interest to examine how learning may interact with structural constraints in an artificial neural network, to generate forms of representation that are "tuned" in different ways.

Plaut (2002) used a distributed "semantic" network with a two-dimensional topology to learn mappings between a variety of input stimuli and output tasks (vision and touch as input, naming and gesturing as output; see figure 4.12). The model had a topological bias, in which short connections were favored over long connections (the magnitudes of the changes made to connect weights during learning were greater for short connections than for long connections; see also Jacobs and Jordan, 1992). With this bias, units in the semantic network that were close to a particular input or output modality were strongly weighted to achieve a particular (modality-specific) mapping, whereas units that were more distant from the different input and output modalities played a more "multimodal" role, and were not differentially involved in particularly input-output mappings. It followed that lesions to the network generated different patterns of performance depending on which units were affected. For example, a pattern of optic aphasia arose (i.e., impaired naming but not gesturing to visually presented objects) from damage to connections to semantic units specialized for mapping visual input onto names (e.g., units in the lower left region of the two-dimensional semantic space in figure 4.12). Problems in gesturing to visual input (i.e., the pattern of visual apraxia) were apparent after damage to connections to units specialized for mapping between visual input and gestural output (i.e., units in the upper left region of the semantic space shown in figure 4.12). Such lesions thus produce a pattern of performance not unlike that of the "dual route" NAM, with functional specialization in the distributed network developing because of the topological constraints (indeed, in control simulations, when the constraints

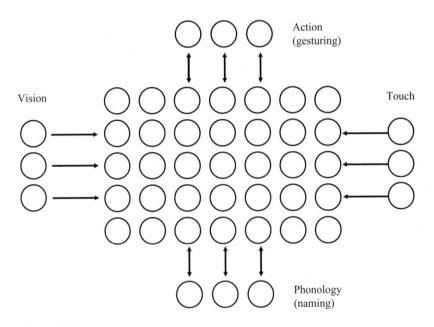

Figure 4.12
Structured distributed semantic memory system proposed by Plaut (2002).

were eliminated, the same patterns of performance did not arise). One difference between NAM and the structured, distributed semantic model of Plaut (2002) is that, in the NAM, visually presented objects must be named through the semantic system—there are no direct connections from visual structural representations of objects to names. In contrast, in Plaut's model, some units can specialize for mapping from vision to names, and indeed lesioning of these units tended to produce optic aphasia. On the other hand, evidence is weak for "direct visual naming of objects" (e.g., instances where patients name an object but cannot retrieve other semantic knowledge; see Hodges and Greene, 1998; Humphreys and Forde, 2005). Thus there is no independent support for the argument that there can be neural specialization for "direct" mapping from vision to names.

Conclusion

Neuropsychological research can provide striking insights into the nature of mental processes, teasing apart processes that are functionally independent of one another. There are instances, however, where the historical assumptions, used to guide theorizing, cannot easily account for some neuropsychological disorders (e.g., visual apraxia). We have argued that, by contrast, explicit computational (and mathematical) models can capture forms of interactivity between processing modules that turn out to be important for understanding human performance. Such models can also provide a framework both for understanding the relations between different neuropsychological disorders and for generating formal accounts of how a brain lesion can selectively affect different processing parameters. Such formal accounts have yielded new insights into the nature of particular disorders. Moreover, the emergent properties of models that incorporate learning and biological constraints into their learning functions can aid our understanding of the relations between brain structure and cognitive function. Computational studies are thus an important tool for cognitive neuroscientific analysis of brain and mind.

Acknowledgments

This work was supported by grants from the Biotechnology and Biological Sciences Research Council, the Engineering and Physical Sciences Research Council, and the Medical Research Council of the United Kingdom to Glyn Humphreys and Dietmar Heinke, and from the British Academy to Eun Young Yoon.

References

Beauvois, M.-F., and Derouesné, J. (1979). Phonological alexia: Three dissociations. *Journal of Neurology, Neurosurgery, and Psychiatry*, *42*, 1115–1124.

Bub, D., Cancelliere, A., and Kertesz, A. (1985). Whole-word and analytic translation of spelling-to-sound in a non-semantic reader. In K. E. Patterson, M. Coltheart, and J. C. Marshall (Eds.), *Surface dyslexia*. London: Erlbaum.

Caramazza, A. (1986). On drawing inferences about the structure of normal cognitive systems from the analysis of patterns of impaired performance: The case for single-patient studies. *Brain and Cognition*, *5*, 41–66.

Coltheart, M. (1984). Editorial. *Cognitive Neuropsychology*, *1*, 1–8.

Coltheart, M. (1985). Cognitive neuropsychology and the study of reading. In M. I. Posner and O. S. M. Marin (Eds.), *Attention and performance XI*. Hillsdale, NJ: Erlbaum.

Coltheart, M., Curtis, B., Atkins, P., and Haller, M. (1993). Models of reading aloud: Dual-route and parallel-distributed-processing approaches. *Psychological Review*, *100*, 589–608.

Coslett, H. B., and Saffran, E. (1991). Simultanagnosia: To see but not two see. *Brain*, *114*, 1523–1545.

De Renzi, E., Faglioni, P., and Sorgato, P. (1982). Modality-specific and supramodal mechanisms of apraxia. *Brain*, *105*, 301–312.

Duncan, J., Bundesen, C., Olson, A., Humphreys, G. W., Chavda, S., and Shibuya, H. (1999). Systematic analysis of deficits in visual attention. *Journal of Experimental Psychology: General*, *128*, 1–29.

Duncan, J., Bundesen, C., Olson, A., Humphreys, G. W., Ward, R., van Raamsdonk, M., Rorden, C., and Chavda, S. (2003). Attentional functions in dorsal and ventral simultanagnosia. *Cognitive Neuropsychology*, *20*, 675–702.

Freund, D. C. (1889). Über optische Aphasie und Seelenblindheit. *Archiv für Psychiatrie und Nervenkrankheiten*, *20*, 276–297.

Funnell, E. (1983). Phonological processing in reading: New evidence from acquired dyslexia. *British Journal of Psychology*, *74*, 159–180.

Gainotti, G., D'Erme, P., Monteleone, D., and Silveri, M. C. (1986). Mechanisms of unilateral spatial neglect in relation to laterality of cerebral lesion. *Brain*, *109*, 599–612.

Habekost, T., and Bundesen, C. (2003). Patient assessment based on a theory of visual attention (TVA): Subtle deficits after a right frontal-subcortical lesion. *Neuropsychologia*, *41*, 1171–1188.

Halligan, P. W., Fink, G. R., Marshall, J. C., and Vallar, G. (2003). Spatial cognition: Evidence from visual neglect. *Trends in Cognitive Sciences*, *7*, 125–133.

Heilman, K. M., Watson, R. T., and Valenstein, E. (1985). Neglect and related disorders. In K. M. Heilman and E. Valenstein (Eds.), *Clinical neuropsychology*. Oxford: Oxford University Press.

Heinke, D., and Humphreys, G. W. (2003). Attention, spatial representation and visual neglect: Simulating emergent attentional processes in the Selective Attention for Identification Model (SAIM). *Psychological Review, 110*, 29–87.

Hillis, A. E., and Caramazza, A. (1995). Cognitive and neural mechanisms underlying visual and semantic processing: Implications from "optic aphasia". *Journal of Cognitive Neuroscience, 7*, 457–478.

Hinton, G. E. (1989). Connectionist learning procedures. *Artificial Intelligence, 40*, 185–234.

Hodges, J. J., Bozeat, S., Lambon Ralph, M. A., Patterson, K., and Spatt, J. (2000). The role of conceptual knowledge in object use: Evidence from semantic dementia. *Brain, 123*, 1913–1925.

Hodges, J. R., and Greene, J. D. W. (1998). Knowing about people and nursing them: Can Alzheimer's disease patients do one without the other? *Quarterly Journal of Experimental Psychology, 51A*, 121–134.

Humphreys, G. W., and Forde, E. M. E. (2005). Naming a giraffe but not an animal: Base-level but not super-ordinate naming in a patient with impaired semantics. *Cognitive Neuropsychology, 22*, 539–558.

Humphreys, G. W., and Heinke, D. (1998). Spatial representation and selection in the brain: Neuropsychological and computational constraints. *Visual Cognition, 5*, 9–47.

Humphreys, G. W., and Riddoch, M. J. (1994). Attention to within-object and between object spatial representations: Multiple sites for visual selection. *Cognitive Neuropsychology, 11*, 207–242.

Humphreys, G. W., and Riddoch, M. J. (1995). Separate coding of space within and between perceptual objects: Evidence from unilateral visual neglect. *Cognitive Neuropsychology, 12*, 283–312.

Humphreys, G. W., and Riddoch, M. J. (2003). From vision to action, and action to vision: A convergent route approach to vision, action and attention. In D. Irwin and B. Ross (Eds.), *The psychology of learning and motivation*. Visual Cognition. Vol. 42. New York: Academic Press.

Jacobs, R. A., and Jordan, M. I. (1992). Computational consequences of a bias toward short connections. *Journal of Cognitive Neuroscience, 4*, 323–336.

Kinsbourne, M., and Warrington, E. K. (1962). A disorder of simultaneous form perception. *Brain, 85*, 461–486.

Lhermitte, F., and Beauvois, M.-F. (1973). A visual-speech disconnexion syndrome: Report of a case with optic aphasia, agnosic alexia and colour agnosia. *Brain, 96*, 695–714.

Lichtheim, L. (1885). On aphasia. *Brain, 7*, 433–484.

McClelland, J. L., and Rumelhart, D. E. (Eds.) (1986). *Parallel distributed processing: Explorations in the microstructure of cognition.* Vol. 2. Cambridge, MA: MIT Press.

Mozer, M. C. (1991). *The perception of multiple objects: A connectionist approach.* Cambridge, MA: MIT Press.

Mozer, M. C., Halligan, P. W., and Marshall, J. C. (1997). The end of the line for a brain-damaged model of unilateral neglect. *Journal of Cognitive Neuroscience, 9,* 171–190.

Patterson, K. E., Seidenberg, M. S., and McClelland, J. L. (1989). Connections and disconnections: Acquired dyslexia in a computational model of reading processes. In R. G. M. Morris (Ed.), *Parallel distributed processing: Implications for psychology and neuroscience.* London: Oxford University Press.

Pilgrim, E., and Humphreys, G. W. (1991). Impairment of action to visual objects in a case of ideomotor apraxia. *Cognitive Neuropsychology, 8,* 459–473.

Pizzamiglio, L., Cappa, S., Vallar, G., Zoccolotti, P., Bottini, G., Ciurli, P., Guariglia, C., and Antonucci, G. (1989). Visual neglect for far and near extrapersonal space in humans. *Cortex, 25,* 471–477.

Pitzalis, S., Di Russo, F., Spinelli, D., and Zoccolotti, P. (2001). Influence of the radial and vertical dimensions on lateral neglect. *Experimental Brain Research, 136,* 281–294.

Plaut, D. C. (2002). Graded modality-specific specialisation in semantics: A computational account of optic aphasia. *Cognitive Neuropsychology, 19,* 603–639.

Plaut, D. C., McClelland, J. L., Seidenberg, M. S., and Patterson, K. E. (1996). Understanding normal and impaired word reading: Computational principles in quasi-regular domains. *Psychological Review, 103,* 56–115.

Posner, M. I., and Cohen, Y. (1984). Components of visual orienting. In H. Bouma and D. G. Bouwhuis (Eds.), *Attention and performance X,* 531–556. Hillsdale, NJ: Erlbaum.

Riddoch, M. J., and Humphreys, G. W. (1987). Visual object processing in optic aphasia: A case of semantic access agnosia. *Cognitive Neuropsychology, 4,* 131–185.

Riddoch, M. J., Humphreys, G. W., and Price, C. J. (1989). Routes to action: Evidence from apraxia. *Cognitive Neuropsychology, 6,* 437–454.

Robertson, I. (1989). Anomalies in the lateralisation omissions in unilateral left neglect: Implications for an attentional theory of neglect. *Neuropsychologia, 27,* 157–165.

Rumelhart, D. E., and McClelland, J. L. (Eds.) (1986). *Parallel distributed processing: Explorations in the microstructure of cognition.* Vol. 1. Cambridge, MA: MIT Press.

Rumiati, R. I., and Humphreys, G. W. (1998). Recognition by action: Dissociating visual and semantic routes to action in normal observers. *Journal of Experimental Psychology: Human Perception and Performance, 24*, 631–647.

Shallice, T., Warrington, E. K., and McCarthy, R. A. (1983). Reading without semantics. *Quarterly Journal of Experimental Psychology, 35A*, 111–138.

Sperling, G. (1960). The information available in brief visual presentations. *Psychological Monographs, 74* (11, Whole no. 498).

Sperling, G. (1967). Successive approximations to a model for short-term memory. In A. F. Sanders (Ed.), *Attention* and *performance I*. Amsterdam: North Holland.

Treisman, A. (1998). Feature binding, attention and object perception. *Philosophical Transactions of the Royal Society London, B353*, 1295–1306.

Yoon, E. Y., Heinke, D., and Humphreys, G. W. (2002). Modelling direct perceptual constraints on action selection: The Naming and Action Model (NAM). *Visual Cognition, 9*, 615–661.

Yoon, E. Y., Humphreys, G. W., and Riddoch, M. J. (2005). Action naming with impaired semantics: Neuropsychological evidence contrasting naming and reading for objects and verbs. *Cognitive Neuropsychology, 22*, 753–767.

5   Skin Conductance: A Psychophysiological Approach to the Study of Decision Making

Nasir H. Naqvi and Antoine Bechara

Overview

Over the last century, psychologists have applied a range of physiological techniques to the body in order to infer the functions of the brain, an approach that is broadly referred to as "psychophysiology." Until the advent of functional neuroimaging, psychophysiological techniques, especially those which measure the functions of the autonomic nervous system, were considered the primary means for addressing the neural processes underlying emotion, attention, learning, and memory. The general philosophy of such an approach is that autonomic responses that reflect cognitive processes are epiphenomenal to the processes themselves; changes in the body are not viewed as necessary for mental processes to be executed— they merely exist as conveniently measurable vestiges of our visceral evolutionary history.

The embodied view of cognition holds that the body and its central representations form the basis for the meaning that we attribute to objects and events in the world (Lakoff and Johnson, 1999). A more specific framework, originally proposed by William James (1884), holds that subjective emotional feeling, a type of meaning, is derived from the bodily consequences of the perception of objects or events that have some innate or acquired relevance to survival. This framework places a special emphasis on the role of the viscera, that is, the tissues that are innervated by the autonomic nervous system, holding that changes within the viscera are intimately linked to the expression of emotions, and that the sensory representations of such visceral changes are essential neural substrates for feeling emotions. More recently, feelings derived from visceral states have come to be considered a central component in the execution of highly complex, goal-oriented behavior (Nauta, 1971; Damasio, 1994). Within this framework, visceral responses are not merely vestiges of our evolutionary past; they are integral components of our rationality, social behavior, and ethics. Accordingly, because it provides information about cognitive processes that cannot be ascertained by any other technique, the psychophysiological measurement of visceral change is an integral tool in the study of cognition, especially cognition of stimuli that guide the making of choices.

This chapter describes how the measurement of a particular type of visceral change, the skin conductance response, can be used to address how humans attribute value to the choices we make. After reviewing the physiological mechanisms that control skin conductance, it describes how we have measured skin conductance in our laboratory. By no means a comprehensive discussion of skin conductance methodology, the description is meant rather to allow experimenters unfamiliar with the technique to replicate our procedures and to extend our methodology into new areas that build upon the principles described below. By presenting the results of our experiments using skin conductance to probe the neural underpinnings of decision making, we hope to illustrate how psychophysiological techniques such as the measurement of skin conductance can be used both to address normal decision making and to characterize the deficits in decision making that result from damage in brain areas that integrate visceral states into goal-directed behavior.

What Is Skin Conductance?

One of several different forms of electrodermal activity, skin conductance refers the degree to which the skin permits the flow of current, and is related to the degree of eccrine sweating, that is, the secretion of electrolyte solution by sweat glands. Skin conductance is measured by applying a small voltage across two electrodes and measuring the resulting current that flows between them. The amplitude of this current is proportional to the skin conductance. Other forms of electrodermal activity include skin resistance (the reciprocal of skin conductance) and skin potential. Skin conductance is the most commonly measured form of electrodermal activity because it is the easiest to measure, and will be the focus of this chapter. The unit of skin conductance is the microsiemens (μS), which is the reciprocal of the kilohm (kΩ).

Although skin conductance is typically measured from the palms of the hands (palmar skin conductance), it can also be measured from the soles of the feet (plantar skin conductance) when the palms are not accessible. The palms and soles, collectively referred to as the "volar surfaces," are unique in that eccrine sweating in these areas is related to mental processes, as opposed to thermoregulation (Kuno, 1956; Boucsein, 1992). These areas are also easily accessible and possess a high density of eccrine sweat glands. Volar sweating is thought to have arisen in evolution as a means of facilitating tactile interaction with the environment. Thus, for example, sweating can increase tactile friction, enhancing the ability to grasp objects (Darrow, 1933); moreover, sweating may also protect the volar surfaces from abrasive injury (Wilcott, 1966). Volar skin conductance may therefore reflect mental preparation to bring objects closer to the body (approach) or to deflect objects away from the body (avoidance).

What Are the Physiological Mechanisms That Control Skin Conductance?

Eccrine sweating is under the exclusive control of the sympathetic nervous system (SNS), which is a branch of the autonomic nervous system. The peripheral neurons of SNS originate in the intermediolateral cell column of the thoracic and lumbar segments of the spinal cord and project to sympathetic ganglia. Here they release acetylcholine, which excites postganglionic neurons through nicotinic acetylcholine receptors. In general, postganglionic sympathetic axons exert their effects on their targets by releasing epinephrine (adrenaline). Eccrine sweating is unique among sympathetically controlled functions in that the postganglionic neurons that innervate eccrine sweat glands release acetylcholine, which binds to muscarinic acetylcholine receptors on the sweat glands. Thus any drug that agonizes or antagonizes peripheral nicotinic or muscarinic cholinergic neurotransmission has the potential to alter eccrine sweating, irrespective of its effects on the central nervous system. This includes both many drugs that are used to treat psychiatric disorders and many that are abused.

Much of the original work on the central control of eccrine sweating was undertaken in cats (for review, see Sequeira-Martinho and Roy, 1993); it focused largely on the functions of the anterior hypothalamus, which receives information both from thermosensory areas within the hypothalamus and from telencephalic areas that mediate higher-order sensory and motor functions. The anterior hypothalamus in turn exerts control over preganglionic sympathetic neurons in the intermediolateral cell column of the spinal cord. The central control over eccrine sweating can be thought to consist of (1) a "lower" system in the brain stem and hypothalamic area, which governs reflex and thermoregulatory control over eccrine sweating; and (2) a "higher" system in the telencephalic areas, including limbic-motor integration centers such as the amygdala, the hippocampus, the basal ganglia, and the prefrontal cortex, which mediates cognitive processes and modulates emotional sweating—and which engages the lower system. Existing for a variety of visceromotor functions, this mode of connectivity facilitates the integration of the visceral state into the planning and execution of behavior (Nauta, 1971; Damasio, 1994); indeed, it may have implications for how visceral responses, including skin conductance response, are deployed in the service of higher cognitive functions, such as decision making.

Earlier lesion studies in severely brain-damaged humans have demonstrated that the telencephalic areas involved in controlling skin conductance include the prefrontal cortex, especially the orbital prefrontal cortex (Luria, Pribram, and Homskaya, 1964; Luria and Homskaya, 1970; Luria, 1973) as well as the amygdala (Lee et al., 1989). Later studies examining the effects of more restricted brain damage have demonstrated that the amygdala and prefrontal cortex play a role in generating skin conductance responses to stimuli with emotional significance (Tranel and Damasio, 1994; Zahn, Grafman, and Tranel, 1999), including stimuli that have acquired emotional value through classical conditioning (LaBar et al., 1995; Bechara et al., 1999), but that these regions are not necessary for the generation of skin conductance responses to nonemotional stimuli, including reflex responses to deep breaths (Tranel and Damasio, 1994) and orienting stimuli (Tranel and Damasio, 1989). This suggests that the visceromotor functions of the amygdala and prefrontal cortex are related specifically to their role in cognitive and emotional processes.

How Is Skin Conductance Recorded?

The procedures used in our laboratory to acquire skin conductance data are adapted from the recommendations of Fowles et al. (1981). For a more thorough review of the technical aspects of skin conductance recording, we refer readers to an excellent volume by Boucsein (1992).

Our laboratory uses the Biopac system (manufactured by Biopac, Inc., Santa Barbara, California) for all psychophysiological data acquisition and analysis. Although we measure multiple physiological channels, including skin conductance, electrocardiogram, respiration, facial electromyogram, electrogastrogram, and finger temperature, our discussion will be restricted to the measurement of skin conductance. This system includes a transducer-amplifier for skin conductance, an interface module, an analog-to-digital converter, and a computer equipped with software for data acquisition and analysis. The Biopac system can also interface with task markers to signal the presentation of stimuli or the behavior of the subject.

As mentioned above, skin conductance is measured from the palmar or plantar surface. Although the palmar surface is usually chosen because it is readily accessible, when skin conductance is measured during fMRI scanning, the plantar surface may be chosen because radio frequency pulses emitted by the scanner may heat electrodes close to the magnet bore. Washing the hands with soap and water and drying them thoroughly is an adequate preparation of the site where the electrodes will be placed. Alcohol and acetone should be avoided because they may dehydrate the skin. Our laboratory measures skin conductance using disposable self-adhesive Ag/AgCl EKG electrodes affixed to the thenar and hypothenar eminences. This placement of palmar electrodes is illustrated in figure 5.1. The electrodes are typically attached to the nondominant hand to allow for manipulation of objects (e.g., a computer mouse) during testing since movement may affect skin conductance. Allowing 10 minutes for the electrodes to "settle" after they are attached will help ensure a more stable recording.

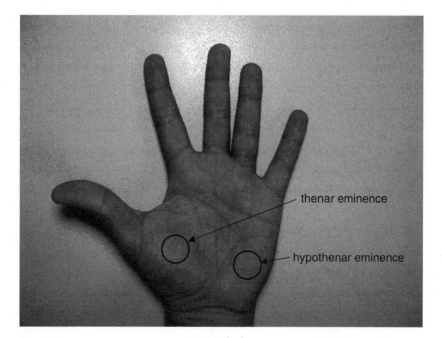

Figure 5.1
Placement of electrodes for recording of palmar skin conductance.

To measure skin conductance, a small command voltage (typically, 0.5 V) is applied across the two electrodes. The skin conductance is proportional to the amplitude of the current that flows between these electrodes. This current is converted into a continuously time-varying output voltage signal that is filtered, amplified, digitized, and stored on a computer. Skin conductance is measured in our laboratory using a DC amplifier, with the low-pass filter set to 10 Hz. The low-pass filter determines the highest frequency of signal to be recorded. Skin conductance is amplified with a gain 5 μS/V, although this may be increased or decreased to accommodate unusually low or high baseline skin conductance levels, respectively. The conditioned output voltage signal is sent from the skin conductance transducer-amplifier to an analog-to-digital converter, which translates this output into units of skin conductance based on the scaling of output voltage to skin conductance. We use a sampling rate of 200 Hz.

What Are Some of the Different Measurements Used in Skin Conductance Recording?

Skin conductance measurements can be broadly categorized into tonic and phasic. The two types of measurements differ both according to the timescales over which they are recorded and according to their causal relationship to an eliciting stimulus. Tonic skin conductance generally refers to changes in skin conductance that are not causally related to an eliciting stimulus and that occur in a period of from tens of seconds to minutes. Phasic skin conductance generally refers to changes that occur within a discrete time window (usually 1–5 seconds) following the presentation of a stimulus.

Examples of tonic skin conductance measurements include skin conductance level (SCL: the average of a series of instantaneous measurements of skin conductance taken over a given interval) and number of nonspecific fluctuations (NNSF: the number of skin conductance increases over a threshold that occur over a given interval). Tonic measurements of skin conductance have been used extensively to address the relationship between autonomic and central nervous system "arousal" (Fowles, 1980; Walschburger, 1986) and between autonomic nervous system activity and "stress" (Lazarus, 1966; Erdmann et al., 1984). They have also been used to assess motivational states that are elicited by a stimulus, but that elaborate over an extended time interval, such as emotional imagery (Stemmler et al., 2003) and cue-induced drug craving (Childress, McLellan, and O'Brien, 1986; Niaura et al., 1989). Such long-term measurements of autonomic function may be more suitable for assessing the relationship between the visceral state and subjective feelings, which may elaborate over a relatively long timescale. Tonic skin conductance measurements are also well suited to be recorded in parallel with brain-imaging techniques that require long acquisition times, such as positron emission tomography (PET; Fredrikson et al., 1998; Damasio et al., 2000).

In contrast, phasic skin conductance measurements are used to address event-related processes, which are recorded over a short time interval and are discretely related to an eliciting stimulus. The most commonly used phasic skin conductance measurement is skin conductance response amplitude (SCR.amp). Strictly speaking, a skin conductance response refers to an increase in skin conductance occurring after the onset of a stimulus. More recently, phasic skin conductance measurements have also been used to address the cognitive processes that precede an event, such as planning of a choice or anticipation of an event (described later in the context of experiments addressing the somatic marker hypothesis of decision making). Because they are recorded over a relatively short timescale, phasic skin conductance response measurements can be applied in parallel with event-related functional imaging techniques, such as functional magnetic resonance imaging (fMRI).

How Are Skin Conductance Responses Measured?

Here we describe the procedures used in our laboratory to record phasic skin conductance measurements. Traditionally, the skin conductance response has been defined as an increase in skin conductance over some threshold value (typically $0.05\,\mu S$ above baseline) occurring within a given time interval after presentation of a stimulus (typically, 5 seconds, beginning 1 second after stimulus onset). Although a variety of parameters can be measured describing the temporal relationship between the stimulus and the skin conductance response, including the latencies of the onset, peak, and decay of the SCR, we will not discuss these here. The most common parameter derived from the skin conductance response is SCR amplitude (SCR.amp), which is defined as the difference between the peak skin conductance value (the high point, where the tangent of the skin conductance curve is zero) within the measurement window and the trough value (the low point, where the tangent of the skin conductance curve is zero) preceding this peak. Using this technique allows one to measure the SCR.amp when the skin conductance response follows a discrete stimulus within a given time interval, as shown in figure 5.2. The technique, which assumes

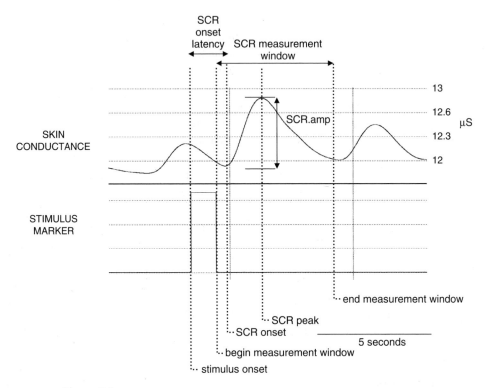

Figure 5.2
Skin conductance response to winning $140 of play money, illustrating the measurement of skin conductance response amplitude (SCR.amp). Here, the response interval begins 1 sec after stimulus onset and ends 5 sec after stimulus onset. Although the peak of the response may occur outside of this interval, the response must initiate within this interval. The tick mark in the task marker channel is 1 sec long.

that the SCR is causally related to the stimulus, is used to address the sensory processing and subsequent evaluation of the stimulus. One may also be interested in the cognitive processes that anticipate an event, such as anticipation of the value of the stimulus and deliberation of the consequences of behavioral choices that may change this value. In this case, it is desirable to measure the physiological responses that precede the onset of a stimulus. Since it may not be possible to identify discrete skin conductance responses occurring before a stimulus, it is useful to be able to measure skin conductance "activity" over an arbitrarily defined prestimulus time interval.

The simplest way to assess skin conductance activity without regard to the onset of a discrete skin conductance response is to measure the area under the curve that represents the change in skin conductance over a given time interval. To obtain this curve, the raw skin conductance trace is first run through a low-pass filter to remove high-frequency noise. In our laboratory, this is done using a moving-average function with a smoothing interval of 1 second. Next, the slow drift in baseline skin conductance level is removed using a moving-difference function with a difference interval of 50 msec (10 points for a 200 Hz sampling rate). The difference function converts every point in the raw skin conductance waveform into the difference between the value of the point and the value of a point located a given interval before it. Although a similar function may also be accomplished during acquisition by setting the high-pass filter of the amplifier to 0.05 Hz, this results in the loss of information about tonic skin conductance level. The area under the curve of the smoothed and differenced function is then measured over an interval that is specified by the task marker using a peak detection function. The area under the curve is measured as the area bounded by the curve and the chord that connects the intersection of the curve with the endpoints of the measurement interval. This includes area both above and below the chord. This area is then divided by the length of the time interval, in seconds, resulting in units of µS/sec. Figure 5.3 illustrates this skin conductance response area under the curve measurement (SCR.auc) and compares it with the traditional method for measuring skin conductance response amplitude (SCR.amp).

The method we use to measure the SCR.auc approximates the that used by Traxel (1957), which measures under the curve of a single skin conductance response. This measurement, which was proposed to index "quantity of affect," takes into account both the amplitude of the response as well as its decay time and may thus have more validity than either of these parameters alone (Boucsein, 1992). The method described here is similar, but allows one to measure multiple responses within the measurement interval; as a further advantage, it can be applied in the same way to the pre- and poststimulus interval. Thus the same measure can be used to address both the cognitive processes leading up to the choice of a behavior and the cognitive processes evaluating the consequences of that behavior once it has been executed. Moreover, the SCR.auc method does not require a subjective judgment as to whether a skin conductance response has occurred, and is thus easily automated.

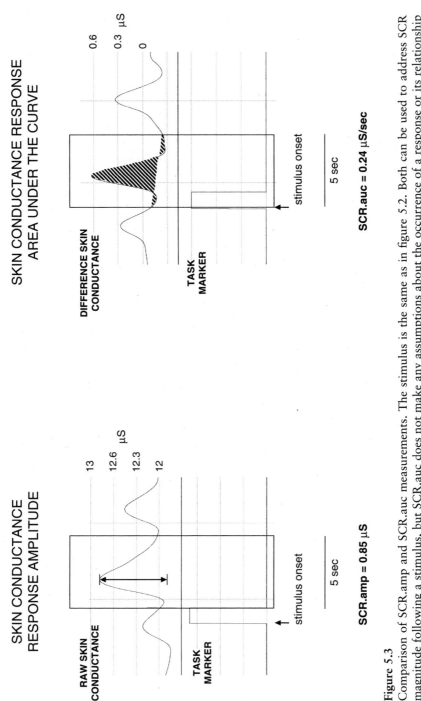

Figure 5.3
Comparison of SCR.amp and SCR.auc measurements. The stimulus is the same as in figure 5.2. Both can be used to address SCR magnitude following a stimulus, but SCR.auc does not make any assumptions about the occurrence of a response or its relationship to an eliciting stimulus. The difference skin conductance trace is derived from the raw skin conductance trace using a moving difference function. Note that the total area measurement includes the area both above and below the chord connecting the measurement interval endpoints.

How Can the Skin Conductance Response Be Used to Address Decision Making?

Traditionally, skin conductance response has been used to address the emotional evaluation of sensory stimuli. Emotions are not just elicited by objects and events in the world, however; they may also be deployed in the process of planning and executing complex behavior. Although such deployment could also be considered a form of emotional evaluation, in this case, the stimuli being evaluated are goals and outcomes that are represented "in mind." Skin conductance response has offered a unique window into the mental processes that represent the value of goals and outcomes. The measurement of skin conductance response has provided support for the somatic marker hypothesis of decision making, which holds that emotions, in particular the visceral manifestations of emotions, are critical components of the process of decision making under conditions of uncertain risk and reward (Damasio, 1994; Bechara, 2001).

The somatic marker hypothesis was originally formulated as a way to explain the deficits in real-life behavior manifested by patients with damage in the ventromedial prefrontal cortex (VMPFC; Damasio, Tranel, and Damasio, 1991), an area comprising the medial portion of the orbitofrontal cortex and the inferior (subgenual) portion of the medial prefrontal cortex. Damage in this part of the brain has been known to lead to highly maladaptive patterns of decision making within personal and social domains, despite normal intelligence and intact reasoning in other domains (Damasio, Tranel, and Damasio, 1990). In particular, patients with VMPFC damage lack the ability to decide advantageously in situations that require them to weigh the positive and negative consequences of their actions under conditions of uncertainty. Although the real-life deficit of these patients is obvious to anyone observing their family life, work life, friendships, and financial affairs, their cognitive abnormality has, until recently, eluded characterization in the laboratory.

To address the impairment caused by this type of brain damage, it was necessary to devise a task that simulated the demands of real-life decision making. The Gambling Task (also known as the "Iowa Gambling Task") was developed in our laboratory to test the hypothesis that patients with damage in the VMPFC are impaired in their ability to decide advantageously in the face of uncertain risk and reward. The Gambling Task has been described in detail elsewhere (Bechara, Tranel, and Damasio, 2000). Briefly, subjects are required to choose between four decks of cards: A, B, C, and D. Choosing from any of the decks always results in the payout of money. Occasionally, choosing from any of the decks can also result in the loss of money. Decks A and B offer a large payout on each choice but also an occasional large loss. Decks C and D offer a small payout on each choice, but also an occasional small loss. These reward and punishment contingencies are designed such that choosing consistently from decks C and D (the advantageous decks) results in an eventual gain of money, whereas choosing consistently from decks A and B (the disadvantageous decks) results in an eventual loss of money. Subjects are instructed to attempt to win as much money as possible; they are told that some of the decks are better than others, but they are not told about the reward and punishment contingencies of each deck. Normal subjects initially sample from both advantageous and disadvantageous decks. Over time, they learn to avoid the disadvantageous decks and to more often choose the advantageous decks, which leads to a higher overall gain of money over the course of the task. Patients with damage in the ventromedial prefrontal cortex continue to choose from the disadvantageous decks, seemingly driven by the certain prospect of receiving a high reward, but undeterred by the uncertain prospect of high punishment.

Further insight into the cognitive deficits of these patients came from the findings, discussed earlier, that patients with damage to the ventromedial prefrontal cortex demonstrate a deficit in the deployment of autonomic responses to emotional stimuli, including skin conductance responses (Tranel and Damasio 1989, 1994). Moreover, patients with damage in the VMPFC also seem to be impaired in their ability to feel certain kinds of emotion (Damasio, 1994). This led to the development of the somatic marker hypothesis, according to which, emotions, in the form of somatic states and their sensory representations within the brain, play an essential role in the process of decision making. They do so by marking the consequences of choices, both anticipated and actual. Preceding a choice, the somatic state triggered during contemplation of the various options functions to mark these options with value. This results in the "gut feeling" or "hunch" that is associated with certain options, and serves to bias decision making in the direction of the advantageous choice. After a choice is made, the somatic state triggered by the receipt of reward or punishment functions to mark the actual outcome of the choice as good or bad. This is necessary for the felt experience of value of the outcome and for forming learned associations between the outcome and the choice that preceded it. According to the somatic marker hypothesis, the VMPFC is a critical substrate for the induction of somatic states during decision making.

To test this hypothesis, it was necessary to acquire somatic measures of the emotional responses during performance of the Gambling Task, specifically, during contemplation of the potential consequences of choices and after the actual consequences of these choices were signaled. Measurement of skin conductance response was ideally suited to this task. To demonstrate the effects of lesions in the VMPFC on skin conductance responses during the Gambling Task, we first used the more traditional SCR.amp measurement, which assumed that skin conductance responses preceding the choice from a deck of cards were related to the deliberation of the consequences of that choice (Bechara et al., 1996, 1997). During these early experiments, we also used a manual version of the Gambling Task with actual decks of cards, fake money, and an experimenter. More recently, however, we have switched to a computerized version of the Gambling Task, and we have adopted the SCR.auc method described above to address questions related to the somatic marker hypothesis of decision making (Bechara et al., 1999, 2001; Bechara, Dolan, and Hindes, 2002; Bechara and Damasio, 2002). The SCR.auc method does not require assumptions about the existence of discrete SCRs before choosing from the decks, and is easily automated.

The two methods yielded highly similar results (figure 5.4 illustrates the recording of skin conductance during the Gambling task; figure 5.5 illustrates the scoring of prechoice and postchoice SCR.auc). Normal subjects were shown to deploy skin conductance responses during the period preceding their choice and to deploy responses that were larger before choosing from the disadvantageous decks than before choosing from the advantageous decks. This suggested that SCR amplitude reflected the anticipated value of the choice that was being made. Moreover, normal subjects deployed skin conductance responses when receiving reward and punishment was signaled after their choice. In contrast to normal subjects, patients with damage to their ventromedial prefrontal cortex did not deploy any skin conductance responses during the period preceding their choices, whereas they continued to deploy skin conductance responses to reward and punishment, although these were somewhat diminished in amplitude and did not discriminate between different levels of reward or punishment. This suggested that damage in the VMPFC resulted in a specific impairment in the ability to emotionally anticipate the future consequence of one's choices, despite a relative sparing of the ability to react emotionally to these consequences when they were ultimately revealed.

Emotional responses to receiving rewards or punishments are hypothesized to play a role in the type of decision making assessed by the Gambling Task. To address whether the emotional responses to reward and punishment were also necessary for normal decision making, our

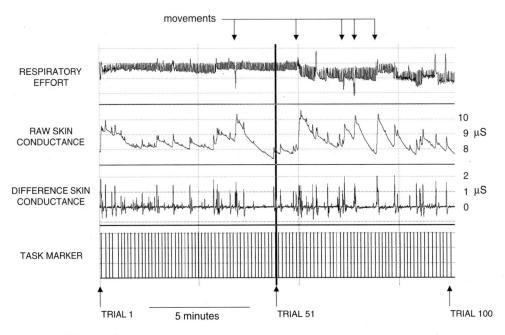

Figure 5.4
Recording of skin conductance concurrently with the Gambling Task. Each tick in
the lower trace represents a choice by the subject. The minimum interval between
each choice has been set to 6 sec in order to allow for measurement of physiological responses. Note slow changes in the conductance level in the raw skin conductance trace and how these are absent in the difference skin conductance trace. These
changes are likely to have been due to movements of the subject, which are evident
in the respiration trace.

laboratory studied a group of patients with damage in another area involved
in emotion, the amygdala. Damage to the amygdala, like damage to the
VMPFC, results in impairments in real-life decision making under conditions of uncertain risk and reward. The amygdala has been identified as a
region involved in emotional evaluation of sensory stimuli (for review see
Adolphs and Tranel, 2000; Ledoux, 2000; Cardinal et al., 2002), and, as
discussed earlier, like the VMPFC, is involved in the emotional control over
visceral function, including skin conductance. Because amygdala has been
implicated in the deployment of quick, automatic emotional responses to
objects and events within the sensory field (for review, see Ledoux, 2000),
we hypothesized that it also mediates the visceral responses to reward and
punishment, which are necessary for representation of the value of the consequences of choices.

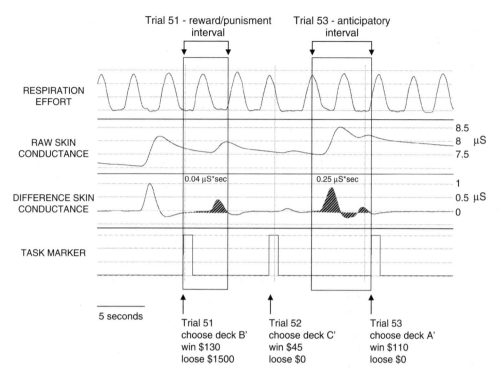

Figure 5.5
Measurement of SCR.auc during the period preceding a choice (anticipatory interval) and after a choice has been made (reward/punishment interval). SCR.auc is measured from the difference skin conductance trace. This is the same recording that was shown in figure 5.4, but with an expanded timescale.

To test this hypothesis, we recorded skin conductance in patients with bilateral damage to the amygdala while they performed the Gambling Task. Like patients with VMPFC damage, patients with amygdala damage performed poorly in the Gambling Task, although the pattern of abnormality in their skin conductance responses suggested a cognitive impairment different from that of patients with VMPFC damage. Specifically, whereas both patients with amygdala damage and patients with VMPFC damage did not show SCRs during the period preceding their choices, patients with amygdala damage also did not show SCRs after receiving reward or punishment (Bechara et al., 1999). These results suggest that the amygdala plays a more basic role in decision making than the ventromedial prefrontal cortex. The lack of emotional responses to winning or losing money indicates that the amygdala mediates the immediate emotional responses to a biologically salient stimulus, in line with its role in the rapid evaluation of the emotional stimuli. The lack of SCRs during the period preceding the choice could reflect one of two possibilities: (1) that the amygdala, in addition to its role in evaluating the emotional significance of reward or punishments, also plays a role in the evaluation of the emotional significance of future consequences, or (2) that the emotional responses to reward and punishment, mediated by the amygdala, are necessary for learning to associate the value of a given outcome with the actions that preceded it. The latter view agrees with the more general idea that the amygdala is necessary for triggering emotional responses in a rapid and relatively automatic fashion, rather than as a consequence of a reasoned deliberation of the emotional significance of events in the future.

From this line of experiments, a model emerged of the role of the amygdala and VMPFC in decision making. Within this model, the amygdala is necessary for triggering rapid and relatively automatic somatic responses to reward and punishment (primary induction); these responses contribute to the encoding of the value of the sensory cues and actions that preceded reward and punishment. Over time, through this encoding, subjects learn the association between a given choice and its outcome. This learning, which may precede explicit awareness of the contingencies between specific choices and their outcome. This is expressed by the VMPFC, which elicits learned representations of the value of a choice in the period before a choice is made, when the outcome of the various choices are weighed against each other as they are each held "in mind." These representations of value are based on the bodily response triggered within the VMPFC (secondary induction), an emotional response that "marks" the value of options for behavior based upon past experience. The somatic state elicited during the period preceding a choice then feeds back to the brain, where it is represented in somatosensory areas and can then influence behavior through a biasing effect. This afferent feedback of the bodily state may also contribute to the subjective experience of a "hunch" or a "gut feeling" during the period preceding a choice.

Conclusion

The somatic marker framework and, specifically, the measurement of skin conductance can be used to elucidate the neurocognitive processes by which normal decision making occurs. These processes are relevant for understanding a range of real-life behaviors—from behaviors related to food, sex, pain, and other natural rewards and punishments to economic and social behaviors—in which the possibilities for future reward and punishment are played against one another while deliberating an uncertain outcome. Moreover, this framework can be applied to help understand the neurocognitive deficits that may underlie the behavioral abnormalities seen in a range of mental disorders that are associated with impairments in emotional processing and decision making. Indeed, it has been now applied to understand the neurocognitive deficits underlying mental illnesses such as drug dependence, in which the ability to weigh the future consequences of one's actions may be compromised (Bechara and Damasio, 2002; Bechara, Dolan, and Hindes, 2002). A similar approach has been used to elucidate the neurocognitive underpinnings of obsessive-compulsive disorder (Cavedini et al., 2002), anorexia nervosa (Cavedini et al., 2004), and certain forms of psychopathy (van Honk et al., 2002). The measurement of skin conductance may also aid in assessing the severity of these disorders, in predicting the response to therapy, and in showing how these disorders are related to the function of brain regions that integrate visceral states into complex goal-oriented behavior.

References

Adolphs, R., and Tranel, D. (2000). Emotion recognition and the human amygdala. In J. P. Aggleton (Ed.), *The amygdala: A functional analysis*, 587–630. New York: Oxford University Press.

Bechara, A. (2001). Neurobiology of decision-making: Risk and reward. *Seminars in Clinical Neuropsychiatry*, 6(3), 205–216.

Bechara, A., and Damasio, H. (2002). Decision-making and addiction. 1. Impaired activation of somatic states in substance dependent individuals when pondering decisions with negative future consequences. *Neuropsychologia*, 40(10), 1675–1689.

Bechara, A., Damasio, H., Damasio, A. R., and Lee, G. P. (1999). Different contributions of the human amygdala and ventromedial prefrontal cortex to decision-making. *Journal of Neuroscience*, 19, 5473–5481.

Bechara, A., Damasio, H. Tranel, D., and Damasio, A. R. (1997). Deciding advantageously before knowing the advantageous strategy. *Science*, 275(5304), 1293–1295.

Bechara, A., Dolan, S., Denburg, N., Hindes, A., Anderson, S. W., and Nathan, P. E. (2001). Decision-making deficits, linked to a dysfunctional ventromedial prefrontal cortex, revealed in alcohol and stimulant abusers. *Neuropsychologia*, 39(4), 376–389.

Bechara, A., Dolan, S., and Hindes, A. (2002). Decision-making and addiction. 2. Myopia for the future or hypersensitivity to reward? *Neuropsychologia*, 40(10), 1690–1705.

Bechara, A., Tranel, D., and Damasio, H. (2000). Characterization of the decision-making deficit of patients with ventromedial prefrontal cortex lesions. *Brain*, *123*(pt.11), 2189–2202.

Bechara, A., Tranel, D., Damasio, H., and Damasio, A. R. (1996). Failure to respond autonomically to anticipated future outcomes following damage to prefrontal cortex. *Cerebral Cortex*, *6*(2), 215–225.

Boucsein, W. (1992). *Electrodermal activity*. New York: Plenum Press.

Cardinal, R. N., Parkinson, J. A., Hall, J., and Everitt, B. J. (2002). Emotion and motivation: The role of the amygdala, ventral striatum and prefrontal cortex. *Neuroscience and Biobehavioral Reviews*, *26*, 321–352.

Cavedini, P., Bassi, T., Zorzi, C., and Bellodi, L. (2004). The advantages of choosing antiobsessive therapy according to decision-making functioning. *Journal of Clinical Psychopharmacology*, *24*(6), 628–631.

Cavedini, P., Riboldi, G., D'Annucci, A., Belotti, P., Cisima, M., and Bellodi, L. (2002). Decision-making heterogeneity in obsessive-compulsive disorder: ventromedial prefrontal cortex function predicts different treatment outcomes. *Neuropsychologia*, *40*(2), 205–211.

Childress, A. R., McLellan, A. T., and O'Brien, C. P. (1986). Role of conditioning factors in the development of drug dependence. *Psychiatric Clinics of North America*, *9*(3), 413–425.

Damasio, A. R. (1994). *Descartes' error: Emotion, reason and the human brain*. New York: Putnam.

Damasio, A. R., Grabowski, T. J., Bechara, A., Damasio, H., Ponto, L. L., Parvizi, J., and Hichwa, R. D. (2000). Subcortical and cortical brain activity during the feeling of self-generated emotions. *Nature Neuroscience*, *3*(10), 1049–1056.

Damasio, A. R., Tranel, D., and Damasio, H. (1990). Individuals with sociopathic behavior caused by frontal damage fail to respond autonomically to social stimuli. *Behavioural Brain Research*, *41*(2), 81–94.

Damasio, A. R., Tranel, D., and Damasio, H. (1991). Somatic markers and the guidance of behaviour. In H. Levin, H. Eisenberg, and A. Benton (Eds.), *Frontal lobe function and dysfunction*, 217–229. New York: Oxford University Press.

Darrow, C. (1933). The functional significance of the galvanic skin reflex and perspiration on the backs of the palms of the hands. *Psychological Bulletin*, *30*, 712.

Erdmann, G., Janke, W., Kochers, S., and Terschlusen, B. (1984). Comparison of the emotional effects of beta-adrenergic blockade and a tranquilizer under different situational conditions. 1. Anxiety-arousing situations. *Neuropsychobiology*, *12*, 143–151.

Fowles, D. C. (1980). The three arousal model: Implication of Gray's two-factor learning theory for heart-rate, electrodermal activity and psychopathy. *Psychophysiology*, *17*(2), 87–104.

Fowles, D. C., Christie, M. J., Edelberg, R., Grings, W. W., Lykken, D. T., and Venables, P. H. (1981). Committee report: Publication recommendations for electrodermal measurements. *Psychophysiology*, *18*(3), 232–239.

Fredrikson, M., Furmark, T., Olsson, M. T., Fischer, H., Andersson, J., and Langstrom, B. (1998). Functional neuroanatomical correlates of electrodermal activity: a positron emission tomographic study. *Psychophysiology*, *35*(2), 179–185.

James, W. (1884). What is an emotion? *Mind*, *9*, 188–205.

Kuno, Y. (1956). *Human perspiration*. Springfield, Il: Thomas.

LaBar, K. S., LeDoux, J. E., Spener, D. D., and Phelps, E. A. (1995). Impaired fear conditioning following unilateral temporal lobectomy in humans. *Journal of Neuroscience*, *15*(10), 6846–6855.

Lakoff, G., and Johnson, M. (1999). *Philosophy in the flesh*. New York: Basic Books.

Lazarus, R. S. (1966). *Psychological stress and the coping process*. New York: McGraw-Hill.

Ledoux, J. E. (2000). Emotion circuits in the brain. *Annual Review of Neuroscience*, *23*, 155–184.

Lee, G. P., Arena, J. G., Meador, K. J., Smith, J. R., Loring, D. W., and Flanigin, H. F. (1989). Changes in autonomic responsiveness following bilateral amygdalectomy in humans. *Neuropsychiatry, Neuropsychology, and Behavioral Neurology*, *1*, 119–130.

Luria, A. R. (1973). The frontal lobes and the regulation of behavior. In K. H. Pribram and A. R. Luria (Eds.), *Psychophysiology of the frontal lobes*, 3–26. New York: Academic Press.

Luria, A. R. and Homskaya, E. D. (1970). Frontal lobes and the regulation of arousal processes. In D. I. Mostofsky (Ed.), *Attention: Contemporary theory and analysis*, 303–330. New York, Appleton-Century-Crofts.

Luria, A. R., Pribram, K. H., and Homskaya, E. D. (1964). An experimental analysis of the behavioral disturbance produced by a left frontal arachnoidal endothelioma (meningioma). *Neuropsychologia*, *2*, 257–280.

Nauta, W. J. (1971). The problem of the frontal lobe: a reinterpretation. *Journal of Psychiatric Research*, *8*(3), 167–187.

Niaura, R., Abrams, D., Demuth, B., Pinto, R., and Monti, P. (1989). Responses to smoking-related stimuli and early relapse to smoking. *Addictive Behaviors*, *14*(4), 419–428.

Sequeira-Martinho, H., and Roy, J. (1993). Cortical and hypothalamo-limbic control of electrodermal responses. In J. Roy and W. Boucsein (Eds.), *Progress in electrodermal research*, vol. 249, pp. 93–114. New York: Plenum.

Stemmler, G., Janig, W., Hamm, A. O., Schupp, H. T., Weike, A. I., Levenson, R. W., Ohman, A., Wiens, S., Hugdahl, K., and Stormark, K. M. (2003). Part II:

Autonomic psychophysiology. In R. J. Davidson, K. R. Scherer, and H. H. Goldsmith (Eds.), *Handbook of affective sciences*, 131–291. Series in Affective Science. London, Oxford University Press.

Tranel, D., and Damasio, H. (1989). Intact electrodermal skin conductance responses after bilateral amygdala damage. *Neuropsychologia*, 27(4), 381–390.

Tranel, D., and Damasio, H. (1994). Neuroanatomical correlates of electrodermal skin conductance responses. *Psychophysiology*, 31(5), 427–438.

Traxel, W. (1957). Über das Zeitß psychogalvanischen Reaktion. *Zeitschrift für Psychologie*, 161, 282–291.

van Honk, J., Hermans, E. J., Putnam, P., Montagne, B., and Schutter, D. J. (2002). Defective somatic markers in sub-clinical psychopathy. *NeuroReport*, 13(8), 1025–1027.

Walschburger, P. (1986). Psychophysiological activation research. In J. Valsiner (Ed.), *The individual subject and scientific psychology*, 311–345. London: Plenum Press.

Wilcott, R. C. (1966). Adaptive value of arousal sweating and the epidermal mechanism related to skin potential and skin resistance. *Psychophysiology*, 2, 249–262.

Zahn, T. P., Grafman, J., and Tranel, D. (1999). Frontal lobe lesions and electrodermal activity: effects of significance. *Neuropsychologia*, 37(11), 1227–1241.

6 Single Neurons and Primate Behavior

Robert H. Wurtz and Marc A. Sommer

Understanding the brain mechanisms mediating cognitive behavior requires combining two experimental steps. First, the brain must actually be engaged in the cognitive behavior under study. Second, the brain activity must be measured during this behavior and the recording sufficiently described to permit replication of the experiment. There are a number of ways of meeting the second prerequisite, many discussed elsewhere in this volume; our chapter will address one with unsurpassed spatial and temporal resolution: the recording of the action potentials of single neurons.

Recording single neurons in the brain is a mature technique that has been used extensively for over a quarter century. In outlining the technique's requirements and comparing them to those of other techniques, we will focus on what has become a cornerstone for the study of brain mechanisms underlying cognitive behavior: single-neuron recording from awake monkeys trained on behavioral tasks. Our description and comments are based on our own experience in studying awake monkeys; we also provide references on specific technical points not addressed in this chapter.

Development

The ability to study the relation of the brain's neural activity to behavior progressed from the outside in, starting with the discovery that the brain's electrical activity could be recorded outside the skull using techniques that evolved into the field of electroencephalography. From the time of Hans Berger's report of the changes in brain activity during sleep and wakefulness in the 1920s (see Brazier, 1961) until the late 1950s, the electroencephalogram (EEG) was the major window into the electrical activity of the brain. This technique was extended to include changes in brain activity in a range of cognitive states including perception, learning, and memory. A series of symposia in the late fifties and early sixties that summarized many of the research directions relating the EEG to cognitive behavior, also noted there were still unresolved problems in using the EEG (see, for example, Wolstenholme, 1958; Jasper and Smirnov, 1960; Fessard, Gerard, and Konorski, 1961). Throughout the era when changes in EEG activity were correlated with behavior, it was uncertain exactly what the EEG was measuring. Was it the summation of action potentials conveyed within a cortical region—or of those between regions? Was it the summation of synaptic potentials—or of dendritic potentials? Moreover, whatever was being measured, it most likely included activity from brain regions substantially larger than those intended, and probably even failed to distinguish between cortical and subcortical activity.

Moving within the skull to study the activity of single neurons solved these problems. The action potential was well understood, and hence there was no ambiguity as to what was being compared to behavior. In addition, because single-neuron activity could only be "seen" within a few hundred microns of its origin, its local origin was assured.

But, in solving one set of problems, single-neuron recording introduced another: how to move the recording electrode near enough to a neuron to record its activity and how to continue this recording during behavior. Jasper, Ricci, and Doane (1958), recognized as the first to record single-neuron activity in an awake, behaving mammal, came up with an ingenious solution—head-mounted microdrives that enabled the investigators to move the electrode while their monkeys performed conditioned response tasks. This was soon followed by other single-neuron research with awake, behaving animals: Hubel (1959, 1960; Hubel et al., 1959) recorded neuronal activity in the visual pathway and auditory cortex of the cat, and Olds (1963) recorded neuronal activity in the rat brain. Figure 6.1 shows an example of one of these early recordings. Further critical advances proceeded from the work of Evarts (Evarts, 1966a, 1968a, 1968b), who pioneered a set of reproducible, highly influential techniques to record from single neurons in the awake monkey.

Equally important, Evarts developed methods for humane, painless restraint; this was critical because, unlike cats or rats, monkeys can simply reach up and dismantle attachments for recording with their fingers. Evarts's detailed description of procedures for recording from single neurons in awake monkeys was the major stimulus for the expansion of recording in awake monkeys that has flourished into the present. Even though almost all of the specific procedures have been extensively modified in laboratories throughout the world, the basic methods were laid out in the three papers cited above, with Evarts's own early experiments

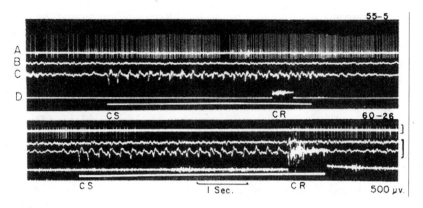

Figure 6.1
Sample of one of the earliest single-neuron recordings from an awake monkey. Records show (A) single-neuron activity, and (B and C) surface electrocorticogram from motor and visual cortex, respectively, (D) electromyogram of monkey's response, and time of conditioned stimulus (CS) and conditioned response (CR). (From Jasper, Ricci, and Doane 1960)

demonstrating the efficacy of the procedures during sleep, wakefulness, and arm movements (Evarts, 1966a, 1966b). These procedures were promptly extended from motor cortex to the oculomotor neurons (Fuchs and Luschei, 1970; Robinson, 1970; Schiller, 1970).

But recording from a single neuron addresses only half the issue; the other half is comparing neuronal activity to behavior, particularly to more complex cognitive behavior. Although many of the initial single-neuron studies simply compared the neuronal activity with spontaneous behavior, Evarts (1966b) showed that he could elicit the same behavior reliably by training monkeys to do controlled movements, allowing him to repeatedly compare the activity of a single neuron to identical behavior. Given the larger minute-to-minute variability in neuronal activity in the awake versus the anesthetized monkey, this was a critical advance in evaluating the consistency of the correlation between neuronal activity and behavior.

Whereas it is impossible to record neuronal activity related to movement from anesthetized, paralyzed animals, it is both possible and even desirable to record neuronal activity related to sensory responses from such animals, simply because they cannot move. Primarily for this reason, application of single-neuron recording techniques in awake, behaving animals came onto the scene later in sensory than in motor research. Difficulties in using behaving primates were particularly acute for the visual system because, in the awake monkey, the eyes make rapid or saccadic eye movements several times per second. Repeatedly directing the visual stimulus to the same place on the retina was therefore not feasible. This problem was solved by using behavioral training techniques that required the monkey to continue fixating at a point on the screen in front of it for several seconds, during which time a visual stimulus could be presented to determine the location of the visual receptive field of the neuron under study (Wurtz, 1969). Again the techniques used to achieve this visual fixation have evolved substantially, especially with improvements in eye movement recording (Robinson, 1963; Judge, Richmond, and Chu, 1980); the use of visual fixation has proven vital to the burgeoning research into cognitive processing in the visual system.

Thus, by the early seventies, the essential techniques required for neuronal recording in awake monkeys were largely worked out and the opportunities for investigating the mechanisms of cognitive processing in the awake monkey had become established. Subsequently, several improved techniques have converted recording in awake monkeys from a harrowing to a standard, albeit challenging, procedure. At the behavioral level, the change has been even more striking: the application of behavioral techniques has transformed the nature of the questions that can be asked in monkey experiments and has opened the door to the analytical study of cognitive questions at the single-neuron level. The old worry many investigators had about whether anything could be learned studying single neurons in the midst of the deluge of neuronal activity in awake, behaving animals has been dispelled; the new worry is whether the technique can address larger issues of cognitive brain function.

Principles

Because, as we noted, single-neuron recording is a mature technique, there are now multiple solutions to many of the technical problems, detailed explanations in the literature, and commercial sources for much of the hardware required. Here we concentrate on the salient principles of the technique, providing references to several especially useful sources of further information for each step.

The most fundamental principle of the method is that the single neurons are recorded extracellularly, with the flow of current generated by the active neurons being detected through the volume of the fluid within the brain. As a consequence, the farther the active neuron is from the electrode the smaller the signal, with the amplitude of the signal declining as the cube of the distance between neuron and electrode. Furthermore, the extracellular fluid acts like a low-pass filter so that the high-frequency band containing action potential signals is reduced the most and the lower-frequency bands are reduced the least. Thus, to isolate the action potentials of a neuron from its neighbors, the electrode tip has to be close to the neuron. The good news is that when the activity of the neuron is isolated from the background activity, we can be certain it relates to the local area under study. The bad news is that larger neurons—which may or may not be more important functionally—tend to be recorded preferentially, leading to inherent sampling biases (a fact rarely discussed by investigators). Although lower frequencies can also be recorded, because they travel over considerably longer distances, they cannot be so narrowly localized.

Basic Methods

As the interface between the brain and the registration of the brain activity, the microelectrode has understandably been a much-investigated topic since the dawn of the single-neuron recording technique. Because of their sturdy structure, metal microelectrodes have been preferred; various metals and alloys have been used, including steel (Green, 1958), tungsten (Hubel, 1957), and platinum-iridium (Wolbarsht, MacNichol, and Wagner, 1960). Although initially made within the laboratory, microelectrodes are now produced commercially and distributed by a number of vendors (see http://www.fh-co.com/ and http://www.thomasrecording.com/pdf/Elektroden.pdf). Basic variables in the microelectrode are the size and shape of the tip exposed to the brain, although the relative importance of these variables remains a matter of discussion. For practical reasons, the impedance of the microelectrode is usually taken as a measure of its quality. The range for metal microelectrodes falls between 100 kilohms and several megohms (at 1,000 Hz): the higher the impedance, the better the isolation, although the fewer neurons isolated, the greater the difficulty in holding the neuron. The microelectrodes are introduced into the brain using microdrives to advance or retract them to the desired depth; these drives are equipped with a coarse control in the millimeter range to move to the approximate depth, and a fine control in the micron range to move to the precise depth. Because of the compliance of the brain to the push of the microelectrode, the smallest step we usually make is five microns. The microelectrode must also be advanced or retracted remotely, so that moving it does not disrupt the monkey's behavior, and positioned not only upward and downward but also in the x-y plane over the brain, so that one actually targets the brain structure of interest. The microdrive has evolved over the years, and a variety of hydraulic and electrical motor devices are now available commercially (see http://www.fh-co.com/; http://www.alphaomega-eng.com/; for construction from drawings, see http://www.lsrweb.net). Although screw drives are occasionally used because of their simplicity and small size, most cannot be controlled remotely (see, for example, Nichols et al., 1998)

The microdrive is typically attached to the monkey only during a recording session, using an implanted base that is screwed or cemented to the skull, or both, in a previous surgery done under general anesthesia. During that initial surgery, the skull inside the base is removed so that the dura is exposed and electrode penetrations can be made into the brain through the dura. We use a circular base into which we insert a grid with holes drilled at one millimeter intervals (see Crist et al., 1988); through these holes, we pass a stainless steel guide tube that either rests close to the surface of the dura or penetrates the dura to allow access to deeper regions of the brain. The grid is at least 0.5 cm thick to ensure that microelectrodes inserted into different holes will follow parallel paths into the brain. We leave the dura intact because it reduces the risk of infection when the recording extends for many months. Alternatively, the dura can be removed and an artificial dura installed (see Arieli, Grinvald, and Slovin, 2002), or only small holes can be drilled in the skull so that a microelectrode always passes through newly exposed dura.

The hardware used to attach the microdrive to the skull and to attach brackets to restrain the head varies widely between laboratories. The hardware developed in our laboratory is typically made from plastic for magnetic resonance imaging (MRI) compatibility. Figure 6.2 shows examples of the hardware we currently use (for a description, see our Web site, http://www.lsr-web.net) and is commercially available (see http://www.cristinstrument.com).

Because the neuron is being recorded at a distance, identification of a single neuron as opposed to several is critical. There are basically two steps in this identification. The first is to observe the change in amplitude and shape of the recorded action potential as the electrode is advanced or retracted. Since the neurons are at different distances from the electrode, movement of the electrode shortens the distance from some neurons and the spike from those neurons becomes larger. A variant of this approach is the use of a tetrode, four separate recording electrodes typically cemented together and applied to four closely spaced recording sites (see Gray et al., 1995). The second step is to discriminate individual neurons based on the amplitude, shape, or both, of their action potentials. The simplest discriminators select individual neurons on the basis of spike amplitude; the

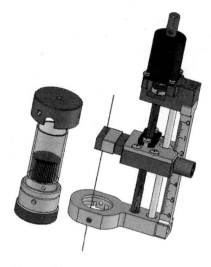

Figure 6.2
Example of single-neuron recording apparatus. On the left, in an exploded view, is
an implanted base, a grid that fits into the base, and a cap that covers the assem-
bly when the microdrive is not attached. On the right is a microelectrode held by
a microdrive with a stepper motor that advances the microelectrode. (Illustration
courtesy of Altah M. Nichols and Thomas W. Ruffner)

addition of multiple thresholds for different phases of the spike and of a
temporal window for width of the spike waveform makes the discrimination more powerful. Other methods, such as relying on principal component analysis for the identification, permit discrimination based on criteria
other than spike amplitude and width, although such analysis usually
requires that discrimination be made after a sample of spikes has been
obtained, that is, after the behavior has been completed. Discrimination by
spike amplitude and width frequently also benefits from post hoc analysis
after preliminary online analysis.

Location of the region of the brain to be studied is now greatly aided
by making an MRI of the monkey's brain before the experiment begins. In
our case, we usually place the recording cylinder base on the skull, install
the grid, and insert several tungsten microelectrodes (for a 1.5 T magnet
and without the stainless steel guide tubes) into the brain to about a centimeter above where we plan to record. If steel electrodes are used, small
marks made by passing current can be seen on the MRI (see Fung, Burstein,
and Born, 1998). This allows us to shift our recordings on the grid so that
the penetrations are centered on the desired target and to more accurately
estimate depth for subcortical targets.

After the experiment, the site of the neurons in the brain can be histologically located by a mark placed at the recording site, usually by passing a 10–20 μA current through the microelectrode depending on the expected survival time of the monkey, the number of marks in the area, and the required precision of the localization. This localization of the recording site is a key requirement of single-neuron recording: an experiment can be replicated only if one accurately determines where the original neurons were. Recovery of the marks is typically accomplished by inspecting alternating cell and fiber stained histological sections no thicker than 50 microns. We frequently code penetrations with a pattern of marks higher up in the penetration as we withdraw the electrode.

We can hardly conclude our consideration of basic methods without emphasizing that the power of single-neuron recording has been immeasurably enhanced by two technical advances. First and foremost, the advent of cheap but powerful computers has enabled the development of sophisticated and easily altered programs for controlling behavioral paradigms and stimulus presentations, recording behavioral and neuronal responses, displaying experimental data online, and analyzing experimental results offline. Second, the availability of structural MRI to verify the recording site, at least approximately, during the experiment has allowed us to explore both new brain areas and multiple areas at the same time, a feat that was exceedingly difficult in the pre-MRI era.

A Trilogy of Techniques

Our description of the basic methods cannot help but leave the impression that the end goal is simply to compare neuronal activity to behavior. But such a goal yields only a correlation of neuronal activity at one point in the brain with a specific cognitive behavior. Although a good start, it is still just a correlation and, as such, would not tell us the degree to which the neurons are part of the brain mechanisms producing behavior. A strength of the single-neuron recording technique is that it can be paired with two other techniques that move it beyond the realm of correlation: stimulation and reversible inactivation of the neurons at the recording site. We refer to the set of techniques—neuronal recording, stimulation, and inactivation—as the "trilogy of techniques," a trilogy that moves single-neuron neurophysiology from the observation of correlations into the study of causation.

Our general approach is to formulate hypotheses about the relation of the neuronal activity to behavior based on single-neuron recordings and then test these hypotheses by altering this neuronal activity by activating or inactivating the neurons.

Neurons can be activated by using an excitatory transmitter or by blocking the continuing action of an endogenous inhibitory transmitter; we have used bicuculline to block the GABA receptors. Alternatively, activation can be accomplished by electrical stimulation of the neurons, by passing an electrical current through the same microelectrode used to record the activity, a method used extensively in cognitively related experiments (Tehovnik, 1996; Cohen and Newsome, 2004). The advantage of electrical stimulation is that, whereas transmitter activation and inactivation alter neuronal activity over a period of time, electrical stimulation can provide activation trial by trial. For inactivation, the optimal method is to suppress the neuronal activity by applying an inhibitory transmitter, and we have relied on the inhibitory transmitter GABA, using either GABA itself or its agonist muscimol. The advantage of the GABA agonist over an anesthetic is that it inactivates only the local neurons but not the fibers of passage (which have no receptors), whereas an anesthetic acts on both (see Lomber, 1999). A promising future direction is the activation or inactivation of a specific subset of neurons using molecular biological techniques (see Tan et al., 2003).

Both activation and inactivation have substantial limits on their interpretation. Activation using electrical stimulation raises questions as to what neurons are altered and at what distance, the extent to which remote neuronal activity is invoked by the stimulation of axons, and the artificial conjunction of activity in neurons that are never normally active together. Inactivation using transmitter agonists, on the other hand, raises questions as to how far the agonist spreads and what neurons are affected by the spread.

Although, taken individually, each of the trilogy of techniques has limitations, used in a coordinated manner, the trilogy is powerful because each technique overcomes at least to some degree the other techniques' limitations. Judicious use allows experimenters to push beyond correlation to causation, maximizing the opportunity available to them.

Innovation

Everyone doing single-neuron recording would happily provide a wish list for innovations that would expand the technique. Here we consider two innovations that address two major problems with single-neuron recording: (1) multielectrode recording, more often referred to as "multichannel recording," to overcome the limitation in area of brain region studied; and (2) anti- and orthodromic stimulation to overcome the difficulty of identifying the connections of neurons studied.

Multichannel recording addresses a central feature of single-neuron recording that may also be considered its central deficiency: recordings are made from only neuron at a time. By introducing multiple electrodes into the brain, more than one neuron can be recorded within a structure or from several different structures. The advantages of multichannel recording are in sampling a larger number of neurons within a population, differentiating the extent to which these neurons are related to a given behavior trial by trial, examining the cross-correlation between neurons, and recording a larger number of neurons on any given set of trials. One method of obtaining these multiple recordings is to insert chronic wire electrodes into the brain (see deCharms, Blake, and Merzenich, 1999; Nicolelis et al., 2003), and this has been used to compare activity between areas along the somatosensory pathway (see, for example, Faggin et al., 1997) and within structures such as motor cortex or the superior colliculus (see Maynard et al., 1999; Hanes et al., 2005). This method has the advantage of allowing experimenters to insert many bundles of electrode wires and to record at many sites. Multichannel systems that record up to 128 channels are available commercially (see http://www.fh-co.com or http://www.alphaomega-eng.com). A disadvantage is the inability to move the electrode, which means that the neurons found are the ones that must be studied, and also that one of the two ways in which unit isolation is verified is lost. A method that preserves the ability to move the electrodes individually is to attach each to a separate micromanipulator. This method has the advantage of verifying the isolation of single neurons and selecting those from the population of interest, but the disadvantage of recording from comparatively fewer neurons. Both multichannel methods introduce the difficulty of characterizing each neuron using tests that could zero in on their individual traits, a difficulty that often results in such characterizations not being made or in a battery of tests being applied to the whole sample en masse. For example, running a fixed pattern of targets for eye movements enables experimenters to identify the visual receptive fields or movement fields of neurons, but how well the field of each neuron is determined depends on how closely spaced the targets are (see Hanes et al., 2005). In general, multichannel recordings are difficult to apply in areas where neurons related to disparate parts of visual or motor space are clustered near each other (such as prefrontal cortex); they are better suited to regions that contain highly predictable maps. The underlying risk in multichannel recordings is that one sacrifices quality (careful characterization of each neuron) for the sake of quantity (a spectacular increase in sample size).

Although experimenters need of course to know where a neuron is located in the brain, they also need to understand its connections. Identification of at least some of these connections can be made through the use of antidromic and orthodromic stimulation, a standard practice in experiments on anesthetized animals but one rarely adopted for experiments on awake, behaving animals. Interestingly enough, however, in some of the first single-neuron recordings made from awake, behaving monkeys, neurons in the skeletomotor and oculomotor frontal cortex were identified as descending output neurons by antidromically stimulating them from lower areas (Evarts, 1966b; Bizzi, 1968). We have recently combined antidromic with orthodromic stimulation to identify relay neurons in the pathway from superior colliculus in the brain stem through the mediodorsal nucleus of the thalamus to the frontal eye field in frontal cortex. Antidromic stimulation from frontal cortex showed that a mediodorsal neuron projected to the frontal cortex, while orthodromic stimulation from the superior colliculus showed that the same neuron received input from the superior colliculus (figure 6.3; Sommer and Wurtz, 2004a, 2004b). Antidromic stimulation is straightforward and simple and relies on the regular, short latency of the antidromic response in the recorded neuron. In contrast, because the orthodromic response in the recorded neuron is subject to multiple interpretations—synaptic activation can take numerous routes— orthodromic stimulation requires added precautions. (These issues are considered in detail in the excellent review by Lemon, 1984.)

A second advantage of antidromic stimulation is that it can correct for sampling biases. Recording as the microelectrode passes through the brain has been compared to shooting fish in a barrel: the larger the fish, the more likely it is to be hit (see Towe and Harding, 1970). With antidromic stimulation, the conduction speed of a neuron can be calculated. Faster speeds imply larger axons and neuronal cell bodies, and therefore estimates of the relative cell sizes can be made. Knowing this distribution of cell sizes allows one to determine the actual distribution of neuronal classes in an area (in terms of the signals they carry) and not just their observed, biased distribution (Humphrey and Corrie, 1978). For example, the seeming prevalence of neurons with activity related to eye movements in the frontal eye field turns out to be, in part, illusory; corrections for sampling bias indicate that such neurons are larger than their neighbors (Sommer and Wurtz, 2000).

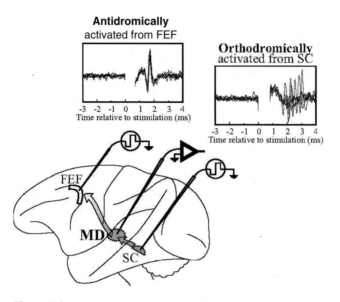

Figure 6.3
Example of antidromic and orthodromic stimulation as used to identify connection of neurons. Stimulating electrodes were implanted with their tips in the frontal eye field (FEF) and the superior colliculus (SC). A single neuron was recorded in the mediodorsal thalamus (MD). At top left, several of the MD neuron's action potentials are aligned to the start of stimulation (at time 0) in the FEF. The highly repeatable activation at invariant latency is indicative of antidromic activation (showing that the neuron projects to the frontal eye field). At top right, action potentials of the same mediodorsal thalamus neuron are aligned to the start of superior collicus stimulation. The jittery activation latency is indicative of orthodromic activation (showing that the neuron receives input from the superior colliculus). (After Sommer and Wurtz, 2004a)

Limitations

The principal limitation of single-neuron recording in cognitive studies is glaringly obvious: studying one neuron at a time in a brain mass of billions of neurons. No behavior we are aware of in vertebrates results from the activity of a single neuron or of small, localized groups of neurons. Even machinelike functions such as the stabilization of the visual scene by ocular following, which has one of the shortest latencies in the primate visual system (70 msec at most), probably arise from the activity of a population of cortical (Takemura et al., 2001) and subcortical neurons. Few would doubt that more cognitive functions such as visual perception and the planning of action must result from the activity of far larger populations of neurons over a series of steps in the brain.

A possible solution to this problem is the growing use of functional magnetic resonance imaging to assess the activity of brain regions during cognitive behavior. The problem of activity related to only a few neurons is solved: the fMRI indicates phases of the hemodynamic response secondary to neuronal activity, and thus of necessity covers a large population of neurons. The noninvasive nature of fMRI also permits researchers to study these populations of neurons in the human brain during demanding cognitive tasks. The disadvantage is that the fMRI does not measure electrical activity directly, and how the hemodynamic response correlates with various phases of activity (e.g., synaptic potentials vs. action potentials) remains controversial. Moreover, this hemodynamic response introduces a temporal filter, currently on the order of one second at best, a time that far exceeds that required for many cognitive functions. For example, a subject can look at a scene, select what aspect is important, make an eye movement to it, and repeat this two to three times within the time needed to obtain an fMRI response. For examination of the mechanisms in the brain that underlie cognition, fMRI cannot compete with single-neuron recording. The sequential application of fMRI and single-neuron recording in monkeys, however, holds great promise. Functional MRI could identify regions of the brain that are involved in cognitive processes without any indication of the underlying mechanism, while follow-up single-neuron recordings could decipher the code for those mechanisms.

At the opposite end of the continuum, a second limitation of single-neuron recording is that microcircuitry and local connections (e.g., along the dendrites) cannot be determined with this in vivo, extracellular technique. The synaptic activity of a neuron and its degree of membrane depolarization are simply inaccessible to the extracellular microelectrode. With slice and cell culture preparations, these limitations are overcome. For example, in studying the superior colliculus in rodent brain slices, Hall and Isa and their collaborators (see, for example, Hall and Lee, 1997; Lee et al., 1997; Isa, Endo, and Saito, 1998; Isa and Saito, 2001) have measured the distance over which inhibition can be obtained and the extent to which superficial layers functionally activate the intermediate layers, factors that extracellular recording had not determined over the preceding 30 years. Hall and Lee (1997) have also been able to photoactivate specific identified neurons, which is impossible to do in the behaving monkey. On the other hand, creating a slice cuts the inputs and outputs to the colliculus from the rest of the brain and decouples the activity from its relation to behavior. Again, combining information from both techniques sharpens the insights gained from each.

The point is that single-neuron recording, though in itself a limited technique, can be a powerful investigative tool when used in conjunction with other, complementary techniques.

Integration

If we want to know about the brain mechanisms that underlie cognitive behavior, we need to study the smallest individual elements of brain circuits: single neurons. Knowing the detailed characteristics of neuronal activity will require recording from individual neurons both separately and together with others, and the better the connections of these neurons can be determined, the stronger the conclusions that can be drawn. These are all correlations, however, and to move beyond the correlations, it is essential to combine single-neuron recording with stimulation and inactivation of the neurons. The understanding derived from this "trilogy of techniques" in turn can be strengthened by fMRI measurements, which reflect large populations of neurons, and by in vitro approaches, which provide insight into the microcircuitry underlying neuronal activity. Although we do not know what technical breakthroughs lie beyond our horizon, we do know that advances in understanding the brain have always relied on a combination of techniques, and single-neuron recording is no exception.

References

Arieli, A., Grinvald, A., and Slovin, H. (2002). Dural substitute for long-term imaging of cortical activity in behaving monkeys and its clinical implications. *Journal of Neuroscience Methods*, *114*, 119–133.

Bizzi, E. (1968). Discharge of frontal eye field neurons during saccadic and following eye movements in unanesthetized monkeys. *Experimental Brain Research*, *6*, 69–80.

Brazier, M. A. B. (1961). *A history of the electrical activity of the brain: The first half-century*. London: Pittman.

Cohen, M. R., and Newsome, W. T. (2004). What electrical microstimulation has revealed about the neural basis of cognition. *Current Opinion in Neurobiology*, *14*, 169–177.

Crist, C. F., Yamasaki, D. S. G., Komatsu, H., and Wurtz, R. H. (1988). A grid system and a microsyringe for single cell recording. *Journal of Neuroscience Methods*, *26*, 117–122.

deCharms, R. C., Blake, D. T., and Merzenich, M. M. (1999). A multielectrode implant device for the cerebral cortex. *Journal of Neuroscience Methods*, *93*, 27–35.

Evarts, E. V. (1966a). Methods for recording activity of individual neurons in moving animals. In R. F. Rushmer (Ed.), *Methods in medical research*, 241–250. Chicago: Year Book.

Evarts, E. V. (1966b). Pyramidal tract activity associated with a conditioned hand movement in the monkey. *Journal of Neurophysiology, 29*, 1011–1027.

Evarts, E. V. (1968a). A technique for recording activity of subcortical neurons in moving animals. *Electroencephalography and Clinical Neurophysiology, 24*, 83–86.

Evarts, E. V. (1968b). Relation of pyramidal tract activity to force exerted during voluntary movement. *Journal of Neurophysiology, 31*, 14–27.

Faggin, B. M., Nguyen, K. T., and Nicolelis, M. A. (1997). Immediate and simultaneous sensory reorganization at cortical and subcortical levels of the somatosensory system. *Proceedings of the National Academy of Sciences, USA, 94*, 9428–9433.

Fessard, A., Gerard, R. W., and Konorski, J. (1961). *Brain mechanisms and learning.* Springfield, IL: Charles C. Thomas.

Fuchs, A. F., and Luschei, E. S. (1970). Firing patterns of abducens neurons of alert monkeys in relationship to horizontal eye movement. *Journal of Neurophysiology, 33*, 382–392.

Fung, S. H., Burstein, D., and Born, R. T. (1998). In vivo microelectrode track reconstruction using magnetic resonance imaging. *Journal of Neuroscience Methods, 80*, 215–224.

Gray, C. M., Maldonado, P. E., Wilson, M., and McNaughton, B. (1995). Tetrodes markedly improve the reliability and yield of multiple single-unit isolation from multi-unit recordings in cat striate cortex. *Journal of Neuroscience Methods, 63*, 43–54.

Green, J. D. (1958). A simple microelectrode for recording from the central nervous system. *Nature, 182*, 962.

Hall, W. C., and Lee, P. (1997). Interlaminar connections of the superior colliculus in the tree shrew. 3. The optic layer. *Visual Neuroscience, 14*, 647–661.

Hanes, D. P., Smith, M. K., Optican, L. M., and Wurtz, R. H. (2005). Recovery of saccadic dysmetria following localized lesions in monkey superior colliculus. *Experimental Brain Research, 160*(3), 312–325.

Hubel, D. H. (1957). Tungsten microelectrode for recording from single units. *Science, 125*, 549–550.

Hubel, D. H. (1959). Single unit activity in striate cortex of unrestrained cats. *Journal of Physiology, 147*, 226–238.

Hubel, D. H. (1960). Single unit activity in lateral geniculate body and optic tract of unrestrained cats. *Journal of Physiology, 150*, 91–104.

Hubel, D. H., Henson, C. O., Rupert, A., and Galambos, R. (1959). "Attention" units in the auditory cortex. *Science, 129*, 1279–1280.

Humphrey, D. R., and Corrie, W. S. (1978). Properties of a pyramidal tract neuron system within a functionally defined subregion of primate motor cortex. *Journal of Neurophysiology, 41*, 216–243.

Isa, T., Endo, T., and Saito, Y. (1998). The visuo-motor pathway in the local circuit of the rat superior colliculus. *Journal of Neuroscience, 18*, 8496–8504.

Isa, T., and Saito, Y. (2001). The direct visuo-motor pathway in mammalian superior colliculus: Novel perspective on the interlaminar connection. *Neuroscience Research, 41*, 107–113.

Jasper, H., Ricci, G. F., and Doane, B. (1958). Patterns of cortical neuronal discharge during conditioned responses in monkeys. In G. E. W. Wolstenholme and Cecilia M. O'Connor (Eds.), *Neurological basis of behaviour*. London: Churchill.

Jasper, H., Ricci, G., and Doane, B. (1958). Microelectrode analysis of cortical cell discharge during avoidance conditioning in the monkey. In H. H. Jasper and G. D. Smirnov (Eds.), *The Moscow colloquium on encephalography of higher nervous activity*. *Electroencephalography and Clinical Neurophysiology*, suppl. 13.

Jasper, H. H., and Smirnov, G. D. (Eds.) (1960). *The Moscow colloquium on encephalography of higher nervous activity. Electroencephalography and Clinical Neurophysiology*, suppl. 13.

Judge, S. J., Richmond, B. J., and Chu, F. C. (1980). Implantation of magnetic search coils for measurement of eye position: An improved method. *Vision Research, 20*, 535–538.

Lee, P. H., Helms, M. C., Augustine, G. J., and Hall, W. C. (1997). Role of intrinsic synaptic circuitry in collicular sensorimotor integration. *Proceedings of the National Academy of Sciences, USA, 94*, 13299–13304.

Lemon, R. (1984). *Methods for neuronal recording in conscious animals*. IBRO Handbook Series: Methods in the Neurosciences, vol. 4. New York: Wiley.

Lomber, S. G. (1999). The advantages and limitations of permanent or reversible deactivation techniques in the assessment of neural function. *Journal of Neuroscience Methods, 86*, 109–117.

Maynard, E. M., Hatsopoulos, N. G., Ojakangas, C. L., Acuna, B. D., Sanes, J. N., Normann, R. A., and Donoghue, J. P. (1999). Neuronal interactions improve cortical population coding of movement direction. *Journal of Neuroscience, 19*, 8083–8093.

Nichols, A. M., Ruffner, T. W., Sommer, M. A., and Wurtz, R. H. (1998). A screw microdrive for adjustable chronic unit recording in monkeys. *Journal of Neuroscience Methods, 81*, 185–188.

Nicolelis, M. A., Dimitrov, D., Carmena, J. M., Crist, R., Lehew, G., Kralik, J. D., and Wise, S. P. (2003). Chronic, multisite, multielectrode recordings in macaque monkeys. *Proceedings of the National Academy of Sciences, USA, 100*, 11041–11046.

Olds, J. (1963). Mechanisms of instrumental conditioning. *Electroencephalography and Clinical Neurophysiology*, suppl. 24, 219–225.

Robinson, D. A. (1963). A method of measuring eye movement using a scleral search coil in a magnetic field. *IEEE Transactions on Biomedical Engineering*, *10*, 137–145.

Robinson, D. A. (1970). Oculomotor unit behavior in the monkey. *Journal of Neurophysiology*, *33*, 393–404.

Schiller, P. H. (1970). The discharge characteristics of single units in the oculomotor and abducens nuclei of the unanesthetized monkey. *Experimental Brain Research*, *10*, 347–362.

Sommer, M. A., and Wurtz, R. H. (2000). Composition and topographic organization of signals sent from the frontal eye field to the superior colliculus. *Journal of Neurophysiology*, *83*, 1979–2001.

Sommer, M. A., and Wurtz, R. H. (2004a). What the brain stem tells the frontal cortex. 1. Oculomotor signals sent from superior colliculus to frontal eye field via mediodorsal thalamus. *Journal of Neurophysiology*, *91*, 1381–1402.

Sommer, M. A., and Wurtz, R. H. (2004b). What the brain stem tells the frontal cortex. 2. Role of the SC-MD-FEF pathway in corollary discharge. *Journal of Neurophysiology*, *91*, 1403–1423.

Takemura, A., Inoue, Y., Kawano, K., Quaia, C., and Miles, F. A. (2001). Single-unit activity in cortical area most associated with disparity-vergence eye movements: Evidence for population coding. *Journal of Neurophysiology*, *85*, 2245–2266.

Tan, E. M., Horwitz, G. D., Albright, T. D., and Callaway, E. M. (2003). A genetic method for selective and quick reversible silencing of mammalian neurons in vivo. *Society of Neuroscience Abstracts*, *29*, 125.122.

Tehovnik, E. J. (1996). Electrical stimulation of neural tissue to evoke behavioral responses. *Journal of Neuroscience Methods*, *65*, 1–17.

Towe, A. L., and Harding, G. W. (1970). Extracellular microelectrode sampling bias. *Experimental Neurology*, *29*, 366–381.

Wolbarsht, M. L., MacNichol, E. F. J., and Wagner, H. G. (1960). Glass insulated platinum microelectrode. *Science*, *132*, 1309–1310.

Wolstenholme, G. (1958). *The neurological basis of behavior*. Boston: Little, Brown.

Wurtz, R. H. (1969). Visual receptive fields of striate cortex neurons in awake monkeys. *Journal of Neurophysiology*, *32*, 727–742.

7 Grid Computing and the Future of Neuroscience Computation

John D. Van Horn, James Dobson, Michael Wilde, Jeffrey Woodward, Yong Zhao, Jens Voeckler, and Ian Foster

Since the introduction of computing as a vital tool in scientific research, we have seen several distinct generations of systems architectures come and go. With the earlier generations, it was uncommon for individual researchers to have computers on their desks, let alone computers dedicated solely to their particular research purposes. Mainframe, vector, and time-shared VMS or UNIX computers served as shared resources supporting the concurrent analyses of many researchers. Today, of course, computers are ubiquitous in many parts of the scientific world; researchers typically have one or more personal computers at their disposal. The days of large, monolithic systems are over, and individual computers are the rule. Recently, however, a new computing paradigm has emerged that will again alter the way data computations are performed. Innovative infrastructure technologies including high-speed networking, inexpensive hardware solutions, and open-source, standards-based software have brought a paradigm shift in how computational research is performed. Using local high-density central processing units (CPUs) as well as geographically distributed systems, the high-throughput processing of large quantities of neuroimaging data, in particular, can be completed on the order of minutes rather than hours. This is a fundamental concept behind Grid computing and is causing considerable excitement in the scientific community (Foster, 2003; Foster and Kesselman, 1998).

Large-scale computing has clear advantages for the analysis of many types of large scientific data sets—from particle physics to gene expression, from geospace to astrophysics. For the neurosciences, Grid computing has direct applicability for the analyses of the terabytes of neuroimaging data contained in public archives such as the fMRI Data Center (fMRIDC; see http://www.fmridc.org), based at Dartmouth College (Van Horn et al., 2001). This publicly available repository includes complete data sets from published studies of human cognition using functional magnetic resonance imaging (fMRI). Data sets include four-dimensional functional image volume time course data (e.g., EPI, Spiral), high-resolution brain anatomy–imaging data (e.g., SPGR, MPRAGE), study metadata, and supporting data collected as part of the study. The fMRIDC curates, anonymizes, and packages these data sets for open dissemination; researchers around the world may then use the data sets to conduct novel analyses, test alternative hypotheses, explore new means of data visualization, or use them in education and training. But this ever increasing collection of study data sets can also be compared en masse across studies to identify patterns of cognitively induced signal change unseen in any individual study. Such comparative studies will enable neuroscientists to better understand how particular combinations of brain regions contribute to the processing of cognitive information across different individual task paradigms, and where those paradigms share particular cognitive components.

This chapter discusses the concepts of distributed high-performance and high-throughput Grid computing systems and presents specific examples of their application in the large-scale processing of functional neuroimaging data. Featuring data sets from the fMRI Data Center, we demonstrate the improvement in throughput that may be obtained in (1) using highly parallel clustered processing systems; and (2) utilizing geographically distributed cluster computing power for the analysis of brain-imaging data. We describe a promising opportunity to leverage the capabilities of two rapidly evolving and closely paradigms in information technology, Grid computing and virtual data, to provide the tools, techniques, and resources to make the fMRIDC archive an indispensable community resource for driving advances in neuroscience research. We also describe how Grid computing can harness multiple distributed computing facilities to solve large problems, and how the Virtual Data Model of computing can help scientists utilize the Grid environment with mechanisms for expressing workflows in a high-level language that frees them from distributed computing concerns and at the same time creates accurate, sharable, re-executable descriptions of how every step in a complex, long-running data analysis effort was carried out.

More specifically, we explain how highly optimized anatomical brain-warping processing pipelines can be made to run on the order of minutes rather than hours, and how complex multistage analyses of terabytes—thousands of gigabytes—of data can be distributed across multiple processors and systems. These processes do not require specialized hardware and can often be controlled from laptop computers using Web-enabled interfaces. We also describe how "virtual data–based" workflow systems can serve as an enabling interface to the Grid to facilitate reproducible data analyses and knowledge-intensive collaboration.

As neuroscience researchers make increasing use of functional neuroimaging for the mapping of cognitive activity, they will come to rely more and more on Grid computing. Our chapter provides an overview of what we believe to be a critical aspect in the future of functional neuroimaging data analysis.

Development

Although the advent and development of MRI technology over the past two decades have resulted in a quantum leap in our ability to measure the brain's capabilities, this technology has also vastly increased the amount of data brain researchers must manipulate, manage, and store. In contrast to those typical for positron-emission tomography (PET) studies, data sets for functional MRI studies are large, often exceeding several gigabytes (GB) in size. As advances are made in MRI scanner technology to permit the more rapid acquisition of data, functional imaging experiments will consist of ever greater amounts of data per unit of time over the same scan duration. And as cognitive neuroscientists ask ever more sophisticated questions about fundamental brain processes, they will undoubtedly collect data on an ever greater number of subjects and fMRI time courses per subject.

Data Archiving

Indeed, within the next decade, neuroimaging data archives containing several petabytes—several million gigabytes—are not out of the question and will likely become the norm. A number of individual fMRI data sets already rival the full size of many extant large genetic (Benson et al., 2003) and protein (Berman et al., 2002) science data archives. For instance, the complete study data set from Buckner et al., 2000, exceeds 20 GB. It can be expected that, as advances are made in the spatiotemporal resolution of MRI scanners, the amount of published brain image data will routinely rival the amount contained in the human genome database. A challenge therefore exists in devising efficient means for comparing and contrasting these data on a large scale but within reasonable time.

With these issues in mind, the fMRI Data Center was established as a public archive for fMRI study data and the associated experimental metadata (Van Horn et al., 2004). The fMRIDC began receiving data from researchers in 2000 and made data sets publicly available in 2001. At present, the archive contains more than 100 complete data sets, which researchers may request online and have shipped to them free of charge. Authors of fMRI studies are asked to provide the details of their experiments across several levels, including scanner imaging protocols, subject demographics, and experimental design. The principal intent of obtaining such complete information about each study is to permit researchers to reconstruct the results reported in the literature by the original authors.

The average fMRIDC data set contains approximately 18 gigabytes of uncompressed data and may contain over 30,000 files. A typical functional run is composed of a time series of three-dimensional ANALYZE-compatible volumes, where each ANALYZE volume/header pair represents a single point of time in the time series. A functional run may have 200 files or more where the volumetric data are around 1 megabyte per volume. Recent studies have grown much larger: the fMRIDC holds one anatomical study with over 300 subjects, and a recent functional study comprising over 100 subjects. This scale of data represents a tremendous opportunity for the sharing, and growth, of knowledge in the field. It also presents a significant challenge: to make this information both available to and usable by the neuroscience research community, we must first solve many problems in data transport and storage and in making available and usable the computational tools and resources to make further use of the archived study data.

Grid Computing

As archives of neuroscience data expand, the computational needs required to process the immense volume of data also increase. In terms of the memory and processor speed requirements, individual desktop workstations are now no longer suitable for analyzing potentially gigabytes worth of data at a time. What is needed is to combine effort from across multiple, distributed processing elements and take advantage of the collective power they possess toward analyses of these neuroscientific resources on a massive scale.

The Grid is an emerging paradigm in the computer science community based around distributed systems of computers, data, tools, and people (Foster, 2003). The term *Grid* was coined in the mid-1990s to denote a proposed distributed computing infrastructure for advanced science and engineering. The specific challenge that motivates interest in Grid computing is the coordination of resource sharing and problem solving in dynamic, multi-institutional, spatially dispersed, virtual organizations. Strictly speaking, this does not refer to file exchange, but rather to direct access to computers, software, data, and other resources, as required by a range of collaborative problem-solving and resource-brokering strategies emerging in industry, science, and engineering. This sharing is, necessarily, highly controlled, with resource providers and consumers defining clearly, carefully, and exactly what is shared, who is allowed to share, and the conditions under which sharing occurs. The related term *data Grid* was coined to denote a Grid system that has an additional strong emphasis on the sharing of large amounts of data and data storage resources.

The internal organization or fabric of the Grid is evolving with standards and practices emerging from organizations such as the Global Grid Forum (GGF; see http://www.ggf.org). Although the Grid is a framework for collaboration between virtual organizations on a large, geographically diverse, scale, we should note that the Grid need not have a centralized infrastructure and makes minimal assumptions of computing systems homogeneity. Its underlying architecture is being specifically designed for distributed authentication, authorization, storage, and computation. These guidelines and software protocols will enable technologies from multiple research projects and vendors to interoperate on the shared Grid infrastructure.

Most fMRI data are processed using a series of computational algorithms that "pipeline"—apply spatial realignment, slice-timing adjustment, spatial normalization, filtering, and other such operations on—the data. Pipelined processing operations are designed to take one or more fMRI time series and prepare the image volume data for later statistical processing. These multistage pipelines can typically be run on the Grid with the simple inclusion of some basic code infrastructure for locating data and understanding job dependencies. Thus data-intensive sciences such as functional neuroimaging can utilize Grids for analysis of data sets on scales not possible using local computation.

As researchers' needs exceed the computing power available in a desktop environment, they typically turn toward shared departmental or collaboration-run systems ranging from the departmental servers of a few years ago, to supercomputers, to the computing clusters of today. Although cluster computing at various scales has rapidly replaced both departmental servers and supercomputers, the concept of the Grid has spanned all of these changes. Originally termed *metacomputing* (Catlett and Smarr, 1992), the Grid first consisted of geographically separated supercomputers linked to work on single problems in a loosely coordinated fashion, yet its principles remain much the same even as it links distributed computing clusters to form a single, large "cluster of clusters."

A typical Grid cluster consists of a set of distinct computers, typically similar or identical, called "worker nodes," which provide the computing power of the cluster. A "head node" computer runs a software application called a "scheduler," which distributes computing jobs to the worker nodes. The scheduler maintains a "job queue" of work for the worker nodes. Typically the running of a program or script, a job involves sending the program and input files to a worker node, running the program, and sending the resulting output files back to the user. Some jobs may use a single node to run a program, whereas others, using parallel programming tools such as the "message-passing interface" (MPI) may harness a set of nodes running concurrently and exchanging messages to coordinate and perform parallel computations. A file server provides a file system that is typically shared among all worker nodes and the head node. Files going to and from jobs may reside on this shared file system, or on private file systems that reside on each worker node. Finally, a network such as commodity Ethernet or the higher-speed Myrinet (see http://www.myri.com) is required to link these computers together. For researchers using a Grid cluster, the Grid appears as modeled below in figure 7.1.

Grids and their user communities are often organized as "virtual organizations" (VOs), which consist of groups of collaborating users, typically from multiple real-world organizations such as university departments and laboratory divisions or corporate departments, that are working together to solve a problem or related set of problems (Foster, Kesselman, and Tuecke, 2001). The member organizations that make up a VO may also contribute resources for community use, such as allocation of computing clusters and network-accessible storage, or in some cases, a physical instrument of significant scale and community value such as an electron microscope, a particle accelerator, a fusion reactor, or an earthquake engineering "shake table." Virtual organizations may have no physical resources of their own, but may be granted allocations of resources

Figure 7.1
(*a*) Researcher's view of the Grid. Users submit compute jobs using the virtual data language and drawing from a virtual data catalog. Resources from distributed sites are dedicated (e.g., fully supporting Grid-related activity) or shared (e.g., local jobs given priority) and supply contributed Grid services toward job completion. Note that Grids may vary in size to include the computers in a single laboratory, a building, a campuswide system, or an entire country. (*b*) Grid3 currently consists of 30+ sites in the United States and South Korea.

(a)

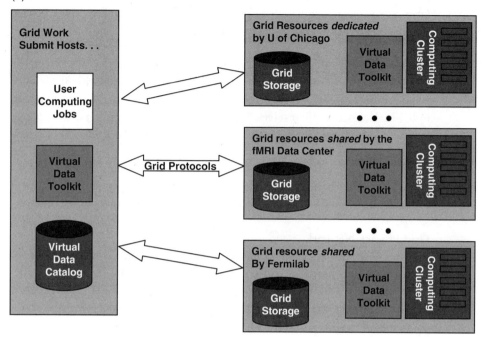

(b)

contributed by other communities or funding agencies. Several large-scale Grid VO projects are worth noting for their scale as well as their broad-based, research-oriented resource sharing.

TeraGrid

A virtual computing infrastructure funded by the National Science Foundation (NSF), the TeraGrid is built from five (ultimately, nine or more) individual clusters (themselves built from smaller computers, or nodes), having nearly 1 petabyte of networked disk storage and linked by a *cross-continent* network backbone with a transmission speed of 40 gigabytes per second—four times faster than the fastest *local* area commodity networks currently in use. Its name reflects the scale of the computing power that it provides: 20 teraflops—a trillion floating point operations per second.

Grid Physics Network

A large-scale project also funded by the NSF, GriPhyN was created to explore ways to harness Grid computing to enhance the scientific productivity of large-scale, collaborative, data-intensive physics experiments. GriPhyN applies the concept of "virtual data" to make scientific data-processing workflows and the utilization of distributed resources as easy for individuals and collaborations to use as a single, local computing system.

International Virtual Data Grid Laboratory, Particle Physics Data Grid, and Grid3

Two other large-scale users of the Grid, IVDGL and PPDG have worked in close collaboration with GriPhyN to create Grid3—a large-scale international test Grid of unprecedented scale, pooling the resources of over 30 sites to form an aggregate computing resource with over 3500 CPUs and many terabytes of storage (figure 7.1b). Examples of several such Grid3 projects currently under way are listed in table 7.1.

European Data Grid, Large Hadron Collider Grid, and Enabling Grids for E-Science in Europe

A project sponsored by the European Commission to develop tools for data-intensive science, the European Data Grid (EDG) was created to serve the needs of the high-energy physics community in analyzing data acquired from the Large Hadron Collider (LHC), based at CERN in Geneva. The EDG evolved in 2004 into a new project, Enabling Grids for E-Science in Europe (EGEE; see http://public.eu-egee.org), which combines earlier high-energy physics with biomedical applications.

Table 7.1
Several leading Grid3 projects for high-volume, high-throughput distributed computing

Project Name	Description and URL
ATLAS	"A Torroidal LHC Apparatus"—a high-energy physics experiment at the Large Hadron Collider (LHC) at CERN http://atlas.web.cern.ch/Atlas/Welcome.html
BTeV	"B-Physics at the Tevatron"—a high-energy physics experiment being conducted at Fermilab to explore so-called B-Physics. http://www-btev.fnal.gov
CMS	"Compact Muon Solenoid"—a high-energy physics experiment at the Large Hadron Collider (LHC) at CERN http://cmsinfo.cern.ch/Welcome.html
LIGO	The Laser Interferometer Gravitational Wave Observatory—a coalition of research centers for analyzing gravitational wave data. http://www.ligo.org
SDSS	The Sloan Digital Sky Survey—a project to map and analyze all celestial objects in a given region of the sky. http://www.sdss.org
GADU	Genomics Analysis and Database Update http://compbio.mcs.anl/gov

Each Grid site or resource provider brings a set of services, typically, storage elements (SEs) and compute elements (CEs). For instance, there are currently 30 sites on Grid3, each contributing computational and data resources, with more expected soon. Such projects demonstrate the utility of the Grid for bringing together consortia of researchers all interested in drawing from the shared pool of research data and computing resources they all have to offer. Community-oriented fMRI research collaboratives, individually possessing large data sets (e.g., BIRN), or distributed researchers seeking to combine effort in drawing from large-scale data repositories (e.g., the fMRIDC), are prime candidates for neuroscience-oriented Grid VOs.

Principles

Components of the Grid

The Grid requires a rigorously designed collection of protocols and standards by which data and services may be utilized. Many different technologies exist to provide Grid users with catalogs that describe what resources are present at the different sites of a Grid. These include the Monitoring and Discovery Service (MDS) of the Globus Toolkit, as well other Grid-specific catalogs (see http://www.ivdgl.org/grid2003). Here we describe the principal software components of Grid computing, from which the Grids described above are constructed.

Globus Toolkit

Providing a large set of services for the creation of Grid systems and is produced by the Globus Alliance (see http://www.globus.org), the Globus Toolkit (Foster and Kesselman, 1998) has gone through several major releases, each of which have brought new standards and interfaces for interaction with distributed resources.

Public Key Infrastructure

Grid security is based on the Public Key Infrastructure (PKI), and uses methods of public/private key pairs to give Grid users a "single sign-on" capability: authenticate once, and create a long-lived "proxy" certificate that can be presented to gain access to Grid services such as the ability to run a job on a remote cluster or to transfer files between clusters. A service from the European Data Grid called the "Virtual Organization Membership Service" (VOMS) is used to map identities from the individual VOs to a local UNIX account.

Grid Resource Allocation and Management

The fundamental component for running computer jobs on the Grid is an element of the Globus toolkit called "Grid Resource Allocation and Management" (GRAM). A site's resources may be managed by schedulers such as Condor, the Portable Batch System (PBS), the Load-Sharing Facility (LSF), and many others. GRAM provides Grid users with a single, uniform interface that permits them to execute and manage jobs on any site of a Grid, without knowing the details of the specific cluster that schedules the software managing the resources of those sites. GRAM provides mechanisms for transporting input data to remotely running jobs and for retrieving output back from them; it is supplemented by Condor-G (Frey et al., 2002), which provides the user with a local queue of jobs being sent into the Grid, the ability to manage the relative priorities and submission rates of jobs in that queue, and several other important features.

Grid File Transfer Protocol

A file transfer service based on the Internet RFC standard file transfer protocol, the GridFTP has extensions to support high-volume data traffic. The

Globus GridFTP server supports the Grid Security Infrastructure (GSI) system to enable single sign-on access to data from any site on the Grid. Many large "data challenge" tests have been conducted using GridFTP to transfer at a rate of many gigabytes per second. Indeed, the entire fMRIDC multiterabyte data archive is accessible via GridFTP. This service is used by remote jobs to transfer data to the site where the computation is performed. GridFTP contains many capabilities that provide the high-performance data transfer required of large-scale data-intensive scientific and engineering applications, including sending multiple streams of data between two servers, strapping multiple servers together, and being able to restart a transfer from any point within a large file. GridFTP serves, for batch jobs running across the Grid, as a ubiquitous data transfer protocol, capable of moving data from any Grid site to any other.

Replica Location Service
The strategy of caching or *replication* is supported in Grid by a cataloging system called the "Replica Location Service" (RLS) component of the Globus Toolkit. This service uses a relational database to create local "replica catalogs," which describe what files exist on the site, and index services, which help speed up lookups for a naming service that can scale to tens or hundreds of millions of file entries Grid-wide. The RLS can also be shared by a distributed group of scientists to specify a common input data set and a name space created for the individual output files from experimentation.

Virtual Data Model

Having outlined the basic groundwork by describing both the mission and nature of the fMRIDC and the Grid computing paradigm and tool sets, we now move on to describe first, how the Virtual Data Model serves to make Grid computing easier and scientific data management more conducive to active research, and then (in the "Applications" section) how this concept has been applied to explore the benefits of Grid computing to fMRI research and data management.

Virtual Data Toolkit
Underlying software technology is needed to deliver data to different groups collaborating across sites, to keep the various sites involved in joint projects in sync, and to serve as a technology transfer vehicle to still other collaborations. The Virtual Data Toolkit (VDT) provides just such software technology.

Virtual Data Language

"Virtual data" is a concept that builds on, automates, and seeks to supplement and eventually to replace the traditional practice of recording the steps of a data analysis effort in a logbook or in ad hoc online records. The process of "virtualizing" data involves describing the steps needed (or used) to produce a data object, using a methodical, high-level, declarative specification. Several important benefits derive from this approach, and serve as a productivity lever in the scientific data analysis process. They enable a data object to be produced anywhere in a distributed environment such as the Grid, while freeing the scientist from implementing the complex mechanics of such "location-independent computing." Moreover, they serve to keep accurate, high-fidelity records of how each data object was produced and how data analysis routines and transformation tools were used. They enable intermediate or even "final" data to be discarded and re-created later if necessary (hence making such data "virtual"). The tool set, which enables the use of the virtual data paradigm, is called the "Virtual Data System" (VDS; see http://griphyn. org/vds) and is bundled into the Virtual Data Toolkit to facilitate both the use and the construction of Grid computing environments.

At the heart of the Virtual Data Model is the virtual data language (VDL; Foster et al., 2002) used to express computational procedures for data derivation. The VDL consists of elements to process declarations of workflows and a virtual data catalog in which to store VDL declarations and records of workflow execution. "Planners" map VDL-specified workflows into a sequence of concrete actions for a specific computing environment such as a local system or a distributed Grid. With VDL, the individual computation actions that one defines are typically the invocation of a single application program, query, or Web service. These "atomic" actions are then linked into workflows of arbitrary complexity using VDL statements to declare data derivation steps and functional compositions of these steps. Depending on the level at which the Virtual Data System tool set is used, scientists may either work directly with VDL, or with tools that produce and execute VDL workflows for them.

Most scientific analysis processes to which the Virtual Data Model would be applied involve a "workflow": a series of interdependent steps that lead from input data through a series of data transformations, reductions, filtrations, and so on, to the data sets needed to support and present scientific findings and conclusions. A straightforward workflow typically resembles a "pipeline"—that is, a series of sequential steps in data processing. More complex workflows are described in terms of graphs (from

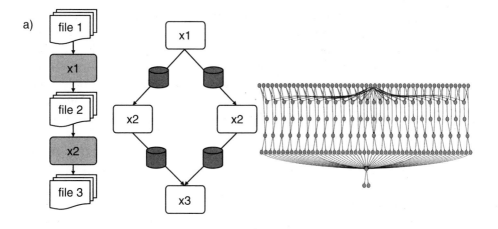

```
b)    TR tr1(in a1, out a2) {
          argument stdin = ${a1};
          argument stdout = ${a2}; }
      TR tr2(in a1, out a2) {
          argument stdin = ${a1};
          argument stdout = ${a2}; }
      DV x1->tr1(a1=@{in:file1}, a2=@{out:file2});
      DV x2->tr2(a1=@{in:file2}, a2=@{out:file3});
```

Figure 7.2
(*a*) Workflow patterns are routinely visualized in the form of directed acyclic graphs (DAGs), shown here of increasing complexity from left to right. (*b*) Virtual data language (VDL) pseudo-code representation of simple data-processing pipeline DAG.

discrete mathematics) that link a set of data objects with a set of processing steps in arbitrarily complex patterns. Workflows that proceed from beginning to end, with no loops or backtracking ("cycles"), can be expressed as "directed acyclic graphs" (DAGs; figure 7.2). Note that DAGs can be used to indicate both data and control flow dependencies, and, of particular use in distributed computing, to determine which steps of a workflow can be executed in parallel. This is presented in the leftmost DAG in figure 7.2a, where both transformations "× 2" in the diamond can be executed in parallel (figure 7.2b), as can each level of transformation tasks in the middle and rightmost multinode DAGs.

Virtual data language provides two basic declaration statements: transformations and derivations. Transformations encapsulate or "wrap" an application program by providing a specification of the input files read by the application, the output files produced by it, and the arguments it accepts and requires. Transformations are like function declarations in that they specify a template for invoking an application. Declaring the inputs and outputs of the application is the key to enabling applications to run transparently anywhere in the Grid. Derivations provide the argument values necessary to invoke a transformation. Like function calls in a programming language, derivations can executed immediately, or can be stored for later, possibly repetitive execution. A sample of virtual data language is shown in figure 7.3. The VDL transformation (TR) statement defines a transformation, and the derivation (DV) statement, a derivation. (Note that the TR in a VDL program has no connection at all with the MRI concept of "repetition time"; VDL is an independent, application-neutral language.)

Virtual Data Catalog

This provides a database called a "virtual data catalog" (VDC) for storing transformation and derivation definitions and the invocation records that are created each time a derivation is executed. The VDC serves as a central focal point of scientific data analysis, collaboration, and information recording and sharing. It plays the role of a specialized metadata catalog that contains information about the interfaces of application programs (arguments, input files, and output files), the "recipes" for calling these

```
TR air::alignlinear( in standard_hdr, in standard_img,
                     in reslice_hdr, in reslice_img,
                     out airfile, none args) {
   argument = ${standard_hdr};
   argument = ${reslice_hdr};
   argument = ${airfile};
   argument = args;
}
DV fmridc::2-2004-1234JD-01_run1->air::alignlinear(
   standard_hdr = @{in:"100-3_anonymized.hdr"},
   standard_img = @{in:"100-3_anonymized.img"},
   reslice_hdr  = @{in:"100-5_anonymized.hdr"},
   reslice_img  = @{in:"100-5_anonymized.img"},
       airfile  = @{out:"100-5_anonymized.air"},
          args   =  "-m 6 -t1 80 -t2 80 -s 81 27 3 -q"
);
```

Figure 7.3
Virtual data language derivation to invoke the declarations of an automated image registration (AIR) transformation. The transformation (TR; not to be confused with repetition time in MRI imaging) defines the operation to be performed and the derivation (DV) actually carries out that operation. Derivations may be strung together in workflow scripts to form more complex data-processing pipelines and build up a catalog of commonly used processing operations (e.g., spatial realignment).

applications to perform specific tasks and for deriving data files, logs records on how, when, and where the applications were invoked, how they performed, and how specific data files were produced. The VDC can be queried to provide this information, and such knowledge can play a key role in the process of organizing, specifying, documenting, assessing, or reproducing a data analysis effort.

To begin, researchers require a virtual data catalog, typically in the form of a database hosted by a PostgreSQL, MySQL, or eXist server. They also require a client workstation on which the Virtual Data System is installed and a "submit host" on which to initiate Grid jobs. User authentication credentials are required in the form of a Grid certificate that is authorized to use one or more Grid sites that provide computing and storage resources. The final component is access to a replica location service to catalog input and output files for a workflow.

The application programs to be executed are first described with virtual data language transformation statements, and these definitions are stored in a virtual data catalog. Once the transformations are cataloged, derivation (DV) statements to invoke them can be coded and cataloged in the VDC. Derivations are typically coded manually for initial tests, and then later generated on a larger scale using a script to process an entire data set. Languages such as Perl and Python are well suited for this task. Although generator scripts form an essential part of the current process, their use will gradually diminish as higher-level descriptive constructs are added to the VDL to iterate over various forms of application-specific data set structures.

Workflow "procedures" can be defined in virtual data language by grouping transformations together into workflow patterns that can be reused multiple times within a larger workflow. For example, to perform a multistage spatial filtering procedure on each file of a large data set, the filter pattern could be defined as a "compound transformation," which is then executed using one (opposed to many) derivation statement for each data set member.

From the definitions in a virtual data catalog, "abstract" workflows are then derived using graph traversal tools that use cataloged derivation definitions to create a graph of logical transformation invocations, creating a requested set of data files. This graph traversal recursively searches the catalog for definitions of the steps needed to produce the requested output data products, thus creating a specification of all the derivation steps needed to create the requested data. We call the output of this stage an "abstract" workflow because it is completely location independent: its steps are tied neither to any specific computing site nor to any specific physical file names at these sites (either for data files or executable applications). A "concrete planner" is then applied to the abstract workflow and generates an executable workflow for either a local environment (typically for testing VDL) or for a Grid environment. The Virtual Data System planners that create Grid-executable workflows employ a variety of strategies for when and how they decide where in the Grid to run each derivation.

Certain workflows may consist of a huge number of steps, and may take many days, or, in some cases that we have worked on, many months, of Grid-wide computing to complete. Such large virtual data language workflows are often used in particle physics (Mambelli et al., 2004), astrophysics (Annis et al., 2002; Deelman et al., 2003), and genomics (Rodriguez et al., 2004). In recent work, including the explorations using fMRI described below, we employed prototype tools that provide higher-level interfaces for executing such workflows on the Grid. With these tools, once an abstract workflow is created, with the location-independent steps of a scientific process, then all remaining steps are automated: initiating execution on the Grid, tracking the progress of the workflow, and recording for diagnostic assessment any errors that occur.

Applications

To uncover and assess the issues involved in applying Grid virtual data techniques to typical computing problems in fMRI data analysis, we have conducted some preliminary experiments on Grid3 using the Virtual Data System. We focused our examinations on using raw neuroimaging data from the fMRI Data Center, on understanding how Grid resources could be leveraged to perform large-scale analyses that would be too time consuming on the resources available to most researchers in the field, and on determining how the procedures and derived data products from such efforts could be shared as a community resource. Three workflow patterns were chosen for more in-depth assessment: (1) the building of an averaged "template" brain, (2) a spatial normalization, and (3) an independent components analysis.

In our applications, we used application programs from the "Automated Image Registration" (AIR) package (Woods et al., 1998a, 1998b) for performing spatial realignment and warping of brain image data. A virtual data language transformation such as "AIR::alignlinear" was used to describe the various arguments used in a run of typical linear alignment. The input and output file arguments were specified in such statements, and where useful, default argument values were assigned. VDL transformations were created and cataloged for six different utilities from the AIR toolkit:

"align_warp," "definecommon_air," "alignlinear," "reslice," "reslice_warp," and "softmean," as well as several tools from FSL and other packages. The VDL "name space" capability (the string "AIR::" in the example above) was used to separate simple, unstructured tool names into different packages, both to avoid collisions and to serve as additional documentation and a convenient search key. VDL derivation statements were then created to execute the "alignlinear" tool on a specific set of input files. When executed, the output files from such derivations were listed in a replica catalog and an "invocation record" describing the run-time environment and resource utilization of the invocation was saved in the virtual data catalog.

Our sample data sets were drawn from files from two published and fMRIDC-catalogued studies: Buckner et al., 2000, and Head et al., 2004 (fMRIDC accession nos. 2-2000-1118W and 2-2004-1168X, respectively). Since our purpose was to explore analysis methodology using the Grid, rather than to test specific neuroscience hypotheses, we focused at this point in our assessment of virtual data solely on software tool usage modalities and on exploring how the fMRI research community might interact with the Grid tools. In some instances, synthetic data sets that mimicked the directory structure of the file system as well as the file types and sizes of the actual archived accessions under study were utilized for testing purposes.

Two data management tasks were required when moving from a locally executed virtual data language workflow to running on the Grid, and these were both assisted by utilities that we either enhanced or developed as part of our work. First, the application program (or suite of tools) needed to be installed at all Grid sites where we sought to execute. This was, as mentioned earlier, performed by a script that iterated over all (or set of) Grid sites. The second task involved making the input files of the workflow accessible to Grid jobs, which might be running at any site in the Grid, in a location-independent manner. This was accomplished by scripts that copied the input file set to a file system served by the Grid file transfer protocol, and then cataloged the files in the replica location server that served our study. This effort, too, was heavily automated and assisted by utility scripts that will be incorporated into the Virtual Data System, to make the copy-and-catalog steps as simple as an ordinary secure copy (scp) command from the SSH Communications Security tool set (Ylonen et al., 2001).

Our first sample application was a workflow for functional MRI analysis of the spatial normalization of data to a known brain template space. The input files for this workflow are high-resolution anatomical volumes. We created a workflow that would reorient and spatially normalize the data to the standardized brain atlas from the Montreal Neurological Institute (MNI). Since the volumes needed to be in a similar orientation we selected a single study with a large number of anatomical volumes. This study (fMRIDC accession no. 2-2004-1168X) had four anatomical volumes per subject with 120 subjects. An example of a resulting spatially normalized image volume is shown in figure 7.4a. Using these same anatomical images in a second sample application, we designed a workflow to create an average normalized brain from the whole population of subjects. Figure 7.4b shows a less-detailed view of the directed acyclic graph for this process as well as the normalized "average brain" from this study.

Finally, in a third sample application, designed to demonstrate the processing throughput advantages of using the Grid, we constructed an independent components analysis workflow, which we then applied to a large fMRIDC data set (fMRIDC accession no. 2-2000-1118W) to extract interesting spatiotemporal features from the raw data (figure 7.5). Independent components analysis has proven to be a useful tool for understanding underlying functional systems in the brain, in particular, for assessing the role of baseline levels of brain activity (Greicius et al., 2004).

In our case, the use of ICA, though not necessarily intended to examine the brain systems underlying cognitively induced signal change in systems of distributed brain regions, was deemed to be a useful means for benchmarking Grid performance. We used MELODIC 2.0 (Beckmann and Smith, 2004), from the Oxford Center for Functional Magnetic Resonance Imaging of the Brain (FMRIB), as distributed as part of the FMRIB Software Library (FSL) tool suite. The MELODIC code requires a four-dimensional ANALYZE or NIFTI data set as input. We ran this workflow extracting 36 components from a 160-volume time course for a single subject in a study drawn from the fMRIDC archive: Buckner et al., 2000 (fMRIDC accession no. 2-2000-1118W-01).

To characterize the computational performance of this workflow, we compared its performance to that expected from a standard Unix (bash) shell script (table 7.2). Although the workflow and shell script have similar time scales for processing a single time course, the number of jobs performed in serial using a shell script would take a theoretical 162 hours (nearly a week) of processing time to produce a complete set of independent components analysis results for 30 such time courses. In contrast, using the Virtual Data System, regardless of the number of processing jobs submitted to the Grid, would take less than 6 hours. This is an obvious advantage of parallel versus serial computing, although it should be remembered

(a)

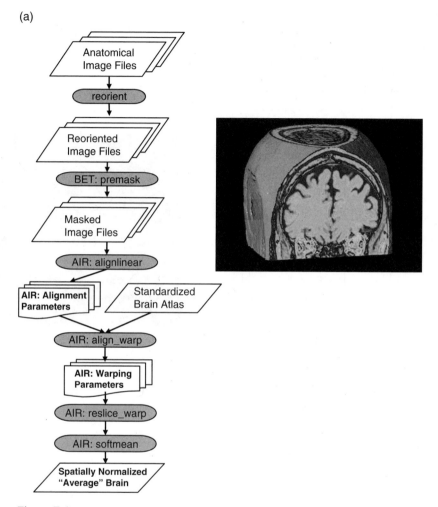

Figure 7.4

(*a*) Detailed directed acyclic graph (DAG) to spatially normalize a subject's anatomical brain image data to the Montreal Neurological Institute (MNI) brain template atlas. The cutaway anatomical template image was constructed using this workflow and data available from the fMRIDC. (*b*) A Higher-level view of a workflow DAG to spatially normalize multiple brain image volumes to the MNI template atlas and create a population-based average. Only the first few of the number of subject image volumes input to the workflow are shown here for illustrative purposes. The resulting "average brain" (with skull partially removed) is also shown.

(b)

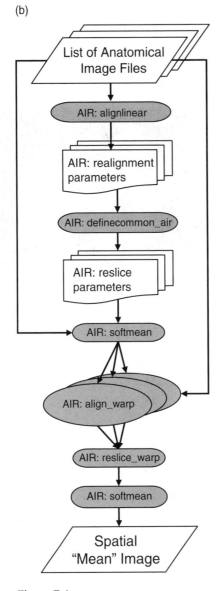

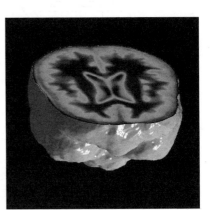

Figure 7.4
(continued)

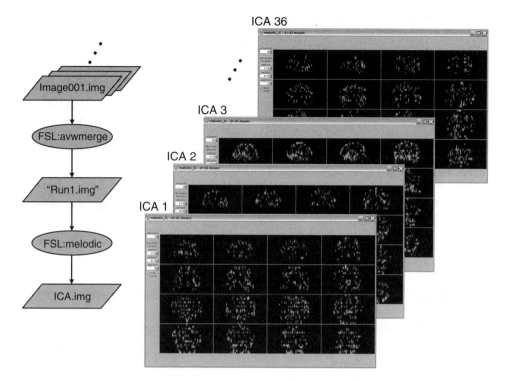

Figure 7.5
Directed acyclic graph (DAG) for performing an independent components analysis (ICA) using the FMRIB Software Library (Oxford) Melodic 2.0 routine and for use in benchmarking Grid performance on neuroimaging data. Any Analyze- or Nifti-compatible image viewer, such as the Java-based, Web-enabled viewer from the fMRIDC, can be used to view output images.

Table 7.2
Speedup chart for FMRIB Software Library independent components analysis using the Grid (hours : minutes)

Number of Processing Jobs	Shell Script Duration	Estimated Virtual Data System Duration
1	5:24	5:28
10	54:00	5:28
20	108:00	5:28
30	162:00	5:28

Timings based on 2.8 GHz Intel Xeon, 512 MByte RAM processors. Dataset was a single fMRI run having 160 volumes, $79 \times 95 \times 68$ voxels, 16-bit integer precision. It was assumed that (1) all systems were identically configured; (2) all queued jobs were executed immediately; and (3) the time needed to transfer data was identical between Grid sites. Virtual Data System overhead: Condor-G + Globus GRAM + SGE overhead: 90 seconds; pre- + postprocessing (for the selected data set): 160 seconds.

that the computational hardware for running the VDS does not reside locally and is available only as a consequence of using Grid. The Virtual Data System also has the benefits of queries, provenance tracking, parameter specification, as well as having the ability to create "compound workflow functions," whereas traditional shell scripting may not.

Limitations

The following observations from our experience with using virtual data techniques for fMRI analysis address both the potential advantages of the approach and the next steps we have identified for making the approach useful to the fMRI research community.

Scalability and Location-Independent Computing

Perhaps our most important finding is that the data and parameter encapsulation provided by virtual data language and the virtual data approach lends itself quite well to a powerful and valuable model of "location-independent computing." Specifically, when a sequence of analysis steps in a science workflow is described in VDL rather than in an ad hoc script, the precise declarations of the workflow's input and output files enable the use of automated "planner" and "executor" services. These Virtual Data System components handle all the tedious, error-prone work involved in dynamically selecting an execution locale for each step of the workflow. They automatically perform all of the explicit load balancing, data moving, data lookup, and cataloging actions required in a distributed environment.

Data Provenance Queries

Once studies have been run on the Grid using the Virtual Data System, a great deal of useful information on workflow structure, tool relationships, and data derivation attributes can be found in the virtual data catalog. From answers to specific queries, researchers can determine what parameters were used in deriving the datum in question, discover the derivations employed, and use this information to assess the derived object's validity. For example, they can ascertain whether a specific result was derived from an input brain image that had been anonymized, or had been registered by a linear alignment using a specific affine model.

Processing Data Sets

Presently, the virtual data language operates on individual files. To operate on structured, multifile or multidirectory data sets such as those in the fMRIDC archive, which are common throughout the field of fMRI and imaging studies in general, we frequently employ a "generator"—a script typically written in a higher-level scripting language such as Perl or Python. A generator serves, in part, as a "higher-level transformation": given a data set (a subset of the files in a directory tree), it performs a Virtual Data Toolkit transformation on each member of the data set, and operates by producing VDL *derivations* with the appropriate argument substitution.

File- and Directory-Naming Conventions

An area critical to the fMRI data set model is to establish natural, uniform conventions for the expression and manipulation of the file names and directory paths with a large archive and among the intermediate and final outputs of the workflow. To facilitate the use of fMRIDC data sets on the Grid, a flexible but general set of file name conventions is needed, one that can serve the entire user community (e.g., Nifti).

Community Setup and Usability

From our efforts, a picture is emerging of the type of community infra-structure needed to bring the benefits of virtual data methods and Grid computing to fMRI researchers. A logical next step in our continuing studies will be to Grid-enable the fMRIDC archival file server with the Grid file transfer protocol (GridFTP) service. An initial installation of this has been completed, which will enable us to grant secure and high-speed access to the entire fMRIDC archive with the GridFTP. A dedicated fMRIDC replica location service is being established that will enable portions of the archive to be cached throughout a Grid such as Grid3. As the studies proceed in parallel, significant network data transfer reduction can thus be expected from this caching model.

Our explorations have demonstrated great benefits from the auto-mated site selection and load balancing mechanisms that are part of various research tools within the Virtual Data System. Preliminary work on pre-dicting completion times for workflows will be highly valuable to science users. Continued enhancement of such fault-tolerant recovery mechanisms is critical in a Grid environment, as are diagnostics that permit end users and administrators to easily determine what may have failed in a long-running workflow, and what corrective actions are required.

Integration

With the collection of neurobiological data into large databases and the availability of Grid-enabled means for large-scale data processing, a new form of discovery-oriented neuroscience is on the horizon. Researchers are increasingly wanting to examine vast and disparate collections of data in their hunt for unseen patterns that might provide clues to underlying biological mechanisms. By providing input for pattern-seeking and other relevant algorithms (see Ma, Tromp, and Li, 2002; Jones and Swindells, 2002; Schutte et al., 2002), the terabytes of data being collected in many fields can provide further insights into complex processes. The well-known successes of molecular biology, biomedicine, and astrophysics infrastructures have enabled experts in computer science, mathematics, and statistics to make significant contributions to these fields, from which most of their expertise would otherwise have been excluded. The need to build on these successes and to extend them to a wider set of scientific research arenas is an ever-present theme (see Altman, 2003; Brookes, 2001; Persson, 2000).

A discovery science for brain function will undoubtedly be located at the interface between large-scale archives of primary data and Grid computing capability. Indeed, we contend that functional neuroimaging could become a leading example of this phenomenon, whereby patterns of brain activity present across multiple subjects and dozens of studies can be systematically extracted and examined using Grid-based tools. The data from a published fMRI experiment contributed to a public repository such as the fMRIDC can be directly examined using Grid-capable tools by students and researchers who devise new and more sophisticated algorithms for analyzing the functional time courses. But where to begin? How can we move toward this vision?

In the first place, it is not difficult to envision the development of collections of Virtual Data System–based MRI processing tools that enable users to easily analyze data from the fMRIDC study data archive. The VDS would provide the virtual data catalog for many commonly used neuroimaging data transformation and derivation definitions, as well as basic scripts to instantiate many commonly used multistep data-processing pipelines (e.g., three-dimensional image registration). Utilities would be provided to users so that the might easily set up Grid workflow runs, transfer and catalog fMRI datasets, and monitor remote program execution. Users could draw from the library of virtual data scripts provided or contribute their own virtual data transformations and scripts with accompanying directed acyclic graphs. More than just a repository for code, virtual data language pipelines performing like operations (e.g., spatial normalization) could be benchmarked for speed and accuracy and ranked accordingly. Those most highly ranked could become the "industry standards," determined not by committee, but by community, through usage statistics and rigorous assessment across multiple published data sets. In contributing their published studies to the fMRIDC, rather than providing a full-fledged data-processing narrative, authors could simply provide the virtual data language transformations, derivations, and scripts to the archive. Thus each study would have not only gigabytes of data, but also a ready means of replicating the exact analysis steps used by the original study authors. Variations on the order of transformations or pipelined operations could be tried to assess the properties of the resultant statistical outcomes (see, for example, LaConte et al., 2003). Finally, virtual data language scripts could also maximally leverage study metadata to process data contingent on various study, subject, or protocol parameters. For instance, the spatial normalization VDL script could be weighted by subject age and the data processed using an age-stratified brain template atlas. In this way, subject structural image volumes would be "normalized" to age-appropriate brain templates rather than some, supposedly, "ageless" stereotactic atlas.

As for computing resources, users already have what it takes to begin such Grid-level analyses now, with no need for large computers and massive disk arrays per se. Virtual data language–based algorithms are run on "virtual" fMRI data and submitted to the Grid, which transparently distributes the data-processing workload to geospatially distributed computers.

Rapid processing of large quantities of data in this way will lead to new scientific outcomes and patterns of results not envisioned through the examination of each study individually. Such patterns can suggest fundamental mechanisms, and the mechanisms can, in turn, suggest testable biological experiments to foster new hypothesis-driven research. Confirmed mechanisms add to the knowledge base of neurobiological science and provide the basis for further experimentation and the generation of still more valuable data that can be included in still greater analyses. This greater knowledge about fundamental cognitive processes will then suggest new and testable hypotheses that will lead to novel fMRI experimentation, the data from which will be contributed back into the publicly available archive.

Such a cycle of science (figure 7.6) thus becomes a driving force behind the research endeavor and accelerates the growth of accumulated knowledge. It fosters greater use of costly and complex sets of brain imaging data, broadens the scope of the findings published in the literature, and serves to educate the next generation of neuroscientists.

Conclusion

Publicly available archives of primary fMRI data and distributed Grid computing are already playing important roles. The interface between these two domains promises unique neuroscientific outcomes giving rise to discovery science and broadening the scope of education. Moreover, with further refinements to standards and protocols for Grid computing, many forms of fMRI analyses may soon not be run on local machines at all, but will instead be performed using the resources of many geographically distributed computers. With more data present in these valuable archives and sophisticated Grid-based applications, greater opportunities for the genesis of new hypotheses and real scientific progress are just around the corner.

Acknowledgments

The fMRI Data Center (fMRIDC) Project is supported by a P20 grant from the National Institute of Mental Health Human Brain Project. The Grid Physics Network (GriPhyN) and the International Virtual Data Grid Laboratory (iVDGL) are supported by the National Science Foundation; the Particle Physics Data Grid (PPDG) and the Globus Alliance are supported by the U.S. Department of Energy Office of Science. We wish to thank the following persons and institutions for their contributions: fMRIDC team members Sarene Schumacher, John Wolfe, Autumn Agnoli, Michael Schmitt, Bennet Vance, Katherine Clemans, and Wendy Starr; Luiz Meyer, Federal University of Rio de Janeiro (UFRJ); the University of Chicago; GriPhyN and iVDGL team members Ewa Deelman, Gaurang Mehta, and Karan Vahi at the Information Services Institute, Marina del Rey, California; Miron Livny and Alan Roy at the University of Wisconsin; GriPhyN, iVDGL, and PPDG management team members Paul Avery, Rick Cavanaugh, Ruth Pordes, Doug Olson, and Richard Mount; and iVGDL operations team members Leigh Grundhoefer and Jorge Rodriguez. We also

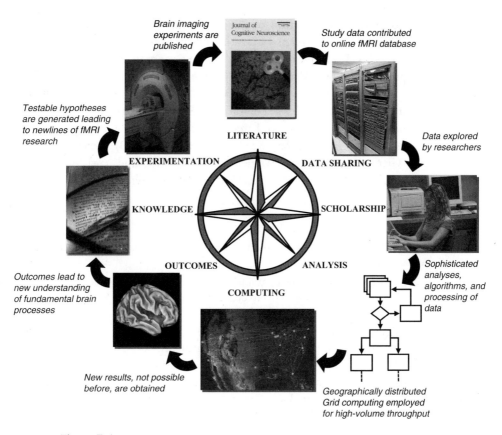

Figure 7.6
Cycle of a discovery science for neuroimaging made possible using large-scale data archiving and Grid-based computing. The availability of complete study data in online archives is enhanced by researchers being able to rapidly create novel processing methods for new analyses that utilize the Grid. Outcomes from these analyses broaden the collective knowledge base of fundamental brain function, may lead to new publications in their own right, and foster novel avenues for research and fMRI experiments. Data from these analyses are contributed to the archive and the cycle begins a new.

wish to thank Scott Grafton of the Dartmouth Brain-Imaging Center for consultation on the design of spatial normalization workflows; Natalia Maltsev, Alex Rodriquez, Dinanath Sulhake, and Veronica Nefedova for applying the GriPhyN Virtual Data System to genomics research; Jim Annis, Neha Sharma, Vijay Sekhri, and Michael Milligan for their Virtual Data System work on the Sloan Digital Sky Survey; Albert Lazzarini, Scott Koranda, Kent Blackburn, and many others for their work on the Laser Interferometer Gravitational Wave Observatory (LIGO) project; Ed May, Jerry Gieraltowski, Marco Mamelli, Rob Gardner, and Yuri Smirnov for their work on ATLAS (A Toroidal Large hadron collider Apparatus).

References

Altman, R. B. (2003). The expanding scope of bioinformatics: Sequence analysis and beyond. *Heredity, 90,* 345.

Annis, J., Zhao, Y., Voeckler, J., Wilde, M., Kent, S., and Foster, I. (2002). Applying Chimera virtual data concepts to cluster finding in the Sloan Sky Survey. In *Proceedings of Supercomputing 2002.* Baltimore.

Beckmann, C. F., and Smith, S. M. (2004). Probabilistic independent component analysis for functional magnetic resonance imaging. *IEEE Transactions on Medical Imaging, 23,* 137–152.

Benson, D. A., Karsch-Mizrachi, I., Lipman, D. J., Ostell, J., and Wheeler, D. L. (2003). GenBank. *Nucleic Acids Research, 31,* 23–37.

Berman, H. M., Battistuz, T., Bhat, T. N., Bluhm, W. F., Bourne, P. E., Burkhardt, K., Feng, Z., Gilliland, G. L., Iype, L., Jain, S., Fagan, P., Marvin, J., Padilla, D., Ravichandran, V., Schneider, B., Thanki, N., Weissig, H., Westbrook, J. D., and Zardecki, C. (2002). The Protein Data Bank. *Acta Crystallographica, D58,* 899–907.

Brookes, A. J. (2001). Rethinking genetic strategies to study complex diseases. *Trends in Molecular Medicine, 7,* 512–516.

Buckner, R. L., Snyder, A. Z., Sanders, A. L., Raichle, M. E., and Morris, J. C. (2000). Functional imaging of young, nondemented and demented older adults. *Journal of Cognitive Neuroscience, 12* (suppl. 2), 24–34.

Catlett, C., and Smarr, L. (1992). Metacomputing. *Communications of the ACM (Association of Computing Machinery), 35,* 44–52.

Deelman, E., Kesselman, C., Mehta, G., Meshkat, L., Pearlman, L., Blackburn, K., Ehrens, P., Lazzarini, A., Williams, R., and Koranda, S. (2002). GriPhyN and LIGO, Building a Virtual Data Grid for Gravitational Wave Scientists. *Proceedings of the 11th IEEE International Symposium on High Performance Distributed Computing (HPDC'02),* p. 225, http://csdl2.computer.org/persagen/DLAbsToc.jsp?resource Path=/dl/proceedings/&toc=comp/proceedings/hpdc/2002/1686/00/1686toc.xml& DOI=10.1109/HPDC.2002.1029922

Foster, I. (2003). The Grid: Computing without Bounds. *Scientific American, 288*(3), 78–85.

Foster, I., and Kesselman, C. (1998). Globus: A metcomputing infrastructure toolkit. *International Journal of Supercomputer Applications, 11*(2), 115–129.

Foster, I., Kesselman, C., and Tuecke, S. (2001). The anatomy of the Grid: Enabling scalable virtual organizations. *International Journal of Supercomputer Applications, 15*(3), 200–222.

Foster, I., Voeckler, J., Wilde, M., and Zhao, Y. (2002). Chimera: A virtual data system for representing, querying, and automating data derivation. In *Fourteenth International Conference on Scientific and Statistical Database Management.* Edinburgh.

Frey, J., Tannenbaum, T., Foster, I., Livny, M., and Tuecke, S. (2002). Condor-G: A computational management agent for multi-institutional Grids. *Cluster Computing, 5*, 237–246.

Greicius, M. D., Srivastava, G., Reiss, A. L., and Menon, V. (2004). Default-mode network activity distinguishes Alzheimer's disease from healthy aging: Evidence from functional MRI. *Proceedings of the National Academy of Sciences, USA, 101*, 4637–4642.

Head, D., Snyder, A. Z., Girton, L. E., Morris, J. C., and Buckner, R. L. (forthcoming). Frontal-hippocampal double dissociation between normal aging and Alzheimer's disease. *Cerebral Cortex.*

Jones, D. T., and Swindells, M. B. (2002). Getting the most from PSI-BLAST. *Trends in Biochemical Science, 27*, 161–164.

LaConte, S., Anderson, J., Muley, S., Ashe, J., Frutiger, S., Rehm, K., Hansen, L. K., Yacoub, E., Hu Xiaoping, Rottenberg, D., and Strother, S. C. (2003). The evaluation of preprocessing choices in single-subject BOLD fMRI usings NPAIRS performance metrics. *Neuroimage, 18*, 10–27.

Ma, B., Tromp, J., and Li, M. (2002). Pattern Hunter: Faster and more sensitive homology search. *Bioinformatics, 18*, 440–445.

Mambelli, M., Gardner, R., Smirnov, Y., Zhao, X., Gieraltowski, G., May, E., Vaniachine, A., Baker, R., Deng, W., Nevski, P., Severini, H., De, K., McGuigan, P., Ozturk, N., and Sosebee, M. (2004). ATLAS data challenge production on Grid 3. Paper delivered at the Computing in High-Energy Physics conference, 2004 (CHEP'04). Interlaken, Switzerland.

Persson, B. (2000). Bioinformatics in protein analysis. *Exs, 88*, 215–231.

Rodriguez, A., Sulakhe, D., Marland, E., Nefedova, V., Wilde, M., and Maltsev, N. (2004). Grid-enabled server for high-throughput analysis of genomes. Paper delivered at the Workshop on Case Studies on Grid Applications. Berlin.

Schutte, B. C., Mitros, J. P., Bartlett, J. A., Walters, J. D., Jia, H. P., Welsh, M. J., Casavant, T. L., and McCray, P. B., Jr. (2002). Discovery of five conserved beta-defensive gene clusters using a computational search strategy. *Proceedings of the National Academy of Sciences, USA, 99*, 2129–2133.

Van Horn, J. D., Grafton, S. T., Rockmore, D., and Gazzaniga, M. S. (2004). Sharing neuroimaging studies of human cognition. *Nature Neuroscience*, 7, 473–481.

Van Horn, J. D., Grethe, J. S., Kostelec, P., Woodward, J. B., Salam, J. A., Rus, D., Rockmore, D., and Gazzaniga, M. S. (2001). The fMRIDC: The challenges and rewards of large-scale data basing of neuroimaging studies. *Philosophical Transactions of the Royal Society, London, B356*, 1323–1339.

Woods, R. P., Grafton, S. T., Holmes, C. J., Cherry, S. R., and Mazziotta, J. C. (1998a). Automated image registration. 1. General methods and intrasubject, intramodality validation. *Journal of Computer-Assisted Tomography*, 22, 139–152.

Woods, R. P., Grafton, S. T., Watson, J. D., Sicotte, N. L., and Mazziotta, J. C. (1998b). Automated image registration. 2. Intersubject validation of linear and non-linear models. *Journal of Computer-Assisted Tomography*, 22, 153–165.

Ylonen, T., Kivinen, T., Saarinen, M., Rinne, T., and Lehtinen, S. (2001). SSH transport layer protocol. Internet Engineering Task Force. Internet draft.

Ylonen, T., Kivinen, T., Saarinen, M., Rinne, T., and Lehtinen, S. (2001). SSH Protocol Architecture. *Proceedings of the Internet Engineering Task Force. Report from the Network Working Group.* Available online at: http://www.letf.org/proceedings/Olmar/index.html.

8 Eye Movements

John M. Henderson

This chapter considers the measurement of eye movements as a methodology in cognitive science. There are at least four reasons why this topic is important. First, a complete theory of human cognition must include an account of eye movements. Human vision is a dynamic process in which the perceiver actively seeks out visual information in the service of ongoing mental and behavioral activity. Indeed, virtually all animals with developed visual systems actively control their gaze using eye, head, and body movements, singly or in combination (Land, 1999). Active vision ensures that high-quality visual information is available as needed to support perceptual and cognitive processing as well as behavioral activity, and can simplify a large variety of otherwise difficult computational problems in vision and cognition (Ballard, 1996; Ballard, et al., 1997; Churchland, Ramachandran, and Sejnowski, 1994). A complete theory of human cognition therefore requires that we understand (1) how visual and cognitive processes control, in real time, the direction of the eyes in the service of the mind (the issue of gaze control); and (2) how visual and cognitive processes are affected by where the eyes are directed at any given moment.

Second, a complete theory of visual attention must include an account of eye movements. It has been well known since the emergence of psychology as a scientific discipline that attention plays an important role in our ability to take in and process visual information. Although visuospatial attention can be investigated independently of eye movements, the more natural case is one in which covert attentional systems (internal attention systems not related to physical changes in the orientation of the receptors) and the overt eye movement system work together. Indeed, it has recently been argued that studying attention independently of eye movements is misguided and misleading (Findlay and Gilchrist, 2003). Whether this is true or not, there is no doubt that, in the more natural case, the control of attention and gaze control are tightly linked if not identical.

Third, a complete theory of visual processing must include an account of eye movements. Until recently, it has been less well appreciated that limits to attention are imposed by the physical properties of the visual receptors themselves, with factors such as visual acuity and lateral masking placing severe restrictions on the amount and type of information that can be acquired from a complex visual scene during a given eye fixation. This fact is perhaps most easily recognized in reading, where the need to extract high spatial frequencies from text in alphabetic languages makes it imperative to fixate most words. By way of informal demonstration, the reader is invited to fixate the following "X" and attempt to read the text four lines above without making an eye movement. Because letter perception is restricted to a very narrow region around fixation, the eyes must be actively guided through the text during reading (Rayner, 1998); acquisition of fine detail from the larger visual world is similarly limited.

The phenomenon of "change blindness" provides an excellent empirical demonstration of the principle that the encoding of visual information from a real-world scene is tightly tied to the position of fixation (Hollingworth and Henderson, 2002). In the first reports of change blindness, apparently obvious changes to a visual stimulus went unnoticed when those changes took place across a saccade during reading (Rayner, 1975; McConkie and Rayner, 1975) and picture viewing (Bridgeman, Hendry, and Stark, 1975; see also Currie et al., 2000; Grimes, 1996; Henderson and Hollingworth, 2003a). For example, presented with a complex photograph, subjects usually failed to notice that the heads of two men were exchanged during a saccade (Grimes, 1996). Interestingly, change blindness across saccades is essentially eliminated when the changed object is fixated (and concurrently attended) before and after the change (Hollingworth and Henderson, 2002; see also Hollingworth, Schrock, and Henderson, 2001) because visual memory is also strongly tied to fixation location (Nelson and Loftus, 1980). These results highlight the fact that, presented with a complex scene, our visual processing proceeds, not equivalently and in parallel, but rather preferentially and around the fixation point where acuity is best and attention is typically focused.

Fourth, as a methodological tool, eye movements provide an unobtrusive, sensitive, real-time behavioral index of ongoing visual and cognitive processing. This fact has been exploited to a considerable degree in the study of perceptual, cognitive, and linguistic processes in reading (see Rayner, 1998), and to a lesser but still significant degree in the study of real-world scene perception (see Henderson, 2003; Henderson and Hollingworth, 1998). In the last few years, eye movements have also been used to study an increasingly wide variety of visual and cognitive processes such as visual search (Findlay, 2004), chess playing (Reingold et al., 2001), and music reading (Truitt et al., 1997), to name only a few. Most recently, eye movement recording has become a central tool in the study of natural language production and comprehension as participants use language to describe and understand their environment (Tanenhaus et al., 1995).

This chapter will review the use of eye tracking as a behavioral methodology in cognitive science. It will focus on recent work in currently active areas, touching on the types of measures derived from eye tracking and what they reflect about the architecture of mind and brain.

Principles

To understand how inferences about the nature of cognition can be drawn from eye-tracking data, it is important to gain an appreciation for the basics of how the eyes behave during complex visuocognitive activity. Of particular interest are saccadic eye movements, in which a distinction is drawn between two functionally important temporal phases: (1) fixations, when gaze position is held relatively still so that the foveae remain directed at a particular point in space; and (2) saccades, when the eyes move rapidly to change fixation from one spatial location to another. Other major types of eye movements include smooth pursuit movements, which support visual tracking by keeping a moving object at fixation, vergence movements, which direct the eyes to a common point in depth, vestibular-ocular reflex (VOR) movements, which keep the eyes stably oriented despite head movements, and optokinetic nystagmus movements, which keep the eyes stably oriented over large-scale movements of the environment. All of these types of eye movements are important, and disruptions to the systems that support them can reveal cognitive abnormalities (see Shaw and David, chapter 2, this volume). However, with the potential exception of smooth pursuit, these types of eye movements have typically not been used to reveal the basic underlying properties of cognition.

Saccadic eye movements are very fast (e.g., 700 degrees per second or faster; Carpenter, 1988). To a good approximation, the duration of a saccade is a linear function of its amplitude, captured by the equation $D = 2.2A + 21$, where D is the duration in milliseconds and A is the amplitude in degrees (Carpenter, 1988). For example, a 2-degree saccade typical of reading would have a duration of about 25 msec. In general, saccade durations are about an order of magnitude shorter than the durations of fixations. Due to a combination of visual masking and central suppression, visual uptake of useful information is essentially shut down during a saccade, a phenomenon generically known as "saccadic suppression" (Thiele et al., 2002; Matin, 1974; Volkman, 1986). Interestingly, there is also evidence that some cognitive processes, particularly those associated with spatial cognition, are also suppressed during saccades (Irwin, 2004). The phenomenon of transsaccadic change blindness discussed earlier in the chapter, in which seemingly obvious scene changes go unnoticed when they take place during a saccade, occurs in part because visual processing does not take place during the saccade itself.

The fundamental task of eye tracking is to determine the point in space at which a viewer's foveae are directed and the amount of time (measured in msec) that they are directed there. The quality of the visual information available to visual and cognitive systems during a fixation falls off rapidly and continuously from the center of gaze (the fixation point) due to the optical properties of the cornea and lens and the neuroanatomical structure of the retina and visual cortex. The highest quality visual information is acquired from the foveal region of a viewed scene, a spatial area subtending roughly 2 degrees of visual angle at and immediately surrounding the fixation point. Centered at the optical axis of the eye where light is focused, the fovea has a high density of cones with minimal spatial summation. Although sensitive to the differences in wavelength that give rise to the perception of color and able to preserve the high spatial frequency changes in reflected light over space that support the perception of fine detail, the cones require a relatively high luminance level to operate. Furthermore, a disproportionately large amount of primary visual cortex is devoted to the fovea (a property known as cortical magnification), providing the neural machinery needed for initial visual computation that can take advantage of this high-resolution input.

Eye tracking can be accomplished in a number of ways. The most popular current systems typically illuminate the eye with infrared light and capture the reflection of that light with the charge-coupled device (CCD) array of a digital video camera. The video images are then processed by image-processing hardware and software that compute the location of the center of the pupil, either by itself or in conjunction with that of the corneal reflection (the first Purkinje image). Limits in such systems are typically imposed by the spatial resolution of the CCD array in the camera and the temporal resolution of the video raster scan. For example, a CCD array with 512 sensors vertically and horizontally could at best detect 512×512 different eye positions. Standard video raster rate is 60 Hz, but systems that operate at 240 Hz are becoming common, allowing for eye position to be updated about once every 4 msec. Both the spatial and temporal resolutions of video trackers have been rapidly increasing with improving video technology, and this advancement is likely to continue. Dual Purkinje image trackers, typically considered to produce the highest spatial and temporal resolution for human use, capture the reflected first and fourth Purkinje images (images from the front surface of the cornea and the back surface of the lens) and track those points using an optical-mechanical servo system (figure 8.1). Analog voltages related to the positions of mirrors that are used to keep those images stable on a photocell are produced as output. In both video and dual Purkinje image eye trackers, the concept is to measure reflections from the eye that are systematically related to the orientation of the eyes in the head. When a system for tracking head position is also used, head movement can be accommodated as well. Other types of eye-tracking systems, such as magnetic scleral search coils, sclera trackers, and electrooculograms (EOGs), have also been used in research, but are becoming less favored for use with humans for reasons of invasiveness, difficulty of use, and low spatial and temporal resolution.

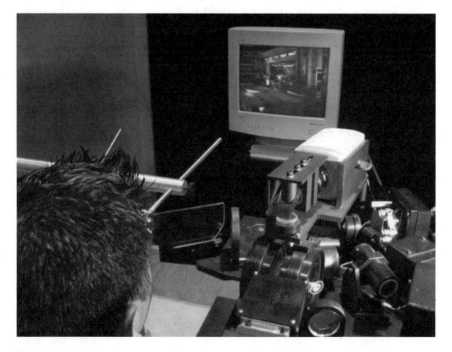

Figure 8.1
Participant on a modern dual Purkinje image eye tracker. (Figure originally published in Henderson, 2004)

Once the orientation of the eye in the head has been determined, that orientation can be mapped onto world coordinates. Typically, this mapping is generated via a calibration procedure in which the observer is asked to fixate specific targets, and the output of the eye tracker corresponding to those targets in eye tracker coordinates is mapped onto the known world coordinates for those same targets. Some method is then used to interpolate between the calibrated points. Eye trackers with linear output are preferred because interpolation is more straightforward. When the head of the observer and the world remain stable with respect to each other, the mapping from eye tracker coordinates to world coordinates is relatively straightforward, which is one reason that many uses of eye tracking require that the participant's head be held as still as possible (e.g., with a forehead or chin rest, or a bite bar) or that some method be used to compensate for small head movements (e.g., using the corneal reflection or an image of reference points in the world as a measure of head translation and rotation; Buswell's eye-tracking apparatus used a chromium bead for this purpose). Keeping the head and world stable also makes separating different eye movement behaviors (e.g., saccadic and smooth pursuit movements, and fixations) easier to automate. And because eye tracker coordinates can be mapped directly onto unchanging world coordinates, automatic data-scoring methods can be used to determine where and for how long areas of the world are fixated. That is, because when the head is still, eye tracker coordinate X_e, Y_e always maps onto world coordinate X_w, Y_w, software can be developed for directly analyzing the eye tracker output in world coordinates of interest.

For mobile eye tracking where the viewers are free to move their head or body (figure 8.2), mapping eye tracker coordinates onto world coordinates is more challenging. Typically, free-movement eye trackers include a scene camera that is used to record an image of the scene that is directly in front of the viewer. The eye-tracking coordinates are then calibrated against the image captured by this scene camera rather than directly against the world. The region of the environment visible to the observer and preserved by the scene camera changes as the observer rotates and translates in space. In this case, eye tracker coordinate X_e, Y_e always maps onto a given scene camera coordinate X_c, Y_c, but neither of these coordinates will necessarily map onto a given world coordinate X_w, Y_w. Concretely, if a viewer is looking straight ahead at a penny on the viewer's desk, the scene camera will capture the desktop with the penny in the center, and the eye tracker will place fixation on the particular x,y pixel coordinate in that image where the penny is to be found. If the viewer then turns to fixate a quarter that is now straight

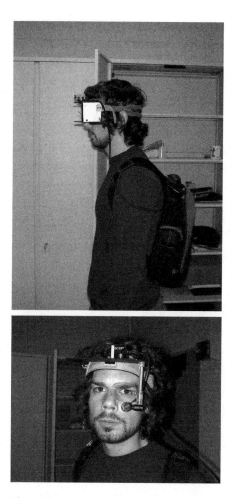

Figure 8.2
Participant wearing a portable, free-movement eye tracker. These eye trackers are lightweight and allow the viewer freedom of head and body movement. The top panel shows the electronics backpack and head goggles for outdoor use. The bottom panel shows a close-up of the lightweight optics for indoor use.

ahead on the desk, the quarter will be centered on the scene camera, and the eye tracker will produce exactly the same x,y coordinate as output (the coordinate corresponding to visual straight ahead). Thus the eye tracker output is not informative about what in the world is being fixated. Given that computer vision is still some ways away from open-ended automatic object and scene recognition, the eye tracker operator is required to hand-score the resulting video output to map the eye tracking data onto the real world, an often tedious, laborious, and time-consuming process. An important concern for increasing the use of eye tracking in real-world applications, then, will be to develop automated data analysis methods for free-movement eye trackers.

Eye tracking has proved to be one of the richest and most important sources of information about the perceptual, cognitive, and linguistic processes that take place during reading. Furthermore, much that has been learned about these processes generalizes to cognition more generally. Two important issues for understanding eye movements in complex activity are where fixation tends to be directed and how long it typically remains there. For example, the finding that the duration of the initial fixation on a word is longer if the word has a lower frequency in the language suggests not only that lexical frequency is an important psycholinguistic variable, but also that the cognitive system is highly sensitive to the relative frequency of environmental stimuli more generally. The literature on eye movements in reading is vast and justice cannot be done to it in the space provided here. Interested readers are directed to the extensive review provided by Rayner (1998), as well as the succinct overviews by Rayner and Liversedge (2004), and Starr and Rayner (2001).

During reading, the eyes move across the page at a rate of about four fixations per second. Most words in a text are fixated, and many words receive more than one fixation. Shorter, higher-frequency, and more highly constrained words tend to be skipped more often than longer, lower-frequency, and less-constrained words. The majority of saccades carry the eyes forward (rightward in English) through the text, though backward or regressive eye movements are not uncommon. Average fixation durations are about 225 msec and average forward saccade amplitudes are about 8 character spaces or 2 degrees at a typical reading distance. Importantly, there is considerable variability around these means within an individual and across individuals. The durations of individual fixations on a word as well as the cumulative durations of all initial fixations (gaze durations) are related to the perceptual and cognitive processes associated with that word. For example, the initial or first fixation duration on a word is affected by lexical factors (e.g., word length and word frequency), syntactic factors (e.g., syntactic frequency), and discourse processes (e.g., anaphor resolution).

Development

In his book *The Psychology and Pedagogy of Reading*, Edmund Huey (1908) noted that the earliest reports on the nature of eye movements in reading were published by Emile Javal in 1878 and 1879, and by Alexander Brown in 1895. Indeed, the use of the term *saccade* to mean a rapid, jerky movement of the eyes as they moved to fixate a new position was coined by Javal from his early observations of eye movements. Although these studies represent the first use of "eye tracking" to study visual and cognitive processes, as Huey noted, they consisted simply of watching a subject's eyes (directly or in a mirror) as the subject engaged in an activity such as reading and of observing the nature and number of related eye movements. Huey pointed out that, because such observation was difficult and error prone, more objective methods were required to produce a lasting record of the movements of the eyes. The earliest attempts at creating eye trackers that recorded eye movements involved mechanical devices. For example, a cup (ivory or plaster of Paris) was attached to the eyeball, and changes in eye position were recorded by physically connecting a recording stylus or brush to the cup that traced eye movements on a physical medium such as smoked paper (e.g., Delabarre, 1898; Huey, 1908). Although no doubt unpleasant for the user, many of the basic facts about eye movements in reading were correctly established using these methods.

A photographic technique for recording eye movements was developed in the 1920s by Guy Buswell at the University of Chicago (see figure 8.3), one approaching the unobtrusive methods of modern eye tracking (see also Tinker, 1936). Buswell recorded the light reflected from the cornea onto a rotating photographic drum; he quantized the reflection with the moving blades of a fan so that durations of eye movement behaviors could be determined. Buswell used this technique to record eye movements during reading (Buswell, 1922) and viewing different types of pictorial images (Buswell, 1935). Buswell's 1935 study was the first to bring these techniques to the study of vision more generally, demonstrating that the eyes tend to fixate informative image regions. In a later, better-known study, the Russian physiologist Alfred Yarbus (1967) also reported eye movement data from subjects viewing a wide variety of pictorial stimuli.

Following these initial studies, which marked the "first era" of eye movement research (Rayner, 1998), there was a significant fall off in

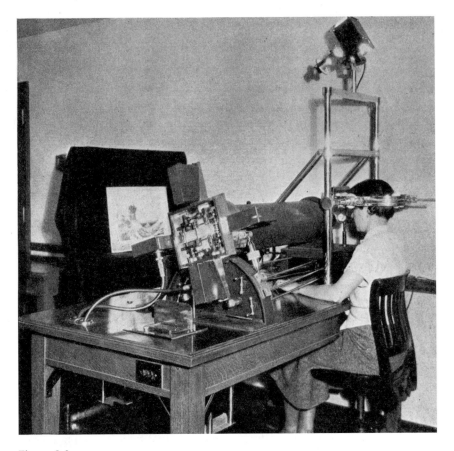

Figure 8.3
Eye-tracking apparatus used by Buswell in his 1935 eye movement study of how people look at pictures. Figure originally published in Buswell, 1935.

interest in eye tracking in psychology. The "second era," which began in the late 1960s and early 1970s with a resurgence of interest in eye tracking, was brought about by a convergence of factors including the decline of behaviorism and the ascent of the cognitive paradigm within psychology, the development of new eye-tracking devices based on video technology and the dual Purkinje image method, and the availability of computer systems that could be interfaced with eye trackers to collect and record large amounts of data automatically. This new era led to a plethora of published studies on eye movements related both to reading (e.g., Just and Carpenter, 1980; McConkie and Rayner, 1975; see also Rayner, 1998) and to picture perception (e.g., Antes, 1977; Friedman, 1979; Loftus and

Mackworth, 1978; Mackworth and Morandi, 1967; Parker, 1978; see also Henderson and Hollingworth, 1998).

Although the use of eye tracking to study perceptual and language processes in reading has continued relatively unabated from the mid-1970s until today, its use to study complex scene perception fell off in the 1980s before enjoying a sharp upswing in the mid-1990s. Two significant developments in eye tracking that have opened up the study of eye movements in scene perception are the ability to interface sophisticated graphics systems with eye trackers, allowing investigators to display complex photorealistic images on a computer monitor, and the development of portable, free-movement eye trackers that allow participants to move about and interact with the environment while their eye movements are precisely tracked.

As mentioned above, a major driving force behind the development of methods to record eye movements has been the study of skilled reading. An important methodological development in the study of reading was the eye-contingent display change technique (McConkie and Rayner, 1975; Rayner, 1975), in which an eye tracker and display device are interfaced with a computer, and the text displayed on the monitor is changed contingent on characteristics of a reader's eye position or movement. This technique provides a powerful method for investigating central issues in vision and attention related to eye movements. For example, initial investigations of the perceptual span, defined as the distance beyond fixation from which useful information can be acquired during fixation, involved the use of the tachistoscope. Estimates of the perceptual span in reading derived from the tachistoscope were found to be misleading, however (Rayner, 1975, 1998). To circumvent the problems associated with brief stimulus presentations, McConkie and Rayner (1975) developed the moving window paradigm, a version of the eye-contingent display change technique in which the text surrounding fixation is displayed normally but the text farther from fixation is degraded in some way. Because the display is updated based on the signal from the eye tracker, the region of text within the window moves with the eyes, providing clear text wherever the reader looks and degraded text elsewhere. By manipulating the size of the window of clear text and the nature of the degradation outside the window, investigators can infer the size of the perceptual span in reading for various sorts of information such as letter identities, letter features, and word spaces (see Rayner, 1998). The inverse of the moving window, a moving mask at fixation that creates an artificial scotoma, has also bee used to study basic visual processes in reading. These studies demonstrate the critical importance of foveal vision in normal reading (Rayner and Bertera, 1979; Rayner et al., 1981).

Eye movements during more general visual perception have traditionally been studied using pictures. In two classic studies, reported by Buswell (1935) and Yarbus (1967), viewers were shown a wide variety of pictures including photographs of paintings, sculpture, and individual objects. These early studies established that eye movements during viewing of complex visual stimuli are regular and systematic. Thus, for example, viewers tend to fixate meaningful and informative regions of a picture at the expense of visually uniform and semantically uninformative regions, and their task influences what areas of a picture receive fixations (figure 8.4).

Following the Buswell and Yarbus studies, in the late 1960s through the 1970s, eye movements were primarily studied using line drawings of simple scenes. The falloff noted above in studies that investigated eye

Figure 8.4
Scan pattern of a single viewer looking at a picture while searching for people in the scene. The circles represent fixations and are scaled by fixation duration (shown in milliseconds). The lines represent saccades. The subject began the trial by looking at the center of the picture (the fixation lasting 194 msec) and the scan pattern unfolded from there. The scan pattern illustrates that only scene areas relevant to the task (those likely to contain people) were fixated.

movements during complex scene viewing was caused in large part by the difficulty of presenting, under precise experimental control, depictions of complex visual stimuli that could reasonably stand in for the natural visual environment, and by the difficulty of studying eye movements in the natural environment itself. The display devices that allowed for the study of eye movements in reading, including cathode-ray tubes (CRTs), were initially not capable of presenting images more complex than simple line drawings or cartoons. Thus, too, the resurgence of the study of eye movements in complex scene perception in the mid-1990s was generated in large part by the advent of high-quality digital imaging and digital display devices that enable investigators to present realistic images such as high-resolution digital color photographs and photorealistic computer renderings of three-dimensional scene models.

Studies of scene perception using pictures have shown that both fixation durations and saccade amplitudes tend to be longer in picture viewing than in reading, with average fixation durations of about 300 msec and average saccade amplitudes of about 3 degrees. As with reading, there is considerable variability in these characteristics both within and across individuals (see Henderson and Hollingworth, 1998; Rayner, 1998). The increased average fixation duration apparent in picture viewing seems to be due to a longer tail in the distribution rather than to a shift in the mode, with a greater number of longer fixations in picture viewing than in reading (Henderson and Hollingworth, 1998). (For a relatively complete review of the use of eye tracking to study scene perception, see Henderson and Hollingworth, 1998; for a brief introduction, see Henderson, 2004.)

As with scene perception, eye movements during face perception have primarily been studied using pictures. In an important study, Yarbus (1967) presented illustrations of viewers' eye movement patterns on a number of pictures of faces. For example, the viewing pattern on the profile bust of the Egyptian Queen Nefertiti showed that eye movements were concentrated on the outside bounding contours of the face (figure 8.5, top panels), whereas the viewing pattern on a second face viewed from straight on showed them to be concentrated on the internal features of the face (figure 8.5, middle panels), though there continued to be fixations on the outer contours as well (see plate 2). An often overlooked aspect of Yarbus study is that these demonstrations were often based on a single participant viewing a given image for a very long period of time. There is now considerable evidence that eye movements tend to be directed predominantly to internal facial features during both face learning and face recognition (Groner, Walder, and Groner, 1984; Henderson, Williams, and Falk, 2005;

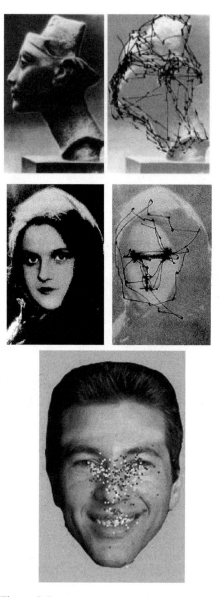

Figure 8.5
Examples of eye movements during face perception. The first two examples show the eye movement traces of a single viewer examining a bust of Nefertiti and a straight-on view of a face, both adapted from Yarbus, 1967. The final example shows all fixations generated by 20 viewers each during identity (yellow), mood (red), and gender (blue) recognition tasks. See plate 2 for color version.

Walker-Smith, Gale, and Findlay, 1977; see figure 8.5, bottom panel). For example, Henderson et al. (2001) reported that close to 60 percent of fixation time was spent on the eyes in a face recognition task, and that about 90 percent of fixation time was spent on the eyes, nose and mouth. These eye movements appear to play a functional role: Henderson, Williams, and Falk (2005) demonstrated that face recognition was greatly impaired when viewers were restrained from making eye movements during face learning compared to when they were free to move their eyes, holding viewing time constant.

Innovation

Moving beyond the use of photographic stimuli, investigators have recently begun to study visual perception in the real environment using portable free-movement eye trackers (Land and Hayhoe, 2001). This innovative use of eye tracking involves lightweight, head-mounted optics and portable electronics that allow viewers to move naturally and freely without being tethered to any stationary equipment. Although research using these devices is still relatively new, it has become apparent that there are important differences in eye movements for pictures of the environment and for the environment itself. For example, there is some evidence that distributions of fixation durations and saccade amplitudes differ for the two conditions, with average saccade amplitudes significantly greater for the environment (Land and Hayhoe, 2001). Free-movement eye tracking allows investigators to study the nature of the eye movements that are made in the service of everyday tasks such as driving (Land and Horwood, 1995) and tea and sandwich making (Hayhoe et al., 2003; Land, Mennie, and Rusted, 1999). Free-movement eye tracking has also proved to be a very powerful technique for investigating theoretical issues in language production and comprehension, and for understanding the interaction between the language and visual processing systems (Tanenhaus et al., 1995; see also review chapters in Henderson and Ferreira, 2004, and Trueswell and Tanenhaus, 2005). And although significant progress has been made in these areas, the use of free-movement eye tracking is in many ways still in its infancy, and can be expected to progress as new methods for automated data analysis are developed.

Limitations

One of the most important limitations on the use of eye tracking in the past has concerned expanding the methodology to less constrained and more natural situations in which viewers are free to move within and interact with the natural environment. As noted above, recent eye-tracking technologies have provided for mobile, free-movement eye tracking. A limitation of these trackers, though, is that they tend to be less accurate than their stationary counterparts; moreover, data collected from them are much more difficult to analyze because, as discussed in the "Principles" section, they require that video data be hand-scored. Given the advances needed in artificial vision systems before automated data scoring becomes possible, it is unclear whether this latter problem will be solved in the near future. Continuing progress in the study of eye movements in perception and cognition is thus likely to involve converging evidence from both highly accurate stationary eye trackers and free-movement eye trackers.

Integration

An important burgeoning area of integration in the study of eye movements in cognitive science and in cognitive neuroscience involves the use of formal modeling. The two domains in which eye movement modeling has played the most apparent role in the past few years are reading and complex scene viewing. In both cases, the aim is to account for the spatial and temporal characteristics of eye movements and their relationship to perceptual and cognitive factors. In reading, current computational and mathematical models are focused on predicting the basic statistics of eye movement control such as the means and frequency distributions of fixation durations and saccade amplitudes (e.g., Reichle et al., 1998). In these models, specification of the relationship between covert attention and eye movements, and the degree to which lexical processing is serial versus parallel, are issues of current critical concern. In complex scene viewing, recent computational models have been inspired by known response properties of neurons in visual cortex, and the primary focus has been to determine where and in what order fixations will be placed in a scene (Itti and Koch, 2000), whereas issues of fixation durations have tended to be ignored (Henderson, 2003). An important focus for future modeling in both domains will be to capture a more complete set of eye movement characteristics.

A second area that is ready for significant progress is the integration of sophisticated eye tracking with methods of functional neuroimaging (see Bandettini, chapter 9, and Singh, chapter 12, this volume). For example, even though many scanners used for fMRI research have eye trackers installed in them, most of these eye trackers have been used to determine whether the viewers are maintaining fixation, or at best to determine whether a saccade has been executed in a specific direction at a specific time, as in the antisaccade task (Hallett, 1978). Although these uses are important, they barely scratch the surface of the utility of the method for determining where and when perceptual, attentional, and cognitive processes have been deployed over a given complex visual stimulus. The combined integration of sophisticated eye tracking to measure the locus of eye fixations over time with methods for examining neural activity related to specific fixations (or saccades), whether with fMRI or other techniques such as event-related potentials (ERPs) and magnetoencephalography (MEG), would seem to offer tremendous opportunity for advancing our knowledge of mind and brain.

Conclusion

The active control of eye fixation plays an important functional role in all perceptual and cognitive tasks. Active vision ensures that visual input is available to the cognitive system as it is needed. The measurement of eye movements provides an unobtrusive, noninvasive, sensitive, behavioral window into the operation of the cognitive system as it unfolds in real time.

Acknowledgments

Preparation of this chapter was supported by grants from the National Science Foundation (BCS-0094433) and the Army Research Office (W911NF-04-1-0078) to John M. Henderson, the Michigan State University (MSU) Foundation to Fernanda Ferreira and John M. Henderson, and the National Institute of Mental Health (R01-MH63146) to Joel Nigg, John M. Henderson, and Fernanda Ferreira. Thanks to Brendon Hsieh and Michael Mack for modeling in figures 8.1 and 8.2, to Monica Castelhano for figure 8.4, and to Aaron Pearson for the last panel in figure 8.5.

The opinions expressed in this chapter are mine and do not necessarily represent the views of the Department of the Army or any other governmental organization. Reference to or citation of trade or corporate names does not constitute explicit or implied endorsement of those entities or their products either by me or by the Department of the Army.

References

Antes, J. R. (1977). Recognizing and localizing features in brief picture presentations. *Memory and Cognition, 5*, 155–161.

Ballard, D. H. (1996). On the function of visual representation. In K. Akins (Ed.), *Perception: Vancouver studies in cognitive science*, 111–131. Oxford: Oxford University Press.

Ballard, D. H., Hayhoe, M. M., Pook, P. K., and Rao, R. P. (1997). Deictic codes for the embodiment of cognition. *Behavioral and Brain Sciences*, 20, 723–767.

Bridgeman, B., Hendry, D., and Stark, L. (1975). Failure to detect displacements of the visual world during saccadic eye movements. *Vision Research*, 15, 719–722.

Buswell, G. T. (1922). *Fundamental reading habits: A study of their development.* Chicago: University of Chicago Press.

Buswell, G. (1935). *How people look at pictures: A study of the psychology and perception in art.* Chicago: University of Chicago Press.

Carpenter, R. H. S. (1988). *Movements of the eyes.* London: Pion.

Churchland, P. S., Ramachandran, V. S., and Sejnowski, T. J. (1994). A critique of pure vision. In C. Koch and S. Davis (Eds.), *Large-scale neuronal theories of the brain*, 23–60. Cambridge, MA: MIT Press.

Currie, C., McConkie, G., Carlson-Radvansky, L. A., and Irwin, D. E. (2000). The role of the saccade target object in the perception of a visually stable world. *Perception and Psychophysics*, 62, 673–683.

Dodge, R. (1900). Visual perceptions during eye movements. *Psychological Review*, 7, 454–465.

Delabarre, E. B. (1898). A method of recording eye movements. *American Journal of Psychology*, 9, 572–574.

Findlay, J. M. (2004). Eye scanning and visual search. In J. M. Henderson and F. Ferreira (Eds.), *The interface of language, vision, and action: Eye movements and the visual world.* New York: Psychology Press.

Findlay, J. M., and Gilchrist, I. D. (2003). *Active vision: The psychology of looking and seeing.* Oxford: Oxford University Press.

Friedman, A. (1979). Framing pictures: The role of knowledge in automatized encoding and memory for gist. *Journal of Experimental Psychology: General*, 108, 316–355.

Grimes, J. (1996). On the failure to detect changes in scenes across saccades. In K. Akins (Ed.), *Perception: Vancouver studies in cognitive science*, 89–110. Oxford: Oxford University Press.

Groner, R., Walder, F., and Groner, M. (1984). Looking at faces: Local and global aspects of scanpaths. In A. G. Gale and F. Johnson (Eds.), *Theoretical and applied aspects of eye movement research*, 523–533. Amsterdam: Elsevier.

Hallett, P. E. (1978). Primary and secondary saccades to goals defined by instructions. *Vision Research*, 18, 1279–1296.

Hayhoe, M. M., Shrivastava, A., Mruczek, R., and Pelz, J. B. (2003). Visual memory and motor planning in a natural task. *Journal of Vision*, 3, 49–63.

Henderson, J. M. (2003). Human gaze control in real-world scene perception. *Trends in Cognitive Sciences*, *7*, 498–504.

Henderson, J. M., and Castelhano, M. S. (2005). Eye movements and visual memory for scenes. In G. Underwood (Ed.), *Cognitive processes in eye guidance*. Oxford: Oxford University Press.

Henderson, J. M., and Ferreira F. (Eds.) (2004). *The interface of language, vision, and action: Eye movements and the visual world*. New York: Psychology Press.

Henderson, J. M., and Hollingworth, A. (1998). Eye movements during scene viewing: An overview. In G. Underwood (Ed.), *Eye guidance in reading and scene perception*, 269–283. Oxford: Elsevier.

Henderson, J. M., and Hollingworth, A. (2003a). Global transsaccadic change blindness during scene perception. *Psychological Science*, *14*, 493–497.

Henderson, J. M., and Hollingworth, A. (2003b). Eye movements and visual memory: Detecting changes to saccade targets in scenes. *Perception and Psychophysics*, *65*, 58–71.

Henderson, J. M., Williams, C. C., and Falk, R. J. (2005). Eye movements are functional during face learning. *Memory and Cognition*, *33*, 98–106.

Hollingworth, A., and Henderson, J. (2002). Accurate visual memory for previously attended objects in natural scenes. *Journal of Experimental Psychology: Human Perception and Performance*, *28*, 113–136.

Hollingworth, A., Schrock, G., and Henderson, J. M. (2001). Change detection in the flicker paradigm: The role of fixation position within the scene. *Memory and Cognition*, *29*, 296–304.

Huey, E. B. (1908). *The psychology and pedagogy of reading*. New York: Macmillan. Reprint, Cambridge, MA: MIT Press, 1968.

Irwin, D. E. (2004). Fixation location and fixation duration as indices of cognitive processing. In J. M. Henderson and F. Ferreira (Eds.), *The interface of language, vision, and action: Eye movements and the visual world*, 105–133. New York: Psychology Press.

Itti, L., and Koch, C. (2000). A saliency-based search mechanism for overt and covert shifts of visual attention. *Vision Research*, *40*, 1489–1506.

Just, M. A., and Carpenter, P. A. (1980). A theory of reading: From eye fixations to comprehension, *Psychological Review*, *87*, 329–354.

Land, M. F. (1999). Motion and vision: Why animals move their eyes. *Journal of Comparative Physiology*, *A185*, 341–352.

Land, M. F., and Hayhoe, M. (2001). In what ways do eye movements contribute to everyday activities? *Vision Research*, *41*, 3559–3565.

Land, M. F., and Horwood, J. (1995). Which part of the road guides steering? *Nature*, *377*, 339–340.

Land, M. F., Mennie, N., and Rusted, J. (1999). Eye movements and the roles of vision in activities of daily living: Making a cup of tea. *Perception, 28,* 1311–1328.

Loftus, G. R., and Mackworth, N. H. (1978). Cognitive determinants of fixation location during picture viewing. *Journal of Experimental Psychology: Human Perception and Performance, 4,* 565–572.

Mackworth, N. H., and Morandi, A. J. (1967). The gaze selects informative details within pictures. *Perception and Psychophysics, 2,* 547–552.

Matin, E. (1974). Saccadic suppression: A review and an analysis. *Psychological Bulletin, 81,* 899–917.

McConkie, G. W., and Rayner, K. (1975). The span of the effective stimulus during a fixation in reading. *Perception and Psychophysics, 17,* 578–586.

Nelson, W. W., and Loftus, G. R. (1980). The functional visual field during picture viewing. *Journal of Experimental Psychology: Human Perception and Performance, 6,* 391–399.

Parker, R. E. (1978). Picture processing during recognition. *Journal of Experimental Psychology: Human Perception and Performance, 4,* 284–293.

Rayner, K. (1975). The perceptual span and peripheral cues in reading. *Cognitive Psychology, 7,* 65–81.

Rayner, K. (1998). Eye movements in reading and information processing: Twenty years of research. *Psychological Bulletin, 124,* 372–422.

Rayner, K., and Bertera, J. H. (1979). Reading without a fovea. *Science, 206,* 468–489.

Rayner, K., Inhoff, A. W., Morrison, R., Slowiaczek, M. L., and Bertera, J. H. (1981). Masking of foveal and parafoveal vision during fixations in reading. *Journal of Experimental Psychology: Human Perception and Performance, 7,* 167–179.

Rayner, K., and Liversedge, S. P. (2004). Visual and linguistic processing during eye fixations in reading. In J. M. Henderson and F. Ferreira (Eds.), *The interface of language, vision, and action: Eye movements and the visual world,* 59–104. New York: Psychology Press.

Reichle, E. D., Pollatsek, A., Fischer, D. F., and Rayner, K. (1998). Toward a model of eye movement control in reading. *Psychological Review, 105,* 125–157.

Reingold, E. M., Charness, N., Pomplun, M., and Stampe, D. M. (2001). Visual span in expert chess players: Evidence from eye movements. *Psychological Science, 12,* 48–55.

Starr, M. S., and Rayner, K. (2001). Eye movements during reading: Some current controversies. *Trends in Cognitive Sciences, 5,* 156–163.

Tanenhaus, M. K., Spivey-Knowlton, M. J., Eberhard, K. M., and Sedivy, J. E. (1995). Integration of visual and linguistic information in spoken language comprehension. *Science, 268,* 632–634.

Thiele, A., Henning, M., Buischik, K., and Hoffman, P. (2002). Neural mechanisms of saccadic suppression. *Science*, *295*, 2460–2462.

Tinker, M. A. (1936). Reliability and validity of eye-movement measures of reading. *Journal of Experimental Psychology*, *19*, 732–746.

Trueswell, J. C., and Tanenhaus, M. K. (Eds.) (2005). *Approaches to studying world-situated language use*. Cambridge, MA: MIT Press.

Truitt, F. E., Clifton, C., Pollatsek, A., and Rayner, K. (1997). The perceptual span and the eye hand span in sight reading music. *Visual Cognition*, *4*, 143–162.

Volkmann, F. (1986). Human visual suppression. *Vision Research*, *26*, 1401–1416.

Walker-Smith, G. J., Gale, A. G., and Findlay J. M. (1977). Eye movement strategies involved in face perception. *Perception*, *6*, 313–326.

Yarbus, A. L. (1967). *Eye movements and vision*. New York, Plenum Press.

9 Functional Magnetic Resonance Imaging

Peter A. Bandettini

The idea of using magnetic resonance imaging (MRI) to assess human brain activation noninvasively, rapidly, and with relatively high spatial resolution, was, before 1990, pure fantasy. The arrival of functional MRI (fMRI) was marked by the publication of the groundbreaking paper by Belliveau et al. (1991) in November of 1991. Although innovative and generating considerable excitement, the "Belliveau technique," which involved two bolus injections of gadolinium-DTPA to characterize blood volume changes with activation, was effectively made obsolete as a brain activation assessment method by the time it was published. It was replaced by a completely noninvasive MRI-based technique using endogenous functional contrast associated with localized changes in blood oxygenation during activation.

Between the late spring and early fall of 1991, the first successful experiments were carried out at the Massachusetts General Hospital (May), University of Minnesota (June), and Medical College of Wisconsin (September) using endogenous MRI contrast to assess brain activation. These experiments were published within two weeks of each other in the early summer of 1992.

The mechanism of endogenous contrast on which the activation assessments were based was pioneered by Ogawa et al. (1990), who coined the term *blood oxygenation level–dependent* (BOLD), and by Turner et al. (1991), who discovered the contrast while searching for changes in the diffusion coefficient among apnea patients. In a prescient comment in 1990—two years before the first successful experiments were published and about a year before the first successful experiments were performed—Ogawa et al. (1990) predicted the beginning of a new method to assess brain activation.

A still earlier brain study using positron-emission tomography (PET; Fox and Raichle, 1986) had demonstrated an activation-induced decrease in the oxygen extraction fraction, thus predicting an increase in the MRI signal with activation. And, indeed, as researchers would find, the BOLD fMRI signal did increase with an increase in brain activation.

Another noninvasive fMRI technique, emerging almost simultaneously with BOLD fMRI, is known as "arterial spin labeling" (ASL; Williams et al., 1992). The contrast in ASL arises from cerebral blood flow and perfusion, independent of blood oxygenation. Other techniques, allowing noninvasive assessment of activation-induced changes in cerebral blood volume (Lu et al., 2003) and oxidative metabolic rate (Davis et al., 1998; Hoge et al., 1999) have since been developed.

BOLD fMRI is currently the brain activation–mapping method of choice for almost all neuroscientists because it is easiest to implement and the functional contrast to noise is 2 to 4 times higher than the other methods. Functional contrast to noise (defined as the ratio of signal change to background fluctuations) ranges from 2 to about 6 at higher field strengths when BOLD contrast is used. Currently, the need for sensitivity outweighs the need for specificity, stability over long periods of time, quantitation, or baseline state information—all of which are advantages inherent to ASL, and all of which come at the price of sensitivity.

Since these first discoveries, hardware, methodology, signal interpretability, and applications have been advancing synergistically. Advances in hardware include scanners with increased magnetic field strength, improved radiofrequency coils, and subject interface devices; those in methodology include pulse sequences, postprocessing, multimodal integration, and improved paradigm design. Advances in signal interpretability include improved understanding of the relationship between underlying neuronal activity, on the one hand, and simultaneous direct measures of neuronal activity and precise modulation of its dynamics and magnitudes obtained through use of BOLD fMRI, on the other; in applications, advances have been directed both at understanding brain organization and at complementing clinical diagnoses and characterizing neurological and psychiatric disorders. Generally, advances in any one of these domains have furthered advances in the others; the needs of one domain have in many instances driven the development of the others. (This exciting, highly interdisciplinary coevolution is described in the "Development" section.)

Even though fMRI is nearly 15 years old, unknowns remain regarding the physiological and biophysical factors influencing fMRI signal changes. New insights into the principles of BOLD and other fMRI contrast mechanisms as well as image acquisition and postprocessing are published at a steady rate. (The latest information regarding the acquisition, processing, and interpretation of fMRI signal changes is presented in the "Principles" section.)

Functional MRI is continually being shaped by innovations in hardware, methodology, interpretation, and applications. Scanner field strength and image acquisitions hardware grow ever more sophisticated—allowing greater sensitivity, speed of acquisition, and resolution. Paradigm design and postprocessing methods continually evolve as applications demand. New methods for integrating fMRI with other brain activation assessment techniques have emerged, allowing more precise interpretation of fMRI signal changes and introducing novel applications. Although most fMRI applications remain in the research domain, with continuing improvements in robustness and interpretability, especially in regard to activation maps and signal change dynamics of specific patient populations, fMRI is poised to make a clinical impact as well. (All these topics are covered, and highlights of fMRI development described, in the "Development" section.)

That the sources of contrast in functional MRI—cerebral blood flow, volume, and oxygenation changes—are secondary to brain activation places an inherent limitation on the upper spatial and temporal resolution and on the interpretability of the technique. Other fMRI limitations include sensitivity to subject motion, signal dropout in specific regions, and temporal instability within and across scanning sessions. (These limitations are described, and to overcome them outlined, methods in the "Limitations" section.)

The scope and success of the best fMRI research and applications are defined by how well the paradigms, processing, and interpretation of results are integrated with other brain function assessment techniques. This integration has yielded far greater insights into human brain function than any that fMRI could provide on its own. Techniques successfully integrated with fMRI include behavioral measures, electroencephalography (EEG), magnetoencephalography (MEG), physiological measurements, optical imaging, electrophysiological measurements, and transcranial magnetic stimulation (TMS). (The basics of how these techniques are used in conjunction with fMRI, and of the insights gained, are presented in the "Integration" section.)

Development

It is important first to put fMRI development in context. In 1991, brain activation studies were being performed by a handful of groups using techniques involving ionizing radiation or electroencephalography. Although these techniques are still quite useful today, providing complementary information, functional MRI, as it came into common use in the early nineties, represented a huge leap in ease and flexibility of brain-mapping experimentation. After 1992, investigators undertaking brain activation studies had simply to put their subjects in the scanner, have them perform a task during time series image collection, and look for MRI changes. This proved to be both a blessing and a curse for the burgeoning brain-mapping community.

On the "curse" side, easy access to this powerful tool has given rise to many poorly planned, executed, and analyzed experiments filled with overinterpretation of artifactual signal changes (although fewer today, with rapid improvements in the collective expertise of the imaging community). Moreover, the frantic rush to pick the scientific "low-hanging fruit" that began in earnest with the introduction of functional imaging continues in many contexts today. Most fMRI researchers, myself included, have been caught up in the exciting sense of urgency to use this extraordinarily powerful technique, whose potential we have only glimpsed.

On the "blessing" side, however, fMRI has brought unique insights into how the human brain is organized, how it changes over time (from seconds to years) and varies across populations, and has steadily advanced our understanding of human cognition. Most important, it has given rise to a much larger collective effort toward using brain-mapping technology for research—and to the start of an effort toward applying fMRI to diagnose and treat clinical populations.

Circa 1992, only a handful of laboratories could perform fMRI: it required not only an MRI scanner but also the capability of performing high-speed MRI—known as "echo planar imaging" (EPI). With EPI, neuroimagers could collect an entire image (or "plane") with the use of a single radio frequency (RF) pulse and subsequent signal "echo," hence the name "echo planar." Typical clinical MRI sequences use at least 128 RF pulses for a single image. One pulse typically yields a "line" of data. To collect an image with one RF pulse requires that the imaging gradients (used to spatially encode the data and thus to create an image) be oscillated very rapidly since the usable signal only lasts for about 100 msec. Because a waiting period is required between RF pulses, called the "repetition time" (TR— typically 100 msec to 2 sec), and also because clinical images typically have at least 128 lines, such an image takes on the order of several seconds to several minutes to collect. An important point is that not only do clinical images take time, but because of signal fluctuations with repeated collection of the same image, their temporal stability is relatively low, with cardiac

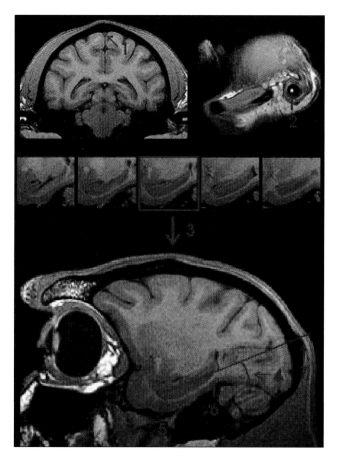

Plate 1

T1-weighted MR images obtained from a young adult rhesus monkey. Images show the brain in the coronal plane (top left) and several parasagittal planes (all others). The arrows and numerals highlight landmarks used to plan MRI-guided longitudinal surgical approaches to the hippocampus. (Reprinted from Hampton et al., 2004)

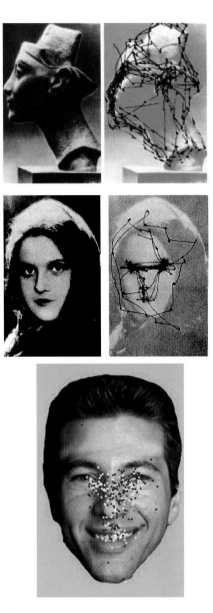

Plate 2
Examples of eye movements during face perception. The first two examples show the eye movement traces of a single viewer examining a bust of Nefertiti and a straight-on view of a face, both adapted from Yarbus, 1967. The final example shows all fixations generated by 20 viewers each during identity (yellow), mood (red), and gender (blue) recognition tasks.

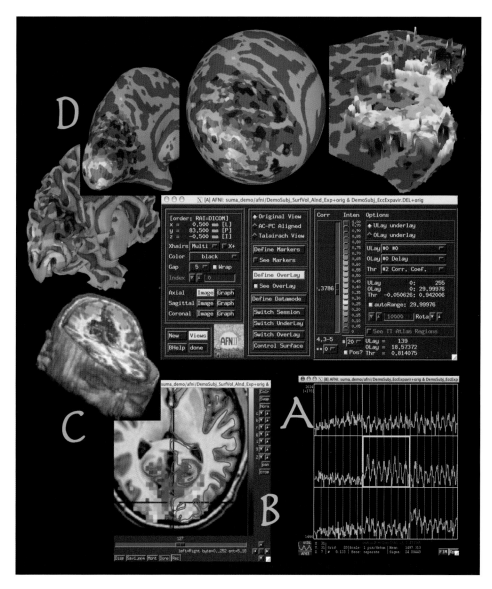

Plate 3
Example of how the same fMRI data, in their various forms, can be simultaneously and interactively visualized. See body of text for figure legend.

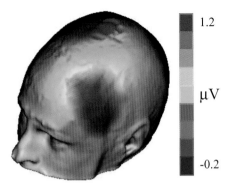
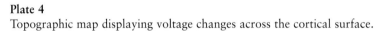

Plate 4
Topographic map displaying voltage changes across the cortical surface.

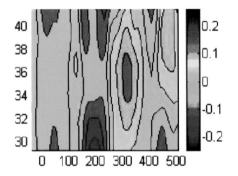

Plate 5
Time-frequency representation (TFRs) of event-related reduction in alpha (8–13Hz) activity at approximately 150msec poststimulus.

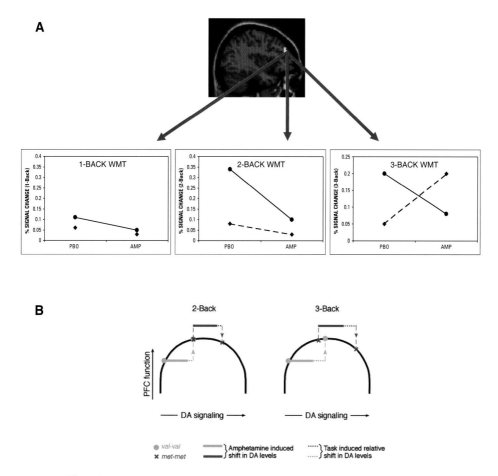

Plate 6
(*A*) Mattay et al. (2003), using BOLD fMRI, demonstrate a complex drug x COMT genotype interaction in the left prefrontal cortex (PFC) during the N-Back working memory task. While subjects homozygous for the val allele (solid line) showed a more efficient PFC response on amphetamine (i.e., greater PFC activity on placebo than on amphetamine) irrespective of task difficulty, subjects homozygous for the met allele (broken line) became inefficient on amphetamine at the highest working memory demand (i.e., they show more PFC activity on amphetamine than on placebo during the 3-Back working memory (WM) task). This paradoxical decrease in efficiency on the 3-Back task in the met/met homozygous subjects was associated with a significant decrement in performance (decreased accuracy and increased reaction time). We suggest that the combined effects of amphetamine and high WM load push PFC dopamine levels in these individuals beyond the critical threshold at which compensation can be made. (*B*) Schema of our proposed theoretical model to account for variable effects of the COMT genotype, WM load, and amphetamine on dopamine signaling and PFC function. See body of text for figure legend.

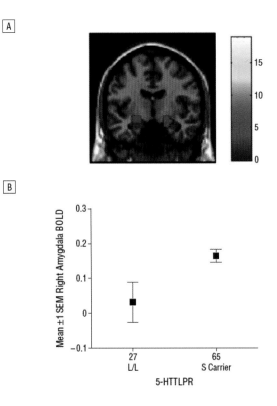

Plate 7
Hariri et al. (2005), using BOLD fMRI, demonstrate 5-HTTLPR effects on amygdala reactivity to environmental threat. Individuals homozygous for the s allele (s carriers) of the serotonin transporter gene, who presumably have greater synaptic serotonin levels, exhibit greater amygdala neuronal activity during the perceptual processing of fearful and threatening facial expressions than individuals homozygous for the l allele, who presumably have lower synaptic serotonin levels. This genetically driven differential excitability of the amygdala may contribute to the increased fear and anxiety typically associated with the s allele.

A

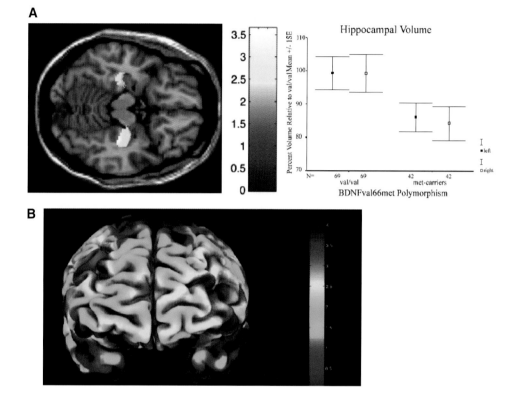

B

Plate 8

Pezawas et al. (2004), using optimized voxel-based morphometry (VBM), demonstrate volume differences in BDNF met carriers relative to BDNF val/carriers in the hippocampus (*A*) and prefrontal cortex (*B*). Consistent with the role of BDNF in cortical development and with the cellular and clinical effects of the BDNF val66met polymorphism, met carriers have relatively reduced gray matter volume in these brain regions.

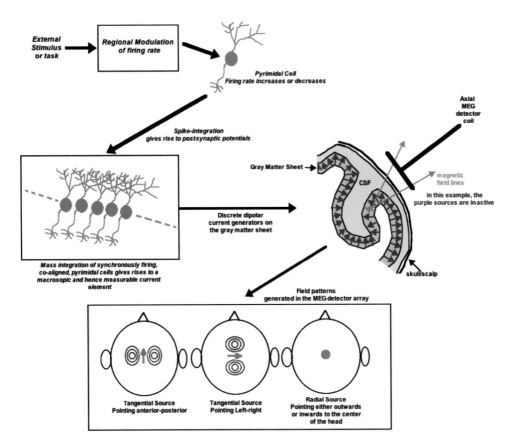

Plate 9
Schematic showing the generation of measurable neuromagnetic fields from a synchronous population of aligned dendritic processes. The bottom panel shows the magnetic field contours that would be generated in an axial measurement array, from a single focal neuronal source (known as a dipole), as the orientation of the source changes. Red indicates magnetic field lines entering the head, blue indicates field lines exiting the head. Note that for a radial source, no field is measured.

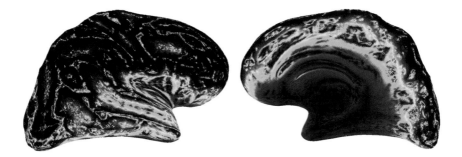

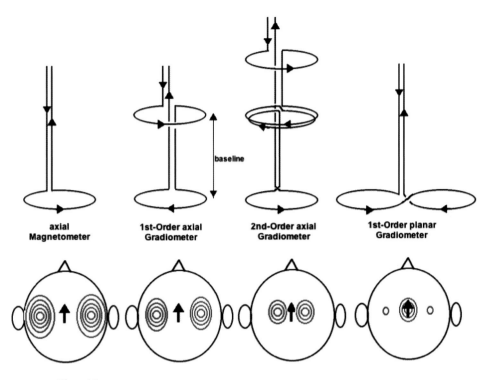

Plate 11

Typical configurations of axial magnetometers/gradiometers and the planar gradiometers used in a typical thin-film system. Under each device, cartoons of the typical field patterns generated in each coil configuration are shown, assuming a single tangential dipolar current source at the vertex. Red indicates magnetic field lines entering the head, blue indicates field lines exiting the head. Note how, with the axial devices, the contour maps become spatially tighter for higher-order gradiometers. One advantage of the planar gradiometer is that it gives a maximum detection signal directly above the source.

◄ opposite   **Plate 10**

Simulation data showing the current dipole strength needed, at each point in the brain, to accurately localize a source at that point, at least 70 percent of the time (Hillebrand and Barnes, 2002). It can be seen that relatively small regions on the crest of each gyrus are difficult to localize because of the radial nature of the currents. The figure also clearly shows that sources become increasingly difficult to localize accurately in deeper regions of the brain. (Figure courtesy of Arjan Hillebrand)

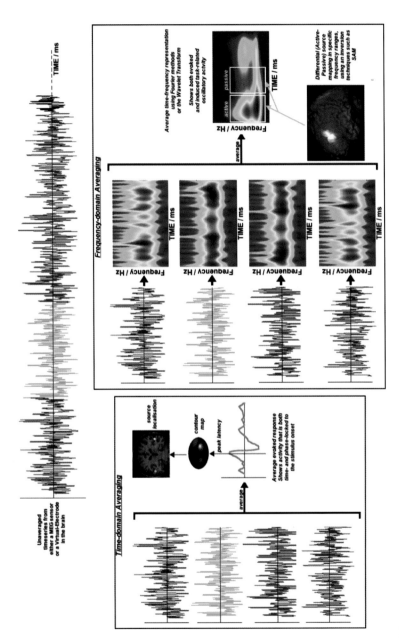

Plate 12

Schematic showing how the MEG data shown at the top of the figure can be analyzed using either time-domain averaging to reveal phase-locked evoked activity or frequency-domain averaging to reveal both evoked and induced oscillatory power changes. For the purposes of illustration only 4 epochs are averaged and each is color coded (red, green, blue, and purple).

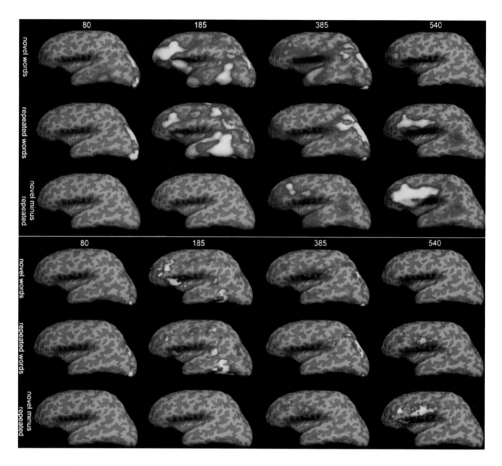

Plate 13

Demonstration of the utility of fMRI constraints in the analysis of MEG data, taken from (Dale et al., 2000; with permission). The data are from a single subject, performing a cognitive task in which the subject was presented with written concrete nouns (objects and animals) and had to decide whether the named object was more than a foot long. Identical fMRI and MEG experiments were performed using a trial-based evoked-response paradigm. To allow the hemodynamic response to decay back to baseline, a 16sec intertrial interval was used in both modalities, even though it is not necessary for the MEG experiment. Each brain image shows the inflated gray matter sheet for this individual at four different latencies after stimulus onset (80, 185, 385, and 540msec). The top panel of the figure displays the MEG data, analyzed using a noise-normalized inverse and constrained using only the anatomical gray matter sheet. The time course of activation is clearly visible. The bottom panel displays the same data analyzed using the same inversion algorithm, but with fMRI data also used to constrain the solution. Increased spatial resolution is clearly evident.

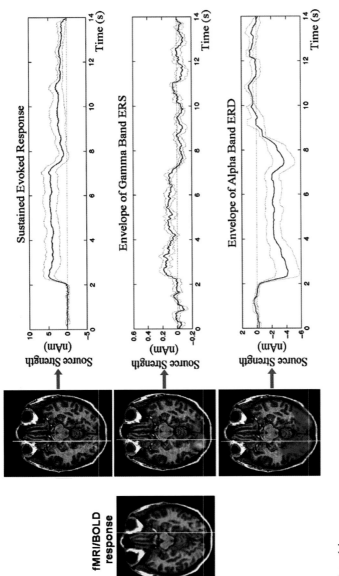

Plate 14

Results from a single subject of an fMRI-MEG comparison experiment in which the subject was shown a static checkerboard visual stimulus for 6sec (Brookes et al., 2005). Orange colors depict power increases, blue/pink colors depict task-related power decreases. During the stimulus presentation (2–8sec), three neuro-electric effects were detected in a SAM analysis of the MEG data: (1) a sustained and evoked shift in the DC baseline (top panel); (2) an induced increase in gamma-band (55–70Hz) power (middle panel); and (3) an induced decrease in alpha (8–13Hz) power (bottom panel). These effects are in a similar location to the BOLD response found in an identical MRI experiment (far left panel). (Figure courtesy of Matt Brookes)

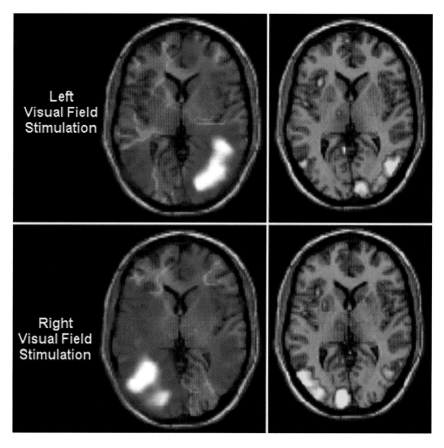

Plate 15
MEG-fMRI comparison experiment showing activation to a visual stimulus consisting of a field of coherently moving dots (n = 11). On the left, SAM analysis of the MEG data shows beta (15–25Hz) power decreases in extrastriate visual cortex, including V5/MT. This ERD is clearly contralateral to the visual field in which the stimulus is presented. On the right, the BOLD fMRI activation to the same task is also shown. There is a clear correspondence between those areas showing a BOLD increase, and those areas showing a beta power decrease.

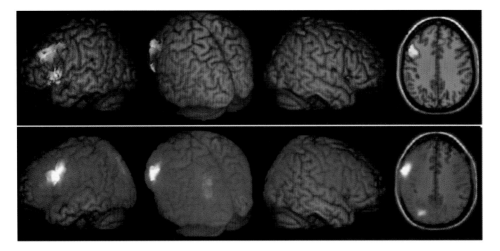

Plate 16
Comparison of the group BOLD response (top row) and the SAM-MEG analysis
(bottom row) of task-related beta (15–25Hz) ERD, for a letter fluency language
task ($n = 6$).

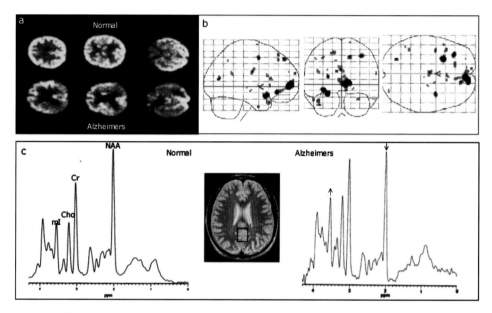

Plate 17

PET, fMRI, and MRS in cognitive chemistry. (*a*) Use of FDG-PET to show glucose metabolism in the healthy population (top) and patients with Alzheimer's disease (bottom) to reflect reduced regional energy demand (modified from Jagust, 2004). (*b*) Use of fMRI to show regions of increased blood supply during the Stroop task, under conditions of serotonin depletion in the brain (modified from Horacek et al., 2005). (*c*) Use of MRS to determine the difference in grey matter spectrum metabolite ratio in Alzheimer's disease (*right*) compared to normal (*left*), showing reduced NAA and increase mI. The center brain image shows a typical voxel for gray matter (red) and white matter (green) acquisition (adapted from Danielsen and Ross, 1999).

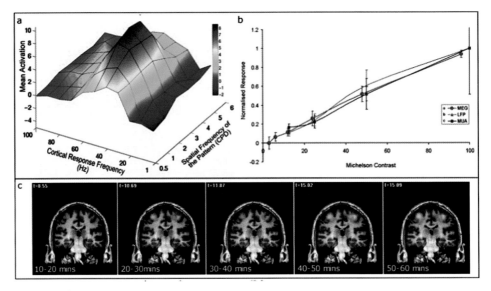

Plate 18
Visual gamma and pharmaco-MEG. Modulation of gamma oscillatory activity
in the human visual cortex in response to visual stimulation, showing that peak
oscillatory power is observed at 3cpd (*a*) and 100 percent contrast (*b*) (Adjamian et
al., 2004b, and Hall et al., 2005). Use of the pharmaco-MEG (*c*) to observe changes
in beta (15–25Hz) activity in the motor cortex over a 60-minute period following
administration of diazepam.

and respiratory effects producing nonrepeatable image artifacts. Collecting an entire image in 30 msec with EPI, however, "freezes" these physiological processes, causing artifacts to be more or less precisely replicated from image to image over time (with some exceptions)—thus substantially increasing temporal stability. It should be noted that, although some early studies adopted artifact correction strategies that used non-EPI techniques, using EPI and, more generally, "single-shot" techniques using one RF pulse per image is the most common and successful strategy. Hardware for performing EPI was not available on clinical systems until about 1996. Before that time, centers that performed EPI made use of low-inductance gradient coils built in-house or, if they were fortunate enough collaborated with small companies whose systems, also built in-house, allowed rapid gradient switching. Hardware availability remains an issue to this day. The most innovative technology for performing fMRI is at least several years ahead of what is available on clinical scanners. Because functional MRI remains a nonclinical technique, vendors simply choose to apply their research and development efforts elsewhere. This is certain to change when fMRI's clinical utility becomes more apparent.

Figure 9.1 shows the results of a science citation index reference search on fMRI-related papers published since 1992. The number of papers published appears to grow exponentially until 2001, before dropping into a steep, but arching second phase of growth from 2002 on. Papers published before 1996 were typically performed on systems developed in-house. After 1996, the number of groups performing fMRI expanded rapidly. To add a dimension of perspective to this plot, table 9.1 shows a list of the fifty most

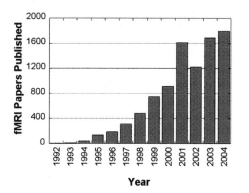

Figure 9.1
Bar graph of the approximate number of fMRI papers published, as determined by a Medline search for the keywords "fMRI" or "functional MRI" after 1993.

Table 9.1
Fifty most frequently cited papers on functional MRI (as of December 2004)

Rank	Citations per Year	Total Citations	Authors	Type
1	114	1485	Kwong et al., 1992	M
2	112	448	Logothetis et al., 2001	I
3	101	507	Cabeza and Nyberg, 2000	A
4	84	1095	Ogawa et al., 1992	M
5	82	655	Kanwisher et al., 1997	A
6	71	857	Bandettini et al., 1993	M
7	67	336	Bush et al., 2000	A
8	60	419	Carter et al., 1998	A
9	58	231	Egan et al., 2001	A
10	57	458	Cohen et al., 1997	M/A
11	57	509	Cox, 1996	M
12	55	497	Martin et al., 1996	A
13	53	745	Belliveau et al., 1991	M
14	53	691	Bandettini et al., 1992	M
15	52	523	Sereno et al., 1995	M/A
16	50	348	Wagner et al., 1998	A
17	50	348	Whalen et al., 1998	A
18	48	428	Worsley et al., 1996	M
19	47	233	Corbetta et al., 2000	A
20	44	174	O'Doherty et al., 2001	A
21	44	87	Egan et al., 2003	A
22	43	173	Fletcher and Henson, 2001	A
23	43	427	Tootell et al., 1995	M/A
24	42	419	Shaywitz et al., 1995	A
25	42	418	Worsley and Friston, 1995	M
26	41	446	Pellerin and Magistretti, 1994	I
27	40	359	Breiter et al., 1996	A
28	40	319	Binder et al., 1997	A
29	40	317	Braver et al., 1997	M/A
30	39	393	D'Esposito et al., 1995	A
31	39	391	Friston et al., 1995	M
32	39	348	Boynton et al., 1996	I
33	39	348	Malonek and Grinvald, 1996	I/A
34	38	384	Karni et al., 1995	A
35	38	114	Corbetta and Shulman, 2002	A
36	38	455	Ogawa et al., 1993	I
37	38	303	Courtney et al., 1997	M/A
38	37	185	Haxby et al., 2000	A

Table 9.1
(continued)

Rank	Citations per Year	Total Citations	Authors	Type
39	37	443	Rao et al., 1993	A
40	37	368	Buckner et al., 1995	A
41	37	365	Forman et al., 1995	M
42	36	181	Hopfinger et al., 2000	A
43	36	253	Kelley et al., 1998	A
44	36	249	Corbetta et al., 1998	A
45	35	317	Courtney et al., 1996	A
46	34	344	Demb et al., 1995	A
47	34	271	Dale and Buckner, 1997	M
48	34	203	Friston et al., 1999	M
49	33	200	Botvinick et al., 1999	A
50	33	231	Courtney et al., 1998	A

Based on science citation search of "fMRI" or "functional MRI." "A" papers focus on application of FMRI toward a specific neuroscience or clinical question; "M," papers on methods development; and "I" papers, on the relationship between neuronal activity and fMRI signal changes; some papers are combinations of these types. See reference list for full publication information.

frequently cited fMRI papers since 1991. It is worth noting that many of the studies labeled "M/A," indicating that they specifically employed fMRI to derive a novel insight into brain organization, were carried out by neuroscientists who have worked closely with individuals in methodology development. This serves to highlight the multidisciplinary nature of fMRI and the fact that many cutting-edge applications are still closely tied to advances in methodology. It is also worth noting, however, that, since the title search keywords were simply "fMRI" or "functional MRI," many relevant papers were likely missed.

After about 1996, with the rapid proliferation of EPI-capable MRI scanners incorporating whole-body gradients, functional magnetic resonance imaging arrived at the operating platform that is still "standard" today—sequence: gradient-echo EPI; echo time (TE): 40 msec; matrix size: 64 × 64; field of view: 24 cm; slice thickness: 4 mm. Typically, whole-brain volume coverage is achieved using a repetition time (TR) of 2 seconds, with time series lasting on the order of 5 to 8 minutes and with about 7 time series collected per subject-scanning session. Multisubject studies usually settle on assessing about 12 such sessions. And typically, a whole-brain, single quadrature RF coil is used; around 2002, the "standard" field strength was increased from 1.5 T to 3 T.

Beyond basic collection, standards begin to diverge; paradigm design and postprocessing are still evolving steadily. Nevertheless, "typical" paradigm design methods are either "boxcar," involving steady-state activation periods of 10 seconds or more, or more commonly, "event-related" designs, enjoying the flexibility inherent to brief activation periods interspersed within a given time series. For processing, SPM is the most common software, followed closely by software platforms such as Brain Voyager, FSL, and AFNI. The most common techniques use "reference" functions for statistical map creation; when multisubject data are involved, statistical maps are spatially smoothed and transformed to a standardized space for comparison or averaging. Recent technological advances have made possible the unprecedented visualization and navigation of fMRI data (see figure 9.2, plate 3).

Figure 9.2
Example of how the same fMRI data in their various forms can be simultaneously and interactively visualized. Data are from a retinotopy experiment (expanding ring); processing and visualization were performed using AFNI and SUMA (Cox, 1996) and surface models created with FreeSurfer (Dale, Fischl, and Sereno, 1999). Central panel shows AFNI's main controller window used to select and control data to be visualized. (A) Echo planar imaging (EPI) time series from voxels in the occipital cortex during cyclic visual stimulation. Of the 9 voxels shown here, some show clear modulation at the main frequency of the stimulus; others do not. (B) Statistical maps in color overlaid atop high-resolution anatomical data. The colored voxels represent response delay of significantly activated voxels and the cross hair represents the location of the central voxel in (A). Contours of pial and white matter/gray matter boundary surface models are shown in blue and red lines. (C) Three-dimensional volume rendering of the data shown in panel B with cutouts revealing the calcarine sulcus. (D) Functional imaging data projected on models of the same cortical surface with varying degrees of deformation. From left to right we have the white matter/gray matter boundary surface, an inflated version that reveals buried portions of sulci, a spherical version that can be warped into a standard coordinate space for surface-based group analysis (Fischl et al., 1999; Van Essen and Drury, 1997; Saad et al., 2004) and a flattened version of the occipital cortex with the data represented in color and relief form. Note that all panels were created simultaneously and interactively. For example, a change of statistical threshold in the main AFNI controller, will affect all displays in panels (B) through (D). A selection of a new location on the flat map in (D) will cause all other viewers to jump to the corresponding new location. (Figure and caption provided courtesy of Ziad Saad, Ph.D., Statistical and Scientific Computing Core Facility, National Institute of Mental Health) See plate 3 for color version.

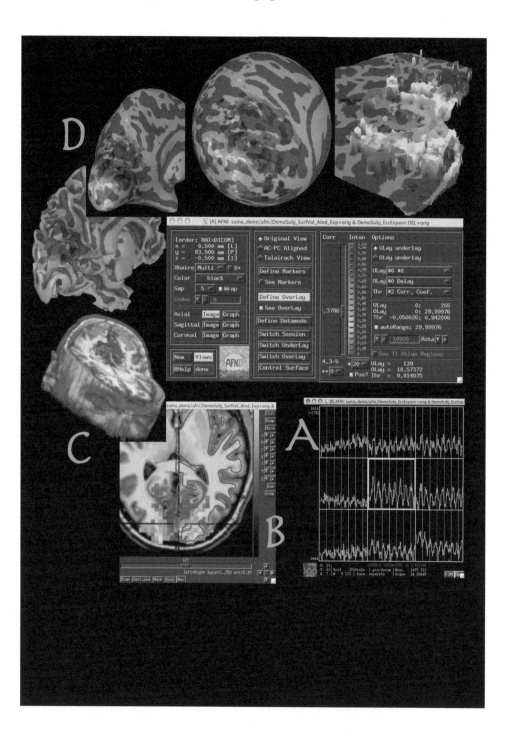

Overall, the evolution of fMRI has been punctuated by novel techniques, findings, and controversies. For a sense of perspective, here are just eleven of the more prominent developments in fMRI before 2003:

- Parametric manipulation of brain activation demonstrates that BOLD contrast roughly follows the level of brain activation in the visual system (Kwong et al., 1992), the auditory system (Binder et al., 1994), and the motor system (Rao et al., 1996).
- Event-related fMRI is first demonstrated (Blamire et al., 1992), then applied to cognitive activation (Buckner et al., 1996; McCarthy et al., 1997). Mixed event-related and block designs are developed (Visscher et al., 2003); paradigms are demonstrated in which the activation timing of multiple brain systems timing was orthogonal, allowing multiple conditions to be cleanly extracted from a single run (Courtney et al., 1997).
- High-resolution maps are created for spatial resolution in ocular dominance columns (Menon et al., 1997; Cheng, Waggoner, and Tanaka, 2001); activation maps are created for cortical layers (Logothetis et al., 2002). Extraction of information at high spatial frequencies within regions of activation is demonstrated (Haxby et al., 2001); timings from one to hundreds of milliseconds are extracted for temporal resolution (Ogawa et al., 2000; Menon, Luknowsky, and Gati, 1998; Henson et al., 2002; Bellgowan, Saad, and Bandettini, 2003).
- "Deconvolution" methods are developed for rapid presentation of stimuli (Dale and Buckner, 1997).
- Early BOLD contrast models (Ogawa et al., 1993; Buxton and Frank, 1997), are followed by more sophisticated models that more fully integrate the latest data on hemodynamic and metabolic changes (Buxton et al., 2004).
- Continuous variation of visual stimuli parameters as a function of time is proven to be a powerful method for fMRI-based retinotopy (Engel et al., 1994; DeYoe et al., 1994; Sereno et al., 1995).
- "Clustered-volume" acquisition is developed to avoid scanner noise artifacts (Edmister et al., 1999).
- Functionally related resting states are correlated (Biswal et al., 1995) and regions consistently showing deactivation described (Binder et al., 1999; Raichle et al., 2001).
- The "pre-undershoot" in fMRI is observed (Hennig et al., 1997; Menon, Ogawa, and Ugurbil, 1995; Hu, Le, and Ugurbil, 1997) and correlated with optical imaging (Malonek and Grinvald, 1996).
- Simultaneous use of fMRI and direct electrophysiological recording in nonhuman primate brain during visual stimulation elucidates the rela-

tionship between fMRI and BOLD fMRI contrast (Logothetis et al., 2001). Simultaneous electrophysiological recordings in animal models reveal a correlation between negative signal changes and decreased neuronal activity (Shmuel et al., 2002). Simultaneous electrophysiological recordings in animal models provide evidence that inhibitory input can cause an increase in cerebral blood flow (Mathiesen et al., 1998).

•   Structural equation modeling is developed for fMRI time series analysis (Buchel and Friston, 1998).

This list is only a sampling of the tremendous number of novel developments that have established fMRI as a powerful tool for investigating and quantitating human brain activity.

Principles

With functional magnetic resonance imaging, neuroimagers are able to map the following types of physiological information: baseline cerebral blood volume (Rosen et al., 1991), changes in cerebral blood volume (Belliveau et al., 1991; Lu et al., 2003), quantitative measures of baseline and changes in cerebral perfusion (Wong et al., 1999), changes in cerebral blood oxygenation (Bandettini et al., 1992; Blamire et al., 1992; Frahm et al., 1992; Kwong et al., 1992, Ogawa et al., 1992), the resting-state cerebral oxygen extraction fraction (An et al., 2001), and changes in the cerebral metabolic rate for oxygen ($CMRO_2$) (Davis et al., 1998; Hoge et al., 1999).

BOLD Contrast

Let us consider first the basic mechanism for BOLD fMRI signal changes with brain activation. In brain tissue during resting state, blood oxygenation in capillaries and veins is lower than that of arteries due to the extraction of oxygen from the blood. Deoxyhemoglobin (deoxy-Hb) has a different susceptibility from surrounding brain tissue and water, whereas oxyhemoglobin (oxy-Hb) has the same susceptibility. An object, a deoxy-Hb molecule, say, or a capillary or vein containing deoxy-Hb molecules, that has a different susceptibility from its surrounding tissue creates a magnetic field distortion when placed in a magnetic field. Water molecules (the primary signal source in MRI), also called "spins," precess at a frequency that is directly proportional to the magnetic field they are experiencing. Within a voxel, if spins are precessing at different frequencies, they rapidly become out of phase. The strength of the MRI signal is directly proportional to the coherence of spins: when they are completely out of phase, destructive addition takes place and there is no signal; when they are completely in phase, there is maximal signal. During resting state, enough spins are out of phase, due to the many microscopic field distortions in each voxel, to cause the MRI signal to be attenuated somewhat relative to when there is no deoxy-Hb present.

By contrast, and for reasons not fully understood, during activation, cerebral blood flow increases locally such that there is an overabundance of oxygenated blood delivered to the active regions. This causes the amount of deoxy-Hb, and thus also the magnitude of the magnetic field distortions, to decrease, which increases the coherence of spins within each voxel and leads to an MRI signal increase of a few percent.

The signal begins to increase approximately 2 seconds after neuronal activity begins, and plateaus in the "on" state after about 7 to 10 seconds. Although a "pre-undershoot" is sometimes observed, a "post-undershoot" is more commonly observed. These effects are likely due to transient mismatches between either cerebral blood volume or the cerebral metabolic rate for oxygen ($CMRO_2$) before and after respective increases and decreases in blood flow occur. The dynamics, location, and magnitude of the MRI signal are highly influenced by the vasculature in each voxel. If voxels happen to capture large vessel effects, the magnitude of the signal may be large (up to an order of magnitude greater than that for capillary effects), the timing somewhat more delayed than average (up to 4 seconds more delayed than for capillary effects), and the location of the signal somewhat distal (up to a centimeter) from the true region of activation. Although improvements in methodology have minimized the effects of this variability, the problem of variable vasculature and hemodynamic coupling nevertheless remains at all field strengths in fMRI, limiting the depth and range of questions that can be addressed using this technique.

Perfusion Contrast

Introduced at almost the same time as BOLD functional MRI was the noninvasive method for mapping perfusion in the human brain known as "arterial spin labeling" (ASL). The technique generally involves applying a radio frequency pulse (or continuous RF excitation) below the imaging plane (in the neck area). Without blood flow, the magnetization applied to brain tissue would simply decay and not influence the MRI signal where the images were being collected. With blood flow, however, the altered magnetization of the "labeled" blood affects the longitudinal magnetization (T1) in the imaging slices as it flows, and as water spins mix and exchange magnetization, in the imaged brain tissue. A second set of images is obtained either with the label applied above the brain or not applied at all. Therefore these second images are not affected in the same manner by magnetization of inflowing spins. The last step is to perform pairwise subtraction on the two sets of images, removing all the anatomical signal from each image pair, leaving behind only the effect on the signal by the label. Because of the low signal to noise inherent to this type of contrast, an average of typically several hundred "label-minus-no-label" pairs are obtained to create a map of baseline perfusion.

A strong determinant of perfusion contrast with the ASL technique is the time between the labeling pulse and the subsequent image collection, designated as "TI." If the TI is 200 msec, only the effects of the most rapidly flowing blood can be observed (typically, in arteries). As the TI approaches 1 second, slower perfusing spins in and around capillaries appear. Above 1 second, the magnetization of the label decays significantly. A time series of these "label-minus-no-label" pairs can be collected for the purpose of functional imaging of brain activation. Arterial spin labeling has not achieved the success of BOLD functional MRI mostly because of limitations in the number of slices obtainable, temporal resolution, and decreased functional contrast to noise of the technique relative to BOLD fMRI. Nevertheless, the superior functional specificity and stability of arterial spin labeling over long periods of time, along with its quantitative information, have made it useful for many applications where BOLD fMRI falls short.

Sensitivity

A primary struggle in fMRI is to increase sensitivity. This is achieved by increasing the magnitude of the signal change or by decreasing the effects of noise. This struggle has also been the impetus for imaging at ever higher field strengths. With an increase in field strength, signal to noise increases proportionally and both BOLD and perfusion contrast increase—BOLD contrast increasing with greater changes in transverse relaxation relative to activation, and perfusion contrast increasing with increases in the T1 of blood, which allows the magnetization of the labeled blood to remain longer. Aside from system instabilities, however, higher field strengths result in generally poorer images at the base of the brain due to greater effects of poor shimming and to greater physiological fluctuations. Methods for removing these fluctuations remain imperfect. That said, a primary advantage of imaging at higher field strengths (e.g., 7 T) is that the lower limit of signal to noise is achieved with a much smaller voxel volume, thus allowing much higher imaging resolution (down to $1\,mm^3$) at functional contrast levels comparable to those of imaging at 3 T with voxel volumes of $3\,mm^3$. This increase in resolution without prohibitive losses in sensitivity may explain why imaging of ocular dominance column activation has been successful at 4 T but not at lower field strengths. Currently, successful results in imaging humans have been obtained at 7 T (Vaughan et al., 2001; Pfeuffer et al., 2002b; Yacoub et al., 2001); such results are certain to multiply rapidly.

Other processing steps for increasing sensitivity include temporal and spatial smoothing. Because of the inherent temporal autocorrelation in the signal from hemodynamics or other physiological processes, temporal smoothing is performed so that the temporal degrees of freedom may be accurately assessed. Spatial smoothing can be performed if high spatial frequency information is not desired and as a necessary prespatial normalization step (matching effective resolution with the degree of variability associated with spatial normalization techniques) for multisubject averaging and comparison. An often overlooked fact is that higher temporal sensitivity with less image warping due to a shorter readout window is achieved, not by spatially smoothing the maps after data collection, but by collecting the images at the desired spatial resolution in the first place. Indeed, in many instances, spatial smoothing is clearly *not* desired—particularly when high spatial frequency information in individual maps is compared (Haxby et al., 2001).

Once images are collected, and after motion correction is performed, a time series analysis is carried out voxel by voxel. Typically, a model function or functions are used as regressors, and the significance of the correlation of the time series data with the regressors calculated, again voxel by voxel. If the expected activation timing is not known, a more open-ended approach to analysis is taken, such as independent component analysis (Beckmann and Smith, 2004).

Innovation

The quantity and impact of innovations, and the proportion of truly high quality work, in functional magnetic resonance imaging have continued to grow as the field has matured, making it nearly impossible to stay abreast of the latest and the most interesting advances. Whereas the "Development" section touched on major, "established" innovations of the past 14 years, to give a sense of the vibrancy of the fMRI field, and of its potential for expanding in ever new, exciting directions, this section will highlight emerging innovations that may or may not pan out and make a major impact.

Imaging Technology

Recent innovations in acquisition hardware and imaging strategy may take functional magnetic resonance imaging to new levels of sensitivity, resolution, and speed. Typical acquisition hardware uses a single-quadrature, whole-brain RF coil feeding into one acquisition channel, and collects single-shot echo planar imaging data at 64×64 resolution. Recently, the ability to acquire MRI data with simultaneous multiple high-bandwidth channels (Bodurka et al., 2004), feeding in from multiple RF coils, has resulted, above all, in a dramatic increase in the image signal-to-noise ratio. Figure 9.3 illustrates the gains in sensitivity with multiple RF coils. Sensitivity is approximately proportional to the size of the RF coil used. In the past, some neuroimaging researchers chose to sacrifice brain coverage for sensitivity by using a single, large, "surface" RF coil for acquisition. Today, the use of multiple, small RF coils allows full brain coverage, at significantly higher sensitivity than one large RF coil. Recently, the Massachusetts Hospital Group constructed a brain-imaging device with 32 RF coils, leading to as much as a sixfold increase in signal to noise for an individual image, although, after taking into consideration unfilterable physiological noise, the gains are likely to be only about threefold. What the optimal number of coils might be with regard to increases in sensitivity remains uncertain.

Multichannel acquisition can also be conjoined with a novel image acquisition/reconstruction strategy that uses the spatially distinct sensitive region of each RF coil to help spatially encode the data—with only a small cost in signal to noise. This strategy is known as "SENSE [SENSitivity Encoding] imaging" (de Zwart et al., 2002). When coil placement is used to aid in spatial encoding, less time is needed to create an image of a given resolution. This advantage can be used in either of two ways: (1) the readout window width can be held the same, but the image resolution increased substantially; or (2) the image resolution can be held the same, but the width of the readout window decreased substantially. This reduction in readout window width allows a small increase in the number of EPI slices to be collected in a given repetition time (TR), therefore allowing a reduction in TR for a given number of slices, more slices for a given TR (allowing thinner slices perhaps), or an increase in brain coverage for a given TR (if a shorter TR had previously

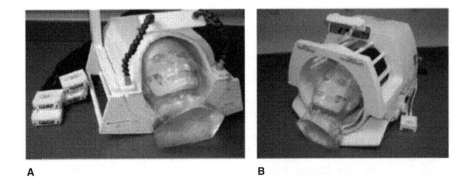

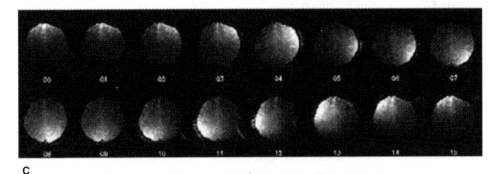

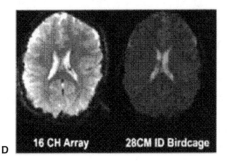

Figure 9.3

Comparison of image signal intensity of MR images created with single- and multichannel systems. (*A*) sixteen-channel coil system (NOVA Medical RF coil combined with NIH in-house parallel acquisition system. (*B*) Single-channel GE Medical Systems quadrature RF coil. (*C*) Display of distinct region of sensitivity for each of the 16 small RF coils within the NOVA Medical RF coil. (*D*) Image on the left was created by addition after reconstruction of the 16 individual images in panel C; image on the right was created from the GE Medical Systems quadrature RF coil. The two images being compared have been normalized such that the noise levels match. The signal intensity therefore gives a relative measure of signal to noise. (Figure provided courtesy of Jerzy Bodurka, Ph.D., Functional MRI Core Facility. The NOVA Medical 16 channel coil was designed by Jeff Duyn, Ph.D., Section on Advanced MRI, NINDS) limited brain coverage). Incorporating this imaging strategy at field strengths above 3 T may allow robust single-shot echo planar imaging with a $1 mm^3$ matrix size and a high-enough signal to noise for fMRI.

Free Behavior and Natural Stimuli Paradigms

A second innovation direction for fMRI lies in the domain of paradigm design. An ongoing challenge in fMRI is to have subjects perform tasks in a predictable and repeatable manner. This is not only impossible in many instances but limits the type of questions that can be addressed using fMRI. One common solution to this problem (described in the "Integration" section) is to keep track of the responses of subjects to specific tasks, then perform post hoc data averaging based on the responses. A potentially powerful extension of this idea is to collect a continuous measure of the subjects' free behavior. In this manner, a natural parametric variation in the response parameters can be used to guide data analysis. Any continuous measure will suffice. Subjects need simply to move a joystick or to track ball or to have their eye position or skin conductance monitored. They can be following an object, for example, or determining certainty, expectation, anxiety, or subjective perception of motion. The data collected can then be analyzed by calculating the moment-to-moment measurement and using it as a regressor in the analysis.

Related to paradigms that measure subjects' free behavior are those which measure their response to natural stimuli, as when viewing a movie, for example. Regressors can be calculated from various salient aspects of the movie presentation such as color, motion, volume, speech, or even the interaction of continuously measured eye position with these variables. A recently published study on movie viewing (Hasson et al., 2004) employed a highly novel processing technique, tailored to a specific paradigm. This technique was based on the understanding that, because the movie had many, unpredictable variables, it would be difficult to generate a set of reference functions for determining the similarly activated regions across subjects. What was done instead was to play precisely the same movie sequence at least twice for each subject and across all subjects. The assumption was that a distinct, repeatable temporal pattern would be manifest. Rather than attempting to choose an appropriate ideal reference function and comparing subsequent activation maps, Hasson and colleagues determined the correlation in the time series fMRI across subjects. Because this technique makes no assumption about what the data should look like— only that they show a repeatable change—it can be effectively applied for the same subject across identical time series collections (see Levin and Uftring, 2001).

Real-Time fMRI Incorporating Feedback to the Subject

A technical challenge in fMRI is to perform basic analysis on data as they are being collected (Cox, Jesmanowicz, and Hyde, 1995). This approach is important for several reasons. A primary reason is to ensure data quality during the scan, an essential requirement if fMRI is to be incorporated into daily clinical practice. A secondary reason, and one just beginning to be explored, is to allow the person scanning or the subject being scanned to guide experimental process in real time. In this regard, some truly unique twists have recently been reported. Weiskopf et al. (2003) have determined that, when a measure of brain activation in specific regions activated by a cognitive (but not sensorimotor) task is fed back to subjects being imaged, they can learn, subjectively, to either increase or decrease the level of activation. This finding offers the fascinating possibility of humans interacting directly with and through computers through simple thought process regulation. Weiskopf's research group has trained subjects to play "pong" using mental control of a "paddle" in which the vertical location was simply proportional to the degree of activation in the controllable brain regions being activated. With two scanners collecting data simultaneously, subjects are able to successfully play "brain pong" using subjective control of their fMRI signal changes.

In a second study of this type of subjective control, DeCharms et al. (2004) instructed patients experiencing chronic pain to reduce the fMRI signal intensity in regions that had been associated with pain perception in a previous experiment. As in the "brain pong" experiment, the subjects were provided with feedback regarding the level of fMRI signal in these regions and were instructed to use whatever strategy they could come up with to decrease the signal. Not only did the experiment result in a subjective decrease in pain perception for most subjects, but this effect also appeared to last months after the experiment was carried out.

Direct Neuronal Current Imaging

A hope among brain imagers is for a technique that would allow direct mapping of brain activity with spatial resolution on the order of a cortical column *and* temporal resolution on the order of an action potential, or at least of a postsynaptic potential. Recent work has established that, in ideal conditions, the minimal magnetic field change detectable with MRI is on the order of 1 ten billionth of a tesla (0.1 nT; Bodurka and Bandettini, 2002). Approximate calculations based on magnetoencephalography (MEG) measurements of 100 quadrillionths of a tesla (100 fT) at the surface of the skull estimate the magnetic field surrounding a dipole is also on the order of 0.1 nT. An increase in neuronal activity should be manifest as a highly localized, extremely transient magnitude decrease or phase shift in the MRI signal (Bandettini, Petridou, and Bodurka, forthcoming). Experimental groups attempting to detect this effect in humans have obtained mixed results, although some have claimed success (Konn et al., 2004; Xiang et al., 2003). Even if detecting the effect proves feasible, however, the utility of doing so will likely be limited, at least initially, by the extremely small size of the effect and the relatively small range of experiments possible using it due to the necessity for specific time-locked averaging. Nevertheless, because research efforts toward this goal have only begun, it is difficult to predict the ultimate success of this novel contrast approach.

Limitations

How accurately functional magnetic resonance imaging can assess brain activation is fundamentally limited by two major factors: (1) the method by which images are collected; and (2) the relationship between neuronal activity and hemodynamic changes.

Temporal Resolution

Echo planar images typically have an acquisition time of 30 msec. Assuming an echo time of 40 msec (the center of the readout window), data acquisition typically ends after 55 msec. About 15 msec is usually required to apply fat saturation at the beginning of the sequence and to apply gradients at the end to eliminate residual magnetization. Allowing for about 15 images to be collected in a second, the total time per plane for single-shot EPI time series collection is about 65 msec. For volume collection, which typically consists of 30 slices, a repetition time of 2 seconds is therefore required. It is also possible to collect one image (as opposed to multiple images) in a volume at a rate of 15 images per second over time.

As described, the hemodynamic response behaves like a low-pass filter for neuronal activity. At on/off frequencies of 6 sec on / 6 sec off (0.08 Hz), BOLD responses begin to be attenuated relative to longer on/off times. At on/off frequencies of 2 sec on/2 sec off (0.25 Hz), the BOLD response is almost completely attenuated. Even though BOLD attenuates these rapid on/off responses, activity of extremely brief duration can be observed. Activity durations as brief as 16 msec have been shown to cause robust BOLD signal changes, indicating that there is no apparent limit to the brief-ness of detectible activation. It is also heartening that, when repeated experiments are performed, the hemodynamic response in each voxel only shows a variability on the order of 100 msec.

Functional brain imagers wish not only to spatially resolve activated regions but also to determine the precise timing of activation in these regions relative both to the stimulus or input and to each other. The temporal resolution required for this type of assessment is on the order of at least tens of milliseconds. But, with BOLD contrast, the latency of the hemodynamic response has a range of 4 seconds due primarily to unchar-acterized spatial variations in the underlying hemodynamics or neurovas-cular coupling from voxel to voxel, even within the same region of activity. If a voxel captures mostly larger venous vessels, the response is typically more delayed than if the voxel captures mostly capillaries, although the precise reasons for latency variations are as yet undetermined.

Of the methods proposed to solve the latency problem, the most direct (whose accuracy also remains undetermined, however) is to try to identify larger vessels by thresholding based on percent signal change or temporal fluctuation characteristics. Another solution is to use pulse sequences sensitive only to capillary effects. Arterial spin labeling techniques are more sensitive to capillaries, but the practical limitations of lower functional contrast to noise and longer interimage waiting time (due to the additionally required TI of about 1.5 sec) make this unworkable for most studies. Spin-echo sequences performed at very high field strengths or with velocity-nulling gradients (both of which eliminate intravascular large vessel effects) are also sensitive to capillary effects. On the other hand, since the reduction in functional contrast to noise is about a factor of 2 with spin-echo, and an additional factor of 3 with velocity-nulling gradients to remove intravascular signal, the contrast is likely too low to be useful.

An alternate strategy is to focus on localized *changes* in latency and width associated with task timing changes. As mentioned, within a voxel, the hemodynamic response varies on the order of 100 msec allowing sig-nificantly more accurate assessment when activation timing varies within a region. When neuroimagers use a task modulation that causes a difference in reaction time, and one region of the brain shows an increased width and another shows an increased delay, then it follows that the region showing the width change is spending additional time to process information and the region showing the increased delay is downstream from the region showing the width change, having to wait until processing is complete in that node in order to receive any information. Although oversimplified, this scenario shows how temporal information may be extracted in fMRI. The key is task timing modulation and observation of hemodynamic changes, voxel by voxel.

Figure 9.4 (adapted from Bellgowan, Saad, and Bandettini, 2003) illustrates the point made above. Subjects performed a word recognition task in which the stimuli included both words and nonwords presented at varying rotation angles. Bellgowan, Saad, and Bandettini observed that subjects took longer to recognize nonwords than words, and longer to identify a word when it was rotated. The hypothesis is that the region performing word rotation and the region performing word recognition are likely to be spatially distinct. Figure 9.4 shows average time courses from the left anterior prefrontal cortex—typically associated with word generation. It appears that the hemodynamic response during word processing is about 500 msec wider than that during nonword processing, which suggests that activity in this region is of longer duration during the nonword recognition process.

Spatial Resolution

The upper in-plane resolution of standard single-shot echo planar imaging is about $2 \, mm^2$. The use of multishot EPI (at a cost in time and stability) or of strategies incorporating multiple radiofrequency coils to aid in spatial encoding of data can achieve functional image resolutions of about $1 \, mm^3$.

As with temporal resolution limits, spatial resolution limits are chiefly determined by the spatial spread of oxygenation and perfusion changes that accompany focal brain activation, not by limits in acquisition. Although the "hemodynamic point-spread function" has been empirically determined to be on the order of $3 \, mm^3$ (Engel, Glover, and Wandell, 1997), the effects of draining veins have been observed to be as distal as 1 cm from focal regions of activation identified using perfusion contrast.

The pulse-sequence solutions for dealing with the variations in hemodynamics have proved as effective as those for dealing with temporal resolution limits. Moreover, working with hypercapnia comparisons, Bandettini and Wong (1997) and Cohen et al. (2004) have proposed spatial calibration methods. Using BOLD fMRI methods based on cerebral perfusion and blood volume, other brain imagers have delineated ocular dominance

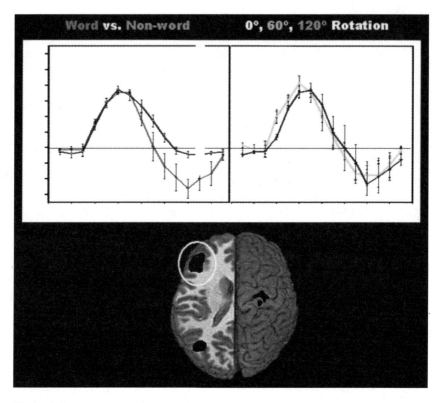

Figure 9.4
Averaged time courses from the left anterior prefrontal cortex during a word recognition task in which the words were presented at varying rotation angles. When word and nonword processing are compared, the width of the hemodynamic response is wider by about 500 msec, suggesting that there is longer duration of activity in this region during the nonword recognition process. When angles of rotation are compared, the onset of activation in this region appears delayed as a function of angle of rotation, suggesting that this region is downstream from the region associated with word rotation. (Adapted from Bellgowan, Saad, and Bandettini, 2003)

columns (1 mm³; Cheng, Waggoner, and Tanaka, 2001; Goodyear and Menon, 2001) and cortical layers (< 0.5 mm³; Logothetis et al., 2002), although, with BOLD contrast (thought to have the lowest resolution), columnar and layer specificity was achieved only by subtracting activation from tasks activating interspersed yet distinct regions (i.e., columns or layers). An ongoing issue with regard to the upper resolution of fMRI is whether or not *fine* delineation necessarily translates to *accurate* delineation—meaning that detailed activation maps may not precisely register underlying function.

Interpretation

Considerable effort has been directed toward understanding the precise relationship between fMRI signal changes and neuronal activity. Strategies for overcoming limits to interpretation of the data gathered have included

•   animal models and the simultaneous use of other measures of neuronal activity such as multiunit electrodes or more precise measures of hemodynamic changes, such as optical imaging;
•   parametric modulation of magnitude or timing of activation in humans with corresponding measurement of fMRI signal changes;
•   simultaneous measures of neuronal activity (implanted electrode or EEG) and fMRI signal changes;
•   nonsimultaneous MEG or EEG measures of neuronal activity and fMRI signal changes; and
•   modeling the hemodynamic response and comparing model outputs to precise activation magnitude, timing, or pharmacological manipulations of brain tissue.

In summary, even though fMRI is limited to a lesser degree by scanner technology and to a greater degree by the unknowns regarding the spatial, temporal, and magnitude relationships between neuronal activity and hemodynamic signal changes, steady progress is being made in overcoming these limitations. A primary avenue by which the limitations of functional magnetic resonance imaging can be overcome is integration with other brain activation assessment techniques.

Integration

Functional MRI data collection and even the experimental process itself can be greatly enhanced in precision, depth, impact, and certainty if researchers effectively incorporate other brain activation assessment techniques ranging from behavioral to other imaging approaches (Dale and Halgren, 2001).

Techniques that can be simultaneously carried out during time series collection of fMRI data include

- behavioral measures such as performance, reaction time, skin conductance, and eye position;
- electroencephalography (EEG);
- embedded electrodes or multielectrode arrays;
- near-infrared spectroscopy (NIRS) or optical imaging;
- transcranial magnetic stimulation (TMS); and
- physiological measures such as respiration, heart rate, end tidal carbon dioxide, and skin conductance.

Although simultaneity is desirable, complementary experimental measures can be effectively integrated without it. It is only necessary that they be precisely repeatable. Techniques in which the data are collected before or after fMRI experimentation include not only those listed above but also

- positron-emission tomography (PET) and
- magnetoencephalography (MEG).

Although this section describes the methodology and utility of only several of many ways that fMRI experimentation, analysis, and results can be integrated with other modalities, readers are encouraged to consult the relevant chapters in this volume for a more detailed discussion of the specific techniques.

Behavioral Measures

Depending on the hypothesis posed, substantial inferences about brain activity can be made from simple measures of response accuracy and response time, although, since the beginnings of functional MRI experimentation, behavioral response data have also been collected to ensure that the subjects are actually engaged in the experimental tasks assigned them. Subject interface devices such as button boxes or joysticks have been and typically still are used. With the onset of rapid event-related fMRI, however, the ability to selectively average data based on behavioral responses from moment to moment has further increased the range of experiments possible with fMRI.

Two studies, both of processes associated with memory but using different methodologies, serve to illustrate effective integration of behavioral measures with fMRI. In Wagner et al., 1998, subjects were presented with lists of words during the time series collection of fMRI data, which were selectively binned, based on whether the subjects recalled the words after the scanning process. Results revealed that the ability to later remember a verbal experience was predicted by the magnitude of activation in left prefrontal and temporal cortices during that experience.

In Pessoa et al., 2002, fMRI was used to investigate how moment-to-moment neural activity contributed to success or failure on individual trials of a visual working memory task. Different nodes of the network involved with working memory were found to be activated to a greater extent for correct than for incorrect trials during stimulus encoding, memory maintenance during delays, and at test. A logistic regression analysis revealed that the fMRI signal amplitude during the delay interval in a network of frontoparietal regions predicted successful performance trial by trial. Differential activity during the delay periods when working memory was active occurred even on trials when BOLD activity during encoding was strong, demonstrating that such differential activity was not a simple consequence of effective versus ineffective encoding. Study results further demonstrated that accurate memory depends on strong, sustained signals that span the delay interval of working memory tasks. These results could not have been achieved without precise measures of behavior either after the scanning process (testing for long-term memory) or during the scanning process (testing for working memory).

In general, some of the most insightful fMRI results have resulted from tight integration of moment-to-moment behavioral measures with time series collection, which allows researchers to selectively bin relevant fMRI data. Other behavioral measures have included reaction time, eye position, measures of decision processes, and continuous measures of performance or mental state such as those obtained by the use of a joystick or trackball.

Electroencephalography and Magnetoencephalography

The signals produced by EEG and MEG are more direct measures of neuronal activity than those produced with functional MRI, reflecting the electric potential (EEG) and the magnetic field (MEG) resulting from synaptic currents in neuronal dendrites. On the other hand, because of the inherently ill posed "inverse problem" regarding localization of the dipole sources contributing to the electrical potentials and magnetic fields on the surface of the skull, the resolution or, rather, the certainty of localization for both EEG and MEG is generally quite low. Integration of these two techniques and fMRI, however, allows neuroimagers to map brain activity at the higher spatial resolution of fMRI (effectively constraining the "inverse problem"), but also at the higher temporal resolution afforded by MEG and EEG. This will be discussed in greater detail when describing integration with MEG below (see also Singh, chapter 12, this volume). Also, simultaneous use of EEG with fMRI can enhance the ability of neuroimagers to map spontaneous and transient processes only detectible by EEG but mappable using hemodynamic responses that occur 3 to 10 seconds after a signature EEG response.

The complementary use of EEG and fMRI is a burgeoning field in itself: since 1997, over 200 papers have been published on this topic alone. A primary use of simultaneous EEG and fMRI data collection is for the accurate measurement of hemodynamic changes associated with spontaneously occurring and transient events measurable with EEG (see Lemieux, 2003). Another use of these simultaneous measures has been to compare the time-locked, averaged, evoked response characteristics with the hemodynamic response characteristics in order to better understand the neuronal correlates of fMRI. These experiments do not require simultaneous EEG and fMRI but the results derived with simultaneous acquisition are likely to be more accurate since no experiment is replicated perfectly inside and outside of the scanner.

A promising clinical application of simultaneous EEG and fMRI is the more accurate localization of epileptic foci. In specific clinical populations, these foci exhibit spontaneous, irregular EEG activity. The use of simultaneous EEG and fMRI allows neuroimagers to selectively average functional images based on when this signature activity occurs.

In another unique application, simultaneous EEG and fMRI can be used to determine the neuronal correlates of spontaneously changing brain activity associated with specific EEG frequencies. After simultaneously measuring EEG and fMRI, neuroimagers create the power spectrum of the EEG traces for each repetition time (TR) period. They then convolve the amplitude of the power spectrum at a specific frequency range (for example, alpha frequencies: 8–12 Hz, and beta frequencies: 17–23 Hz) at each TR with a hemodynamic response function, used as a regressor in fMRI time series analysis. Taking this approach, Goldman et al. (2001) and Laufs et al. (2003a, 2003b) have been able to accurately map regions that exhibit changes in the hemodynamic response that correlate with spontaneous changes in oscillatory activity.

Simultaneous use of EEG and fMRI data is challenging because the concomitant collection of echo planar imaging data creates a substantial artifact in the EEG trace whenever magnetic field gradients are applied. Several strategies have succeeded in filtering out this artifact however: simply discarding EEG points that occur during image collection; using hardware-based filters or more sophisticated postprocessing techniques; and using what is known as "spike-triggered fMRI scanning", in which unique EEG activity (i.e., spiking) triggers the scanner to collect images.

Efforts to integrate MEG and fMRI (see Dale and Halgren, 2001) have begun to increase as MEG systems become more available, and as the interpretive limits of using fMRI alone become more apparent. Because MEG and fMRI data cannot be collected simultaneously, however, the effectiveness of the integration depends on precise experimental replicability.

Another highly challenging but potentially promising procedure integrating MEG or EEG and fMRI uses fMRI activation maps to help determine dipole locations. The potential information gained by this procedure is significant: when dipole sources for a given cognitive process are precisely determined, the inverse problem can be replaced by a much more readily solvable forward problem. Starting with the dipole locations, the relative dynamics of measured fields at the surface of the skull can then be used to infer the dipole source timings with millisecond accuracy (Ahlfors et al., 1999).

While the promise of precisely determining dipole sources with fMRI data is exciting, many problems remain. First, if there exist mismatches between fMRI activation foci and the true dipole sources, substantial misestimates in timing will result. In this sense, the timing estimation is quite "brittle" in that any errors in dipole estimation render the results almost uninterpretable. Growing evidence exists that there are, in fact, substantial differences between fMRI activation maps and MEG visible dipole sources. With MEG, opposing dipoles may cancel each other, rendering their effects invisible to fMRI. With fMRI, false positives are ubiquitous in individual data, and, likewise, it is not certain whether all MEG-sensitive effects contribute to hemodynamic changes. Also, cognitive tasks typically involve highly distributed networks within and across distributed regions that generally defy simplification to a set of dipoles. Currently, effort is being made to estimate the certainty of the dipole sources, and thus to increase the flexibility and robustness of this approach.

A central issue in the integration of EEG or MEG and fMRI data and, more generally, in the interpretation of fMRI signal changes is that of clarifying the relationship between neuronal activity and fMRI signal changes.

To this end, substantial effort has been applied using other modalities to better understand fMRI contrast. Fruitful studies representing only a small fraction of this effort include those using MEG (Singh et al., 2002), EEG (Horovitz, Skudlarski, and Gore, 2002), optical imaging (Grinvald, Slovin, and Vanzetta, 2000; Villringer, 1997; Cannestra et al., 2001; Boas, Dale, and Franceschini, 2004), electrophysiological recording in humans (Huettel et al., 2004) and animal models (Logothetis et al., 2001; Duong et al., 2000; Devor et al., 2003) and microscopic oxygen probes in animal models (Thompson, Peterson, and Freeman, 2003, 2004).

Transcranial Magnetic Stimulation

In TMS, a highly localized, rapidly oscillating magnetic field is directed at specific circuits of the brain. This rapid oscillation induces neuronal activity, thereby disrupting normal function for what is thought to be a very brief period of time. The power of this technique is its ability to probe the necessity of specific nodes in a network as they relate to specific processes. Because a central problem in the interpretation of brain activation maps is that of determining causality, TMS is highly complementary to brain mapping techniques. Thus it is not apparent from such maps which nodes are activated as a result of actually performing the task and which are activated in order to perform the task. By allowing specific nodes of an activation network to be temporarily disabled, observation of behavior associated with the application of TMS can tease apart the causality of the network involved (Lomarev et al., 2000). The additional dimension of neuronal timing can also be explored by modulating the TMS application time relative to stimulus and response timing. Typically, the TMS timing is titrated to determine the interval that most effectively interferes with a specific behavioral process, thereby revealing neuronal communication rates.

Typically, with TMS and fMRI integration, a brain activation map is first produced and then used to guide TMS stimulation outside of the scanner. Some groups, however, by performing TMS *during* collection of fMRI time series data, have been able to probe the effects of TMS, in itself, on brain activation and thereby to assess functional connectivity against the assumption that if one node is activated, then the nodes it is functionally associated with will also be activated (Bohning et al., 2000a, 2000b). This application, one should note, is highly challenging and may be risky since the torque generated by interaction of the strong electrical currents of a TMS device (typically a figure-eight loop of wire) with the scanner magnetic field can be substantial, depending on the orientation (Bohning et al., 2003).

Because, relatively speaking, TMS devices are inexpensive, easy to operate, and noninvasive, and because the information this technique provides is highly complementary to the data provided by fMRI, TMS is growing rapidly in popularity.

Physiological Measures

A growing trend in fMRI data collection has been not only toward simultaneous recording of behavioral responses but also toward simultaneous collection of physiological measures such as heart and respiration waveforms, end tidal carbon dioxide, and skin conductance. The information gleaned from these measures ranges from assessment and reduction of artifactual influences on the BOLD response to assessment and use of measures of arousal and attention.

Respiration and cardiac pulsations are known to contribute to artifactual signal changes in fMRI, from changes in the magnetic field caused either by the chest cavity movement (respiration; Windischberger et al., 2002; Pfeuffer et al., 2002a) or by localized acceleration of blood, cerebral spinal fluid, and brain tissue (cardiac pulsations; Dagli, Ingeholm, and Haxby, 1999). By simply recording respiration with a chest bellows and cardiac pulsation with a pulse oximeter, neuroimagers can use these artifactual waveforms as "nuisance" regressors, thereby effectively increasing functional contrast to noise and reducing false positive results.

A challenge in removing cardiac effects is that the repetition time is typically too low to sample the cardiac waveform sufficiently. Methods have been proposed to work around this problem (Frank, Buxton, and Wong, 2001; Menon, 2002; Noll et al., 1998). For some fMRI studies, the movement artifacts caused by cardiac pulsations, particularly at the base of the brain, are prohibitive—particularly when attempting to image very small structures that may displace several voxels with each cardiac cycle. This problem has been effective solved by a novel method involving cardiac gating, which subsequently corrects T1-related fluctuations from irregular repetition time values (Guimaraes et al., 1998).

An ongoing study of spontaneous end tidal carbon dioxide fluctuations (Wise et al., 2004) has revealed useful information about the nature of BOLD time series fluctuations. Maps generated using spontaneous changes in end tidal carbon dioxide appear to delineate the spatial distribution of resting-state venous blood volume, indicating the potential for

BOLD signal changes at the voxel level. This study also gives strong evidence that simple changes in breathing rate and depth during an experiment can influence BOLD signal changes. The above three measures may prove to have a complementary impact on the expanding research into resting-state fluctuations to elucidate functionally correlated resting networks (see Lowe, Mock, and Sorenson, 1998; Gusnard et al., 2001; Biswal et al., 1995).

A fourth physiological measure, skin conductance, is a sensitive indicator of states such as arousal, attention, and anxiety. Skin conductance data have also been successfully collected at the same time as fMRI time series data (Critchley et al., 2000; Patterson, Ungerleider, and Bandettini, 2002, Williams et al., 2000; Shastri et al., 2001).This has been done to serve two distinct reseach ends: (1) to ensure that subjects are exhibiting the appropriate response to specific stimuli; and (2) to demonstrate the neuronal correlates of skin conductance in specific mental states or during resting state. Figure 9.5 shows time course plots from an experiment that involved conditioning subjects to expect a shock when they heard a tone presented during the conditioned-stimulus (CS) period (Knight, Nguyen, and Bandettini, 2005).

To serve the second research end, simultaneous measures of skin conductance are used is in much the same way as simultaneous EEG measures, only in this case, SCR time course data are correlated with fMRI time series data. Thus Patterson, Ungerleider, and Bandettini (2002) measured spontaneous skin conductance changes continuously during specific tasks and resting state. Using the spontaneous skin conductance measurement as a regressor, they identified a specific set of regions that showed activity that was correlated with skin conductance changes independent of the task being performed.

Conclusion

This chapter represents only a grainy snapshot of a rapidly changing scene. Its aim has been to give at least some sense of the history, development, limits, and more innovative ideas of functional MRI, and of the general excitement surrounding this rapidly advancing technique. Integration of fMRI with other techniques is steadily contributing to our understanding of how the human brain is organized, how it changes from moment to moment and year to year, and how it varies across clinically relevant populations. Although it is still too early to tell what the ultimate impact of fMRI will be have on the fields of neuroscience and medicine, one thing is

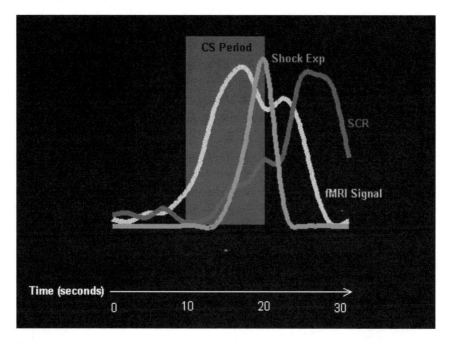

Figure 9.5
Time course plots from an experiment (Knight, Nguyen, and Bandettini, forthcoming) involved conditioning subjects to expect a shock when they heard a tone during the conditioned stimulus (CS) period. Subjects controlled a dial according to subjective expectation level; their skin conductance response (SCR) was also continuously measured. (Figure provided courtesy of David Knight, Ph.D., Section on Functional Imaging Methods, NIMH)

already clear: functional magnetic resonance imaging is a maturing technique with extraordinary potential.

Acknowledgments

This work was supported by the National Institute of Mental Health (NIMH), Division of Intramural Research Programs. My thanks to Ziad Saad, Scientific and Statistical Core Facility; David Knight, Section on Functional Imaging Methods; and Jerzy Bodurka, Functional MRI Core Facility, all of the NIMH, for their contributions of figures to this chapter.

References

Ahlfors, S. P., Simpson, G. V., Dale, A. M., Belliveau, J. W., Liu, A. K., Korvenoja, A., Virtanen, J., Huotilainen, M., Tootell, R. B. H., Aronen, H. J., and Ilmoniemi,

R. J. (1999). Spatiotemporal activity of a cortical network for processing visual motion revealed by MEG and fMRI. *Journal of Neurophysiology, 82,* 2545–2555.

An, H. Y., Lin, W. L., Celik, A., and Lee, Y. Z. (2001). Quantitative measurements of cerebral metabolic rate of oxygen using MRI: A volunteer study. *NMR in Biomedicine, 14,* 441–447.

Bandettini, P. A., Jesmanowicz, A., Wong, E. C., and Hyde, J. S. (1993). Processing strategies for time-course data sets in functional MRI of the human brain. *Magnetic Resonance Medicine, 30,* 161–173.

Bandettini, P. A., Petridou, N., and Bodurka, J. (2006). Direct detection of neuronal activity with MRI: Fantasy, possibility, or reality? *Applied Magnetic Resonance, 29,* 65–85.

Bandettini, P. A., and Wong, E. C. (1997). A hypercapnia-based normalization method for improved spatial localization of human brain activation with fMRI. *NMR in Biomedicine, 10,* 197–203.

Bandettini, P. A., Wong, E. C., Hinks, R. S., Tikofsky, R. S., and Hyde, J. S. (1992). Time course EPI of human brain functioning during task activation. *Magnetic Resonance in Medicine, 25,* 390–397.

Beckmann, C. F., and Smith, S. A. (2004). Probabilistic independent component analysis for functional magnetic resonance imaging. *IEEE Transactions on Medical Imaging, 23,* 137–152.

Bellgowan, P. S. F., Saad, Z. S. and Bandettini, P. A. (2003). Understanding neural system dynamics through task modulation and management. *Proceedings of the National Academy of Sciences, USA, 100,* 1415–1419.

Belliveau, J. W., Kennedy, D. N., McKinstry, R. C., Buchbinder, B. R., Weisskoff, R. M., Cohen, M. S., Vevea, J. M., Brady, T. J., and Rosen, B. R. (1991). Functional mapping of the human visual cortex by magnetic resonance imaging. *Science, 254,* 716–719.

Binder, J. R., Frost, J. A., Hammeke, T. A., Bellgowan, P. S. F., Rao, S. M., and Cox, R. W. (1999). Conceptual processing during the conscious resting state: A functional MRI study. *Journal of Cognitive Neuroscience, 11,* 80–93.

Binder, J. R. Frost, J. A., Hammeke, T. A., Cox, R. W., Rao, S. M., and Prieto, T. (1997). Human brain language areas identified by functional magnetic resonance imaging. *Journal of Neuroscience, 17,* 353–362.

Binder, J. R., Rao, S. M., Hammeke, T. A., Frost, J. A., Bandettini, P. A., and Hyde, J. S. (1994). Effects of stimulus rate on signal response during functional magnetic resonance imaging of auditory cortex. *Cognitive Brain Research, 2,* 31–38.

Biswal, B., Yetkin, F. Z., Haughton, V. M., and Hyde, J. S. (1995). Functional connectivity in the motor cortex of resting human brain using echo-planar MIR. *Magnetic Resonance in Medicine, 34,* 537–541.

Blamire, A. M., Ogawa, S., Ugurbil, K., Rothman, D., McCarthy, G., Ellermann, J. M., Hyder, F., Rattner, Z., and Shulman, R. G. (1992). Dynamic mapping of the human visual cortex by high-speed magnetic resonance imaging. *Proceedings of the National Academy of Sciences, USA, 89,* 11069–11073.

Boas, D. A., Dale, A. M., and Franceschini, M. A. (2004). Diffuse optical imaging of brain activation: Approaches to optimizing sensitivity, resolution and accuracy. *NeuroImage, 23,* S275–S288.

Bodurka, J., and Bandettini, P. A. (2002). Toward direct mapping of neuronal activity: MRI detection of ultraweak, transient magnetic field changes. *Magnetic Resonance in Medicine, 47,* 1052–1058.

Bodurka, J., Ledden, P. J., van Gelderen, P., Chu, R. X., de Zwart, J. A., Morris, D., and Duyn, J. H. (2004). Scalable multichannel MRI data acquisition system. *Magnetic Resonance in Medicine, 51,* 165–171.

Bohning, D. E., Denslow, S., Bohning, P. A., Walker, J. A., and George, M. S. (2003). A TMS coil positioning/holding system for MR image-guided TMS interleaved with fMRI. *Clinical Neurophysiology, 114,* 2210–2219.

Bohning, D. E., Shastri, A., McGavin, L., McConnell, K. A., Nahas, Z., Lorberbaum, J. P., Roberts, D. R., and George, M. S. (2000a). Motor cortex brain activity induced by 1 Hz transcranial magnetic stimulation is similar in location and level to that for volitional movement. *Investigative Radiology, 35,* 676–683.

Bohning, D. E., Shastri, A., Wassermann, E. M., Ziemann, U., Lorberbaum, J. P., Nahas, Z., Lomarev, M. P., and George, M. S. (2000b). BOLD-fMRI response to single-pulse transcranial magnetic stimulation (TMS). *Journal of Magnetic Resonance Imaging, 11,* 569–574.

Botvinick, M., Nystrom, L. E., Fissell, K., Carter, C. S., and Cohen, J. D. (1999). Conflict monitoring versus selection-for-action in anterior cingulated cortex. *Nature, 402,* 179–181.

Boynton, G. M., Engel, S. A., Glover, G. H., and Heeger, D. J. (1996). Linear systems analysis of functional magnetic resonance imaging in human V1. *Journal of Neuroscience, 16,* 4207–4221.

Braver, T. S., Cohen, J. D., Nystrom, L. E., Jonides, J., Smith, E. E., and Noll, D. C. (1997). A parametric study of prefrontal cortex involvement in human working memory. *NeuroImage, 5,* 49–62.

Breiter, H. C., Etcoff, N. L., Whalen, P. J., Kennedy, W. A., Rauch, S. L., Buckner, R. L., Strauss, M. M., Hyman, S. E., and Rosen, B. R. (1996). Response and habituation of the human amygdala during visual processing of facial expression. *Neuron, 17,* 875–887.

Buchel, C., and Friston, K. J. (1998). Dynamic changes in effective connectivity characterized by variable parameter regression and kalman filtering. *Human Brain Mapping, 6,* 403–408.

Buckner, R. L., Bandettini, P. A., O'Craven, K. M., Savoy, R. L., Petersen, S. E., Raichle, M. E., and Rosen, B. R. (1996). Detection of cortical activation during averaged single trials of a cognitive task using functional magnetic imaging. *Proceedings of the National Academy of Sciences, USA, 93*, 14878–14883.

Buckner, R. L., Petersen, S. E., Ojemann, J. G., Miezin, F. M., Squire, L. R., and Raichle, M. E. (1995). Functional anatomical studies of explicit and implicit memory retrieval tasks. *Journal of Neuroscience, 15*, 12–29.

Bush, G., Luu, P., and Posner, M. I. (2000). Cognitive and emotional influences in anterior cingulate cortex. *Trends in Cognitive Science, 4*, 215–222.

Buxton, R. B., and Frank, L. R. (1997). A model for the coupling between cerebral blood flow and oxygen metabolism during neural stimulation. *Journal of Cerebral Blood Flow and Metabolism, 17*, 64–72.

Buxton, R. B., Uludag, K., Dubowitz, D. J., and Liu, T. T. (2004). Modeling the hemodynamic response to brain activation. *NeuroImage, 23*, S220–S233.

Cabeza, R., and Nyberg, L. (2000). Imaging cognition II: An empirical review of 275 PET and fMRI studies. *Journal of Cognitive Neuroscience, 12*, 1–47.

Cannestra, A. F., Pouratian, N., Bookheimer, S. Y., Martin, N. A., Beckerand, D. P., and Toga, A. W. (2001). Temporal spatial differences observed by functional MRI and human intraoperative optical imaging. *Cerebral Cortex, 11*, 773–782.

Carter, C. S., Braver, T. S., Barch, D. M., Botvinick, M. M., Noll, D., and Cohen, J. D. (1998). Anterior cingulate cortex, error detection, and the online monitoring of performance. *Science, 280*, 747–749.

Cheng, K., Waggoner, R. A., and Tanaka, K. (2001). Human ocular dominance columns as revealed by high-field functional magnetic resonance imaging. *Neuron, 32*, 359–374.

Cohen, E. R., Rostrup, E., Sidaros, K., Lund, T. E., Paulson, O. B., Ugurbil, K., and Kim, S. G. (2004). Hypercapnic normalization of BOLD fMRI: Comparison across field strengths and pulse sequences. *NeuroImage, 23*, 613–624.

Cohen, J. D., Perlstein, W. M., Braver, T. S., Nystrom, L. E., Noll, D. C., Jonides, J., and Smith, E. E. (1997). Temporal dynamics of brain activation during a working memory task. *Nature, 386*, 604–608.

Corbetta, M., Akbudak, E., Conturo, T. E., Snyder, A. Z., Ollinger, J. M., Drury, H. A., Linenweber, M. R., Petersen, S. E., Raichle, M. E., Van Essen, D. C., and Shulman, G. L. (1998). A common network of functional areas for attention and eye movements. *Neuron, 21*, 761–773.

Corbetta, M., and Shulman, G. L. (2002). Control of goal-directed and stimulus-driven attention in the brain. *Nature Reviews Neuroscience, 3*, 201–215.

Corbetta, M., Kincade, J. M., Ollinger, J. M., McAvoy, M. P., and Shulman, G. L. (2000). Voluntary orienting is dissociated from target detection in human posterior parietal cortex. *Nature Neuroscience, 3*, 292–297.

Courtney, S. M., Petit, L., Maisog, J. M., Ungerleider, L. G., and Haxby, J. V. (1998). An area specialized for spatial working memory in human frontal cortex. *Science, 279*, 1347–1351.

Courtney, S. M., Ungerleider, L. G., Keil, K., and Haxby, J. V. (1996). Object and spatial visual working memory activate separate neural systems in human cortex. *Cerebral Cortex*, 6, 39–49.

Courtney, S. M., Ungerleider, B. G., Keil, K., and Haxby, J. V. (1997). Transient and sustained activity in a distributed neural system for human working memory. *Nature*, 386, 608–611.

Cox, R. W. (1996). Software for analysis and visualization of functional magnetic resonance neuroimages. *Computers and Biomedical Research*, 29, 162–173.

Cox, R. W., Jesmanowicz, A., and Hyde, J. S. (1995). Real-time functional magnetic resonance imaging. *Magnetic Resonance in Medicine*, 33, 230–236.

Critchley, H. D., Elliott, R., Mathias, C. J., and Dolan, R. J. (2000). Neural activity relating to the generation and representation of galvanic skin conductance response: A functional magnetic resonance imaging study. *Journal of Neuroscience*, 20, 3033–3040.

Dagli, M. S., Ingeholm, J. E., and Haxby, J. V. (1999). Localization of cardiac-induced signal change in fMRI. *NeuroImage*, 9, 407–415.

Dale, A. M., and Buckner, R. L. (1997). Selective averaging of rapidly presented individual trials using fMRI. *Human Brain Mapping*, 5, 329–340.

Dale, A. M., Fischl, B., and Sereno, M. I. (1999). Cortical surface-based analysis. 1. Segmentation and surface reconstruction. *NeuroImage*, 9, 179–194.

Dale, A. M., and Halgren, E. (2001). Spatiotemporal mapping of brain activity by integration multiple imaging modalities. *Current Opinion in Neurobiology*, 11, 202–208.

Davis, T. L., Kwong, K. K., Weisskoff, R. M., and Rosen, B. R. (1998). Calibrated functional MRI: Mapping the dynamics of oxidative metabolism. *Proceedings of the National Academy of Sciences*, USA, 95, 1834–1839.

DeCharms, R. C., Christoff, K., Glover, G. H., Pauly, J. M., Whitfield, S., and Gabrieli, J. D. E. (2004). Learned regulation of spatially localized brain activation using real-time fMRI. *NeuroImage*, 21, 436–443.

Demb, J. B., Desmond, J. E., Wagner, A. D., Vaidya, C. J., Glover, G. H., and Gabrieli, J. D. (1995). Semantic encoding and retrieval in the left inferior prefrontal cortex–A functional MRI study of task difficulty and process specificity. *Journal of Neuroscience*, 15, 5870–5878.

D'Esposito, M., Detre, J. A., Alsop, D. C., Shin, R. K., Atlas, S., and Grossman, M. (1995). The neural basis of the central executive system of working memory. *Nature*, 378, 279–281.

Devor, A., Dunn, A. K., Andermann, M. L., Ulbert, I., Boas, D. A., and Dale, A. M. (2003). Coupling of total hemoglobin concentration, oxygenation, and neural activity in rat somatosensory cortex. *Neuron*, 39, 353–359.

DeYoe, E. A., Bandettini, P., Neitz, J., Miller, D., and Winans, P. (1994). Functional magnetic resonance imaging (fMRI) of the human brain. *Journal of Neuroscience Methods*, 54, 171–187.

de Zwart, J. A., van Gelderen, P., Kellman, P., and Duyn, J. H. (2002). Application of sensitivity-encoded echo-planar imaging for blood oxygen level–dependent functional brain imaging. *Magnetic Resonance in Medicine*, 48, 1011–1020.

Duong, T. Q., Kim, D. S., Ugurbil, K., and Kim, S. G. (2000). Spatio-temporal dynamics of the BOLD fMRI signals in cat visual cortex: Toward mapping columnar structures using early negative response. *Magnetic Resonance in Medicine*, 44, 231–242.

Edmister, W. B., Talavage, T. M., Ledden, P. J., and Weisskoff, R. M. (1999). Improved auditory cortex imaging using clustered volume acquisitions. *Human Brain Mapping*, 7, 89–97.

Egan, M. F., Goldberg T. E., Kolachana, B. S., Callicott, J. H., Mazzanti, C. M., Straub, R. E., Goldman, D., and Weinberger, D. R. (2001). Effect of COMT Val(108/158) Met genotype on frontal lobe function and risk for schizophrenia. *Proceedings of the National Academy of Sciences*, 98, 6917–6922.

Egan, M. F., Kojima, M., Callicott, J. H., Goldberg, T. E., Kolachana, B. S., Bertolino, A., Zaitsev, E., Gold, B., Goldman, D., Dean, M., Lu, B., and Weinberger, D. R. (2003). The BDNF val66met polymorphism affects activity-dependent secretion of BDNF and human memory and hippocampal function. *Cell*, 112, 257–269.

Engel, S. A., Glover, G. H., and Wandell, B. A. (1997). Retinotopic organization in human visual cortex and the spatial precision of functional MRI. *Cerebral Cortex*, 7, 181–192.

Engel, S. A., Rumelhart, D. E., Wandell, B. A., Lee, A. T., Glover, G. H., Chichilnisky, E. J., and Shadlen, M. N. (1994). fMRI of human visual cortex. *Nature*, 369, 525–525.

Fischl, B., Sereno, M. I., Tootell, R. B. H., and Dale, A. M. (1999). High-resolution inter-subject averaging and a coordinate system for the cortical surface. *Human Brain Mapping*, 8, 272–284.

Fletcher, P. C., and Henson, R. N. A. (2001). Frontal lobes and human memory—Insights from functional neuroimaging. *Brain*, 124, 849–881.

Forman, S. D., Cohen, J. D., Fitzgerald, M., Eddy, W. F., Mintun, M. A., and Noll, D. C. (1995). Improved assessment of significant activation in functional magnetic resonance imaging (fMRI)—Use of a cluster-size threshold. *Magnetic Resonance Medicine*, 33, 636–647.

Fox, P. T., and Raichle, M. E. (1986). Focal physiological uncoupling of cerebral blood flow and oxidative metabolism during somatosensory stimulation in humans. *Proceedings of the National Academy of the Sciences, USA*, 83, 1140–1144.

Frahm, J., Bruhn, H., Merboldt, K.-D., Hanicke, W., and Math, D. (1992). Dynamic MR imaging of human brain oxygenation during restand photic stimulation. *JMRI: Journal of Magnetic Resonance Imaging*, 2, 501–505.

Frank, L. R., Buxton, R. B., and Wong, E. C. (2001). Estimation of respiration—induced noise fluctuations from under sampled multislice fMRI data. *Magnetic Resonance in Medicine*, 45, 635–644.

Friston, K. J., Holmes, A. P., Poline, J. B., Grasby, P. J., Williams, S. C., Frackowiak, R. S., and Turner, R. (1995). Analysis of fMRI time-series revisited. *NeuroImage*, 2, 45–53.

Friston, K. J., Holmes, A. P., Price, C. J., Buchel, C., and Worsley, K. J. (1999). Multisubject fMRI studies and conjunction analyses. *NeuroImage*, 10, 385–396.

Goldman, R., Stern, J., Engel, J., and Cohen, M. (2001). Tomographic mapping of alpha rhythm using simultaneous EEG/fMRI. *NeuroImage*, 13, S1291–S1291.

Goodyear, B. G., and Menon, R. S. (2001). Brief visual stimulation allows mapping of ocular dominance in visual cortex using fMRI. *Human Brain Mapping*, 14, 210–217.

Grinvald, A., Slovin, H., and Vanzetta, I. (2000). Non-invasive visualization of cortical columns by fMRI. *Nature Neuroscience*, 3, 105–107.

Guimaraes, A. R., Melcher, J. R., Talavage, T. M., Baker, J. R., Ledden, P., Rosen, B. R., Kiang, N. Y. S., Fullerton, B. C., and Weisskoff, R. M. (1998). Imaging subcortical activity in humans. *Human Brain Mapping*, 6, 33–41.

Gusnard, D. A., Akbudak, E., Shulman, G. L., and Raichle, M. E. (2001). Medial prefrontal cortex and self-referential mental activity: Relation to a default mode of brain function. *Proceedings of the National Academy of Sciences, USA*, 98, 4259–4264.

Hasson, U., Nir, Y., Levy, I., Fuhrmann, G., and Malach, R. (2004). Intersubject synchronization of cortical activity during natural vision. *Science*, 303, 1634–1640.

Haxby, J. V., Gobbini, M. I., Furey, M. L., Ishai, A., Schouten, J. L., and Pietrini, P. (2001). Distributed and overlapping representations of faces and objects in ventral temporal cortex. *Science*, 293, 2425–2430.

Haxby, J. V., Hoffman, E. A., and Gobbini, M. I. (2000). The distributed human neural system for face perception. *Trends in Cognitive Science*, 4, 223–233.

Hennig, J., Janz, C., Speck, O., and Ernst, T. (1997). Is there a different type of MR-contrast in early phases of functional activation. In *Advances in experimental medicine and biology*, vol. 413, pp. 35–42. Optical Imaging of Brain Function and Metabolism II. New York: Plenum Press.

Henson, R. N. A., Price, C. J., Rugg, M. D., Turner, R., and Friston, K. J. (2002). Detecting latency differences in event-related BOLD responses: Application to words versus non-words and initial versus repeated face presentations. *NeuroImage*, 15, 83–97.

Hoge, R. D., Atkinson, J., Gill, B., Crelier, G. R., Marrett, S., and Pike, G. B. (1999). Linear coupling between cerebral blood flow and oxygen consumption in activated human cortex. *Proceedings of the National Academy of Sciences, USA*, 96, 9403–9408.

Hopfinger, J. B., Buonocore, M. H., and Mangun, G. R. (2000). The neural mechanisms of top-down attentional control. *Nature Neuroscience*, 3, 284–291.

Horovitz, S. G., Skudlarski, P., and Gore, J. C. (2002). Correlations and dissociations between BOLD signal and P300 amplitude in an auditory odd ball task: A parametric approach to combining fMRI and ERP. *Magnetic Resonance Imaging*, *20*, 319–325.

Hu, X. P., Le, T. H., and Ugurbil, K. (1997). Evaluation of the early response in fMRI in individual subjects using short stimulus duration. *Magnetic Resonance in Medicine*, *37*, 877–884.

Huettel, S. A., McKeown, M. J., Song, A. W., Hart, S., Spencer, D. D., Allison, T., and McCarthy, G. (2004). Linking hemodynamic and electrophysiological measures of brain activity: Evidence from functional MRI. *Cerebral Cortex*, *14*, 165–173.

Kanwisher, N., McDermott, J., and Chun, M. M. (1997). The fusiform face area: A module in human extrastriate cortex specialized for face perception. *Journal of Neuroscience*, *17*, 4302–4311.

Karni, A., Meyer, G., Jezzard, P., Adams, M. M., Turner, R., and Ungerleider, L. G. (1995). Functional MRI evidence for adult motor cortex plasticity during motor skill learning. *Nature*, *377*, 155–158.

Kelley, W. M., Miezin, F. M., McDermott, K. B., Buckner, R. L., Raichle, M. E., Cohen, N. J., Ollinger, J. M., Akbudak, E., Conturo, T. E., Snyder, A. Z., and Petersen, S. E. (1998). Hemispheric specialization in human dorsal frontal cortex and medial temporal lobe for verbal and nonverbal memory encoding. *Neuron*, *20*, 927–936.

Knight, D. C., Nguyen, H. T., and Bandettini, P. A. (2005). The role of the human amygdala in the production of conditioned fear. *NeuroImage*, *26*, 1193–1200.

Konn, D., Leach, S., Gowland, P., and Bowtell, R. (2004). Initial attempts at directly detecting alpha wave activity in the brain using MRI. *Magnetic Resonance Imaging*, *22*, 1413–1427.

Kwong, K. K., Belliveau, J. W., Chesler, D. A., Goldberg, I. E., Weisskoff, R. M., Poncelet, B. P., Kennedy, D. N., Hoppel, B. E., Cohen, M. S., Turner, R., Cheng, H. M., Brady, T. J., and Rosen, B. R. (1992). Dynamic magnetic resonance imaging of human brain activity during primary sensory stimulation. *Proceedings of the National Academy of Sciences, USA*, *89*, 5675–5679.

Laufs, H., Kleinschmidt, A., Beyerle, A., Eger, E., Salek-Haddadi, A., Preibisch, C., and Krakow, K. (2003a). EEG-correlated fMRI of human alpha activity. *NeuroImage*, *19*, 1463–1476.

Laufs, H., Krakow, K., Sterzer, P., Eger, E., Beyerle, A., Salek-Haddadi, A., and Kleinschmidt, A. (2003b). Electroencephalographic signatures of attentional and cognitive default modes in spontaneous brain activity fluctuations. *Proceedings of the National Academy of Sciences, USA*, *100*, 11053–11058.

Lemieux, L. (2004). Electroencephalography-correlated functional MR imaging studies of epileptic activity. *Neuroimaging Clinics of North America*, *14*, 487–506.

Levin, D. N., and Uftring, S. J. (2001). Detecting brain activation in fMRI data without prior knowledge of mental event timing. *NeuroImage*, *13*, 153–160.

Logothetis, N. K., Merkle, H., Augath, M., Trinath, T., and Ugurbil, K. (2002). Ultra-high-resolution fMRI in monkeys with implanted RF coils. *Neuron*, *35*, 227–242.

Logothetis, N. K., Pauls, J., Augath, M., Trinath, T., and Oeltermann, A. (2001). Neurophysiological investigation of the basis of the fMRI signal. *Nature*, *412*, 150–157.

Lomarev, M., Shastri, A., Ziemann, U., Wassermann, E. M., McConnell, K. A., Nahas, Z., Lorberbaum, J. P., Vincent, D. J., George, M. S., and Bohning, D. E. (2000). Can interleaved TMS and fMRI demonstrate changes in an activated circuit? In *Biological Psychiatry Annual Conference*, *47*, 97S (no. 323).

Lowe, M. J., Mock, B. J., and Sorenson, J. A. (1998). Functional connectivity in single and multislice echoplanar imaging using resting state fluctuations. *NeuroImage*, *7*, 119–132.

Lu, H. Z., Golay, X., Pekar, J. J., and van Zijll, P. C. M. (2003). Functional magnetic resonance imaging based on changes in vascular space occupancy. *Magnetic Resonance in Medicine*, *50*, 263–274.

Malonek, D., and Grinvald, A. (1996). Interactions between electrical activity and cortical microcirculation revealed by imaging spectroscopy: Implications for functional brain mapping. *Science*, *272*, 551–554.

Martin, A., Wiggs, C. L., Ungerleider, L. G., and Haxby, J. V. (1996). Neural correlates of category-specific knowledge. *Nature*, *379*, 649–652.

Mathiesen, C., Caesar, K., Akgoren, N., and Lauritzen, M. (1998). Modification of activity-dependent increases of cerebral blood flow by excitatory synaptic activity and spikes in rat cerebellar cortex. *Journal of Physiology*, *512*, 555–566.

McCarthy, G., Luby, M., Gore, J., and Goldman-Rakic, P. (1997). Infrequent events transiently activate human prefrontal and parietal cortex as measured by functional MRI. *Journal of Neurophysiology*, *77*, 1630–1634.

Menon, R. S. (2002). Post-acquisition suppression of large-vessel BOLD signals in high-resolution fMRI. *Magnetic Resonance in Medicine*, *47*, 1–9.

Menon, R. S., Luknowsky, D. C., and Gati, J. S. (1998). Mental chronometry using latency-resolved functional magnetic resonance imaging. *Proceedings of the National Academy of Sciences, USA*, *95*, 10902–10907.

Menon, R. S., Ogawa, S., Strupp, J. P., and Ugurbil, K. (1997). Ocular dominance in human V1 demonstrated by functional magnetic resonance imaging. *Journal of Neurophysiology*, *77*, 2780–2787.

Menon, R. S., Ogawa, S., and Ugurbil, K. (1995). High-temporal-resolution studies of the human primary visual cortex at 4T: Teasing out the oxygenation contribution in fMRI. *International Journal of Imaging Systems and Technology*, *6*, 209–215.

Noll, D. C., Genovese, C. R., Vazquez, A. L., O'Brien, J. L., and Eddy, W. F. (1998). Evaluation of respiratory artifact correction techniques in functional MRI using receiver operator characteristic analysis. *Magnetic Resonance in Medicine*, 40, 633–639.

O'Doherty, J., Kringelbach, M. L., Rolls, E. T., Hornak, J., and Andrews, C. (2001). Abstract reward and punishment representations in the human orbitofrontal cortex. *Nature Neuroscience*, 4, 95–102.

Ogawa, S., Lee, T. M., Kay, A. R., and Tank, D. W. (1990). Brain magnetic resonance imaging with contrast dependent on blood oxygenation. *Proceedings of the National Academy of Sciences*, USA, 87, 9868–9872.

Ogawa, S., Lee, T. M., Stepnoski, R., Chen, W., Zhu, X. H., and Ugurbil, K. (2000). An approach to probe some neural systems interaction by functional MRI at neural time scale down to milliseconds. *Proceedings of the National Academy of Sciences*, USA, 97, 11026–11031.

Ogawa, S., Menon, R. S., Tank, D. W., Kim, S. G., Merkle, H., Ellermann, J. M., and Ugurbil, K. (1993). Functional brain mapping by blood oxygenation level–dependent contrast magnetic resonance imaging: A comparison of signal characteristics with a biophysical model. *Biophysical Journal*, 64, 803–812.

Ogawa, S., Tank, D. W., Menon, R., Ellermann, J. M., Kim, S. G., Merkle, H., and Ugurbil, K. (1992). Intrinsic signal changes accompanying sensory stimulation: Functional brain mapping with magnetic resonance imaging. *Proceedings of the National Academy of Sciences*, USA, 89, 5951–5955.

Patterson, J. C., Ungerleider, L. G., and Bandettini, P. A. (2002). Task-independent functional brain activity correlation with skin conductance changes: An fMRI study. *NeuroImage*, 17, 1797–1806.

Pellerin, L., and Magistretti, P. J. (1994). Glutamate uptake into astrocytes stimulates aerobic glycolysis—A mechanism coupling neuronal activity to glucose utilization. *Proceedings of the National Academy of Sciences*, 91, 10625–10629.

Pessoa, L., Gutierrez, E., Bandettini, P. A., and Ungerleider, L. G. (2002). Neural correlates of visual working memory: fMRI amplitude predicts task performance. *Neuron*, 35, 975–987.

Pfeuffer, J., Van de Moortele, P. F., Ugurbil, K., Hu, X. P., and Glover, G. H. (2002a). IMPACT: Image-based physiological artifacts estimation and correction technique for functional MRI. *Magnetic Resonance in Medicine*, 47, 344–353.

Pfeuffer, J., Van de Moortele, P. F., Yacoub, E., Shmuel, A., Adriany, G., Andersen, P., Merkle, H., Garwood, M., Ugurbil, K., and Hu, X. P. (2002b). Zoomed functional imaging in the human brain at 7 tesla with simultaneous high spatial and high temporal resolution. *NeuroImage*, 17, 272–286.

Raichle, M. E., MacLeod, A. M., Snyder, A. Z., Powers, W. J., Gusnard, D. A., and Shulman, G. L. (2001). A default mode of brain function. *Proceedings of the National Academy of Sciences*, USA, 98, 676–682.

Rao, S. M., Bandettini, P. A., Binder, J. R., Bobholz, J. A., Hammeke, T. A., Stein, E. A., and Hyde, J. S. (1996). Relationship between movement rate and functional magnetic resonance signal change in human primary motor cortex. *Journal of Cerebral Blood Flow and Metabolism, 16*, 1250–1254.

Rao, S. M., Binder, J. R., Bandettini, P. A., Hammeke, T. A., Yetkin, F. Z., Jesmanowicz, A., Lisk, L. M., Morris, G. L., Mueller, W. M., Estkowski, L. D., et al. (1993). Functional magnetic resonance imaging of complex human movements. *Neurology, 43*, 2311–2318.

Rosen, B. R., Belliveau, J. W., Aronen, H. J., Kennedy, D., Buchbinder, B. R., Fischman, A., Gruber, M., Glas, J., Weisskoff, R. M., Cohen, M. S., Hochberg, F. H., and Brady, T. J. (1991). Susceptibility contrast imaging of cerebral blood volume: Human experience. *Magnetic Resonance in Medicine, 22*, 293–299.

Saad, Z. S., Reynolds, R. C., Argall, B., Japee, S., and Cox, R. W. (2004). An interface for surface based intra- and inter-subject analysis with AFNI. In *Proceedings of the 2004 IEEE International Symposium on Biomedical Imaging*, 1510–1513.

Sereno, M. I., Dale, A. M., Reppas, J. B., Kwong, K. K., Belliveau, J. W., Brady, T. J., Rosen, B. R., and Tootell, R. B. H. (1995). Borders of multiple visual areas in human revealed by functional magnetic resonance imaging. *Science, 268*, 889–893.

Shastri, A., Lomarev, M. P., Nelson, S. J., George, M. S., Holzwarth, M. R., and Bohning, D. E. (2001). A low-cost system for monitoring skin conductance during functional MRI. *Journal of Magnetic Resonance Imaging, 14*, 187–193.

Shaywitz, B. A., Shaywitz, S. E., Pugh, K. R., Constable, R. T., Skudlarski, P., Fulbright, R. K., Bronen, R. A., Fletcher, J. M., Shankweiler, D. P., Katz, L., et al. (1995). Sex differences in the functional organization of the brain for language. *Nature, 373*, 607–609.

Shmuel, A., Yacoub, E., Pfeuffer, J., Van de Moortele, P. F., Adriany, G., Hu, X. P., and Ugurbil, K. (2002). Sustained negative BOLD, blood flow and oxygen consumption response and its coupling to the positive response in the human brain. *Neuron, 36*, 1195–1210.

Singh, K. D., Barnes, G. R., Hillebrand, A., Forde, E. M. E., and Williams, A. L. (2002). Task-related changes in cortical synchronisation are spatially coincident with the haemodynamic response. *NeuroImage, 16*, 103–114.

Thompson, J. K., Peterson, M. R., and Freeman, R. D. (2003). Single-neuron activity and tissue oxygenation in the cerebral cortex. *Science, 299*, 1070–1072.

Thompson, J. K., Peterson, M. R., and Freeman, R. D. (2004). High-resolution neurometabolic coupling revealed by focal activation of visual neurons. *Nature Neuroscience, 7*, 919–920.

Tootell, R. B. H., Reppas, J. B., Kwong, K. K., Malach, R., Born, R. T., Brady, T. J., Rosen, B. R., and Belliveau, J. W. (1995). Functional analysis of human Mt and related visual cortical areas using magnetic resonance imaging. *Journal of Neuroscience, 15*, 3215–3230.

Turner, R., Le Bihan, D., Moonen, C. T. W., Despres, D., and Frank, J. (1991). Echo-planar time course MRI of cat brain oxygenation changes. *Magnetic Resonance in Medicine*, 22, 159–166.

Van Essen, D. C., and Drury, H. A. (1997). Structural and functional analyses of human cerebral cortex using a surface-based atlas. *Journal of Neuroscience*, 17, 7079–7102.

Vaughan, J. T., Garwood, M., Collins, C. M., Liu, W., DelaBarre, L., Adriany, G., Andersen, P., Merkle, H., Goebel, R., Smith, M. B., and Ugurbil, K. (2001). 7T vs. 4T: RF power, homogeneity, and signal to noise comparison in head images. *Magnetic Resonance in Medicine*, 46, 24–30.

Villringer, A. (1997). Functional neuroimaging. Optical approaches. *Advances in Experimental Medicine and Biology*, 413, 1–18.

Visscher, K. M., Miezin, F. M., Kelly, J. E., Buckner, R. L., Donaldson, D. I., McAvoy, M. P., Bhalodia, V. M., and Petersen, S. E. (2003). Mixed blocked/event-related designs separate transient and sustained activity in fMRI. *NeuroImage*, 19, 1694–1708.

Wagner, A. D., Schacter, D. L., Rotte, M., Koutstaal, W., Maril, A., Dale, A. M., Rosen, B. R., and Buckner, R. L. (1998). Building memories: Remembering and forgetting verbal experiences as predicted by brain activity. *Science*, 281, 1188–1191.

Weiskopf, N., Veit, R., Erb, M., Mathiak, K., Grodd, W., Goebel, R., and Birbaumer, N. (2003). Physiological self-regulation of regional brain activity using real-time functional magnetic resonance imaging (fMRI). *NeuroImage*, 19, 577–586.

Whalen, P. J., Rauch, S. L., Etcoff, N. L., McInerney, S. C., Lee, M. B., and Jenike, M. A. (1998). Masked presentations of emotional facial expressions modulate amygdala activity without explicit knowledge. *Journal of Neuroscience*, 18, 411–418.

Williams, D. S., Detre, J. A., Leigh, J. S., and Koretsky, A. P. (1992). Magnetic resonance imaging of perfusion using spin inversion of arterial water. *Proceedings of the National Academy of Sciences, USA*, 89, 212–216.

Williams, L. M., Brammer, M. J., Skerrett, D., Gordan, E., Rennie, C., Kozek, K., Olivieri, G., and Peduto, T. (2000). The neural correlates of orienting: An integration of fMRI and skin conductance orienting. *NeuroReport*, 11, 3011–3015.

Windischberger, C., Langenberger, H., Sycha, T., Tschernko, E. A., Fuchsjäger-Mayerl, G., Schmetterer, L., and Moser, E. (2002). On the origin of respiratory artifacts in BOLD-EPI of the human brain. *Magnetic Resonance Imaging*, 20, 575–582.

Wise, R. G., Ide, K., Poulin, M. J., and Tracey, I. (2004). Resting fluctuations in arterial carbon dioxide induce significant low-frequency variations in BOLD signal. *NeuroImage*, 21, 1652–1664.

Wong, E. C., Buxton, R. B., and Frank, L. R. (1999). Quantitative perfusion imaging using arterial spin labeling. *Neuroimaging Clinics of North America*, 9, 333–342.

Worsley, K. J., and Friston, K. J. (1995). Analysis of FMRI time-series revisited—Again. *NeuroImage*, 2, 173–181.

Worsley, K. J., Marrett, S., Neelin, P., Vandal, A. C., Friston, K.J., and Evans, A. C. (1996). A unified statistical approach for determining significant signals in images of cerebral activation. *Human Brain Mapping*, 4, 58–73.

Xiong, J. H., Gao, J. H., and Fox, P. T. (2003). Directly mapping magnetic field effects of neuronal activity by MRI. *Human Brain Mapping*, 20, 41–49.

Yacoub, E., Shmuel, A., Pfeuffer, J., Van de Moortele, P. F., Adriany, G., Andersen, P., Vaughan, J. T., Merkle, H., Ugurbil, K., and Hu, X. P. (2001). Imaging brain function in humans at 7 tesla. *Magnetic Resonance in Medicine*, 45, 588–594.

10 Electroencephalography

Gina Rippon

This chapter considers electroencephalography (EEG) from two broad perspectives. The "structural" perspective, which addresses questions such as "How is it measured?" "How are the data analyzed?" and "Where does it come from?" comprises relatively straightforward descriptions of the principles of EEG, focusing rather more on theory and analysis than on equipment per se, but also touching on the potential integration of EEG with other techniques. By contrast, the "functional" perspective, addressing rather harder questions such as "What is it for?" and "What can it tell us about how the brain works?" links EEG more specifically to cognitive neuroscience as a whole.

Although discussions of EEG may include theories of electronics to explain the characteristics of amplifiers, for example, or detailed mathematical equations to understand the differences between linear and nonlinear dynamics, Bayesian statistics and mutual information, these will only be referred to in passing. My chapter is chiefly addressed to cognitive neuroscientists using different but possibly complementary techniques and to novice electroencephalographers seeking an overview of the method, its underlying principles, and its potential applications.

Development

Electroencephalography has the longest history of all brain-imaging techniques. In 1929, Hans Berger (figure 10.1) described a signal measured from small electrodes attached to the scalp. The frequency of this signal was 8–13 cycles per second (Hz) and Berger termed it the *alpha rhythm*. Since then, the development and application of EEG techniques almost exactly parallels the development of cognitive neuroscience. This has been a process of mutually beneficial exchanges. Cognitive neuropsychologists elegantly deconstructed complex cognitive processes such as language and

Figure 10.1
Hailed as the "father of electroencephalography," Dr. Hans Berger (1873–1941)
produced the first recording of electrical activity in the human brain in 1924.

memory to produce hierarchical models of discrete subprocesses (see
Humphreys, Heinke, and Yoon, chapter 4, this volume). These models
could be tested and adjusted using the output of EEG signal-averaging techniques, which had produced clearly delineated response waveforms offering temporal resolution on the millisecond timescale. As early cognitive
science models evolved, their demands drove technical advances in EEG.
The evolution of complex source localization models, for example, drove
the development of multichannel EEG systems. New ways of describing
brain activity supported the evolution of brain models from patterns of specialized modular structures to distributed neuronal assemblies characterized
by transient dynamic couplings. Such models could then be tested by the
increasingly sophisticated analysis of EEG activity. As we will see, interest
in EEG has to some extent now come full circle, from the early interest in
alpha waves to the highly complex interpretations of cortical and subcortical oscillations, hailed as a "renaissance" for alpha waves in particular
and EEG as a whole (Başar et al., 1997; Fernandez et al., 1998).

Principles

The EEG signal reflects the electric potential differences in neuronal dendrites from transmembrane currents. It is generally assumed that the

primary source of the signal is current flow in the apical dendrites of pyramidal cells in the cerebral cortex. Located solely in gray matter, these cells are oriented perpendicularly in the cortex. The value of these postsynaptic potentials continually vary, even when the brain is "at rest," and it is this fluctuating activity which is described in terms of different frequencies.

Originally, EEG measurement entailed the attachment of conducting electrodes (commonly silver chloride) of a fixed size to the scalp at standard locations. The comparison between two active recording sites is known as a "bipolar derivation." Single active electrodes may be compared to common inactive reference electrodes for comparison; these may be noncephalic sites, such as the earlobes, mastoids, or the tip of the nose. The electrodes are coupled to high-impedance amplifiers, with signals analyzed at standard sampling rates; the higher the sampling rate, the better the signal resolution. Since the medium frequencies are generally of interest to the electroencephalographer, the signal is also fed through high- and low-frequency filters (commonly 0.1 to 70+ Hz). This screening out of infraslow (DC shifts) and ultrafast (600+ Hz) frequencies of the level that can be seen in epileptic foci was originally due to technical limitations that have now been overcome.

Contemporary EEG systems may now include nonmetallic electrodes such as carbon and carbon fiber to make them compatible with the requirements of other imaging systems such as functional magnetic resonance imaging (fMRI) and magnetoencephalography (MEG), or electrodes may be mounted in plastic pedestals with scalp contact via electrolyte-soaked sponges (as manufactured by Electrical Geodesics, Inc.). Electrodes may also be premounted in elasticated caps or held in place by a geodesic net system (figure 10.2).

For standard clinical EEGs, electrodes are attached at locations determined by an internationally agreed system. This standardized placement is known as the "10/20 system." The distance from the patient's nasion to inion and between the preauricular points is measured. Each electrode is placed at 10/20 percent intersections along these distances. This results in a montage combining 21 recording and 1 reference electrode. Electrode placements are referred to by an initial letter indicating their location (F = frontal; P = parietal; T = temporal; O = occipital) and a number, with odd numbers referring to left hemisphere electrodes and even numbers to right hemisphere electrodes, or the letter "z" indicating a vertex site (figure 10.3).

Signal artifacts, which may arise from eye movement activity, muscle activity, or cardiovascular activity, have to be screened out. Indeed, because

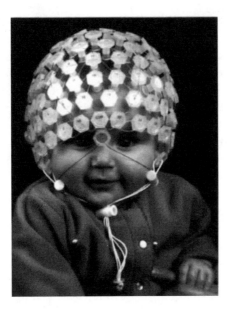

Figure 10.2
Multichannel electroencephalography (EEG) electrode array using the geodesic net system (manufactured by Electrical Geodesics, Inc.).

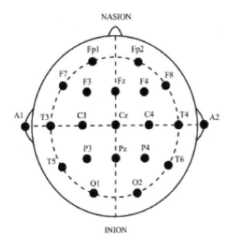

Figure 10.3
Diagrammatic representation of standard 10–20 location of electrodes for EEG measurement.

the large slow wave frontal activity associated with eye movements can seriously contaminate EEG data (Picton et al., 2000), eye movement correction or rejection is a key aspect of EEG data analysis. Eye movements are measured by the placement of electrodes above and below and at the outer canthus of each eye. Eye movement rejection consists of the removal from further analysis of any channels showing signals of greater than $100 \mu V$; eye movement correction consists of the interpolation of projected data to replace rejected data. There are several recognized procedures, the most commonly used being that devised by Gratton, Coles, and Donchin (1983).

Currently, research techniques are moving toward an increasing density of electrodes to provide data for sophisticated analyses of EEG data, such as topographic mapping or source localization, where the smaller the distance between electrodes, the more accurate the mapping. Arrays of 128 and 256 channels are not uncommon (see figure 10.2). Investigating the effect of the number of electrodes on accuracy of source localization, Michel et al. (2004) reported that precision increased dramatically from 25 up to about 100, but leveled out somewhat beyond that number (accuracy was assessed by comparison with the strong focal sources in epileptic patients).

Intracranial electroencephalograms (iEEGs) are recorded from grids of electrodes implanted on the cortex in patients awaiting surgery, commonly for epilepsy (for review, see Lachaux, Rudrauf, and Kahane, 2003). They provide a unique insight into the origin of electrical signals, without the need to generate realistic head models to calculate the distorting effects of conduction from source to scalp. In combination with cognitive paradigms carefully designed to deconstruct the subprocesses of the cognitive skill under scrutiny, they can provide detailed spatiotemporal maps of the underlying neuronal processes. Despite typically low participant numbers, and despite the possibility that preexisting pathology may induce cortical reorganization, intracranial electroencephalography (iEEG) has the potential to provide independent verification of alleged neuronal sources.

Standard EEG analysis ranges from a straightforward description of signal characteristics such as frequency or amplitude to a more detailed description of how the signal and variations in its characteristics are distributed as a function of the electrode location or region of interest, referred to as "occipital alpha," "left parietal beta," and so on.

The best-known description of EEG activity is in terms of different frequencies. This information can be extracted by spectral analysis, whereby amplitude characteristics of the frequency domain of the EEG signal can be assessed using a technique known as "fast Fourier transform" (FFT);

simpler waveforms of specific frequency bands are identified and the signal amplitude within each of these wavebands calculated. In addition to Berger's alpha rhythm, there are the slow delta waves (<4 Hz) associated with eye movements or sleep; theta waves (4–7 Hz), beta waves (14–30 Hz), and gamma waves (30–50 Hz, although sometimes simply described as 40 Hz). More recently, these traditional frequencies have been subdivided into smaller bands such as slow and fast alpha (8–10 Hz and 11–13 Hz), beta 1 (13–16 Hz), beta 2 (16–20 Hz) and beta 3 (20 Hz and above). Klimesch (1996) has also noted individual differences in alpha activity, identifying individual alpha frequencies (IAFs) for each experimental subject. There are other brain wave rhythms associated with specific areas, such as tau (auditory cortex) and mu (somatosensory cortex). Frequency activity can be described as a function of the amplitude or power (square root of amplitude) of the signal within a given frequency band. Different frequencies have characteristic ranges of amplitude (alpha is generally between 25 and 100 μV; beta, less than 20 μV).

Also of interest are the spatial characteristics of the EEG signal, its distribution over the cortex and the changes in this distribution as a function of time, task demands, individual differences, and so on. A contemporary technique that allows online inspection of spatial characteristics of the EEG is topographic mapping, whose simplest form provides amplitude maps for each of the classical frequencies, with either color-coded or grayscale maps depicting the variations in amplitude of the given frequency over the cortex at a particular point in time (figure 10.4, plate 4). Power maps indicate the intensity of the signal in given frequencies at different

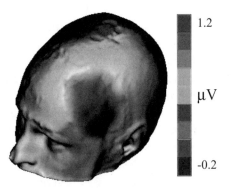

1.2

μV

-0.2

Figure 10.4
Topographic map displaying voltage changes across the cortical surface. See plate 4 for color version.

locations. In addition, statistical maps can be produced with the values from the statistical comparisons mapped at the relevant points on the cortex, providing an "instant snapshot" of areas where statistically significant changes have occurred.

Topographic maps have provided the kind of instant visibility missing from the early, chart-gazing approach, although they must be viewed with caution. The production of these maps involves an interpolation procedure whereby the values lying between the electrodes are statistically estimated in order to produce a value of best fit. These estimated values do not reflect real EEG data, however.

Using an analytic process called "microstate segmentation" (Lehmann, 1987), contemporary topographic mapping techniques can assess differences over time between different topographic distributions of the brain's electrical field. Because field configurations, though changing rapidly and discontinuously, remain stable for brief periods, these periods are interpreted as an index of specific brain functions. Field configurations are measured by the locations of the positive and negative centroids, shown on isopotential contour maps (figure 10.5). This analysis allows a sequential presentation of different activation patterns paralleling the time course of the relevant cognitive process, which can be statistically analyzed to provide measures of strength and duration of the different microstates (Pascual-Marqui, Michel, and Lehmann, 1995).

The analysis of any signal measured from the surface of the head must deal with the "inverse problem," namely, that there are potentially an infinite number of possible sources within the brain that could produce the given signal configuration (Fender, 1987; Michel et al., 2004). In special cases, such as epilepsy, where clearly defined epileptic foci are known, the use of iEEG can provide some independent verification of the source of a given signal, but such applications are obviously limited to a few individuals and a restricted range of protocols. Moreover, for signals generated within the head, estimation of the sources needs to take into account the shape of the head and the conductivity of intervening tissue. Although simple, spherical head models are computationally more straightforward, they are potentially inaccurate; realistic, constrained head models, for their part, are difficult to generate and incorporate. Source localization techniques can be broadly divided into focused- and distributed-source models; examples of each are outlined below.

Dipole fitting involves the application of electromagnetic field theory (Fender, 1987). The changes in polarization of nerve cells produce electrical potentials and magnetic fields that are directly related to the activation

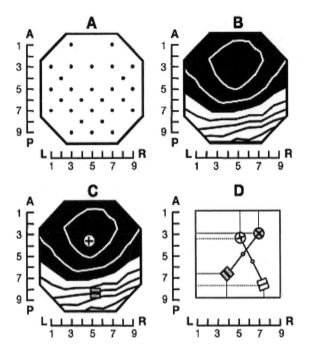

Figure 10.5
Spatial feature extraction and analysis in space-oriented ERP analysis. (*A*) Schematic of electrode array. (*B*) At each time point, a potential distribution map is constructed using linear interpolation between the electrodes; isopotential contour lines in steps of 1.0 μV, positive area in black, negative area in white. (*C*) At each time point, the locations of the negative (square) and the positive (circle) centroids can be used to reduce and characterise the ERP field topography. (*D*) At each time point, the spatial configuration of a momentary map is numerically expressed by 4 coordinate values (*L-R* and *A-P* locations of the positive and negative centroid). The *L-R* and *A-P* locations can be tested for differences between conditions (gray vs. white symbols). The small circles show the locations of the point of gravity of the absolute map voltages. (Adapted from Lavric et al., 2001)

patterns of the underlying nerve cell populations. If neurons are conceived of as dipoles, electrical sources that project positive and negative fields in opposite directions, EEG signals can be modeled as arising from specific dipole current sources. The orientation of these dipoles with respect to the surface of the cortex where recording is taking place will determine the positivity or negativity of the signal being measured. Using a moving-dipole technique, one can calculate the source of any signal.

Dipole techniques have proved effective in studies of sensory processing but are restricted by the necessary a priori assumptions regarding a limited number of sources. Any processes potentially involving a widespread cortical network are difficult to model in this way. Distributed-source models do not make any a priori assumptions regarding the number of sources underlying any given signal; they can produce a volumetric grid of potential locations, which can then be analyzed to estimate a configuration of activity that matches the observed one. Under this heading come minimum norm and weighted minimum norm techniques as well as the beamformer approaches, of which synthetic aperture magnetometry (SAM), a nonlinear form, is currently favored by magnetoencephalography (MEG) researchers (see Singh, chapter 12, this volume).

As well as identifying single or distributed sources of EEG signals, researchers are interested in the interconnectivity between the sources. Coherence analysis computes the correlations between electrodes or groups of electrodes as a function of frequency. Variations in the size and sign of the correlation coefficient are taken as a measure of the "coupling" or "uncoupling" of the respective areas. Coherence values vary from 0 (uncorrelated) to 1 (fully correlated). Early studies used rather simplistic linear assumptions; more recent metrics incorporate nonlinear methods.

The coherence analysis technique is not without its critics, the outcome of the measures potentially being affected by the use of inappropriate reference electrodes, for example (French and Beaumont, 1984). More complex versions of simple coherence have evolved in an attempt to capture the variations in apparent collaborations across the cortex, depicting the distance between correlated sources and the changes in correlations over time, both within and between different frequencies (e.g., Weiss and Mueller, 2003). More contemporary models of connectivity suggest that coherence does not accurately reflect the "chaotic," nonlinear nature of electrical activity in the brain (David, Cosmelli, and Friston, 2004).

Following Berger's lead, early cognitive EEG researchers used frequency variations as the dependent variables while investigating, for example, the relationship between alpha and attention. They attached little functional significance to these variations, however, and made little attempt to apply such findings to the emerging cognitive science models, where complex processes were being deconstructed and described in terms of distributed networks of modules and serial or parallel processing. Instead, a technique that arose from the availability of more powerful computational assistance for EEG analysis was the EEG metric of choice. Averaging techniques can combine the EEG responses from large numbers of stimulus repetitions to produce an average evoked response or potential. It is assumed that the responses are consistent and that they are time locked to the stimulus event; averaging will cancel out the "random" background EEG activity. The resultant waveforms are described in terms of their polarity (P = positive; N = negative) and their latency (e.g., "N100" is a negative-going potential occurring approximately 100 msec after stimulus onset). The baseline-to-peak or peak-to-peak amplitude of the waveforms can also be measured (figure 10.6).

Potentials evoked in association with sensory processes are usually called "evoked potentials" (EPs), hence the term *visual evoked potential* (VEP). Latencies are usually short (<100 msec) and amplitudes small (<1 μV). They have proved a useful measure of the integrity of sensory pathways and hence can be a valuable clinical tool. Evoked potentials associated with cognitive processes are commonly termed *event-related potentials* (ERPs). They have longer latencies (100–600 msec) and can be measured in tens of microvolts. Until recently, ERPs have been the main tool in the application of EEG to cognitive neuroscience research; their fine temporal resolution allows neuroscientists to examine behavioral processes that occur over millisecond timescales. As variations in latencies and polarities became

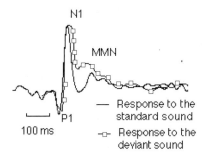

Figure 10.6
Characteristic ERP waveform, showing positive and negative changes at approximately 100 msec and Mismatch negativity (MMN) response to standard and deviant stimuli.

associated with individual cognitive processes, a specific taxonomy arose, with ERPs of differing latencies or polarities named, for example, after the cognitive process that was purportedly being indexed (e.g., "mismatch negativity—MMN"), the characteristics of the cognitive situation ("novelty P300"; "incongruity response—N400"), or the paradigm within which they were elicited ("oddball P300").

Changes in amplitude or power could be associated with different aspects of the relevant process; for example, repeated or successfully recalled items in a memory test were found to elicit larger ERPs than new or unsuccessfully recalled items (Rugg and Coles, 1995). Changes in the amplitude of specific components have been interpreted as indices of the allocation of specific cortical resources to the task, with increases taken as an index of increased, and decreases as an index of decreased, allocation. A paradigm involving the use of "probe" stimuli evolved in association with this interpretation. A simple stimulus is presented while a particular task (e.g., memorizing a list of words) is ongoing; variations in the amplitude of the EP/ERP are analyzed as a function of variations in task complexity. It is commonly found that with increasing complexity, a reduction in EP or ERP amplitude is noted. This can be interpreted as an index of a diversion of processing resources from the simple stimulus to the cognitive task (e.g., Lavric et al., 2000). These changes in amplitude can be interpreted as associated with changes in amount of recruitment of underlying cortical areas, although the acceptance of this interpretation is subject to the same caveats as all source-related interpretations of EEG data.

With the development of multichannel EEG systems, it became possible to combine analysis of the waveform components of ERPs with topographic mapping techniques to produce a temporal map, apparently "tracking" the different stages of a cognitive process. These data could be interpreted in terms of both time and space. Thus, if the amplitude of an ERP was observed to increase in frontal sites prior to an increase in parietotemporal sites, this could be construed as tracking the activity of a frontoparietal system.

ERP techniques proved fruitful for EEG cognitive scientists at the end of the last century, when almost all cognitive processes were examined applying ERP methodology (Rugg and Coles, 1995). Two of the best known are referred as the "mismatch negativity (MMN) response" and the "P300" or "P3," respectively.

Initially identified as a measure of preattentive processing and subsequently much researched by Näätänen et al. (2001), the MMN response is the outcome of a template-matching procedure, with comparisons made between an established neuronal model and incoming stimuli. The greater the deviation between the characteristics of the incoming stimulus and the template, the greater the amplitude and the shorter the latency of the MMN.

The integrity of the MMN response can be taken as a measure of the efficiency of early auditory processing; psychophysical thresholds can be established as a behavioral correlate. If the extent of deviation necessary before an MMN response occurs is outside the normal range, this can be interpreted as a deficit of the underlying cortical processes. Stimuli can be varied along a number of dimensions, such as frequency, duration, and intensity (Näätänen et al., 2004). According to Deouell, Bentin, and Giard, (1998), the MMN response is generated by two main intracranial processes, in the auditory and the frontal cortices. Because experimental subjects need not process the eliciting stimulus in any way, the MMN response is of tremendous utility in assessing early information processing in the very young or in clinical populations (Näätänen, 2003).

The P300 or P3, a positive-going ERP occurring approximately 300 msec after a stimulus, has received much attention as a potential index of human cognitive processes (Polich and Kok, 1995). An "oddball" P300 is observed when repeated series of identical stimuli are occasionally interspersed with a deviant stimulus, varying along relevant dimensions. The response to the "target" stimulus is compared with that to the "standard" stimulus and is taken as a measure of the processing of the differences between these classes of stimuli or the significance of these differences (Sutton et al., 1965). It has been suggested that the P300 is a measure of the outcome of comparisons between internal expectations or template matching processes and external "reality." Those expectations and consequences of confirmation/violation can be manipulated via task demands and stimulus characteristics.

A "novelty" P300 or P3, sometimes called the "P3a," is observed when an additional stimulus completely different from the task-relevant ones is introduced. It has been associated with the generation a new model of the novel event (Friedman, Cycowicz, and Gaeta, 2001). The P3 response to the target stimulus, which is enhanced if its occurrence requires processing, is called the "P3b." The P3a is commonly frontally distributed as compared to the posterior P3b. Using principal component analysis, Dien, Spencer, and Donchin (2003) suggest that the P3b has sources in the temporoparietal junction, whereas the novelty P3 or P3a has sources in the anterior cingulate cortex.

Although there are other well-researched examples of event-related potentials associated with more specific cognitive processes, such as the

N400 and the ERPs of linguistic violation studies (Kutas and Federmeier, 2000), the MMN response and the P300 have proved adaptable to a wide range of paradigms and valuable as dependent variables in a range of task and subject manipulations. However, although the fine temporal resolution of ERPs is undeniable, spatial interpretations are, of course, equally hostage to the inverse problem and source localization assumptions.

ERPs did much to carry the "timing" torch for EEG throughout the rise of cognitive neuroscience and the evolution of highly sophisticated spatial mapping systems. Findings using ERPs have led to elegant models of complex cognitive processes, and insight into the sequence and duration of associated subprocesses. Noting the close similarity between potential maps generated by ERPs and power distribution maps generated by EEG, Makeig et al. (2004) suggest the possibility of converting the former to the latter.

Innovation

As described above, the underlying assumption of ERPs or event-related frequency analyses is that responses are consistent across all trials, time-locked to each stimulus event. Although it is plausible to assume that a response can be time- and phase-locked in primary motor and sensory cortex, the more complex the process and the more distributed the under-lying cortical network, the less acceptable this assumption would appear to be. Emerging models of brain dynamics focus instead on trial-by-trial reset-ting of underlying EEG frequency oscillations, associated with the activity of multiple sources (see Penny et al., 2002).

An aspect of the renewed interest in EEG frequency studies was their focus on the functional significance of increases and decreases in power within specific frequency bands. Pfurtscheller and Aranibar (1977) coined the term *event-related desynchronization/synchronization* (ERD/S), with variations in amplitude or power hypothesized to arise from variations in the desynchronization/synchronization of the originating neuronal popula-tion, increasing/decreasing power associated with increasing/decreasing synchrony, respectively.

Somewhat confusingly, it has been suggested that the reduction in power termed *event-related desynchronization* is connected with increased activation in a given cortical area, possibly associated with the task-related and transient uncoupling of this area from a larger cortical network. By contrast, the increase in power termed *event-related synchronization* is associated with a reduction in activation of a task-irrelevant area, possibly associated with inhibition. Neuper and Pfurtscheller (2001) further developed this concept and described patterns of "focal ERD with surround ERS," reflecting the activity of a thalamocortical mechanism to enhance focal cortical activation by simultaneous inhibition of other areas. To some extent, the term *event-related desynchronization/synchronization* can be seen to beg the question as to the nature of the activity in the neuronal clusters that gives rise to these spectral power changes. Makeig et al. (2004) have coined the term *event-related spectral perturbation* (ERSP), which seems to avoid this pitfall.

With the emergence of more sophisticated models of brain activity focusing on nonlinear oscillatory dynamics and functional connectivity (Varela, Lachaux, and Martiniere, 2001), there has been renewed interest in the "background" EEG activity and its frequencies. Emergent patterns of activity are now interpreted as quasi-deterministic reorganizations of prestimulus activity, rather than as information superimposed on background noise. Attention is drawn to the distinctions between *evoked* changes in activity, which were assumed to be time-locked to the eliciting event, and *induced* changes in activity, which were assumed to be associated with the eliciting event but not necessarily time-locked to it and to evidence trial-by-trial variations.

The data analysis associated with this approach, though computationally more intense, is actually less restrictive in terms of the paradigms and tasks to which it can be applied. The signals can be summed and averaged to measure the phase- and time-locked changes of evoked activity or considered trial by trial to investigate emerging components that are induced by, but not strictly time-locked to, stimulus onset. This has proved particularly valuable in identifying high-frequency components such as gamma waves, which frequently did not emerge with standard time-locked averaging. The time-frequency characteristics of each epoch can be identified using wavelet analysis and visualized using time-frequency representations (TFRs) or spectrograms (figure 10.7, plate 5). Spatial maps can be produced and coregistered with anatomical data to indicate the cortical sources of distinct local field processes (Makeig et al., 2004).

Such techniques have a reciprocal relationship with emerging models of brain activity. It is now possible to describe frequency-specific oscillations within discrete neuronal areas and to measure temporally transient coupling between such areas. These can be long-distance connections or between closely neighboring sites. Models can be tested using linear or nonlinear approaches (David, Cosmelli, and Friston, 2004). The focus is very much on the frequency characteristics of the EEG signal. It is suggested that

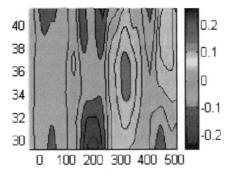

Figure 10.7
Time-frequency representation (TFRs) of event-related inerease in gamma (30–40 Hz) activity at approximately 300 msec poststimulus. See plate 5 for color version. (Adapted from Brown et al., 2005)

it is via these changes or modulations of frequencies that the brain codes and stores the information it is receiving and transmitting (Makeig et al., 2004).

The analytical advance arising from the "event-related brain dynamics" approach focused renewed attention on EEG frequencies, not just as dependent variables but as quasi-deterministic phenomena. It became clear that any attempt to understand how the brain achieves the transient integration of local networks of neurons, which underpins all processes from simple sensation to consciousness itself, would require a better understanding of the role of EEG (or MEG) frequencies in the brain. This focus on frequency has motivated attempts to combine EEG with spatially more powerful techniques such as fMRI in order to localize the source of the frequency changes. Moreover, it has been suggested that, if external influences such as transcranial magnetic stimulation (TMS) can be used to vary (block or attenuate) specific frequencies, perhaps they could also be used to block or enhance specific cognitive processes.

Fernandez et al. (1998) have claimed that different EEG frequencies are propagated by different neural generators. Early research focused on the concept of unique pacemakers, and sought single or simple source solutions (see Michel et al., 1992). More recent conceptualization suggests different frequencies reflect the activity of distributed systems, either locally networked or widely distributed, which resonate together in temporary couplings, dependent on the processing requirements (Nunez, 2000; Başar et al., 1997; Başar, Schurman, and Sakowitz, 2001; Rodriguez et al., 1999).

Research into theta activity is a good example of attempts to discover the functional significance of an EEG frequency by investigating its cortical and cognitive correlates. The theta waveband has been described rather charmingly by Lopes da Silva (1992) as "the finger print of all limbic structures." It is frequently claimed as an index of hippocampal activity (Tesche, Karhu, and Tissari, 1996; Burgess and Gruzelier, 1997). It has been measured in human hippocampal areas using implanted electrodes, with dipole modeling of frontal midline theta reporting sources in the hippocampus, the prefrontal cortex, and the anterior cingulate (Asada et al., 1999). And, indeed, it has been shown to be the dominant rhythm in rat and cat hippocampal structures.

With respect to the behavioral significance, one would therefore expect theta variations to be associated with cognitive processes associated with limbic structures. Unsurprisingly, then, variations in theta have been associated with variations in memory performance (Klimesch et al., 1997, 2001). Burgess and Gruzelier (1997) demonstrated that variations in theta during episodic memory tasks were associated with successful discrimination between "new" and "old" stimuli. More generally, it has been shown that frontal theta varies with success or improvements in task performance. Gevins et al. (1997) have reported changes in theta as a function of practice; Rohm et al. (2001) have reported that theta in the encoding stages of a memory task is a predictor of later successful retrieval; and Rippon and Brunswick (1998, 2000) have reported that successful task performance in dyslexic children is associated with increased levels of frontal theta.

How does oscillatory activity at 4–7 Hz support these cognitive processes? Miller (1991) attributes a priming role to the hippocampus, with hippocampal theta activity priming the circuits of target structures. Associated with this is the Treves and Rolls (1994) model, whereby those parts of the cortex which were active when the memory was laid down are reactivated by hippocampal theta "driving." Başar and colleagues (Başar, Schurmann, and Sakowitz, 2001) posit a similar model whereby a theta "state" modulates the degree of limbic and prefrontal activation.

The alpha rhythm was, of course, the first EEG rhythm to be described and its history therefore partly parallels the history of EEG research. Although there was early interest in its behavioral correlates, the difficulty in inferring the underlying cortical mechanisms reduced the usefulness of the alpha rhythm as a neuroscience research tool. A special edition of the *International Journal of Psychophysiology* in 1997 hailed the "renaissance of alphas" (Başar et al., 1997), with the use of the plural designed to draw attention to the claimed existence of multiple phenomena in the alpha frequency band. The neural origins of alpha waves can be demonstrated by cellular recording. Llinás (1988) reported action potentials in the alpha range in thalamic neurons, and suggested that alpha activity is associated with thalamic pacemakers driving thalamocortical networks (see Steriade et al., 1990). In a review of alpha oscillations in the brain, Başar et al. (1997) refer to a more diffuse and distributed alpha system and identify alpha activity in a variety of networks dependent on the associated behavior.

As with the theta rhythm, the alpha rhythm appears to be associated with specific cognitive processes. Much work by Klimesch and colleagues has indicated its role in memory functions. According to Klimesch (1997), variations in alpha can be taken as an index of individual differences, with good memory performers consistently showing alpha activity at a frequency about 1 Hz higher than that for bad performers. Moreover, within the alpha range, different stages of a memory process appear to be represented with low (8–10 Hz) alpha varying as a function of attentional demands and high (10–12 Hz) alpha as a function of stimulus characteristics and semantic memory processes.

Early observations of the disappearance (or "blocking") of alpha activity with visual stimulation, or of mu activity with somatosensory stimulation, and its replacement by higher-frequency, lower-amplitude activity suggested that alpha activity was a measure of some kind of steady or unengaged cortical state. Thus an increase in alpha power or alpha event-related synchronization (ERS) was taken as a measure of "cortical idling" (Pfurtscheller, Stanak, and Neuper, 1996). This term is perhaps unfortunate since it implies no activity, making reports of alpha ERS in successful or skilled task performance seem paradoxical. However, an alternative interpretation of ERS as a measure of the interruption or inhibition of thalamocortical information transfer and thus the reduction in activity of task-irrelevant networks may explain this apparent paradox (Pfurtscheller, Stancak, and Neuper, 1996).

Beta activity characteristically occurs in situations of specific task demand. Its distribution is less widespread than alpha, and topographic mapping indicates much more focal, localized patterns. Focusing on motor processing, Neuper and Pfurtscheller (2001) contend that beta activity is an index of local activation in sensorimotor areas. They interpret reductions in signal power observable after movement and somatosensory stimulation as the induction of a state of inhibition in these areas, suggesting that neural networks in the primary motor areas are responsible for the generation of oscillatory beta bursts. Lopes da Silva and Pfurtscheller (1999) argue that higher-frequency EEG activity arises from more restricted neuronal pools. Because it appears only on the cortex, beta activity is taken as an exemplar of such restricted synchrony (Lopes da Silva, 1991). Freeman (2004a, b) attributes a "carrier wave" role to beta activity, asserting that beta waves are caused by dendritic currents and determine the firing rate of currently interacting neurons. Moreover, Freeman suggests that, as the counterpart to gamma activity in the "binding" together of relevant neuronal assemblies over short distances, beta activity is responsible for longer-distance synchronization, associated with the activity of long axons of excitatory neurons with high conduction velocities. On the other hand, von Stein and Sarnthein (2000) contend that beta activity plays a more medium-distance role in synchrony, between neighboring cortical areas such as temporal and parietal lobes.

To some extent, current interest in EEG frequencies was stimulated by focus on the gamma rhythm, the high-frequency EEG wave whose presence became easier to determine with improvements in equipment and signal-processing methods. Based on evidence from intracellular recording (Singer and Gray, 1995) and scalp-recorded EEG, Tallon-Baudry and Bertrand (1999) link gamma-band activity with "binding," the integration of functionally discrete activation across the brain; they posit that rhythmic synchronization of neural discharges in the gamma band provide the necessary spatial and temporal links that bind together subprocessing in different areas to build a coherent percept. Studies using illusory or ambiguous figures (Rodriguez et al., 1999; Tallon-Baudry et al., 1999) have shown that successful perception of the figure is associated with bursts of induced (not evoked) gamma activity. Similarly, gamma activity has been associated with activation of internal representations in perception and memory (Tallon-Baudry et al., 1997, 1998). In a review of the role of early-onset (<150 msec) and late-onset (>200 msec) gamma components, Herrmann, Munk, and Engel (2004) propose a potentially unifying model, whereby sensory information is matched with memory contents, with the late-onset component indexing processing outcome such as response selection or context updating.

Early interpretations of the above research claimed gamma activity as the index of consciousness, in that it emerged only when there was a subjective experience or consciousness of a given percept, such as a triangle in the Kanisza figure or a face in the Mooney faces paradigm, that is, when the discrete parts of the percept were experienced as a coherent whole. It was therefore claimed that gamma activity, as a measure of the effective integration or coupling of the neural output from distinct brain regions, was the solution to the "binding" problem (Nunez, 2000). On the other hand, because such synchronization only occurs over distances of a few millimeters, (Steriade, Amzica, and Contreras, 1996), it has been argued that gamma activity's binding role may well be limited to discrete assemblies associated with perception and perceptual representation.

Just as intrafrequency changes can have a cognitive and a biological significance, so, too, can interfrequency changes. For example, Klimesch (1996) observed changes in alpha and theta activity in parallel with encoding and recognition stages of a memory task. Using measures of ERS/ERD in theta and alpha activity, split into narrow (2 Hz) frequency bands in a working memory task, Krause et al. (2000) showed theta event-related synchronization at stimulus recognition stages and ERS/ERD variations between the alpha band frequencies fluctuating as a function of increasing attentional demands and memory load.

As interpeted by von Stein and Sarnthein (2000), high-frequency (gamma) activity reflects activity within localized areas, beta activity reflects activity between neighboring cortical sites, and alpha and theta activity reflect longer-range anterior-posterior pathways. Synchronization over more widely separated cortical areas might be brought about by slower frequencies such as alpha, the difference being due to axonal size and conduction velocities (von Stein and Sarnthein, 2000; Bruns and Eckhorn, 2004). Thus the necessity to couple both local and global processes will involve coupling both high- and low-frequency signals.

It is, perhaps, surprising that frequency bandwidths defined at the outset of EEG research still inform research today, even if they have been subdivided in some cases. They have been abandoned by some researchers who have devised instead descriptors as a function of standard bandwidths, such as "2 Hz" or "10 Hz." The advantage of the classical bandwidths for cognitive neuroscientists is that there is a well-established association between these and a wide range of cognitive processes. It remains to be seen whether a different nomenclature will eventually emerge.

Because the majority of brain processes cognitive scientists are interested in studying operate on a millisecond timescale, only techniques that have such temporal resolution can investigate these processes with any validity. That is the secret of the continued success of electroencephalography in the panoply of available research techniques. Indeed, the availability of EEG has informed the development of contemporary brain models stressing nonlinear dynamics and the interaction of widely and transiently coupled neuronal assemblies (Tononi and Edelman, 1998; Varela, Lachaux, and Martiniere, 2001; David, Cosmelli, and Friston, 2004), models that can be expected to feed back into the ways EEG data are analyzed.

Perhaps the claims to have unlocked the secrets of consciousness through gamma wave research were somewhat premature. Nevertheless, an understanding and accurate characterization of event-related brain dynamics has enormous significance for understanding pathological conditions where functional rather than structural pathology is implicated. One example of this is in research into autism, where it has been possible to test hypotheses of dysfunction in local and global neuronal coupling as underpinning the classic triad of impairments that characterize the behavior of autistic individuals (Grice et al., 2001; Brown et al., 2005). Similar innovative applications can be seen in other developmental disorders and, at the other end of the age scale, in models of normal and abnormal cortical aging (Reuter-Lorenz, 2002). Thus EEG (and with it, MEG) has a clear role to play in exciting new developments in cognitive neuropsychiatry.

Limitations

One undeniable drawback of electroencephalography is its comparatively poor spatial resolution. As described above, along with other neuroimaging techniques such as magnetoencephalography (MEG), EEG suffers from the inverse problem, whereby a signal distribution measured at the surface could arise from a potentially infinite number of different intracranial sources. An additional problem that EEG has, and MEG does not, is that the EEG signal is distorted en route from the intracortical source to scalp. In source localization calculations, an appropriate "head model" thus needs to incorporate estimates of tissue conductivity and consequences for surface mapping of variations in head shape (Michel et al., 2004). Use of intracranial electroencephalographic (iEEG) estimations based on characteristics of signals from known epileptic foci or foci identified by other imaging techniques, animal models and lesion models can give rise to reasonably valid a priori assumptions about underlying cortical sources. As will be discussed below, the integration of EEG with other brain-imaging techniques will go quite some way to overcoming EEG's limitations.

Integration

It might seem surprising to suggest that EEG could be considered complementary to MEG when the latter can be described as "EEG without the problems"—no technical difficulties with electrodes or electrolytes, no head-modeling problems, even finer temporal resolution. Nevertheless, EEG can indeed be considered as complementary to MEG and, in some cases, can even serve as an alternative to it. Thus MEG may have reduced sensitivity to radial sources, which can be effectively accessed by EEG—an important consideration in the accurate presurgical mapping for the treatment of epilepsy. Additionally, because metallic implants preclude the use of MEG, only EEG can be used for brain activity mapping in certain classes of patients.

The coupling of EEG and fMRI combines the superior temporal resolution of the former with the superior spatial resolution of the latter. Simultaneous EEG and fMRI recording is now a possibility, limited mainly by the need to eliminate scanner artifacts from EEG data. To this end, interleaving paradigms have been developed, and spontaneous EEG-fMRI and evoked potential–fMRI studies have been carried out (Salek-Haddadi et al., 2003). The integration of EEG and fMRI can be mutually beneficial, with the fMRI data helping to validate the estimated dipole sources, and with comparisons between the hemodynamic and electrical responses offering insight into the relationships between the two.

Conclusion

The future of EEG in brain research in general and cognitive neuroscience in particular is very promising. EEG provides the link between the cortical and the cognitive/behavioral levels of explanation; indeed, it is clear that EEG activity, far from serving as a mere dependent variable, signals the continuous interplay between these two levels.

That said, mindful of what EEG is actually measuring—cellular activity at the membrane level—we must not lose sight of biological plausibility in our search for the most elegant statistical model. As EEG researchers, we have much to learn from cellular physiologists. Similarly, to ensure rigorous behavioral verification of the processes we are modeling, we must collaborate with clinical and cognitive neuropsychologists to develop appropriate paradigms and output measures. If we do these few things, we can be sure that the oldest of all neuroimaging techniques has much to offer to the study of the mind.

References

Asada, H., Fukuda, Y., Tsunoda, S., Yamaguchi, M., and Tonoike, M. (1999). Frontal midline theta rhythms reflect alternative activation of prefrontal cortex and anterior cingulate cortex in humans. *Neuroscience Letters*, 274(1), 29–32.

Başar, E., Schurmann, M., Başar-Eroglu, C., and Karakas, S. (1997). Alpha oscillations in brain functioning: An integrative theory. *International Journal of Psychophysiology*, 26, 5–29.

Başar, E., Schurmann, M., and Sakowitz, O. (2001). The selectively distributed theta system: Functions. *International Journal of Psychophysiology, 39,* 197–212.

Brown, C., Gruber, T., Boucher, J., Rippon, G., and Brock, J. (2005). Gamma abnormalities during perception of illusory figures in autism. *Correx, 41,* 364–376.

Bruns, A., and Eckhorn, R. (2004). Task-related coupling from high- to low-frequency signals among visual cortical areas in human subdural recordings. *International Journal of Psychophysiology, 51,* 97–116.

Burgess, A., and Gruzelier, J. H. (1997). Short duration synchronisation of human theta rhythm during recognition memory. *NeuroReport, 8,* 1039–1042.

David, O., Cosmelli, D., and Friston, K. J. (2004). Evaluation of different measures of functional connectivity using a neural mass model. *NeuroImage, 21,* 659–673.

Deouell, L. Y., Bentin, S., and Giard, M. H. (1998). Mismatch negativity in dichotic listening: Evidence for interhemispheric differences and multiple generators. *Psychophysiology, 35,* 355–365.

Dien, J., Spencer, K. M., and Donchin, E. (2003). Localisation of the event-related potential novelty response as defined by principal components analysis. *Cognitive Brain Research, 17,* 637–650.

Fender, D. H. (1987). Source localisation of brain electrical activity. In A. S. Gevins and A. Remond (Eds.), *Handbook of electroencephalography and clinical neurophysiology.* Vol. 1: *Methods of analysis of brain electrical and magnetic signals.* Amsterdam: Elsevier.

Fernandez, T., Harmony, T., Silva, J., Galan, L., Diaz-Comas, L., Bosch, J., Rodriguez, M., Fernandez-Bouzas, A., Yanez, G., Otero, G., and Marosi, E. (1998). Relationship of specific EEG frequencies at specific brain areas with performance. *NeuroReport, 9,* 3681–3687.

Freeman, W. J. (2004a). Origin, structure, and role of background EEG activity. Part 1. Analytic amplitude. *Clinical Neurophysiology, 115,* 2077–2088.

Freeman, W. J. (2004b). Origin, structure, and role of background EEG activity. Part 2. Analytic phase. *Clinical Neurophysiology, 115,* 2089–3017.

French, C., and Beaumont, G. (1984). A critical review of EEG coherence studies of hemispheric function. *International Journal of Psychophysiology, 1,* 241–254.

Friedman, D., Cycowicz, Y. M., and Gaeta, H. (2001). The novelty P3: An event-related brain potential (ERP) sign of the brain's evaluation of novelty. *Neuroscience and Biobehavioral Reviews, 25,* 355–373.

Gevins, A., Smith, M. E., McEvoy, L., and Yu, D. (1997). High-resolution EEG mapping of cortical activation related to working memory: Effects of task difficulty, type of processing, and practice. *Cerebral Cortex, 7,* 374–385.

Gratton, G., Coles, M. G. H., and Donchin, E. (1983). A new method for off-line removal of ocular artifact. *Electroencephalography and Clinical Neurophysiology, 55,* 468–484.

Grice, S. J., Spratling, M. W., Kormiloff-Smith, A., Halit, H., Csibra, G., de Haan, M., and Johnson, M. H. (2001). Disordered visual processing and oscillatory brain activity in autism and Williams Syndrome. *Neuroreport, 12,* 2697–2700.

Herrmann, C. S., Munk, M. H., and Engel, A. K. (2004). Cognitive functions of gamma-band activity: Memory match and utilization. *Trends in Cognitive Sciences, 8,* 347–355.

Klimesch, W. (1996). Memory processes, brain oscillations and EEG synchronisation. *International Journal of Psychophysiology, 24,* 61–100.

Klimesch, W. (1997). EEG alpha rhythms and memory processes. *International Journal of Psychophysiology, 26,* 319–340.

Klimesch, W., Doppelmayr, M., Stadler, W., Pollhuber, D., Sauseng, P., and Rohm, D. (2001). Episodic retrieval is reflected by a process specific increase in human electroencephalographic theta activity. *Neuroscience Letters, 302,* 49–52.

Klimesch, W., Doppelmayr, M., Schimke, H., and Ripper, B. (1997). Theta synchronization and alpha desynchronization in a memory task. *Psychophysiology, 34,* 169–176.

Klimesch, W., Schack, B., Schabus, M., Doppelmayr, M., Gruber, W., and Sauseng, P. (2004). Phase-locked alpha and theta oscillations generate the P1-N1 complex and are related to memory performance. *Cognitive Brain Research, 19,* 302–316.

Klimesch, W., Schimke, H., Ladurner, G., and Pfurtscheller, G. (1990). Alpha frequency and memory performance. *Journal of Psychophysiology, 4,* 381–390.

Krause, C. M., Sillanmäki, L., Koivisto, M., Saarela, C., Häggqvist, A., Laine, M., and Hämäläinen, H. (2000). The effects of memory load on event-related EEG desynchronisation and synchronisation. *Clinical Neurophysiology, 111,* 2071–2078.

Kutas, M., and Federmeier, K. D. (2000). Electrophysiology reveals semantic memory use in language comprehension. *Trends in Cognitive Sciences, 4*(12), 470.

Lachaux, J. P., Rudrauf, D., and Kahane, P. (2003). Intracranial EEG and human brain mapping. *Journal of Physiology* (Paris), 97, 613–628.

Lavric, A., Forstmeier, S., and Rippon, G. (2000). Differences in working memory involvement in analytical and creative tasks: An ERP study. *Neuroreport, 11,* 1613–1618.

Lavric, A., Pizzagalli, D., Forstmeier, S., and Rippon, G. (2001). A double-dissociation of English past-tense production revealed by event-related potentials and low-resolution electromagnetic tomography (LORETA). *Clinical Neurophysiology, 112,* 1833–1849.

Lehmann, D. (1987). Principles of spatial analysis. In A. S. Gevins and A. Remond (Eds.), *Handbook of electroencephalography and clinical neurophysiology.* Vol. 1: *Methods of analysis of brain electrical and magnetic signals.* Amsterdam: Elsevier.

Llinás, R. R. (1988). The intrinsic electrophysiological properties of mammalian neurons: Insights into central nervous system function. *Science, 242,* 11654–11664.

Lopes da Silva, F. H. (1991). Neural mechanism underlying brain waves: From neural membranes to networks. *Electroencephalography and Clinical Neurophysiology*, *79*, 81–93.

Lopes da Silva, F. H. (1992). The rhythmic slow activity (theta) of the limbic cortex: An oscillation in search of a function. In E. Başar and T. H. Bullock (Eds.), *Induced rhythms in the brain*. Boston: Birkhauser.

Lopes da Silva, F. H., and Pfurtscheller, G. (1999). Basic concepts of EEG synchronisation and desynchronisation. In G. Pfurtscheller and F. H. Lopes da Silva (Eds.), *Handbook of electroencephalography and clinical neurophysiology*. Vol. 6: *Event-related desynchronisation*. Amsterdam: Elsevier.

Makeig, S., Debener, S., Onton, J., and Delorme, A. (2004). Mining event-related brain dynamics. *Trends in Cognitive Sciences*, *8*(5), 204–210.

Michel, C. M., Lehmann, B., Hemggler, B., and Brandeis, D. (1992). Localisation of the sources of EEG delta, theta, alpha and beta frequency bands using the FFT dipole approximation. *Electroencephalography and Clinical Neurophysiology*, *82*, 38–44.

Michel, C. M., Murray, M. M., Lantz, G., Gonzalez, S., Spinelli, L., and Grave de Peralta, R. (2004). EEG source imaging: Invited review. *Clinical Neurophysiology*, *115*, 2195–2222.

Miller, R. (1991). *Cortico-hippocampal interplay and the representation of contexts in the brain*. Berlin: Springer.

Näätänen, R. (2003). Mismatch negativity: Clinical research and possible applications. *International Journal of Psychophysiology*, *48*, 179–188.

Näätänen, R., Pakarinen, S., Rinne, T., and Takegata, R. (2004). The mismatch negativity (MMN): Towards the optimal paradigm. *Clinical Neurophysiology*, *115*, 140–144.

Näätänen, R., Tervaniemi, M., Sussman, E., Paavilainen, P., and Winkler, I. (2001). Primitive intelligence in the auditory cortex. *Trends in Neurosciences*, *24*(5), 283–288.

Neuper, C., and Pfurtscheller, G. (2001). Event-related dynamics of cortical rhythms: Frequency-specific features and functional correlates. *International Journal of Psychophysiology*, *43*, 41–58.

Nunez, P. L. (2000). Toward a quantitative description of large-scale neocortical dynamic function and EEG. *Behavioural and Brain Sciences*, *23*, 371–437.

Pascual-Marqui, R. D, Michel, C. M., and Lehmann, D. (1995). Low-resolution electromagnetic tomography: A new method to localise electrical activity in the brain. *International Journal of Psychophysiology*, *18*, 49–65.

Penny, W. D., Kiebel, S. J., Kilner, J. M., and Rugg, M. D. (2002). Event-related brain dynamics. *Trends in Neurosciences*, *25*(8), 387–389.

Pfurtscheller, G., and Aranibar, A. (1977). Event-related cortical desynchronization detected by power measurements of scalp EEG. *Electroencephalography and Clinical Neurophysiology*, *42*, 817–826.

Pfurtscheller, G., and Lopes da Silva, F. H. (1999). Event-related EEG/MEG synchronisation and desynchronisation: Basic principles. *Clinical Neurophysiology*, *110*, 1842–1857.

Pfurtscheller, G., Stancak, A., and Neuper, C. (1996). Event-related synchronisation (ERS) in the alpha band—an electrophysiological correlate of cortical idling: A review. *International Journal of Psychophysiology*, *24*, 39–46.

Picton, T. W., Bentin, S., Berg, P., Donchin, E., Hillyard, S. A., Johnson, Jr., R., Miller, G. A., Ritter, W., Ruchkin, D. S., Rugg, M. D., and Taylor, M. J. (2000). Guidelines for using human event-related potentials to study cognition: Recording standards and publishing criteria. *Psychophysiology*, *37*, 127–152.

Polich, J. (1997). On the relationship between EEG and P300: Individual differences, ageing, and ultradian rhythms. *International Journal of Psychophysiology*, *26*, 299–317.

Polich, J., and Kok, A. (1995). Cognitive and biological determinants of P300: An integrative review. *Biological Psychology*, *41*, 103–146.

Ray, W. J., and Cole, H. W. (1985). EEG alpha activity reflects attentional demands and beta activity reflects emotional and cognitive processes. *Science*, *228*, 750–752.

Reuter-Lorenz, P. A. (2002). New visions of the ageing mind and brain. *Trends in Cognitive Sciences*, *6*(9), 394–400.

Rippon, G. M. J., and Brunswick, N. (1998). EEG correlates of phonological processing in dyslexic children. *Journal of Psychophysiology*, *12*, 261–274.

Rippon, G., and Brunswick, N. (2000). State and trait EEG indices of information processing in developmental dyslexia. *International Journal of Psychophysiology*, *36*(3), 251–265.

Rodriguez, E., George, N., Lachaux, J. P., Martiniere, J., Renault, B., and Varela, V. J. (1999). Perception's long shadow: Long-distance synchronisation of human brain activity. *Nature*, *397*, 430–433.

Rohm, D., Klimesch, W., Haider, H., and Doppelmayr, M. (2001). The role of theta and alpha oscillations for language comprehension in the human electroencephalogram. *Neuroscience Letters*, *310*, 137–140.

Rugg, M. D., and Coles, M. G. H. (Eds) (1995). *Electrophysiology of mind: Event-related brain potentials and cognition*. Oxford: Oxford University Press.

Salek-Haddad, A., Lemieux, L., Merschhemke, M., Diehl, B., Allen, P. J., and Fish, D. R. (2003). EEG quality during simultaneous functional MRI of interictal epileptiform discharges. *Magnetic Resonance Imaging*, *21*, 1159–1166.

Schack, B., Vath, N., Petsche, H., Geissler, H. G., and Möller, E. (2002). Phase-coupling of theta-gamma EEG rhythms during short-term memory processing. *International Journal of Psychophysiology*, *44*, 143–163.

Singer, W. (1999). Neuronal synchrony: A versatile code for the definition of relations? *Neuron*, *24*, 49–65.

Singer, W., and Gray, C. M. (1995). Visual feature integration and the temporal correlation hypothesis. *Annual Review of Neuroscience*, *18*, 555–586,

Singh, K. D., Barnes, G. R., Hillebrand, A., Forde, E. M. E., and Williams, A. L. (2002). Task-related changes in cortical synchronisation are spatially coincident with the haemodynamic response. *NeuroImage*, *16*, 103–114.

Steriade, M., Amzica, F., and Contreras, D. (1996). Synchronization of fast (30–40 Hz) spontaneous cortical rhythms during brain activation. *Journal of Neuroscience*, *16*(1), 392–417.

Steriade, M., Gloor, P., Llinas, R. R., Lopes da Silva, F. H., and Mesulam, M. M. (1990). Basic mechanisms of cerebral rhythmic activities. *Electroencephalography and Clinical Neurophysiology*, *76*, 481–508.

Sutton, S., Braren, M., Zubin, J., and John, E. R. (1965). Evoked potential correlates of stimulus uncertainty. *Science*, *150*, 1187–1188.

Tallon-Baudry, C., and Bertrand, O. (1999). Oscillatory gamma activity in humans and its role in object representation. *Trends in Cognitive Sciences*, *3*(4), 151–162.

Tallon-Baudry, C., Bertrand, O., Delpuech, C., and Pernier, J. (1997). Oscillatory gamma-band (30–70 Hz) activity induced by a visual search task in humans. *Journal of Neuroscience*, *17*(2), 722–734.

Tallon-Baudry, C., Bertrand, O., Peronnet, F., and Pernier, J. (1998). Induced gamma-band activity during the delay of a visual short-term memory task in humans. *Journal of Neuroscience*, *18*(11), 4244–4254.

Tesche, C. D., Karhu, J., and Tissari, S. O. (1996). Non-invasive detection of neuronal population activity in human hippocampus. *Cognitive Brain Research*, (4), 39–47.

Treves, A., and Rolls, E. T. (1994). Computational analysis of the role of the hippocampus in memory. *Hippocampus*, *4*, 374–391.

Varela, F., Lachaux, J.-P., Rodriguez, E., and Martiniere, J. (2001). The Brainweb: Phase synchronisation and large-scale integration. *Nature Reviews Neuroscience*, *2*, 229–239.

von Stein, A., and Sarnthein, J. (2000). Different frequencies for different scales of cortical integration: From local gamma to long-range alpha/theta synchronisation. *International Journal of Psychophysiology*, *38*, 301–313.

Weiss, S., and Mueller, H. (2003). The contribution of EEG coherence to the investigation of language. *Brain and Language*, *85*, 325–343.

11 Imaging Genetics

Venkata S. Mattay, Andreas Meyer-Lindenberg, and Daniel R. Weinberger

Imaging genetics, the application of imaging techniques to the identification of genetic effects on neurophysiology, neurochemistry, and brain morphology, is an emerging and promising area of research that could aid in better characterizing the influence of genes on cognition and behavior, as well as the link between genetic susceptibility and neuropsychiatric disorders. This chapter (1) describes the theoretical basis and potential of this novel approach; (2) puts forward some guidelines and principles for its execution and development; (3) reviews recent studies that highlight these principles; and (4) outlines the advantages of imaging genetics over more traditional approaches, such as neuropsychological batteries and personality inventories. (For reviews of some of the concepts and studies highlighted in this chapter, see Hariri and Weinberger, 2003b; Mattay and Goldberg, 2004.)

Development

Scientists and philosophers alike have debated for years about the role of "nature versus nurture" in human cognition, emotion, and behavior. It is now well accepted that both genes and environmental factors contribute to individual differences in brain function and behavior (Krubitzer and Kahn, 2003). Converging evidence also indicates that susceptibility to neuropsychiatric disorders appears to be heritable and that genes appear to be the only consistent risk factors that have been identified across populations (Moldin and Gottesman, 1997). With the recent completion of the working draft of the human genome sequence, researchers can now explore which of the numerous genes expressed in the brain specifically affect cognition, emotion, and behavior, and to what degree. Results from quantitative genetic research in family, twin, and adoption studies lend support to the conclusion that genes not only transmit susceptibility to neuropsychiatric disorders, but also contribute to individual variation in many aspects of cognition, temperament, and personality.

The "candidate gene association approach," or genetic association method, has been a particularly popular strategy for identifying genes involved in mental disorders. In contrast to linkage analysis, which focuses on the position of a tested marker, the genetic association method tests whether a given genetic variant (e.g., a particular allele of a marker or a mutation, specific genotype, or haplotype) is enriched or statistically associated with affected versus unaffected individuals. In other words, the genetic association method explores the relationship between genetic variants and trait differences in a general population. Typically, the method first identifies a biological aspect of a particular disease or condition and a given genetic variant thought to impact on that aspect, or candidate biological process, then explores whether the given genetic variant is enriched in populations having the designated phenotype. A statistically significant increase in frequency of the genetic variant in the selected population is deemed evidence of genetic association. Although the finding of such an association may indicate that the genetic variant is the causative factor for the particular phenotype, it may be spurious because of methodological or population artifacts, or it may, in fact, indicate a linkage to other genetic variants that are the true causative alleles. These are important caveats to the design and interpretation of genetic association studies in general, resulting from studies of ancestral stratification in sampled populations and of linkage disequilibrium with other loci. (For a review of these and other particulars of genetic methodology beyond the scope of this chapter, see Emahazion et al., 2001.)

Imaging genetics is a form of genetic association analysis in which the phenotype is a measure of brain structure (volume), chemistry, or function (physiological response of the brain during information processing), rather than a disease, symptom complex, or behavior. Imaging genetics is based on the assumption that brain structure, chemistry, and function are closer to gene function than trait differences in overt behavior. Technological advances in brain-imaging techniques over the last decade now allow us to measure brain volume and to assay brain function and chemistry noninvasively, with reasonably high spatial and temporal resolution. These techniques can be roughly divided into (1) those which measure regional brain activity through neurophysiological imaging and recording: blood oxygenation level–dependent functional magnetic resonance imaging (BOLD fMRI), positron-emission tomography (PET), magnetoencephalography (MEG), and electroencephalography (EEG); and (2) those which measure the expression and function of specific brain proteins and metabolites through neurochemical imaging: magnetic resonance spectroscopic imaging (MRS), single-photon emission computerized tomography (SPECT), and, again, PET. Thanks to recent technological advances, superior spatial resolution in magnetic resonance imaging enables us to measure individual differences in neuroanatomy, in particular, gray and white matter volumes with voxel-based morphometry (VBM—a sophisticated, fully automated morphological imaging technique; Ashburner and Friston, 2000; Good et al., 2001) and the direction and integrity of white matter tracts with diffusion-tensor imaging (DTI; Moseley, Bammer and Illes, 2002).

Principles

Selection of Genes to Study

Ideally, the application of neuroimaging techniques to the study of genetic effects in the living brain should start from well-defined functional polymorphisms in genes such as COMT, BDNF, and SERT (illustrated below), whose impact has been demonstrated at the level of cell physiology and biochemistry in anatomically specific brain regions and circuits. In the absence of clearly well defined functional polymorphisms, other potential starting points for imaging genetics include candidate genes with identified single-nucleotide polymorphisms (SNPs) or other allele variants in coding or promoter regions with possible functional implications (e.g., nonconservative amino acid substitution or missense mutation in a promoter consensus sequence) that involve discrete neuroanatomical systems. However, when investigating genetic variations with unknown function, it is crucial to exercise caution in the interpretation of differential brain responses or observed changes in brain structure or chemistry.

Task Selection and Design

The interpretation of a potential gene effect at the level of information processing is critically dependent on task selection and design. Task design can test specific hypotheses about the functions of a particular gene in the brain, for example, COMT and working memory during an N-back paradigm, or it can be used in a data-mining approach to explore gene effects in an atheoretical context—although, as we will see, the latter situation may involve no prior probability of an effect and will require more stringent statistical control for false discovery. Another important requirement in the selection of imaging genetics paradigms is that they reliably engage discrete brain circuits and elicit robust signals with variance across subjects. Association of variation in genetic sequence with variation in phenotype requires that the phenotype be variable across subjects. For this reason, it may be beneficial to choose traditional block-designed paradigms that have high efficacy and sensitivity in detecting sustained signal differences associated with different tasks (Birn, Cox, and Bandettini, 2002). Once the effects of genes on specific brain regions have been identified, event-related fMRI designs that allow the study of independent events and subprocesses in the information-processing stream might be considered. An alternate approach would be to use mixed "blocked and event-related" paradigms that incorporate the features and advantages of both designs (Laurienti, Burdette, and Maldojian, 2003).

Matching for Systematic Nongenetic Differences

The effects of an individual gene on brain morphology, chemistry, and function, though possibly more substantial than on behavior, are still expected to be very small. It is therefore critical to control for systematic nongenetic differences between genotype groups that could also have an impact on the phenotype, that is, the imaging data. Relevant nongenetic variables include gender, age, IQ, education, and environmental factors such as illness, injury, substance abuse, and central nervous system disorders. Moreover, because genetic background at other loci in the genome can give rise to effects not related to the candidate gene, and to preclude stratification artifacts related to ethnicity, it is essential to control for ethnic variability across genotype groups, as traditionally done in case-control association studies. Finally, since imaging response goes hand in hand with task performance, and since systematic differences in performance between genotype groups could mask a true gene effect or be mistaken for one, it is important to control for task performance either by matching for performance across genotype groups or by using performance scores as covariates in the analysis. This final point merits further comment. In principle, genes that affect brain structure or function may show these effects in carefully crafted neuroimaging paradigms, provided the effect size is sufficient. Changes in such brain phenotypes may also impact on behavior, again if the effect size is great enough and if compensation at the behavioral level is insufficient. Thus correcting for behavior may be seen as controlling for the gene effect itself. We maintain that such correction is a necessary step in the validation process implicit in imaging genetics, which, by identifying gene effects at the level of brain that cannot be attributed to behavioral artifacts, has the unique potential to validate gene effects in the living brain.

Maintaining High Methodological Standards

To improve sensitivity of imaging and recording techniques in detecting subtle differences, as when comparing patients to healthy controls or when comparing data within subjects over time to assess drug effects, it is common practice now to maintain high standards of quality control. This practice should also be scrupulously observed in imaging genetics, and requires that (1) data with excessive image or motion artifacts be excluded; (2) measures of variance and signal to noise in image data be comparable across individuals; and (3) quality control procedures be routinely performed to ensure optimal performance of the scanner.

Statistical Issues

The application of brain imaging and recording to genetics presents several unique and, as yet, only partially answered challenges to the statistical evaluation of the resulting data. Typically, the data set for a neuroimaging experiment comprises a large number (on the order of several thousand to tens of thousands) of data points acquired sequentially over a time course of several minutes with a sampling rate that varies from milliseconds when using MEG to several minutes when using PET and SPECT. To assess genetic variation, the results from such imaging experiments must first be summarized appropriately for each subject, often by producing a "statistical parametric map" or some other derived measure with known statistical properties. These within-subject statistical maps are then assessed across subjects and related to genotype or haplotype, often taking into account other possible confounding variables such as age, gender, ethnicity, or performance. This second step is exclusively driven by between-subjects variance. Such an analysis is commonly called a "random effects analysis" in the neuroimaging community (although the two steps can also be performed simultaneously in a "mixed effects model," for both conceptual and practical reasons, they are more often performed sequentially, as described; Frackowiak, 2004). Whereas functional neuroimaging studies with a cognitive neuroscience orientation and small numbers of subjects may still disregard the distinction between within-subject and between-subjects sources of variance, it is essential that imaging genetics studies strictly observe this distinction.

As exemplified by the work discussed in detail below, neuroimaging provides access to an intermediate level of phenotypic expression, where the effects of genes become markedly more pronounced than at the level of behavior and diagnosis. Nevertheless, because brain functions are highly interdependent and dynamic, a risk gene variant will only rarely become the major determinant of regional neural processing, and because the effect of genotype on brain functions is expected to remain moderate, imaging genetics must carefully consider questions of sample size and experimental power. Although most imaging genetics studies published thus far report significant effects in groups of from 20 to 40 subjects, many of their results have not yet been replicated. Moreover, a publication bias against negative results is likely in this newly developing field, and recent data indicate that even for the same genetic mechanism the effect size can vary widely depending on which imaging target measure (structural variation, functional activation, or functional connections) is examined. We therefore think it premature to present a formal estimation of the experimental power of imaging genetics in this review, although this remains an important task that should be tackled within the next two years. Rather, we will draw attention to several important issues that arise in the setting where genetic effects of moderate size are investigated in sample sizes that are comparatively large (compared, that is, to the more cognitively oriented studies that dominate the field of neuroimaging as a whole).

A critical question in this context is that of multiple comparison correction (Frackowiak, 2004). Neuroimaging data, as described, often assess effects at many thousands of locations. At commonly used levels of statistical significance, say 5 percent, the large number of tests performed results in an high number of "significant" test results. This raises the problem of adequately suppressing spurious results while remaining sensitive to true experimental variation (Nichols and Hayasaka, 2003). In imaging genetics, how best to do this largely depends on what is known beforehand about the genetic variation under study, and on which neuroimaging paradigm is chosen. For example, if the known data on gene biology do not usefully constrain hypotheses about where brain function should be affected, or if the neuroimaging paradigm chosen is data driven and hypothesis free (e.g., an independent component analysis of an imaging data set), researchers must control for false positives across all brain locations studied. One of the best methods to control error in this situation may be to combine corrections derived from Gaussian random field theory (Frackowiak, 2004) with the recently proposed false discovery rate (FDR) approaches (Genovese, Lazar, and Nichols, 2002) whereby only a specified proportion of the identified positives are considered false positives.

On the other hand, if information on the neurobiological effects of the gene studied or on population variability in the neuroimaging measure employed is available, incorporating it into the analysis will result in a considerable increase in statistical power. If a gene is known to be differentially expressed in a given brain region or to specifically affect this region's function, statistical inference can be restricted to this region, for example, using a masking or small-volume correction approach. If the number of subjects studied with a given paradigm is large enough, the population variability at any given location in the brain using this paradigm can be directly assessed and used for statistical inference. This obviates the need for assumptions of normality and other distributional features required when performing statistics on a small number of probands. We envision that such an approach, combined with bootstrapping (Bullmore et al., 2000) or permutation approaches if necessary to provide large enough sample volumes (Nichols and Holmes, 2002), will help imaging genetics studies define regionally optimal cutoffs for significance testing, especially studies using data-driven or otherwise hypothetically unconstrained methods.

These last two issues could be usefully combined in a Bayesian approach to imaging genetics. Unlike traditional inferential statistics, Bayes' theorem formalizes the fact that each new experiment modifies our prior knowledge, resulting in a new (posterior) state of knowledge (Friston et al., 2002). Applied to imaging genetics, the effect of a finding of significant difference between genotypes will depend on our prior information. Thus, if we know beforehand that the gene has an effect in a particular brain region, and that the imaging experiment we employ reliably activates that region, we will be inclined to accept a moderate result there as a true positive. Conversely, we will be reluctant to accept even a strong result in a region if we know beforehand that the gene is not expressed there, or is not affected by the task. A lack of any prior knowledge, as when a randomly selected single-nucleotide polymorphism is evaluated using a totally data-driven imaging method, would fall in between these extremes. Bayes' theorem formalizes these considerations and allows for the principled incorporation of different kinds of information relevant to imaging genetics. Information both about regional differences in gene action and about the population distribution of experimental effects can be included as a priori constraints into the statistical machinery (Woolrich et al., 2004). Moreover, the Bayesian approach shows promise for the statistically principled assessment of convergent evidence: as detailed below, several studies have shown regional gene effects across imaging modalities—fMRI, MRSI, and structural imaging—and behavior; the intuitively obvious fact that such convergent evidence strengthens the case for the functional relevance of the genetic variation studied can be formally evaluated using Bayesian statistics. Approaches to perform these analyses in a computationally tractable way are being developed (Woolrich et al., 2004).

The next section presents examples of how applying the principles of imaging genetics can lead to novel insights into biological mechanisms underlying complex behavioral traits and susceptibility to neuropsychiatric disorders.

Innovation

All of the studies described below employed neuroimaging techniques to identify the effects of functional genetic polymorphisms at the systems level. All chose genetic polymorphisms that had been previously associated with alterations at the molecular and cellular level and with specific behaviors or disease states. Some targeted genes with clearly defined functional polymorphisms associated with specific physiological effects in distinct brain circuits at the cellular level (e.g., COMT, 5-HTT, and BDNF, discussed below), whereas other studies, in the absence of detailed functional variants, targeted genes with identified single nucleotide polymorphisms (SNPs) or allelic variants with likely functional polymorphisms that involve circumscribed neuroanatomical systems (e.g., MAO A, D4, APOE4, GRM3, also discussed below).

Imaging the Influence of Genes That Affect Catecholaminergic Signaling in the Brain

Converging evidence indicates that dopamine, a critical neurotransmitter related to reinforcement and reward, also plays an important role in focusing and stabilizing prefrontal cortical networks by modulating N-methyl-D-aspartate (NMDA) signals, non-NMDA glutamate signals, and GABAergic currents (Gonzalez-Burgos et al., 2002; Seamans et al., 2001). Evidence also indicates an inverted "U" relationship in the impact of dopamine signaling: whereas either excessive or insufficient dopaminergic activity in the prefrontal cortex impairs cognition, moderate activity results in optimal prefrontal function. These basic findings have stimulated a series of imaging genetics studies of genes that affect dopamine function in the prefrontal cortex (Goldman-Rakic et al., 2000). Recent evidence suggests that catechol-O-methyl transferase (COMT), an enzyme that inactivates released dopamine via enzymatic conversion to 3-methoxytyramine, may play a unique role in regulating dopamine flux in the prefrontal cortex, because of the low abundance and minimal role of dopamine transporters in this brain region (Moron et al., 2002; Lewis et al., 2001; Mazei et al., 2002). In humans, a functional polymorphism in the gene for COMT has been identified: an evolutionarily recent substitution of methionine (met) for valine (val) at codon 108/158 results in a thermolabile protein with 2–4 times lower activity (Mannisto and Kaakkola, 1999). Consistent with this functional polymorphism in the COMT gene and with the evidence that COMT is important in the prefrontal cortex dopamine flux, Egan et al. (2001) demonstrated that met allele carriers had superior performance on an executive cognition task; using fMRI during a working memory task, they found that subjects with the val allele consistently demonstrated a less efficient physiological response in the prefrontal cortex than subjects with the met allele for a fixed level of task performance (i.e., greater PFC activity). Moreover, using a family-based association analysis, they found a significant increase in transmission of the val allele to schizophrenic offspring. Egan and colleagues concluded that, because it increases prefrontal dopamine catabolism, the COMT val allele impairs prefrontal cognition and physiology, slightly increasing the risk of schizophrenia through this mechanism. This effect of COMT val-met genotype on prefrontal cognition has since been replicated by others (Malhotra et al., 2002; Joober et al., 2002; Goldberg et al., 2003).

Recent imaging studies also reveal that the more efficient working memory and frontal lobe information processing associated with the met allele may come at a price, such as adverse response to stimulants like amphetamine and heightened sensitivity to pain (Mattay et al., 2003; Zubieta et al., 2003). Using a double-blind crossover design to compare the effects of amphetamine and placebo, Mattay et al. (2003) monitored activity in the prefrontal cortex with BOLD fMRI while healthy subjects performed a version of the N-back working memory task. Regardless of the difficulty of the task, individuals homozygous for the val allele showed a more efficient frontal lobe response on amphetamine, that is, they showed a more focused PFC activation pattern on amphetamine relative to placebo while maintaining the same level of performance. In contrast, in individuals homozygous for the met allele, the efficiency of PFC response as well as accuracy and reaction time diminished significantly relative to the placebo condition at the most difficult task level, suggesting that information processing in these individuals was compromised. Mattay and colleagues interpreted these results to indicate that the combined effects of amphetamine and high working memory load "pushed" dopamine levels in these individuals beyond the optimal range on the inverted "U" via activation of inhibitory mechanisms, including inactivation of N-type Ca 2+ channels (Yang and Seamans, 1996), activation of GABAergic interneurons (Seamans et al., 2000), and pre- and postsynaptic reduction of glutamate-mediated synaptic responses (Law-Tho, Hirsch, and Crepel, 1994). Providing further evidence of an inverted "U" functional response curve to increasing dopamine signaling in prefrontal cortex, these findings also suggest that individuals with the met158met COMT genotype, though more efficient than the val carriers in PFC function under baseline conditions, appear to be at increased risk of an adverse cognitive response to amphetamine (figure 11.1, plate 6).

Using PET μ-opioid imaging with ^{11}C-carfentanil in concert with questionnaires measuring pain-related sensory and affective qualities (to link subjects' neurochemical response with their physical and psychological experience of painful stimuli), Zubieta et al. (2003) implicated another negative aspect of the met allele. They examined the hypothesis that the different levels of COMT activity produced by val-met polymorphism may have an influence on other functions regulated by catecholamines, including the μ-opioid system responses to noxious stimuli. They found that, in contrast to heterozygous individuals, individuals homozygous for the met allele showed a diminished μ-opioid response in the thalamus and amygdala, together with higher sensory and affective ratings of pain and a negative internal state. Individuals homozygous for the val allele, on the other hand, showed the opposite response. Zubieta and colleagues interpreted

Figure 11.1
(continued)
push PFC dopamine levels in these individuals beyond the critical threshold at which compensation can be made. (B) Schema of our proposed theoretical model to account for variable effects of the COMT genotype, WM load, and amphetamine on dopamine signaling and PFC function. According to this model, at baseline, individuals homozygous for the val allele (who have relatively poorer prefrontal function, greater COMT activity, and presumably less dopaminergic tone) are located on the up slope the inverted "U" curve of the normal range, whereas individuals homozygous for the met allele are located near the peak. In val/val homozygous individuals, amphetamine improves PFC function as dopamine signaling is shifted to more optimal levels at all load conditions. By contrast, in met/met homozygous individuals, amphetamine shifts dopamine levels onto the down slope of the curve, which has no effect or a deleterious effect depending on the magnitude of additional changes in dopamine levels associated with increasing processing demands. These data extend basic evidence of an inverted "U" functional response curve to increasing DA signaling in PFC. See plate 4 for color version.

A

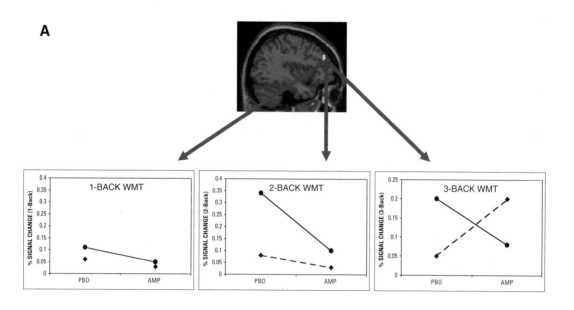

B

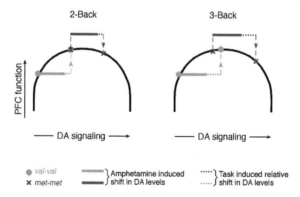

Figure 11.1

(A) Mattay et al. (2003), using BOLD fMRI, demonstrate a complex drug × COMT genotype interaction in the left prefrontal cortex (PFC) during the N-Back working memory task. While subjects homozygous for the val allele (solid line) showed a more efficient PFC response on amphetamine (i.e., greater PFC activity on placebo than on amphetamine) irrespective of task difficulty, subjects homozygous for the met allele (broken line) became inefficient on amphetamine at the highest working memory demand (i.e., they show more PFC activity on amphetamine than on placebo during the 3-Back working memory (WM) task). This paradoxical decrease in efficiency on the 3-Back task in the met/met homozygous subjects was associated with a significant decrement in performance (decreased accuracy and increased reaction time). We suggest that the combined effects of amphetamine and high WM load these results as evidence that (1) the COMT val-met polymorphism confers a variable response to pain across individuals via a downstream effect on regional μ-opioid transmission through interactions with dopaminergic or noradrenergic terminals; and (2) the "efficient" (met) allele confers a lower threshold for pain tolerance (although they did not specify the mechanism of this lower tolerance). It remains to be determined whether the met allele effect is related to pain threshold because of catecholeamine regulation of the opiate system or because met allele individuals are temperamentally less compliant with experimental procedures that inflict pain. Other data suggest that met allele carriers are more anxiety prone and have more obsessive-compulsive characteristics (for a review, see Bilder et al., 2004).

Dopamine, along with norepinephrine, has also been implicated in attentional processes. Fan et al. (2003) tested the hypothesis that polymorphisms linked with variability in aminergic signaling may explain the variation in cortical efficiency in managing incongruent or conflicting stimuli across individuals. Using BOLD fMRI, they demonstrated an effect of a polymorphism in the D4 receptor gene (an insertion/deletion polymorphism in the 5′ region with unknown functional effects) and a polymorphism in the promoter region of the monoamine oxidase A (MAO A) gene (linked with relatively lower expression of the MAO A gene and presumably greater catecholeamine levels) on the response of the anterior cingulate, a region thought to be critical for conflict monitoring or conflict resolution in cortical information processing. More efficient behavior, reflected in shorter reaction time, was associated with greater cingulate activation. The insertion class group in the D4 polymorphism and 4-repeat group in the MAO A polymorphism, demonstrated less conflict (in terms of the reaction time ratio) and greater cingulate activity when compared to the deletion class group in the D4 polymorphism and the 3-repeat group in the MAO A polymorphism. Fan and colleagues concluded that greater regional activity implies greater cortical efficiency, although, with respect to the MAO A polymorphism, the finding was presumably related to lower dopaminergic/noradrenergic signaling. Other neuroimaging studies, whether on effects of the COMT val158met polymorphism (see above; Egan et al., 2001; Mattay et al., 2003) in healthy elderly controls (e.g., Rypma and D'Esposito, 2000), or in patients with Parkinson's disease (e.g., Mattay et al., 2002), have shown that increased cortical activity can be associated with prolonged reaction time, a finding attributed to cortical inefficiency, at least in part to decreased dopaminergic tone. It should be noted, however, that these later studies examined prefrontal cortex in the context of working memory performance and, more specifically, dopamine activity.

Imaging the Influence of Genes that Affect Serotoninergic Signaling in the Brain

The amygdala plays an important role in the generation and regulation of emotional behavior, and several lines of evidence suggest that serotonin is critical for this function (for review, see Hariri and Weinberger, 2003a). A polymorphism in the promoter region of the serotonin transporter gene (5-HTTLPR) has been linked to alterations in 5-HTT transcription and in 5-HT uptake. Individuals homozygous for the long (l) promoter allelic variant express more serotonin transporter messenger RNA (mRNA) and thereby have greater serotonin synaptic uptake than individuals homozygous for the short (s) promoter allelic variant, who have relatively lower expression of the transporter and thereby relatively greater synaptic serotonin levels. Behavioral studies have suggested a relationship between the less efficient s allele, on the one hand, and abnormal levels of anxiety and fear and the increased prevalence of affective disorders, on the other. Their findings have not been consistent, however, possibly reflecting the vagueness and subjectivity of the behavioral measurements (Deary et al., 1999; Ball et al., 1997; Ebstein et al., 1997; Katsuragi et al., 1999; Jacobsen et al., 2000). Proceeding from the premise that the response within the amygdala might be more reliably measurable than behavior, and using BOLD fMRI, Hariri et al. (2002) demonstrated that subjects carrying the less efficient s allele had an exaggerated amygdala response to fearful stimuli compared to those homozygous for the l allele. Based on their findings, they concluded that the increased anxiety and fear associated with individuals possessing the s allele may reflect the hyperresponsiveness of the amygdala to environmental stimuli. More recently, Hariri et al. (2005) confirmed this finding in a larger cohort of healthy controls ($n = 92$) carefully screened for past and present medical or psychiatric illness (figure 11.2, plate 7). In this study, they also observed that the dominant short allele effect was as prominent in men as it was in women, and that neither 5-HTTLPR genotype, amygdala reactivity, nor genotype-driven variability in this reactivity was reflected in harm avoidance scores, a putative personality measure related to trait anxiety. Studies such as this promise to provide valuable insights into the neurobiological mechanisms of abnormal mood and affect associated with variation in 5-HT signaling.

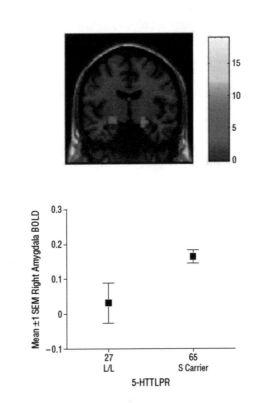

Figure 11.2
Hariri et al. (2005), using BOLD fMRI, demonstrate 5-HTTLPR effects on amygdala reactivity to environmental threat. Individuals homozygous for the s allele (s
carriers) of the serotonin transporter gene, who presumably have greater synaptic
serotonin levels, exhibit greater amygdala neuronal activity during the perceptual
processing of fearful and threatening facial expressions than individuals homozygous for the l allele, who presumably have lower synaptic serotonin levels. This
genetically driven differential excitability of the amygdala may contribute to the
increased fear and anxiety typically associated with the s allele. See plate 7 for color
version.

The mechanism of the effect of the 5-HTTLPR polymorphism remains a matter of some controversy. Although in vitro studies in lymphoblast cell lines (Lesch et al., 1996; Collier et al., 1996) have shown that the promoter activity of the 5-HTT gene is dependent on 5-HTTLPR allelic variants. (the transcriptional activity of the l allele was more than two times that of the s allele), findings from studies in human tissue are less consistent. In perhaps the first "imaging genetics" study, Heinz et al. (2000) used single-photon emission computerized tomography (SPECT) imaging to measure serotonin reuptake transporter (SERT) binding to a radioligand ^{123}I-B-CIT in vivo in the human brain. Their findings were remarkably similar to what in vitro studies had reported, although subsequent reports (Willeit et al., 2001; Heinz et al., 2000; Jacobsen et al., 2000) have been inconsistent. Findings on SERT expression in postmortem human brain tissue as a function of 5-HTTLPR genotype also have been inconsistent (for review, see Hariri and Weinberger, 2003a). Given the positive results of in vitro studies (Lesch et al., 1996; Collier et al., 1996) and human fMRI studies (Hariri et al., 2002) showing a functional effect of this polymorphism, further studies are warranted to reliably characterize the association between the serotonin transporter–linked polymorphisms and 5-HTT binding.

Imaging the Influence of Brain-Derived Neurotrophic Factor

Studies in slice preparations and in experimental animals (see Poo, 2001) have shown that brain-derived neurotrophic factor (BDNF), a critical protein involved in neuronal survival and synaptic growth and plasticity, also plays a critical role in hippocampal long-term potentiation associated with learning and memory. There is a frequent polymorphism resulting in a nonconservative val to met substitution at codon 66 in the human BDNF gene, and recently Egan et al. (2003) have elaborated its effect on BNDF function. They showed in transfected neuronal culture that met alleles are abnormally packaged and trafficked and that their secretion is abnormally regulated. This would suggest that met BDNF would function relatively abnormally in conditions where neuroplasticity was critical for expression of a phenotype. Finding that BDNF affects hippocampal learning and memory and long-term potentiation (LTP), Egan and colleagues further showed that normal met/met homozygous individuals performed less well on episodic memory tasks than did val/val homozygous individuals. Using magnetic resonance spectroscopic imaging (MRSI) to address the mechanism at the neural system level, they found that the met allele is associated with relatively lower levels of N-acetyl aspartate (NAA), a putative marker of neuronal integrity and synaptic abundance, in the hippocampus. When they used fMRI to measure hippocampal activity during a working memory task, which normally leads to relative disengagement of the hippocampus, they found that met carriers failed to show this response. To directly explore the impact of the BDNF polymorphism on memory-related hippocampal activity, Hariri et al. (2003) used BOLD fMRI to measure such activity during encoding and subsequent retrieval of complex, novel scenes by healthy human subjects. They found that subjects homozygous for the met allele exhibited relatively diminished hippocampal activity during both encoding and retrieval processes, in comparison to subjects homozygous for the val allele. Moreover, they demonstrated that the interaction between BDNF val-met genotype and hippocampal activity (as measured by the BOLD response) during encoding accounted for 25 percent of the total variance in recognition accuracy (figure 11.3).

In a third study, using optimized voxel-based morphometry (Ashburner and Friston, 2000; Good et al., 2001), Pezawas et al. (2004) observed that healthy volunteers who were met/met homozygous (met carriers) had reduced gray matter volume in the hippocampus and the prefrontal cortex, regions related to learning and memory, in comparison to normal subjects who were val/val homozygous (figure 11.4, plate 8)—a finding consistent with the cellular and clinical effects of BDNF val66met polymorphism and the role of BDNF in cortical development. Together, these three studies illustrate the potential of a systems-level approach using in vitro, in vivo (brain-imaging), and behavioral measures to successfully delineate the impact of a gene, BDNF in this case, on brain structure and function.

Imaging the Influence of the Apolipoprotein E Allele on Brain Function

Perhaps on the basis of its role in cholesterol metabolism, apolipoprotein E (APOE) is thought to play a role in cell maintenance and repair, including amyloid clearance. It is now well established that the APOE4 allele is associated with increased risk for Alzheimer's disease in a dose-dependent manner (Saunders et al., 1993; Corder et al., 1993). If the deposition of beta-amyloid (assumed to be pathogenic in Alzheimer's) is a chronic and lifelong process that is either accelerated or not ameliorated by APOE4, then it stands to reason that individuals with APOE4 genotypes may have increasingly evident cognitive abnormalities over their life spans. Alternatively, a threshold effect for beta amyloid's impact on information

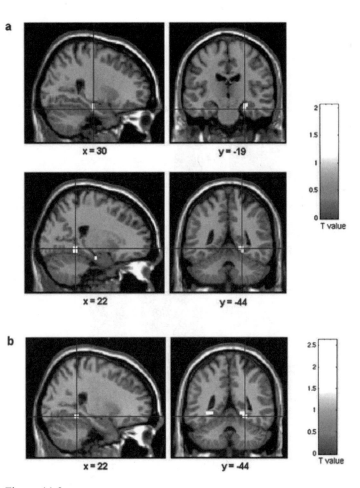

Figure 11.3
Hariri et al. (2003), using BOLD fMRI, demonstrate greater hippocampal activity during (*a*) encoding and (*b*) retrieval of (*c*) novel visual stimuli in subjects homozygous for the val allele of the BDNF gene relative to subjects homozygous for the met allele. Of note, this interaction between BDNF val66met genotype and the hippocampal BOLD response during encoding accounted for almost 25 percent of the variance in recognition memory performance (*d*).

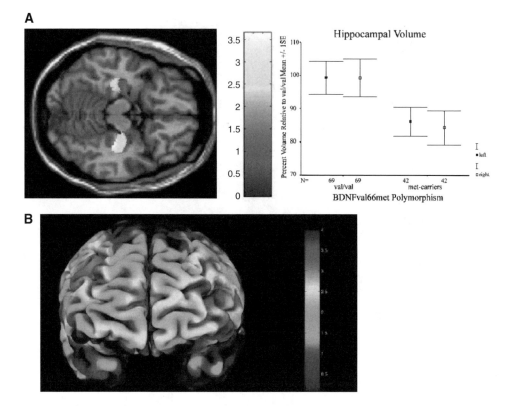

Figure 11.4
Pezawas et al. (2004), using optimized voxel-based morphometry (VBM), demonstrate volume differences in BDNF met carriers relative to BDNF val/carriers in the hippocampus (A) and prefrontal cortex (B). Consistent with the role of BDNF in cortical development and with the cellular and clinical effects of the BDNF val66met polymorphism, met carriers have relatively reduced gray matter volume in these brain regions. See plate 8 for color version.

processing (such that it becomes apparent only after it exceeds some limit) cannot be ruled out. Functional brain-imaging studies have consistently shown APOE4 effects in otherwise normal individuals. Early resting PET studies (Reiman et al., 1996; Small et al., 2000) found widespread reductions in glucose metabolism in otherwise normal APOE4 carriers. Using fMRI, Smith, Sikes, and Levin (1998) showed a reduced BOLD response in APOE4 carriers in the inferotemporal region during fluency and object recognition. On the other hand, Bookheimer et al. (2000) showed increased activity in response to memory tasks in subjects carrying the epsilon4 or E4 allele compared to those without this allele, and interpreted it to reflect a compensatory response via the recruitment of additional cognitive resources in the face of greater task demands. More recently, Petrella et al. (2002) and Burggren et al. (2002) replicated this phenomenon of compensatory increased activity in other brain circuits as well. Using BOLD fMRI during a working memory task in healthy, nondemented elderly individuals, Petrella et al. (2002) demonstrated greater extent and magnitude of activation in the prefrontal cortex in the E4 carriers relative to the E3 carriers. Burggren et al. (2002), on the other hand, examined whether these differences were specific to memory tasks only or could be generalized to any difficult cognitive task. Using fMRI and a modified digit-span task with varying difficulty in carriers and noncarriers of the APOE4 allele, they reported no significant difference in activation patterns at the most difficult task level and suggested that additional cognitive effort in persons at genetic risk for Alzheimer's disease is specific to episodic encoding and is not a reflection of task difficulty per se. Most importantly, Bookheimer et al. (2000) also demonstrated that greater baseline brain activation correlated with subsequent verbal memory decline. When "decline" begins is a key issue, though a study by Reiman et al. (1996) indicates that it may be discernible in individuals from 20 to 40 years old on FDG (^{18}F-fluorodeoxyglucose) PET.

Given that APOE4 confers increased susceptibility to age-related memory problems and that cholinergic system abnormalities are associated with memory problems in the elderly and Alzheimer's patients, Cohen et al. (2003) used ^{18}F-FP-TZTP (^{18}F-labeled-muscarinic-2 selective agonist) to directly measure the effect of APOE4 on the muscarinic component of the cholinergic system. They found increased distribution volumes of the tracer in APOE4 carrying older individuals relative to the noncarriers and this correlated inversely with cerebral blood flow. Cohen and colleagues interpret this finding to reflect an increase in the number of unoccupied muscarinic-2 receptors most likely from lower synaptic acetylcholine concentration in the APOE4 carriers. Taken together, these data from these functional neuroimaging studies support the notion that the effects of APOE4 allele can be discerned well before clinical presentation of disease and that elderly subjects with this allele are possibly more susceptible to future cognitive decline.

Recent advances in radiolabeling of amyloid proteins show promise for in vivo mapping of amyloid plaque density and neurofibrillary tangles in the human brain (Shoghi-Jadid et al., 2002; Small et al., 2002). Specifically, Shoghi-Jadid et al. (2002) reported that greater accumulation and clearance in brain areas rich in amyloid plaque and neurofibrillary tangle correlated with lower performance scores not only in Alzheimer's patients but also in controls. When combined with genetic information these in vivo techniques have the potential to elucidate the relationship between APOE4 allele load affect, amyloid plaque and neurofibrillary tangle density, and susceptibility to future cognitive decline and Alzheimer's disease.

Imaging the Influence of Metabotropic Glutamate Receptor Gene

Glutamate receptor, metabotropic 3 (GRM3) is responsible for multiple regulatory aspects of synaptic glutamate concentrations. Since glutamatergic abnormalities have been observed to play a critical role in the pathophysiology of schizophrenia, GRM3 is a promising candidate gene for schizophrenia. Using a family-based analysis, Egan et al. (2004) reported that a common GRM3 haplotype was strongly associated with schizophrenia. They observed that, within this haplotype, the A allele of the intronic single-nucleoticle polymorphism (SNP) hCV11245618 was associated with a significant increase in transmissions to schizophrenic offspring, and with poorer performance on cognitive intermediate phenotypes involving prefrontal and hippocampal function. Using fMRI, Egan and colleagues also observed that the physiological responses to cognitive processing in both these brain regions showed relatively deleterious effects of the SNP4 A allele. In particular, they observed that this allele was associated with a relatively exaggerated response in the prefrontal cortex during a working memory task suggestive of PFC inefficiency (figure 11.5A). In addition, during the encoding phase of an episodic memory task, they observed decreased activation in the hippocampus (figure 11.5B). Emerging in studies of normal volunteers, these observations were neither artifacts of psychiatric illness nor environmental confounders. Given the presumed positive relationship of hippocampal activation during declarative memory encoding and the improved performance during retrieval, Egan and colleagues concluded that this response reflects a deleterious effect of the A allele or of a nearby variation that was in linkage disequilbrium with the single-nucleotide polymorphism under study. Using MRSI, they observed that this allele also predicted lower prefrontal N-acetyl aspartate (NAA), an in vivo MRI measure of tissue glutamate. In an attempt to explore the cellular mechanisms underlying the above effects, they also measured both GRM3 mRNA and protein levels, as well as the regulation by GRM3 of downstream genes such as the glial glutamate transporter (a critical synaptic regulatory protein that regulates synaptic glutamate concentrations) in postmortem human prefrontal cortical brain tissue. They found that the

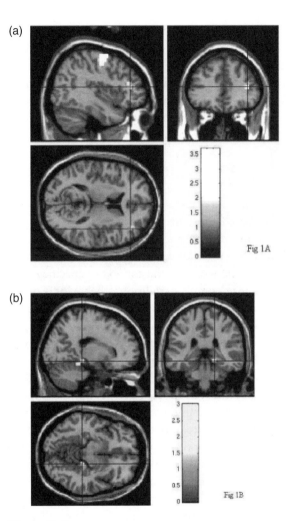

Figure 11.5
Egan et al. (2004), using BOLD fMRI in healthy controls, demonstrate the deleterious effects of the A allele of SNP hCV11245618 in GRM3 on prefrontal and hippocampal physiological responses. (A) Subjects with the A/A genotype showed higher DLPFC activation during a working memory task relative to a combined group of subjects with the A/G and G/G genotypes. (B) On the other hand, subjects with the A/A genotype showed reduced activation during an episodic memory task relative to subjects with the A/G and G/G genotypes. Further, using MRSI, Egan and colleagues observed that the A allele also predicted lower prefrontal NAA, an in vivo MRI measure of tissue glutamate. These data suggest that the A allele of GRM3 genotype, presumably by altering GRM3 expression, affects prefrontal and hippocampal physiological responses via downstream effects on glutamate neurotransmission.

same A allele was associated with a trend toward lower GRM3 mRNA expression, lower protein levels, assayed with a GRM2/3 antibody, and a strong effect on lower mRNA levels of the glial transporter. Based on these converging data, Egan and colleagues proposed that GRM3 variation probably increases risk for schizophrenia by altering GRM3 expression, which, via downstream effects on glutamate neurotransmission, affects prefrontal and hippocampal physiological responses as well as cognition.

Integration

The advantage of imaging genetics over traditional strategies for phenotyping brain function based on neuropsychological tests and personality inventories is that it allows researchers to more directly measure the impact of the gene at the level of information processing and neurochemistry within discrete brain regions and networks in the context of specific informational load. In contrast, the more complex traditional behavioral measures and test scores can be affected by factors such as the use of alternate task strategies, level of cooperation, and so on that can mask potential gene effects on the underlying neural substrates meant to be engaged by the tests. Genes encode for simple molecules within cells, which impact on the molecular processing of cellular information; they do not encode for behavior. Variations in cell processing lead to variation in the development and plasticity of neuronal networks, which handle complex environmental stimuli and information. Imaging genetics attempts to characterize gene effects at the level of the neuronal circuitry, and is thus closer to the biologic effect of genetic variation, at least in comparison to the emergent behavioral properties of functional variation in these networks. Moreover, whole-brain imaging allows researchers to study many individual processes, including those most salient to a trait, whereas behavioral studies typically focus on a single final behavioral measure, which is itself a product of multiple interactive processes. In particular, the superior signal detection power of functional neuroimaging techniques such as fMRI and of electrophysiological techniques such as EEG or MEG allows researchers to acquire several hundreds of measurements of brain function within a single subject in a single session. Moreover, whole-brain imaging techniques allow them to investigate specific effects of genes by exploring their impact on multiple functional systems (e.g., prefrontal, striatal, limbic) in each subject in a single experimental session. These various advantages of imaging genetics strategies have likely contributed to their demonstrated ability to identify significant gene effects on brain function with smaller samples than traditional behavioral measures (tens versus hundreds). The unique capabilities of neuroimaging methods place them in an excellent position among available tools for the in vivo investigation of functional genetic variation.

Conclusion

Human cognition, behavior, and psychiatric disorders involve complex and polygenic modes of inheritance, in which each gene is likely to have only a small effect on variation in manifest behavior. Neuroimaging is a powerful approach to magnifying the effect size of genetic variation at the level of brain development and function. To date, only the effects of single genetic polymorphisms on brain function have been explored with neuroimaging techniques. The functional interactions between multiple gene variants and the environment, and their collective impact on brain function, are yet to be explored.

The striking results of some of the studies reviewed in this chapter illustrate the potential of brain-imaging techniques to unravel the mystery of how genetic polymorphisms both alter brain function, chemistry, and morphology and transmit susceptibility to illness. They also underscore the advantage of a systems-level approach—integrating genetic information with endophenotypic information (regional neurophysiological, neurochemical, and neuroanatomical data obtained through neuroimaging techniques) and with phenotypic information (cognitive and behavioral data) to successfully delineate the influence of genes on the brain.

References

Ashburner, J., and Friston, K. J. (2000). Voxel-based morphometry: The methods. *NeuroImage, 11*, 805–821.

Ball, D., Hill, L., Freeman, B., Eley, T. C., Strelau, J., Riemann, R., Spinath, F. M., Angleitner, A., and Plomin, R. (1997). The serotonin transporter gene and peer-related neuroticism. *NeuroReport, 8*, 1301–1304.

Bilder, R. M., Volavka, J., Lachman, H. M., and Grace, A. A. (2004). The catechol-O-methyltransferase polymorphism: Relations to the tonic-phase dopamine hypothesis and neuropsychiatric phenotypes. *Neuropsychopharmacology, 29*, 1943–1961.

Birn, R. M., Cox, R. W., and Bandettini, P. A. (2002). Detection versus estimation in event-related fMRI: Choosing the optimal stimulus timing. *NeuroImage, 15*, 252–264.

Bookheimer, S. Y., Strojwas, M. H., Cohen, M. S., Saunders, A. M., Pericak-Vance, M. A., Mazziotta, J. C., and Small, G. W. (2000). Patterns of brain activation in people at risk for Alzheimer's disease. *New England Journal of Medicine, 343,* 450–456.

Bullmore, E., Horwitz, B., Honey, G., Brammer, M., Williams, S., and Sharma, T. (2000). How good is good enough in path analysis of fMRI data? *NeuroImage, 11,* 289–301.

Burggren, A. C., Small, G. W., Sabb, F. W., and Bookheimer, S. Y. (2002). Specificity of brain activation patterns in people at genetic risk for Alzheimer's disease. *American Journal of Geriatric Psychiatry, 10,* 44–51.

Cohen, R. M., Podruchny, T. A., Bokde, A. L., Carson, R. E., Herscovitch, P., Kiesewetter, D. O., Eckelman, W. C., and Sunderland, T. (2003). In vivo muscarinic 2 receptor imaging in cognitively normal young and older volunteers. *Synapse, 49,* 150–156.

Collier, D. A., Stober, G., Li, T., Heils, A., Catalano, M., Di Bella, D., Arranz, M. J., Murray, R. M., Vallada, H. P., Bengel, D., Muller, C. R., Roberts, G. W., Smeraldi, E., Kirov, G., Sham, P., and Lesch, K. P. (1996). A novel functional polymorphism within the promoter of the serotonin transporter gene: Possible role in susceptibility to affective disorders. *Molecular Psychiatry, 1,* 453–460.

Corder, E. H., Saunders, A. M., Strittmatter, W. J., Schmechel, D. E., Gaskell, P. C., Small, G. W., Roses, A. D., Haines, J. L., and Pericak-Vance, M. A. (1993). Gene dose of apolipoprotein E type 4 allele and the risk of Alzheimer's disease in late onset families. *Science, 261,* 921–923.

Deary, I. J., Battersby, S., Whiteman, M. C., Connor, J. M., Fowkes, F. G., and Harmar, A. (1999). Neuroticism and polymorphisms in the serotonin transporter gene. *Psychological Medicine, 29,* 735–739.

Ebstein, R. P., Segman, R., Benjamin, J., Osher, Y., Nemanov, L., and Belmaker, R. H. (1997). 5-HT2C (HTR2C) serotonin receptor gene polymorphism associated with the human personality trait of reward dependence: Interaction with dopamine D4 receptor (D4DR) and dopamine D3 receptor (D3DR) polymorphisms. *American Journal of Medical Genetics, 74,* 65–72.

Egan, M. F., Goldberg, T. E., Kolachana, B. S., Callicott, J. H., Mazzanti, C. M., Straub, R. E., Goldman, D., and Weinberger, D. R. (2001). Effect of COMT Val108/158Met genotype on frontal lobe function and risk for schizophrenia. *Proceedings of the National Academy of Sciences, USA, 98,* 6917–6922.

Egan, M. F., Kojima, M., Callicott, J. H., Goldberg, T. E., Kolachana, B. S., Bertolino, A., Zaitsev, E., Gold, B., Goldman, D., Dean, M., Lu, B., and Weinberger, D. R. (2003). A single nucleotide polymorphism in BDNF gene affects regulated secretion of BDNF and human memory and hippocampal function. *Rom Cell, 112,* 257–269.

Egan, M. F., Straub, R. E., Goldberg, T. E., Yakub, I., Callicott, J. H., Hariri, A. R., Mattay, V. S., Bertolino, A., Hyde, T. M., Shannon-Weickert, C., Akil, M., Crook, J., Vakkalanka, R. K., Balkissoon, R., Gibbs, R. A., Kleinman, J. E., and Weinberger, D. R. (2004). Variation in GRM3 affects cognition, prefrontal glutamate, and risk for schizophrenia. *Proceedings of the National Academy of Sciences, USA, 101,* 12604–12609.

Emahazion, T., Feuk, L., Jobs, M., Sawyer, S. L., Fredman, D., St. Clair, D., Prince, J. A., and Brookes, A. J. (2001). SNP association studies in Alzheimer's disease highlight problems for complex disease analysis. *Trends in Genetics, 17,* 407–413.

Fan, J., Fossella, J., Sommer, T., Wu, Y., and Posner, M. I. (2003). Mapping the genetic variation of executive attention onto brain activity. *Proceedings of the National Academy of Sciences, USA, 100,* 7406–7411.

Frackowiak, R. S. J. (Ed.) (2004). *Human brain function.* Amsterdam: Elsevier.

Friston, K. J., Penny, W., Phillips, C., Kiebel, S., Hinton, G., and Ashburner, J. (2002). Classical and Bayesian inference in neuroimaging: Theory. *NeuroImage, 16,* 465–483.

Genovese, C. R., Lazar, N. A., and Nichols, T. (2002). Thresholding of statistical maps in functional neuroimaging. *NeuroImage, 15,* 870–878.

Goldberg, T. E., Egan, M. F., Gscheidle, T., Coppola, R., Weickert, T., Kolachana, B. S., Goldman, D., and Weinberger, D. R. (2003). Executive subprocesses in working memory: Relationship to catechol-O-methyltradsferase Val158Met genotype and schizophrenia. *Archives of General Psychiatry, 60,* 889–896.

Goldman-Rakic, P. S., Muly, E. C., 3rd, and Williams, G. V. (2000). D(1) receptors in prefrontal cells and circuits. *Brain Research: Brain Research Reviews, 31,* 295–301.

Gonzalez-Burgos, G., Kroner, S., Krimer, L. S., Seamans, J. K., Urban, N. N., Henze, D. A., Lewis, D. A., and Barrionuevo, G. (2002). Dopamine modulation of neuronal function in monkey prefrontal cortex. *Physiology and Behavior, 77,* 537–543.

Good, C. D., Johnsrude, I. S., Ashburner, J., Henson, R. N., Friston, K. J., and Frackowiak, R. S. (2001). A voxel-based morphometric study of ageing in 465 normal adult human brains. *NeuroImage, 14,* 21–36.

Hariri, A. R., Drabant, E. M., Munoz, K. E., Kolachana, B. S., Mattay, V. S., Egan, M. F., and Weinberger, D. R. (2005). A susceptibility gene for affective disorders and the response of the human amygdala. *Archives of General Psychiatry, 62,* 146–152.

Hariri, A. R., Goldberg, T. E., Mattay, V. S., Kolachana, B. S., Callicott, J. H., Egan, M. F., and Weinberger, D. R. (2003). Brain-derived neurotropic factor val66met polymorphism affects human memory-related hippocampal activity and predicts memory performance. *Journal of Neuroscience, 23,* 6690–6694.

Hariri, A. R., Mattay, V. S., Tessitore, A., Kolachana, B., Fera, F., Goldman, D., Egan, M. F., and Weinberger, D. R. (2002). Serotonin transporter genetic variation and the response of the human amygdala. *Science, 297,* 400–403.

Hariri, A. R., and Weinberger, D. R. (2003a). Functional neuroimaging of genetic variation in serotonorgic neurotransmission. *Genes and Brain Behavior, 2,* 341–349.

Hariri, A. R., and Weinberger, D. R. (2003b). Imaging genomics. *Brtish Medical Bulletin, 65,* 259–270. Review.

Heinz, A., Jones, D. W., Mazzanti, C., Goldman, D., Ragan, P., Hommer, D., Linnoila, M., and Weinberger, D. R. (2000). A relationship between serotonin transporter genotype and in vivo protein expression and alcohol neurotoxicity. *Biological Psychiatry, 47,* 643–649.

Jacobsen, L. K., Staley, J. K., Malison, R. T., Zoghbi, S. S., Seibyl, J. P., Kosten, T. R., and Innis, R. B. (2000). Elevated central serotonin transporter binding availability in acutely abstinent cocaine-dependent patients. *American Journal of Psychiatry, 157,* 1134–1140.

Joober, R., Gauthier, J., Lal, S., Bloom, D., Lalonde, P., Rouleau, G., Benkelfat, C., and Labelle, A. (2002). Catechol-O-methyltransferase Val-108/158-Met gene variants associated with performance on the Wisconsin Card Sorting Test. *Archives of General Psychiatry, 59,* 662–663.

Katsuragi, S., Kunugi, H., Sano, A., Tsutsumi, T., Isogawa, K., Nanko, S., and Akiyoshi, J. (1999). Association between serotonin transported gene polymorphism and anxiety-related traits. *Biological Psychiatry, 45,* 368–370.

Krubitzer, L., and Kahn, D. M. (2003). Nature versus nurture revisited: An old idea with a new twist. *Progress in Neurobiology, 70,* 33–52.

Laurienti, P. J., Burdette, J. H., and Maldjian, J. A. (2003). Separating neural processes using mixed event-related and epoch-based fMRI paradigms. *Journal of Neuroscience Methods, 131,* 41–50.

Law-Tho, D., Hirsch, J. C., and Crepel, F. (1994). Dopamine modulation of synaptic transmission in rat prefrontal cortex: An in vitro electrophysiological study. *Neuroscience Research, 21,* 151–160.

Lesch, K. P., Bengel, D., Heils, A., Sabol, S. Z., Greenberg, B. D., Petri, S., Benjamin, J., Muller, C. R., Hamer, D. H., and Murphy, D. L. (1996). Association of anxiety-related traits with a polymorphism in the serotonin transporter gene regulatory region. *Science, 274,* 1527–1531.

Lewis, D. A., Melchitzky, D. S., Sesack, S. R., Whitehead, R. E., Auh, S., and Sampson, A. (2001). Dopamine transporter immunoreactivity in monkey cerebral cortex: Regional, laminar, and ultrastructural localization. *Journal of Comparative Neurology, 432,* 119–136.

Malhotra, A. K., Kestler, L. J., Mazzanti, C., Bates, J. A., Goldberg, T., and Goldman, D. (2002). A functional polymorphism in the COMT gene and performance on a text of prefrontal cognition. *American Journal of Psychiatry, 159,* 652–654.

Mannisto, P. T., and Kaakkola, S. (1999). Catechol-O-methyltransferase (COMT): Biochemistry, molecular biology, pharmacology, and clinical efficacy of the new selective COMT inhibitors. *Pharmacological Review, 51,* 593–628.

Mattay, V. S., and Goldberg, T. E. (2004). Imaging genetic influences in human brain function. *Current Opinion in Neurobiology, 14,* 239–247.

Mattay, V. S., Goldberg, T. E., Fera, F., Hariri, A. R., Tessitore, A., Egan, M. F., Kolachana, B., Callicott, J. H., and Weinberger, D. R. (2003). Catechol-O-methyltransferase val158-met genotype and individual variation in the brain response to amphetamine. *Proceedings of the National Academy of Sciences, USA, 100*, 6186–6191.

Mattay, V. S., Tessitore, A., Callicott, J. H., Bertolino, A., Goldberg, T. E., Chase, T. N., Hyde, T. M., and Weinberger, D. R. (2002). Dopaminergic modulation of cortical function in patients with Parkinson's disease. *Annals of Neurology, 51*, 156–164.

Mazei, M. S., Pluto, C. P., Kirkbride, B., and Pehek, E. A. (2002). Effects of catecholamine uptake blockers in the caudate-putamen and subregions of the medial prefrontal cortex of the rat. *Brain Research, 936*, 58–67.

Moldin, S. O., and Gottesman, II (1997). At issue: Genes, experience, and chance in schizophrenia—positioning for the 21st century. *Schizophrenic Bulletin, 23*, 547–561.

Moron, J. A., Brockington, A., Wise, R. A., Rocha, B. A., and Hope, B. T. (2002). Dopamine uptake through the norepinephrine transporter in brain regions with low levels of the dopamine transporter: Evidence from knock-out mouse lines. *Journal of Neuroscience, 22*, 389–395.

Moseley, M., Bammer, R., and Illes, J. (2002). Diffusion-tensor imaging of cognitive performance. *Brain and Cognition, 50*, 396–413. Review.

Nichols, T., and Hayasaka, S. (2003). Controlling the familywise error rate in functional neuroimaging: A comparative review. *Statistical Methods in Medical Research, 12*, 419–446.

Nichols, T. E., and Holmes, A. P. (2002). Nonparametric permutation tests for functional neuroimaging: A primer with examples. *Human Brain Mapping, 15*, 1–25.

Petrella, J. R., Lustig, C., Bucher, L. A., Jha, A. P., and Doraiswamy, P. M. (2002). Prefrontal activation patterns in subjects at risk for Alzheimer's disease. *American Journal of Geriatric Psychiatry, 10*, 112–113.

Pezawas, L., Verchinski, B. A., Mattay, V. S., Callicott, J. H., Kolachana, B. S., Straub, R. E., Egan, M. F., Meyer-Lindenberg, A., and Weinberger, D. R. (2004). The brain-derived neurotrophic factor val66met polymorphism and variation in human cortical morphology. *Journal of Neuroscience, 24*, 10099–10102.

Poo, M. M. (2001). Neurotrophins as synaptic modulators. *Nature Reviews Neuroscience, 2*, 24–32.

Reiman, E. M., Caselli, R. J., Yun, L. S., Chen, K., Bandy, D., Minoshima, S., Thibodeau, S. N., and Osborne, D. (1996). Preclinical evidence of Alzheimer's disease in persons homozygous for the epsilon 4 allele for apolipoprotein E. *New England Journal of Medicine, 334*, 752–758.

Rypma, B., and D'Esposito, M. (2000). Isolating the neural mechanisms of age-related changes in human working memory. *Nature Neuroscience, 3*, 509–515.

Saunders, A. M., Strittmatter, W. J., Schmechel, D., George-Hyslop, P. H., Pericak-Vance, M. A., Joo, S. H., Rosi, B. L., Gusella, J. F., Crapper-MacLachlan, D. R., Alberts, M. J., et al. (1993). Association of apolipoprotein E allele epsilon 4 with late-onset familial and sporadic Alzheimer's disease. *Neurology*, *43*, 1467–1472.

Seamans, J., Gorelova, N., Durstewitz, D., and Yang, C. (2000). Bidirectional dopamine modulation of GABA ergic inhibition in prefrontal cortical pyramidal neurons. *Society of Neuroscience*, *30*, 1430.

Seamans, J. K., Durstewitz, D., Christie, B. R., Stevens, C. F., and Sejnowski, T. J. (2001). Dopamine D1/D5 receptor modulation of excitatory synaptic inputs to layer V prefrontal cortex neurons. *Proceedings of the National Academy of Science, USA*, *98*, 301–306.

Shoghi-Jadid, K., Small, G. W., Agdeppa, E. D., Kepe, V., Ercoli, L. M., Siddarth, P., Read, S., Satyamurthy, N., Petric, A., Huang, S. C., and Barrio, J. R. (2002). Localization of neurofibrillary tangles and beta-amyloid plaques in the brains of living patients with Alzheimer's disease. *American Journal of Geriatric Psychiatry*, *10*, 24–35.

Small, G. W., Agdeppa, E. D., Kepe, V., Satyamurthy, N., Huang, S. C., and Barrio, J. R. (2002). In vivo brain imaging of tangle burden in humans. *Journal of Molecular Neuroscience*, *19*, 323–327.

Small, G. W., Ercoli, L. M., Silverman, D. H., Huang, S. C., Komo, S., Bookheimer, S. Y., Lavretsky, H., Miller, K., Siddarth, P., Rasgon, N. L., Mazziotta, J. C., Saxena, S., Wu, H. M., Mega, M. S., Cummings, J. L., Saunders, A. M., Pericak-Vance, M. A., Roses, A. D., Barrio, J. R., and Phelps, M. E. (2000). Cerebral metabolic and cognitive decline in persons at genetic risk for Alzheimer's disease. *Proceedings of the National Academy of Sciences, USA*, *97*, 6037–6042.

Smith, J. D., Sikes, J., and Levin, J. A. (1998). Human apolipoprotein E allele–specific brain expressing transgenic mice. *Neurobiolical Aging*, *19*, 407–413.

Willeit, M., Stastny, J., Pirker, W., Praschak-Rieder, N., Neumeister, A., Asenbaum, S., Tauscher, J., Fuchs, K., Sieghart, W., Hornik, K., Aschauer, H. N., Brucke, T., and Kasper, S. (2001). No evidence for in vivo regulation of midbrain serotonin transporter availability by serotonin transporter promoter gene. *Biological Psychiatry*, *50*, 8–12.

Woolrich, M. W., Behrens, T. E., Beckmann, C. F., Jenkinson, M., and Smith, S. M. (2004). Multilevel linear modeling for fMRI group analysis using Bayesian inference. *NeuroImage*, *21*, 1732–1747.

Yang, C. R., and Seamans, J. K. (1996). Dopamine D1 receptor actions in layers V–VI rat prefrontal cortex neurons in vitro: Modulation of dendritic-somatic signal integration. *Journal of Neuroscience*, *16*, 1922–1935.

Zubieta, J. K., Heitzeg, M. M., Smith, Y. R., Bueller, J. A., Xu, K., Xu, Y., Koeppe, R. A., Stohler, C. S., and Goldman, D. (2003). COMT val158met genotype affects mu-opioid neurotransmitter responses to a pain stressor. *Science*, *299*, 1240–1243.

12 Magnetoencephalography

Krish D. Singh

The holy grail of functional neuroimaging methods is to provide a complete spatiotemporal description of the distribution of task-related activity within the brain. This would bridge the gap between the microscopic domain of neuronal properties, at the level of both the single cell and the network, and the macroscopic domain of complete human behavior. In addition, recent theories of cognitive function suggest that the interaction between cortical areas, and how these interactions vary over time, may play an important role in the way information from disparate sensory modalities is integrated to form a conscious, unified percept. Unfortunately, no single imaging technique currently has the spatial and temporal accuracy necessary to fulfill all of our requirements.

Cognitive neuroimaging has mostly emphasized the spatial localization of brain activity and has been driven by relatively easy access to excellent tools such as functional magnetic resonance imaging (fMRI), which has good spatial resolution that is essentially uniform across the head. This has led to a virtual explosion in the number of published studies using fMRI to investigate cognitive function in both normal and patient populations. However, fMRI measures an indirect hemodynamic correlate of brain function, namely, task-induced changes in the regional distribution of oxygenated hemoglobin, leading to several unfortunate limitations. First, the coupling of neural activity to the hemodynamic response is not fully understood and may vary across the brain. Second, depending on the relative sensitivity to blood in the capillary bed and draining veins, the site of the hemodynamic response may actually be displaced from the site of true activation. Third, and perhaps most important, because of its slowness, we cannot use the hemodynamic response to study either the temporal sequence of activation or its relationship to temporal measures of behavior at the operating speed of the brain, and thus we cannot use fMRI to study how interactions between cortical regions evolve from one instant to the next.

This chapter will describe a technique known as magnetoencephalography (MEG), which does not suffer from the limitations described above. As we shall see, remarkable innovations in the analysis of MEG data have placed MEG firmly in the realm of noninvasive functional neuroimaging, alongside fMRI, although significant uncertainties remain in our ability to localize the cortical activity generating the MEG signal. Clearly, the best approach will be to combine fMRI and MEG data, taken in parallel experiments where exactly the same experimental protocol is performed using both techniques.

Development

MEG is the measurement of the extremely weak magnetic fields generated by the electrical activity of a population of neurons (for reviews, see Hari and Lounasmaa, 1989; Hämäläinen et al., 1993; Vrba and Robinson, 2001; Hämäläinen and Hari, 2002). Magnetoencephalography in many respects closely resembles electroencephalography (EEG; see Rippon, chapter 10 this volume). In contrast to the neuroelectrical signals associated with EEG, however, the neuromagnetic fields associated with MEG are so weak that four decades of technological development were needed to achieve the measurement sensitivity necessary for brain research with MEG. Using a conventionally wound induction coil, David Cohen (1968) made the first MEG recordings; these were of the human alpha rhythm, perhaps the strongest of all electromagnetic signals from the brain. Recognizing that, to be more generally useful, a more sensitive measurement technology was needed, Cohen (1972) went on to demonstrate the use of superconducting electronics for MEG measurement. All MEG systems since 1972 have been based on the superconducting technology he pioneered. Over the intervening 30 years, significant innovation has taken place both in the hardware associated with MEG and in the algorithms used to analyze its data. The earliest MEG systems consisted of a single magnetometer that needed to be moved over the surface of the head in order to generate a field map. In contrast, modern MEG systems have 200–300 separate superconducting magnetometers distributed over the surface of the head, allowing one-shot whole-head recordings. One of the most intractable problems confronting magnetoencephalography is the localization of the cortical generators, given the brain's external magnetic field. Despite much effort over the last 30 years, and despite enormous progress, this inverse problem remains essentially unresolved for MEG and EEG alike; the advent of multimodal functional neuroimaging represents the best hope for its eventual resolution.

Principles and Limitations

Generation of Neuromagnetic Fields

Any electrical current generates an associated magnetic field perpendicular to the direction of the current; the strength of the field falls off with the square of the distance from the generating current. It is fairly easy to show that the current generated by a single neuron is far too weak to be detected by MEG or EEG; indeed, only the locally synchronous firing of millions of neurons—approximately $25\,mm^2$ of the cortical sheet—can generate a measurable signal (Hämäläinen and Hari, 2002).

Neuroelectric activity in a discrete region of the cortex will be a mixture of transient action potentials and slower synaptic potentials in the dendrites (Nunez, 1981). It is unlikely, however, that the action potentials themselves will give rise to a measurable magnetic field (or electrical) signal. First, action potentials are temporally brief spikes, which are unlikely to sum in a synchronous fashion. Second, as an action potential travels down an axon it can be considered to be two opposing—depolarizing and repolarizing—current sources. These two, closely spaced current sources represent a quadripolar generator, whose magnetic field falls off very rapidly with distance.

It is therefore more likely that the measured external magnetic field of the brain is generated by slower postsynaptic potentials in the dendrites of the neuronal population. However, the situation is complex and the dendritic processes need to be spatially aligned in order to generate a measurable magnetic field (figure 12.1, plate 9). For example, a population of closed cells, in which the dendrites are randomly and uniformly distributed, will not generate a net magnetic field because the bulk current flow is uniformly distributed in all directions. In contrast, the apical dendrites of pyramidal cells are all oriented in a similar fashion, perpendicular to the gray matter surface. If enough aligned pyramidal cells are firing synchronously, they will generate a net current flow sufficiently strong to be detected with MEG or EEG (Hämäläinen and Hari, 2002).

For any given region of the brain, the electric current associated with neuronal activity in that region is known as the "primary current"; it is this

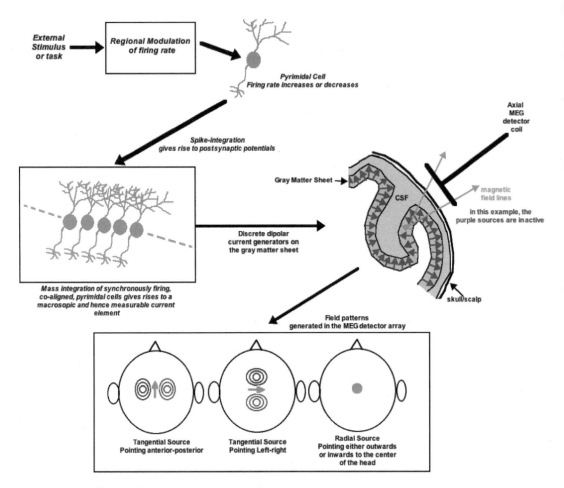

Figure 12.1

Schematic showing the generation of measurable neuromagnetic fields from a synchronous population of aligned dendritic processes. The bottom panel shows the magnetic field contours that would be generated in an axial measurement array, from a single focal neuronal source (known as a dipole), as the orientation of the source changes. Red indicates magnetic field lines entering the head, blue indicates field lines exiting the head. Note that for a radial source, no field is measured. See plate 9 for color version.

direct electrical activity we are most interested in characterizing and local-izing with EEG and MEG. However, because the brain itself is a conduct-ing medium, secondary currents are generated, which travel from the primary site throughout the brain. Indeed, it is these secondary currents, leaking to the surface of the scalp from the primary neuronal generators along variable and essentially unknown pathways, which are measured by EEG. Although both primary and secondary currents generate associated magnetic fields, in an approximately spherical conductor such as the head, the magnetic fields from the secondary currents tend to cancel each other out, rendering MEG most sensitive to the fields from the desired primary currents.

It is worth pointing out that although several simulations studies (see Liu, Dale, and Belliveau, 2002) appear to show that EEG and MEG have similar accuracy of localization, or even that EEG gives more accurate local-ization of source positions than MEG, these studies typically do not model inaccuracies in the conductivity profile of the head. In the analysis of real data, our values for the conductivities of the brain, skull, and scalp are likely to be inaccurate, and the level of error indeterminate. Because of its reduced dependence on the unknown profile, MEG is thus more robust than EEG in real-life situations.

Some of the main criticisms of MEG have to do with its spatial sen-sitivity to neuronal currents in the brain. There are two key criticisms in this regard. First, because magnetic fields fall off rapidly with distance, MEG is held to be insensitive to deep sources within the brain. Recently published data, however, suggest that MEG can detect cortical activity from relatively deep structures such as the hippocampus (Tesche and Karhu, 2000) or amygdala, provided sufficient signal is available compared to the noise in the data. Second, if we assume the head is effectively spherical, then cortical generators that are aligned in a perfectly radial pattern should gen-erate no external measurable magnetic field. MEG's insensitivity to radial sources has led many to suggest that it is only sensitive to sources in the sulcul walls, rather than in the fundus or on the gyral convexities, raising serious questions about MEG's utility altogether. The cortex is a complex and convoluted structure, however; indeed, it can be argued that the pro-portion of gray matter actually aligned radially is likely to be quite small. In a recent simulation study, Hillebrand and Barnes (2002), showed that, for superficial cortex, there are only relatively small regions of the gray matter where MEG's insensitivity to perfectly radial sources leads to its inability to correctly localize cortical activity (figure 12.2, plate 10).

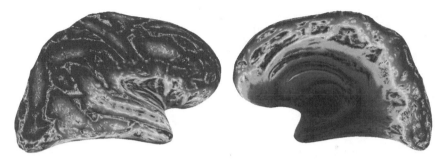

Figure 12.2
Simulation data showing the current dipole strength needed, at each point in the brain, to accurately localize a source at that point, at least 70 percent of the time (Hillebrand and Barnes, 2002). It can be seen that relatively small regions on the crest of each gyrus are difficult to localize because of the radial nature of the currents. The figure also clearly shows that sources become increasingly difficult to localize accurately in deeper regions of the brain. (Figure courtesy of Arjan Hillebrand) See plate 10 for color version.

Measurement of Neuromagnetic Fields

Because the fields are weak (10–12 tesla at best) in a hostile environment of electromagnetic noise, measurement of the external magnetic fields associated with the brain's neural activity is technically challenging. Typically, a car driving on a nearby road will generate a magnetic field that is several orders of magnitude stronger than the neuromagnetic field. Modern buildings containing multiple pieces of electrical equipment are also particularly problematical locations for MEG laboratories. Other troublesome electromagnetic noise sources, such as the heart, are located within the subject's body.

The technology at the core of all modern MEG systems is the superconducting quantum interference device (SQUID). Put simply, a SQUID is a small (2–3 mm) ring of superconducting material in which one or more insulating breaks, known as "junctions," have been made. When the SQUID is immersed in liquid helium (4.2°K), it becomes superconducting and a quantum mechanical tunneling current can flow across the junctions. The current is modulated in a very sensitive fashion by the external magnetic field threading the loop. This makes the SQUID the most sensitive magnetic field detector known, and it is certainly sensitive enough to measure neuromagnetic fields.

The SQUID itself is very small and thus does not collect much in the way of magnetic flux. Because of this, typically, larger pickup coils are used to "collect" the magnetic field over a relatively large area and, by means of inductive coupling, funnel the measured flux into the small SQUID ring. All pickup coils and connecting wires need to be made of a superconducting material (usually niobium) so that the currents generated in the pickup coils can be transported to the SQUID without any resistive losses. Once the SQUID voltage has been formed, however, there is no further need for superconductivity; conventional electronics can be used to further process the signal.

Modern MEG systems (figure 12.3) measure the magnetic field at multiple locations over the whole of the head. It is desirable to measure the field with as high a sampling density as possible, with the newest generation of scanners containing 275–300 separate SQUID detectors. All these detectors and their associated pickup coils have to be housed in a single liquid helium dewar reservoir, which maintains all the superconducting components at 4.2°K. With advanced cryogenic design, the gap between the superconducting pickup coils at 4.2°K and the subject's head at body temperature can be minimized so as to maximize the detection of cortically evoked magnetic fields.

Although SQUIDs coupled to pickup coils near the head provide enough sensitivity to detect these fields, without a noise rejection strategy, the neural signals would be overwhelmed by electromagnetic noise from environmental and physiological sources. The first defense against such noise is to electrically and magnetically isolate the SQUID dewar and subject from the noise environment by placing them in a multilayered shielded room. The room shielding typically consists of at least two complete nested metal enclosures. The first, made from aluminum, is a shield that rejects time-varying electromagnetic fields (>10 Hz) by way of induced eddy currents within the wall of the shield. The second and perhaps third layers are made from a high-permeability alloy, known as "mu-metal," which deflects low-frequency magnetic field around, rather than through, the room contents.

As a second defense against electromagnetic noise, modern MEG systems capitalize on the fact that the magnetic fields from the relatively distant environmental and physiological sources are spatially more uniform, their spatial gradient falling off rapidly with distance from the generating source. By using combinations of oppositely wound coils, instead of a single pickup coil, known as a "magnetometer," the SQUID sensor can be made sensitive to an approximation of the spatial gradient of the magnetic field, rather than to the field itself, thus rendering the sensor differentially sensitive to the closer neural signals. Such a coil configuration is known as a

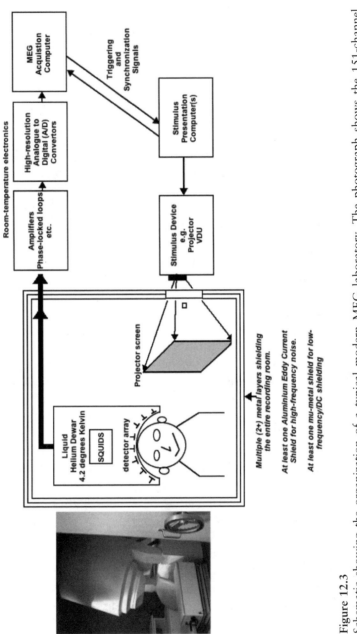

Figure 12.3
Schematic showing the organization of a typical modern MEG laboratory. The photograph shows the 151-channel CTF-Omega system at Aston University, England.

"gradiometer" (Carelli and Leoni, 1986); by using increasingly complex combinations of coils it is possible to make first- second- and third-order gradiometers sensitive to higher-order spatial gradients (figure 12.4, plate 11). The distance between the coil components in the gradiometer array is known as the "baseline"—the smaller the baseline, the more electromagnetic noise is rejected, although the less sensitive the gradiometer becomes to deeper sources within the head.

Gradiometers have to be accurately manufactured so that each coil has the same surface area. The degree of accuracy in this matching is known as the "balance" of a gradiometer and again directly translates into noise

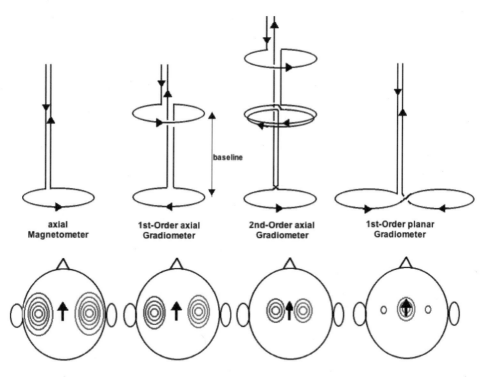

Figure 12.4
Typical configurations of axial magnetometers/gradiometers and the planar gradiometers used in a typical thin-film system. Under each device, cartoons of the typical field patterns generated in each coil configuration are shown, assuming a single tangential dipolar current source at the vertex. Red indicates magnetic field lines entering the head, blue indicates field lines exiting the head. Note how, with the axial devices, the contour maps become spatially tighter for higher-order gradiometers. One advantage of the planar gradiometer is that it gives a maximum detection signal directly above the source. See plate 11 for color version.

rejection performance for the device. Virtual higher-order gradiometers can also be implemented by combining the measured signals in postprocessing software (Vrba and Robinson, 2001).

In configuring an MEG system, there are thus several choices to be made: whether to use magnetometers or gradiometers, axial or planar geometries, and to what degree software gradiometry is to be used. Each MEG manufacturer has its preferred configuration and will argue strongly for the merits of its system supported by a host of software simulations. There is no "best" solution—the relative merits of each design depend strongly on the electromagnetic noise model chosen to illustrate its performance (Vrba and Robinson, 2001). Nevertheless, it would be interesting to look at the publication record of each system design after a few years in use to see whether there was any systematic variation in the detection of activity from each brain area, especially in the case of deep structures.

Forward and Inverse Problems

Given the position, magnitude, and orientation of any hypothetical neuronal current source, together with the conductor geometry of the head, skull, and scalp, it is relatively easy to work out what magnetic field would be measured in any given MEG detector array. This is known as "solving the MEG forward problem" and has a unique solution—there is only one possible magnetic field distribution that can be generated by a given current configuration. Whereas, for accurate solution of the EEG forward problem, one must fully consider the conducting geometry of the brain, skull and scalp, using perhaps the real head shape of the individual, for MEG, one can use much simpler conductivity models, such as a homogeneous sphere or multiple overlapping spheres for each separate MEG detector (Huang, Mosher, and Leahy, 1999)—in either case, the MEG forward problem solution is straightforward.

To be useful as a functional neuroimaging tool, MEG must be able to localize the cortical current generators given an externally measured magnetic field. This is known as "solving the MEG inverse problem" (Sarvas, 1987). Unfortunately, because there are an infinite number of cortical current distributions that could generate any given externally measured magnetic field, the solution of either the MEG or the EEG inverse problem is impossible from the measured data alone. Another way of thinking about this is that there is insufficient information in the external field measurements to tell us the distribution of electrical currents in the brain. This problem is known as "nonuniqueness."

Although nonuniqueness obviously has serious implications for the utility of both EEG and MEG as functional imaging techniques, things are not as bleak as they appear. If we can add any extra information about the spatial or temporal nature of the cortical currents (known as "a priori constraints"), then we can often collapse the space of possible solutions to a single one, which is unique in that context. A good analogy for this comes from stereoscopic vision. Normally, we use our two eyes to view the world. By combining the signals from both eyes, depth information can be extracted, which allows us to use the apparent visual size of an object and its distance from the eyes to estimate the real size of the object. A unique solution can be obtained. On the other hand, when we watch a film, or if we are unlucky enough to lose an eye, we no longer have formal depth information—there is no longer a unique solution to the inverse problem because depth and object size are confounded. Of course, in reality, we watch films quite happily and people with one eye are able, for example, to drive cars safely enough. The reason why our visual functionality is mostly preserved is, of course, that we have a lot of a priori information about the real physical size of objects. Because we know how big a cow is, when we identify the image of one on film or monocularly, we can use that a priori information to estimate how far away from us the object is. Of course, if our a priori information is wrong—perhaps the apparent cow is really a small model of a cow—then our solution will be wrong. This illustrates an important point—solutions to the inverse problem stand or fall on the validity of their a priori constraints.

There are a bewildering array of approaches to the inverse problem for both EEG and MEG data, some of which are described briefly below. Each approach has its advocates and the literature can often be quite confrontational when groups propose a new algorithm and criticize a previous approach. Although a full description of the approaches and algorithms available and of the advantages and disadvantages of each is beyond the scope of this chapter, luckily, there are some excellent modern review articles (see, for example, Baillet, Mosher, and Leahy, 2001; Michel et al., 2001).

It is worth noting that each approach can be applied to either EEG or MEG data—the only difference is that the solution to the forward problem will be different for each modality, which has implications for the relative accuracy of the localization. In either case, three golden rules should always be kept in mind:

1.   There is no magic bullet. Although no algorithm will work in every situation and yield the true current distribution in the head, for each algo-

rithm, it is formally possible to define when it will work perfectly and when it will fail completely. One problem in the literature is that proponents of each algorithm tend to concentrate on situations where their algorithm works best.

2.   There is no "best" algorithm. There are some quite simple inverse problem algorithms, such as the single-current dipole described below, which work perfectly well if the a priori constraints are valid. In other situations, more complicated distributed algorithms will be needed.

3.   There is no way to determine, using MEG alone, which inverse problem algorithm will yield the true current distribution in the head. As we shall see, it is possible for two different algorithms to give very different, but equally valid, solutions to the inverse problem, given the same MEG data set. The only way out of this predicament is to add extra information that will inform our choice of which algorithm to use.

The MEG Experiment: Average Evoked and Induced Effects

Before choosing an inverse problem algorithm, it is necessary to consider the actual design of the MEG experiment and the type of neural activity that is to be measured. In a typical MEG experiment, the system can record data from, say, 275 magnetometer channels at a rate of several thousand samples a second. Typically, these data are recorded in a single run lasting several minutes (figure 12.5, plate 12). During this recording period, the experimental manipulations can take place. The precise timings of all stimuli and tasks need to be logged by the MEG system with millisecond precision. This can then be used to divide the MEG recording into experimentally salient temporal segments, known as "epochs," whose length can vary from a few tens of milliseconds to several tens of seconds or even minutes. The simplest and oldest MEG/EEG experimental paradigm is the average evoked response, in which the time series contained in each epoch is simply averaged. Electromagnetic noise, whether arising from the environment or from the brain, will tend to average out, whereas any reproducible task-related neural activity will tend to average in, and to be reinforced in the final average epoch. Only neural activity that occurs in each epoch and at exactly the same time within each epoch will tend to contribute to the final average. This is known as "phase-locked activity" because it is necessarily locked to the stimulus or trial onset. Typically, evoked response experiments use epochs that are only a few hundred milliseconds long. One reason for this is that the timing of the neural activity in each epoch becomes more variable for delays longer than this, so that

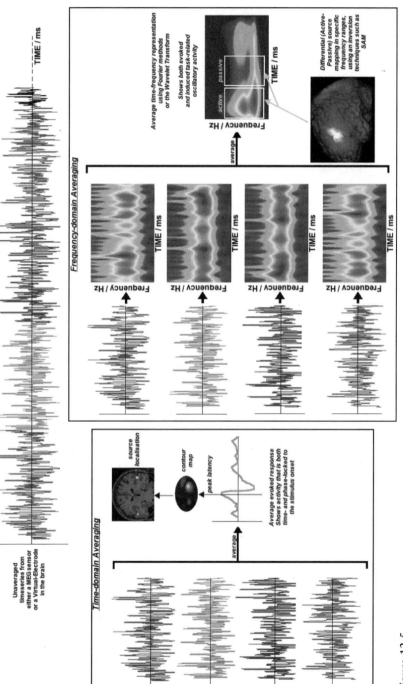

Figure 12.5

Schematic showing how the MEG data shown at the top of the figure can be analyzed using either time-domain averaging to reveal phase-locked evoked activity or frequency-domain averaging to reveal both evoked and induced oscillatory power changes. For the purposes of illustration only 4 epochs are averaged and each is color coded (red, green, blue, and purple). See plate 12 for color version.

the activity does not average in. The net result is that, within the average epoch, there are typically only a few peak components, which are then taken forward for further analyses, such as contour mapping, time-frequency analysis, or solving the inverse problem.

A related approach is the steady state evoked response experiment in which several brief stimulus presentations are presented to the subject at a fixed frequency. The EEG or MEG activity measured as a consequence of this will show driven oscillatory responses at the stimulation frequency or a harmonic of the stimulus frequency. Steady state evoked responses are most often used in studies of the primary sensory cortices, where it appears to be fairly easy to evoke oscillatory responses. For example, an 8 Hz flickering checkerboard stimulus will generate a strong oscillatory signal, at 8 Hz or its multiple, in posterior EEG and MEG sensors.

Although the evoked response paradigm has been the mainstay of EEG and MEG experiments for several decades, it has several disadvantages, the principal one being that only neural activation tightly phase locked to a particular instant of time will be revealed in the average. If the neural response to a stimulus or task "jitters" by only a few milliseconds from trial to trial, the final power in the average response will be drastically reduced (Hillebrand et al., 2005). This has obvious disadvantages for cognitive paradigms where subjects will perform and respond to tasks in a temporally variable or self-paced fashion. Because of this, the evoked response paradigm is really best suited to experiments studying the primary sensory cortices or basic cognitive functions. And because there is little or no temporal resolution with functional magnetic resonance imaging, the cortical response as measured by fMRI is much more robust to jitter in the subjects' processing speed than that measured by MEG, which helps explain why fMRI has been so successful and so wide ranging as a cognitive neuroimaging technique. One of the key reasons why MEG has not been as widely accepted in this role is that, until recently, the experimental paradigm had to be formulated in terms of a brief evoked response design, which is fundamentally limiting. In addition, this design is nonoptimal for fMRI-MEG comparison studies, due to the slowness of the hemodynamic response.

There has been much recent interest in changes in the brain's intrinsic oscillatory rhythms that are time, but not phase, locked to the presence of a stimulus or the execution of a cognitive task (Hari and Salmelin, 1997; Pfurtscheller and Lopes da Silva, 1999; Basar et al., 2001; Pfurtscheller, 2001, Hillebrand et al., 2005), which means that the power in a specific frequency range, say 5–15 Hz, will either increase or decrease during an experimentally salient period of time, such as when subjects view a visual stimulus. A good example, which appears early in the neuroimaging literature, is the large modulation in posterior alpha activity that occurs when subjects open or shut their eyes. On any given trial, the phase of the underlying oscillatory activity is essentially random, such that simple averaging of the epochs in the time domain does not reveal any net neuronal activity, that is, there is no significant evoked response. If, however, the epoch data are instead averaged in the Fourier domain, so that we are averaging the time-frequency content of each trial, then task-related changes in oscillatory power can be revealed (figure 12.5). These task-related and frequency-specific power increases and decreases have been termed *event-related synchronization* (ERS) and *event-related desynchronization* (ERD), respectively (Pfurtscheller and Lopes da Silva, 1999; Pfurtscheller, 2001). Note that the power changes do not have to relate to a particular event or instant in time—the oscillatory power simply has to increase or decrease in one period of time compared to another baseline period. Also, synchronization in this context refers to the local synchronization of neurons within a small region, not a change in synchrony between two distinct cortical regions. All in all, the terms ERS and ERD should be treated with caution because of the above caveats and should always be interpreted simply as oscillatory power increases and decreases. Whatever the terminology, ERS and ERD have been investigated extensively with EEG, and more recently MEG, with some striking results. It seems clear that, as subjects perform a variety of tasks, there are very focal and frequency-specific changes in oscillatory power that occur in response to that task. These results span the full range of cognitive functions, including vision, audition, language, memory, emotion, and sensorimotor functions. One advantage of studying these phenomena is that they can occur in relatively long time windows and need not be phase locked to an instant of time. This means that ERS/ERD effects can be studied using experimental designs in which the subject's response can jitter in time and may be relatively sustained, thus facilitating comparison with an identical fMRI experiment (e.g., Singh et al., 2002).

The Single Equivalent Current Dipole

The simplest inverse problem algorithm assumes that a single small patch of current generates the measured magnetic field (Wood, 1982; Scherg and von Cramon, 1985). Although we know that this patch has to be at least a few square millimeters in size, it is far enough from the detectors to be accurately modeled as a point source of current, known as an "equivalent current dipole" (ECD). For magnetoencephalography, an ECD in a homogenous sphere model is defined uniquely by five parameters; three describing its position within the head, and two defining its tangential orientation and current strength. For any given ECD, the solution to the forward problem is fairly straightforward. The field has a characteristic dipolar shape, with two lobes where the field from the dipole exits the head before looping back into the head (figures 12.1 and 12.4). The ECD is located approximately below the midpoint between the two field maxima at a depth indicated by their separation. Because they have a single detection maximum directly above the position of the ECD (figure 12.4), the field pattern from an array of planar gradiometers is conceptually easier to interpret.

The single equivalent current dipole model for solving the inverse problem is best suited to evoked response experiments where a small number of peak latencies can be identified in the average response. Typically, the user identifies a single latency of interest and the dipole-fitting software will adjust the position, strength, and orientation of a simulated dipole until the calculated magnetic field matches the measured field distribution in the sensor array. A goodness-of-fit criterion is used to accept or reject the fit.

Multiple Equivalent Current Dipole Models

As brain activity becomes more complex, both in space and time, more complex source models are needed. If the magnetic field is not successfully modeled by a single equivalent current dipole, the dipole-fitting software can add increasing numbers of dipoles to the model, each one requiring the iterative fitting of another five dipole parameters. In practice, however, this is only usually successful for fewer than five ECDs because, as more and more dipoles are added to the model, the fit becomes more sensitive to the starting values for each dipole. Choosing slightly different initial positions for each of the modeled sources, for example, can result in radically different positions in the final solution—the model becomes unstable. This oversensitivity to starting conditions can be partially overcome by using multistart approaches (Aine et al., 2000).

The models described above can be extended so that instead of fitting the dipole to a single instance of time, the software can be told to generate a dipole fit that attempts to explain the MEG data over a range of latencies. Within these spatiotemporal models, each equivalent current dipole can either be fixed in position (Scherg and von Cramon, 1985), perhaps representing a fixed region of the gray matter sheet, or be allowed to move during the fitted range of latencies.

Dipole Scanning Approaches

With the advent of increasingly rapid computer technology, the problem of fit instability for multiple dipole models can be partially addressed using "brute force" approaches in which the entire head (or a subvolume of interest) is scanned for possible sources. At each part in the brain, for example, a simulated dipole can be placed and the forward problem used to generate the field in the sensors. This simulated field can be compared to the measured field and a goodness-of-fit measure calculated. This is repeated for each point in the brain in order to generate a volumetric representation of the goodness of fit. Typically, this will have several maxima, which represent putative discrete cortical sources. One popular approach is that of multiple-signal classification (MUSIC), first used in signal processing before adaptation for EEG/MEG (Mosher, Lewis, Leahy, 1992). In MUSIC, dipole components are identified that fit both the spatial and temporal components of a subset of MEG data. This can only work if the sources are in some way independent, and if the contributions of signal and noise are appropriately separated. One problem with MUSIC is that, although it can be easy to identify the strongest dipole contribution, this can mask some smaller components in the signal space. To address this problem, an improvement to MUSIC has been recently proposed, known as "recursively applied and projected MUSIC" (RAP MUSIC), in which the contribution of the strongest dipolar source in the initial MUSIC solution is subtracted from the measured data (Mosher and Leahy, 1999). The whole procedure is then repeated to identify the next largest source, and so on in an iterative fashion.

Beamformer Models

Closely related to dipole scanning algorithms, beamformer models have recently been proposed for the analysis of EEG and MEG data. These models use algorithms based on those of fixed-aperture radar technology, in which any portion of the sky can be scanned using a weighted combination of fixed radar detectors (van Drongelen et al., 1996; Van Veen et al., 1997).

In any MEG detector array, we might have 275 channels of magnetic field data recorded every millisecond or faster. What we are actually interested in is the magnitude and time series of activation of a given point in the brain. This is sometimes described as a "virtual electrode recording" (Vrba and Robinson, 2001; Grave de Peralta-Menendez et al., 2004) because it describes what we might measure if we were to insert a recording micro-electrode at this location in the brain. In beamformer analysis, the virtual electrode output is estimated at any location by summing the MEG detector outputs in a suitably weighted fashion to yield a single time series for the virtual electrode. Because the MEG data has an intrinsic temporal resolution of 1 msec or better, the virtual electrode time series will have the same temporal resolution. The key is, of course, the appropriate determination of the weights (275 numbers in our example) for each location in the brain. In a "perfect" beamformer, for any location in the brain, we would choose our 275 weights so that we were sensitive to activity only at that location and completely insensitive to activity elsewhere. We would then determine our 275 weight values at each location in the brain, enabling us to have a complete map of electrical activity at each point. Of course, we know that nonuniqueness must forbid this level of perfection in any inverse problem algorithm. There are potentially several tens of thousands of separate points in the brain we could probe with our MEG array, yet we only have 275 discrete channels—this fundamentally limits our beamformer resolution. In reality, beamformer models must approximate the optimal weights using minimization algorithms. Typically, in these constrained minimum variance (CMV) beamformer algorithms, the weights are determined from the data covariance matrix such that the limited number of degrees-of-freedom are used in an optimal fashion to suppress the contribution of unwanted sources at each point in the source space. One of the most widely used beamformers for MEG applications is known as "synthetic aperture magnetometry" (SAM; Robinson and Vrba, 1999; Vrba and Robinson, 2001; Gaetz and Cheyne, 2003; for a recent review of SAM applications, see Hillebrand et al., 2005).

Algorithms such as SAM make two key assumptions: (1) the MEG data are generated by a set of discrete dipolar sources and (2) the time series of these sources are uncorrelated. This latter assumption is the main limitation of beamformer approaches: two, perfectly correlated cortical sources will be self-canceling and hence will not be represented in the final beamformer reconstruction. This means that algorithms such as SAM are probably not well suited to the analysis of short-epoch evoked response experiments. On the other hand, simulations and empirical results have shown that these algorithms are robust to moderate levels of source correlations (Van Veen et al., 1997; Gross et al., 2001), suggesting that they may be well suited for the analysis of longer-epoch evoked response experiments, and for experimental designs that do not involve averaging in the time domain.

The advantages of algorithms such as SAM are twofold. First, there is no need to specify the number, initial position, or orientation of dipoles a priori. If the assumptions are valid, the algorithm will correctly reconstruct the number and position of the sources. Second, because the weights are determined from the data covariance matrix, there is no need to average the MEG time series in the time domain. This makes techniques such as SAM ideal for studying time-, but not phase-, locked activity, such as the ERS and ERD oscillatory activity described above.

In a typical SAM analysis, the virtual electrode output is determined for each region in the brain, typically at a scanning resolution of $5 \times 5 \times 5$ mm. This time series can be broken down into discrete epochs, reflecting any number of different experimental conditions. Statistical analysis can then be performed between the epoch groups. For example, the amount of alpha (5–15 Hz) activity could be assessed in the active epochs and compared to that in the passive epochs. In SAM, a difference statistic is computed for each voxel in the brain, which gives rise to a parametric intensity map, conceptually similar to those generated by techniques such as functional magnetic resonance imaging and positron-emission tomography, but with a much higher underlying temporal resolution. The resulting SAM maps can be subject to statistical procedures similar to those developed for fMRI and PET, including statistical inference at the level of the single subject (Barnes and Hillebrand, 2003) and the group (Singh, Barnes, and Hillebrand, 2003). SAM can also be used to localize oscillatory effects that change slowly over time, for example, those generated by pharmacological interventions or by physiological phenomena such as migraine aura (Hall et al., 2004) or swallowing (Furlong et al., 2004).

Distributed Current Algorithms

Because they assume that activity can occur anywhere within the brain, distributed current algorithms (DCAs) do not constrain the spatial extent of the current generators. The whole source space is filled with a dense field of fixed dipoles for which only the vector amplitudes of the dipoles at each point in the source space need to be determined. This can be further simplified if we use anatomical information from the subject's fMRI scan to constrain the position and orientation of each dipole. Now only one parameter, amplitude, needs to be determined for each dipole in the source space. The forward problem for a single instant of time can be written as a simple matrix equation:

$$B = LJ,$$

where J is a $N \times 1$ matrix describing the amplitude of each of the N fixed dipoles in the brain and B is a $1 \times M$ matrix describing the MEG measurement in each of the M channels. The $M \times N$ matrix L is known as the "lead field matrix," and each element of L describes the amount of MEG signal generated in one of the MEG sensors by a dipolar source at one of the source space locations. Hence the calculation of the elements of L requires the forward problem to be solved for each dipole-sensor pair, given the relative positions of the source and MEG coils and the conductivity model being used. L and B are therefore known, or calculable; to solve the inverse problem we need only invert the above equation to calculate the current distribution, J. This is essentially a linear problem that, in principle, can be solved using fairly straightforward matrix inversion algorithms (Hämäläinen and Ilmoniemi, 1984; Fuchs et al., 1999; Baillet et al., 2001; Michel et al., 2001).

Unfortunately, to be useful, the dipole field needs to be defined on a dense, three-dimensional grid, having typically tens of thousands of dipole amplitude parameters. Because, however, we have only 150–300 channels of data, the inverse problem under this approach is massively underdetermined ($N \gg M$). Thus, to be practicable, DCAs need to make additional a priori constraints on the form of the current density.

There are several different approaches to this area of the EEG/MEG inverse problem, one that has generated perhaps the most discussion in the literature. Perhaps the simplest and oldest technique is the minimum-norm least-squares (MNLS) solution (Hämäläinen and Ilmoniemi, 1984), in which a distributed current algorithm solution is found that best fits the MEG data, using a least-squares criterion. As we have seen, in the underdetermined MEG inverse problem, there are many such nonunique solutions. Within the MNLS framework, the solution that has the minimum power is chosen from this solution set.

Note that, although distributed current algorithms have been most often used in the analysis of average evoked response data, they can also be formulated for use in the analysis of oscillatory power changes, such as event-related synchronization and desynchronization (Jensen and Vanni, 2002). In addition, statistical volumetric maps of activation changes between active and passive states, or between experimental conditions, can be constructed using appropriately constructed minimum-norm algorithms (Dale et al., 2000).

A key problem with the minimum-norm least-squares solution is that it generates very smooth solutions and favors superficial distributed current distributions, even if the true source is a deeper, more focal, current generator. Several proposed modifications to the MNLS solution can be shown to do a better job at localizing focal sources of current (Ioannides, Bolton, and Clarke, 1990; Dale and Sereno, 1993; Grave de Peralta-Menedez and Gonzalez-Andino, 1998; Grave de Peralta-Menendez et al., 2004; Fuchs et al., 1999; Dale et al., 2000). In one approach to this key problem, introducing an a priori weighting matrix allows one to change the nature of the final solution. For example, one can use weighting factors to correct for the depth bias, or noise in the data to "normalize" the MNLS solution (Dale et al., 2000), or one can use iterated algorithms in which the initial MNLS solution serves as an a priori weighting matrix for the recalculation of a new minimum-norm solution. Although these algorithms tend to zero in on more focal solutions (Gorodnitsky, George, and Rao, 1995), in some cases, they have been shown to be sensitive to noise in the data (Baillet, Mosher, and Leahy, 2001). In another approach, imposing a smoothness constraint within the inversion, a method known as LORETA (Pascual-Marqui, Michel, and Lehmann, 1994), can be shown to accurately reconstruct the position of focal sources, although at the expense of spatially smearing the reconstructed sources.

It is important to note, however, that we do not actually know whether the generating current source is focal or extended. Figure 12.6a

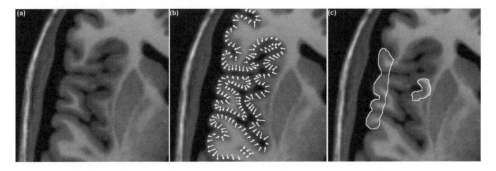

Figure 12.6
Demonstration of source space complexity and nonuniqueness in the frontal lobe/ insula cortex region of the human brain.

shows a particularly complicated part of the cortex, in the region of the inferior frontal lobe and insula cortex. The insula is of interest because it is separate from the neocortex and yet has the same gray matter layers capable of providing a source of externally measured magnetic fields. The complexity of the source space is evident, with several layers of vectors (figure 12.6b), and rapidly changing source orientations. Figure 12.6c shows some hypothetical source locations for the measured field. Unfortunately, a deep focal source in the insula could generate the same magnetic field as that of a distributed superficial source in the frontal lobe. There is no way of choosing between these two options. A single current dipole analysis might be able to quite accurately model the MEG data and would yield a source in the insula. In contrast, an MNLS solution would demonstrate an extended area of activation in the frontal lobe. Other algorithms, such as weighted or iterated minimum-norm solutions, would presumably favor the deeper focal source, or perhaps something in between. The generic inability of inverse problem algorithms both to assess the spatial extent of activation and to localize its position in three dimensions has led some to propose that a more principled approach is to simply use a basic minimum-norm solution on a two-dimensional source space, and accept that the reconstructed source distribution will effectively be a surface projection of the underlying sources (Hauk, 2004). If MEG is to be truly useful as a cognitive imaging tool, however, we need to unambiguously localize activity as coming from, for example, either the frontal lobe or the insular cortex. It follows that we need to be able to provide extra information to the inverse problem algorithm, so that these ambiguities can be resolved.

Applications

The acquisition hardware for MEG will certainly evolve in the next few years, with improved dewar design, greater numbers of channels, new gradiometer design, faster amplifiers, and better A/D converters. Some of the inverse problem algorithms described earlier will be implemented as real-time solutions on fast computer platforms. This will allow cortical activity to be displayed while the subject is actually performing a cognitive task.

One of the key potential application areas for MEG is in research and clinical studies of pediatric populations. For example, MEG can be used to study the neuroelectric correlates of normal development or disorders such as dyslexia, autism, and epilepsy. MEG has advantages in that it is silent, relatively unintimidating (compared to fMRI), there are no safety or ethical issues other than informed consent and MEG can be performed quite rapidly. On the other hand, pediatric MEG has two disadvantages. First, the child must be compliant enough to remain still. Although false "activations" cannot be created by head movement with MEG as they can with fMRI, the magnitude of averaged signals can be reduced and the accuracy of cortical localization compromised by excessive head movement. Muscle artifacts may also be introduced in the MEG sensor array. The use of "soft" inflatable head restraints can help with this, as can the presence of a family member in the shielded room.

Second, in modern MEG systems, the dewar is designed to fit around most of the adult population rather than a child. In some adults with quite large heads this can be quite a tight fit. With children, the opposite problem occurs. Young children's heads are so small, compared to the standard dewar size, that the detectors are not placed optimally close to the head surface (figure 12.7). Although using magnetometers, with their potentially greater depth sensitivity, may help in these situations, their concomitant increased sensitivity to environmental electromagnetic noise may reduce the benefit. For optimum scanning of young children, it is probably desirable, therefore, to construct an MEG system that is directly matched to the head sizes of children in the target age group.

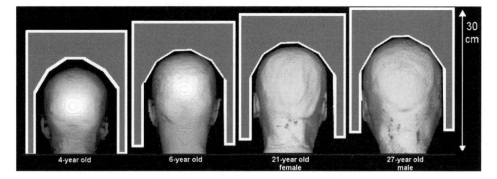

Figure 12.7
Illustration of the problem of designing a generic MEG system for adult and pediatric populations. Each head is rendered from real MRI data from 4 individuals. The MEG helmet is a hypothetical one that closely fits the head of the 27-year-old male subject. The horizontal line represents the shoulders of each person. For the younger, smaller heads, the temporal MEG sensors become increasingly distant from the head, reducing sensitivity. Occipital and frontal channels (not shown) are similarly nonoptimal. (Child data courtesy of Jay Giedd and Clare Mackay)

Integration and Innovation

Integration with Electroencephalography

Because magnetoencephalography and electroencephalography provide complementary information about neuronal current sources (for example, EEG is more sensitive than MEG to radial currents and activity from deeper sources in the brain), a joint EEG-MEG approach can be used to solve the inverse problem (Dale and Sereno, 1993). Most modern MEG systems also come with EEG electrode sets and amplifiers, allowing the simultaneous recording of EEG and MEG data. The two data sets can be used together in a joint solution to the inverse problem, such as a combined distributed current algorithm approach. Within the DCA analysis, the MEG and EEG channels are treated equivalently, all that is needed is for the different lead field functions for EEG electrodes and MEG coils to be specified appropriately in the matrix L. Although the joint use of EEG and MEG reduces the problem of nonuniqueness, it does not abolish it completely.

Coregistration and Integration with Magnetic Resonance Imaging

Because MEG itself provides no anatomical information, MEG localizations must be superimposed or coregistered on the individual's MRI scan. MEG-MRI coregistration is a two-step process. First, the position of the MEG detectors must be ascertained within a head-based coordinate system. A common approach is to use small coils placed on three or more discrete positions on the head, known as "fiducial points." By passing a current through these coils, researchers can use the detectors to localize the position of the coils and hence define a head-based coordinate system for the MEG sensor positions (Erné et al., 1987). Second, the position of that head-based coordinate system must be ascertained within the MRI coordinate system. By placing oil-filled capsules on these same fiducial points, the researcher can easily identify them in the MRI scans and hence bring the two coordinate systems into registration. Unfortunately, even small errors in the location of the fiducial points can lead to significant coregistration errors at cortical locations distant from the fiducial points (Singh et al., 1997). Greater accuracy can be obtained using a surface-matching approach, whereby the surface of the scalp is automatically extracted from the MRI data, then matched by translation and rotation to a head surface that has been digitized in the MEG laboratory. The advantage of this approach is that points over the whole of the scalp are used in the coregistration, so that errors at each point tend to average out, and there is no lever effect, as there is with small numbers of fiducial points. The disadvantage is that a head surface has to be digitized in the MEG laboratory. One digitizing strategy is to move a small coil over the surface of the head and to localize each position within the MEG coordinate system. This yields the maximum accuracy because the scalp head shape is automatically defined with reference to the position of the MEG sensors. The disadvantage of this strategy is that it can be quite time consuming. An alternative strategy is to digitize the subject's head shape using special digitizing equipment, such as the Polhemus three-dimensional digitizer, or photometric, camera-based digitizing techniques within the MEG laboratory. This can be faster, but the problem then remains of linking the position of the digitized head shape with the position of the MEG detectors.

The coregistration problem is the Cinderella of MEG. Although usually addressed as an afterthought (there are relatively few published papers on the topic) when laboratories first acquire an MEG system, the next generation of source localization algorithms will critically depend on accurate coregistration so that the position or orientation of the cortical gray matter sheet and fMRI data can be used as accurate a priori constraints.

Anatomical MRIs are of such high quality that automatic algorithms are now easily able to segment the image of the brain into tissue compartments such as gray matter, white matter, and cerebrospinal fluid (e.g., Dale and Sereno, 1993; Dale et al., 2000). The gray matter can be modeled locally as a two-dimensional sheet, which can then be subdivided into small dipolar elements. The orientation of each dipole can be fixed such that its orientation is perpendicular to the gray-white matter boundary. The use of such a stringent anatomical a priori constraint for the source space dramatically reduces the number of source parameters that need to be determined when solving the inverse problem and results in more spatially localized solutions. It does not, however, get around the problem of nonuniqueness because, for example, extent and depth ambiguities still remain.

One key problem, which is often overlooked, however, is the issue of coregistration accuracy. Again, if we use figure 12.6 as an example, we can see how complex the gray matter sheet is and that areas of quite different source orientations can be physically quite close together. This means that any significant error in MEG-MRI coregistration would result in a highly constrained source model that is displaced from its true position. Consequently, using anatomical a priori constraints could provide erroneous information for the inverse problem solution, which might well be worse than using no anatomical information at all (Hillebrand and Barnes, 2003). The successful use of anatomical MRI a priori constraints depends critically on the accuracy of the coregistration. It is also important to realize that MEG/EEG signals arise not only from the gray matter sheet of the cortex; it is likely that deep brain structures may also generate such signals. Thus it may be necessary to place single dipolar sources in the center of potentially active structures (Dale and Sereno, 1993).

Additional information for solving the MEG inverse problem can potentially be obtained from other functional imaging modalities, such as fMRI. The intention here is to combine the complementary information from the two techniques in a principled fashion, making the best use of the spatial accuracy of fMRI and the high temporal resolution of MEG. A simple approach is to perform the same, or similar, experiment using fMRI and MEG so that the resulting source localizations can be compared to see whether there is a match between the two modalities (e.g., Singh et al., 2002; Moradi et al., 2003).

More formally, after statistical analysis of the fMRI data set, the activation map can be used to "bias" the inverse solution, such that activity is more likely to be localized to the clusters found in the fMRI analysis (Liu, Belliveau, and Dale, 1998; Ahlfors et al., 1999; Dale et al., 2000; figure 12.8, plate 13). The advantage of this approach is that the temporal evolution of activity within the fMRI clusters can now be described using the millisecond resolution of MEG. Given the inherent nonuniqueness of the MEG/EEG inverse problem, this may be our best chance to get close to our "perfect" neuroimaging technique, which yields a nonunique solution in both space and time.

Of course, inevitably, there are some problems with integrating magnetoencephalography with functional magnetic resonance imaging, which mostly derive from the hemodynamic nature of the fMRI BOLD response. Although much progress has been made in understanding the relationship between the underlying neural substrate of the BOLD response (Logothetis et al., 2001), there is much that is still not known. In particular, we cannot guarantee that an activation cluster obtained in an fMRI experiment will have a real counterpart in the MEG data, or vice versa (Ahlfors et al., 1999; Nunez and Silberstein, 2000). This would lead to the fMRI data set being inappropriate as a suitable a priori constraint for the MEG/EEG inverse problem. Recently, Bayesian methodologies have been proposed for the MEG/EEG inverse problem that would allow the fMRI a priori constraint, or indeed any other, to be used in a variable fashion, in which the relative contribution of each constraint would be selected on the basis of whether it truly helps explain the data.

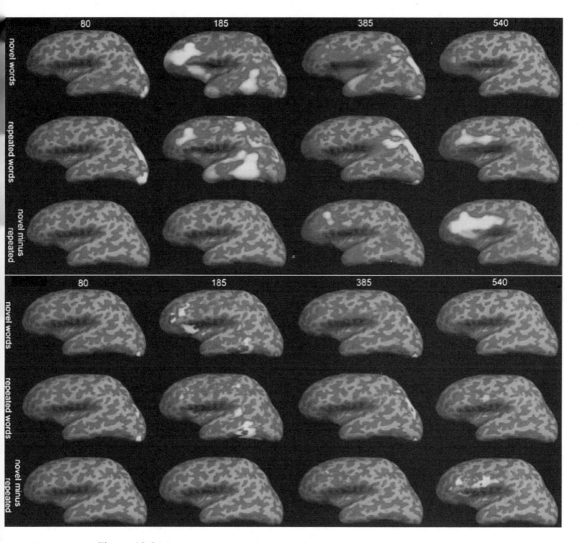

Figure 12.8
Demonstration of the utility of fMRI constraints in the analysis of MEG data, taken from (Dale et al., 2000). The data are from a single subject, performing a cognitive task in which the subject was presented with written concrete nouns (objects and animals) and had to decide whether the named object was more than a foot long. Identical fMRI and MEG experiments were performed using a trial-based evoked-response paradigm. To allow the hemodynamic response to decay back to baseline, a 16 sec intertrial interval was used in both modalities, even though it is not necessary for the MEG experiment. Each brain image shows the inflated gray matter sheet for this individual at four different latencies after stimulus onset (80, 185, 385, and 540 msec). The top panel of the figure displays the MEG data, analyzed using a noise-normalized inverse and constrained using only the anatomical gray matter sheet. The time course of activation is clearly visible. The bottom panel displays the same data analyzed using the same inversion algorithm, but with fMRI data also used to constrain the solution. Increased spatial resolution is clearly evident. See plate 13 for color version.

A related problem is that it is actually quite difficult to perform exactly the same experiment in the two imaging modalities, given the slowness of the hemodynamic response.

It can also be difficult to decide which aspect of activity recorded with MEG/EEG should be compared with the BOLD response. Both evoked and induced oscillatory activity can be generated in the brain and it is not yet clear which neural metric provides the best match to the activation measured with BOLD fMRI. Figure 12.9 (plate 14) shows the results of a recent experiment comparing the fMRI and MEG signals generated by the presentation of a static checkerboard visual stimulus (Brookes et al., 2005). The experiment clearly demonstrates the presence of multiple evoked and induced components, located in similar regions to the BOLD response, in even the simplest of MEG experiments.

Similarly, in a recent experiment, my colleagues and I also used MEG and fMRI to investigate the cortical areas involved in the perception of a simple moving dot pattern (figure 12.10, plate 15). As expected the fMRI data set revealed a network of activated extrastriate visual areas, including the human motion area V5/MT. Previous MEG evoked response experiments have also localized activity in these regions (Lam et al., 2000). In our data, we found beta desynchronization in the same regions as those showing a BOLD response. This again suggests that both evoked and induced components coexist in the same neuronal population showing a BOLD response. Although the SAM analysis is not formally constrained by the fMRI data set, the results give us some faith that, in this experiment, SAM is correctly localizing the current generators.

In a recent cognitive experiment, my colleagues and I (Singh et al., 2002) investigated the relationship between ERS/ERD effects and the BOLD response for a language fluency task, in which subjects had to generate words beginning with a given letter (figure 12.11, plate 16). The design of this experiment is rather unusual for an MEG one in that it is a conventional fMRI boxcar design in which subjects repeatedly performed simple visual fixation for 15 seconds and then performed the language task for 15 seconds. The study is also unusual in that it is one of the first to use the spatial normalization approach for forming group images of ERS/ERD within the synthetic aperture magnetometry framework. This group SAM analysis clearly shows beta ERD in the same regions as those where the BOLD response is found. It appears from the various MEG-fMRI experiments that have been performed thus far that often evoked response activity, localized with MEG, occurs in similar locations to that of the BOLD response (see, for example, figure 12.8). Similarly, studies looking at

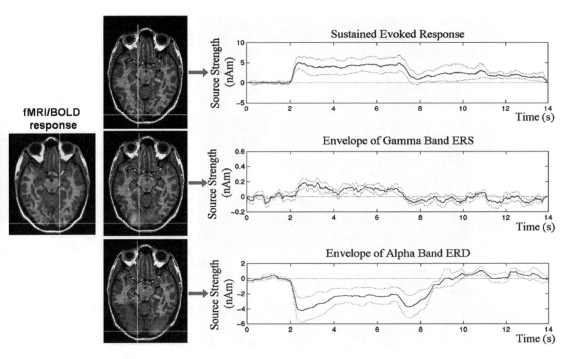

Figure 12.9

Results from a single subject of an fMRI-MEG comparison experiment in which the subject was shown a static checkerboard visual stimulus for 6 sec (Brookes et al., 2005). Orange colors depict power increases, blue/pink colors depict task-related power decreases. During the stimulus presentation (2–8 sec), three neuroelectric effects were detected in a SAM analysis of the MEG data: (1) a sustained and evoked shift in the DC baseline (top panel); (2) an induced increase in gamma-band (55–70 Hz) power (middle panel); and (3) an induced decrease in alpha (8–13 Hz) power (bottom panel). These effects are in a similar location to the BOLD response found in an identical MRI experiment (far left panel). (Figure courtesy of Matt Brookes) See plate 14 for color version.

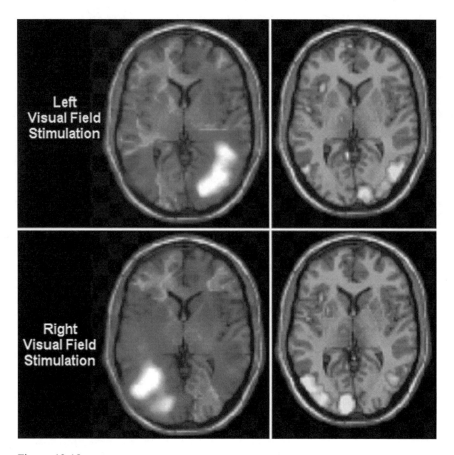

Figure 12.10
MEG-fMRI comparison experiment showing activation to a visual stimulus consisting of a field of coherently moving dots ($n = 11$). On the left, SAM analysis of the MEG data shows beta (15–25 Hz) power decreases in extrastriate visual cortex, including V5/MT. This ERD is clearly contralateral to the visual field in which the stimulus is presented. On the right, the BOLD fMRI activation to the same task is also shown. There is a clear correspondence between those areas showing a BOLD increase, and those areas showing a beta power decrease. See plate 15 for color version.

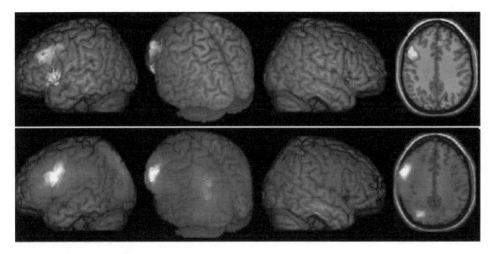

Figure 12.11
Comparison of the group BOLD response (top row) and the SAM-MEG analysis (bottom row) of task-related beta (15–25 Hz) ERD, for a letter fluency language task (*n* = 6). See plate 16 for color version.

ERS/ERD induced effects (figures 12.9, 12.10, and 12.11) show a mixture of correspondences with BOLD effects, with one of the most prevalent being desynchronization in the alpha and beta bands. Although this might, at first, seem puzzling, neuronal modeling studies of ERD have also shown that, as the mean activation level in a population rises, the amount of oscillatory power in lower frequencies, such as alpha and beta, can be seen to decrease (Pfurtscheller and Lopes da Silva, 1999; Pfurtscheller, 2001). In this context, therefore, it appears that event-related desynchronization is actually a correlate of activation, although there is much work to be done in investigating which aspects of neuroelectric activity best correlate with the BOLD response.

Conclusion

One area of research that is likely to be very important in the future is the use of MEG to study the phase relationship between separate cortical areas of the brain. Modern theories of brain function speculate that phase synchronization between cortical areas, and the modulation of this synchrony moment by moment is a fundamental building block of perception and consciousness (Sporns, Tononi, and Edelman, 2000). Several studies have already demonstrated MEG's ability to localize both functionally relevant areas and the phase relationships between them (e.g., Gross et al., 2001).

Thus the future looks bright for MEG, and indeed for all neuroimaging technologies. What is becoming increasingly clear, however, is that, moving away from the simple spatial "blob hunting" paradigm, we need to perform more sophisticated experiments in which we investigate the temporal sequencing of activity in the cortex, the role of interregional synchrony, and the functional significance of task-related modulations of the brain's intrinsic oscillations. Because of the fundamental limitations of each technology, these goals can only be attained by a truly multimodal approach to functional neuroimaging.

References

Ahlfors, S. P., Simpson, G. V., Dale, A. M., Belliveau, J. W., Liu, A. K., Korvenoja, A., Virtanen, J., Huotilainen, M., Tootell, R. B., Aronen, H. J., and Ilmoniemi, R. J. (1999). Spatiotemporal activity of a cortical network for processing visual motion revealed by MEG and fMRI. *Journal of Neurophysiology*, *82*(5), 2545–2555.

Aine, C., Huang, M., Stephen, J., and Christner, R. (2000). Multistart algorithms for MEG empirical data analysis reliably characterize locations and time courses of multiple sources. *NeuroImage*, *12*, 159–172.

Baillet, S. M., Mosher, J. C., and Leahy, R. M. (2001). Electromagnetic brain mapping. *IEEE Signal Processing Magazine*, 14–30.

Barnes, G. R., and Hillebrand, A. (2003). Statistical flattening of MEG beamformer images. *Human Brain Mapping*, *18*, 1–12.

Basar, E., Basar-Eroglu, C., Karakas, S., and Schurmann, M. (2001). Gamma, alpha, delta, and theta oscillations govern cognitive processes. *International Journal Psychophysiology*, *39*(2–3), 241–248.

Brookes, M., Gibson, A., Hall, S. D., Furlong, P. L., Barnes, G. R., Hillebrand, H., Singh, K. D., Holliday, I. E., Francis, S., and Morris. P. A. (2005). GLM-beamformer method demonstrates stationary field: Alpha ERD and gamma ERS co-localisation with fMRI BOLD response in visual cortex. *NeuroImage*, *26*(1), 302–308.

Carelli, P., and Leoni, R. (1986). Localization of biological sources with arrays of superconducting gradiometers. *Journal of Applied Physiology*, *59*, 645–650.

Cohen, D. (1968). Magnetoencephalography: Evidence of magnetic fields produced by alpha-rhythm currents. *Science*, *161*, 784–786.

Cohen, D. (1972). Magnetoencephalography: Detection of the brain's electrical activity with a superconducting magnetometer. *Science*, *175*, 664–666.

Dale, A. M., Liu, A. K., Fischl, B. R., Buckner, R. L., Belliveau, J. W., Lewine, J. D., and Halgren, E. (2000). Dynamic statistical parametric mapping: Combining fMRI and MEG for high-resolution imaging of cortical activity. *Neuron*, *26*, 55–67.

Dale, A. M., and Sereno, M. I. (1993). Improved localization of cortical activity by combining EEG and MEG with MRI cortical surface reconstruction: A linear approach. *Journal of Cognitive Neuroscience*, *5*, 162–176.

Erné, S. N., Narici, L., Pizzella, V., and Romani, G. L. (1987). The positioning problem in biomagnetic measurements: A solution for arrays of superconducting sensors. *IEEE Transactions on Magnetics*, *MAG-23*, 1319–1322.

Fuchs, M., Wagner, M., Köhler, T., and Wischmann, H.-A. (1999). Linear and non-linear current density reconstructions. *Journal of Clinical Neurophysiology*, *16*, 267–295.

Furlong, P. L., Hobson, A. R., Aziz, Q., Barnes, G. R., Singh, K. D., Hillebrand, A., Thompson, D. G., and Hamdy, S. (2004). Dissociating the spatio-temporal characteristics of cortical neuronal activity associated with human volitional swallowing in the healthy adult brain. *NeuroImage*, *22*(4), 1447–1455.

Gaetz, W. C., and Cheyne, D. O. (2003). Localization of human somatosensory cortex using spatially filtered magnetoencephalography. *Neuroscience Letters*, *340*, 161–164.

Gorodnitsky, I. F., George, J. S., and Rao, B. D. (1995). Neuromagnetic source imaging with FOCUSS: A recursive weighted minimum norm algorithm. *Electroencephalography and Clinical Neurophysiology*, *95*(4), 231–251.

Grave de Peralta Menendez, R., Murray, M. M., Michel, C. M., Martuzzi, R., and Gonzalez Andino, S. L. (2004). Electrical neuroimaging based on biophysical constraints. *NeuroImage*, *21*(2), 527–539.

Grave de Peralta-Menendez, R., and Gonzalez-Andino, S. L. (1998). A critical analysis of linear inverse solutions to the neuroelectromagnetic inverse problem. *IEEE Transactions on Biomedical Engineering*, *45*, 440–448.

Gross, J., Kujala, J., Hamalainen, M., Timmermann, L., Schnitzler, A., and Salmelin, R. (2001). Dynamic imaging of coherent sources: Studying neural interactions in the human brain. *Proceedings of the National Academy of Sciences, USA*, *98*(2), 694–699.

Hall, S. D., Barnes, G. R., Hillebrand, A., Furlong, P. L., Singh, K. D., and Holliday, I. E. (2004). Spatio-temporal imaging of cortical desynchronization in migraine visual aura: A magnetoencephalography case study. *Headache*, *44*(3), 204–208.

Hämäläinen M. S., and Hari, R. (2002). Magnetoencephalographic characterization of dynamic brain activation: Basic principles and methods of data collection and source analysis. In A. W. Toga and J. C. Mazziotta (Eds.), *Brain mapping: The methods*, 227–253. San Diego: Academic Press.

Hämäläinen, M. S., Hari, R., Ilmoniemi, R. J., Knuutila, J., and Lounasma, O. V. (1993). Magnetoencephalography: Theory, instrumentation, and applications to noninvasive studies of the working human brain. *Reviews of Modern Physics, 65,* 413–497.

Hämäläinen, M. S., and Ilmoniemi, R. J. (1984). Interpreting measured magnetic fields of the brain: Estimates of current distributions. Report no. TKK-F-A559. Helsinki University of Technology, Helsinki.

Hari, R., and Lounasmaa, O. V. (1989). Recording and interpretation of cerebral magnetic fields. *Science, 244,* 432–436.

Hari, R., and Salmelin, R. (1997). Human cortical rhythms: A neuromagnetic view through the skull. *Trends in Neurosciences, 20,* 44–49.

Hauk, O. (2004). Keep it simple: A case for using classical minimum norm estimation in the analysis of EEG and MEG data. *NeuroImage, 21,* 1612–1621.

Hillebrand, A., and Barnes, G. R. (2002). A quantitative assessment of the sensitivity of whole-head MEG to activity in the adult human cortex. *NeuroImage, 16,* 638–650.

Hillebrand, A., and Barnes, G. R. (2003). The use of anatomical constraints with MEG beamformers. *NeuroImage, 20*(4), 2302–2313.

Hillebrand, A., Singh, K. D., Furlong P. L., Holliday, I. E., and Barnes, G. R. (2005). A new approach to neuroimaging with magnetoencephalography. *Human Brain Mapping, 25*(2), 199–211.

Huang, M. X., Mosher, J. C., and Leahy, R. M. (1999). A sensor-weighted overlapping-sphere head model and exhaustive head model comparison for MEG. *Physics in Medicine and Biology, 44*(2), 423–440.

Ioannides, A. A., Bolton, J. P. R., and Clarke, C. J. S. (1990). Continuous probabilistic solutions to the biomagnetic inverse problem. *Inverse Problems, 6,* 523–542.

Jensen, O., and Vanni, S. (2002). A new method to identify multiple sources of oscillatory activity from magnetoencephalographic data. *NeuroImage, 15*(3), 568–574.

Lam, K., Kaneoke, Y., Gunji A., Yamasaki, H., Matsumoto, E., Naito, T., and Kakigi, R. (2000). Magnetic response of human extrastriate cortex in the detection of coherent and incoherent motion. *Neuroscience, 97*(1), 1–10.

Liu, A. K., Belliveau, J. W., and Dale, A. M. (1998). Spatiotemporal imaging of human brain activity using functional MRI-constrained magnetoencephalography data: Monte Carlo simulations. *Proceedings of the National Academy of Sciences, USA, 95*(15), 8945–8950.

Liu, A. K., Dale, A. M., and Belliveau, J. W. (2002). Monte Carlo simulation studies of EEG and MEG localization accuracy. *Human Brain Mapping, 16,* 47–62.

Logothetis, N. K., Pauls, J., Augath, M., Trinath, T., and Oeltermann, A. (2001). Neurophysiological investigation of the basis of the fMRI signal. *Nature, 412,* 150–157.

Michel, C. M., Thut, G., Morand, S., Khateb, A., Pegna, A. J., Grave de Peralta, R., Gonzalez, S., Seeck, M., and Landis, T. (2001). Electric source imaging of human cognitive brain functions: A review. *Brain Research Reviews*, *36*, 108–118.

Moradi, F., Liu, L. C., Cheng, K., Waggoner, R. A., Tanaka, K., and Ioannides, A. A. (2003). Consistent and precise localization of brain activity in human primary visual cortex by MEG and fMRI. *NeuroImage*, *18*(3), 595–609.

Mosher, J. C., and Leahy, R. M. (1999). Source localization using recursively applied and projected (RAP) MUSIC. *IEEE Transactions on Signal Processing*, *47*, 332–340.

Mosher, J. C., Lewis, P. S., and Leahy, R. M. (1992). Multiple dipole modeling and localization from spatio-temporal MEG data. *IEEE Transactions on Biomedical Engineering*, *39*(6), 541–557.

Nunez, P. (1981). Electric fields of the brain: *The neurophysics of EEG*. New York: Oxford University Press.

Nunez, P. L., and Silberstein, R. B. (2000). On the relationship of synaptic activity to macroscopic measurements: Does co-registration of EEG with fMRI make sense? *Brain Topography*, *13*, 79–96.

Pascual-Marqui, R. D., Michel, C. M., and Lehmann, D. (1994). Low resolution electromagnetic tomography: A new method for localizing electrical activity in the brain. *International Journal of Psychophysiology*, *18*, 49–65.

Pfurtscheller, G. (2001). Functional brain imaging based on ERD/ERS. *Vision Research*, *41*, 1257–1260.

Pfurtscheller, G., and Lopes da Silva, F. H. (1999). Event-related EEG/MEG synchronisation and desynchronisation: Basic principles. *Clinical Neurophysiology*, *110*, 1842–1857.

Robinson, S. E., and Vrba, J. (1999). Functional neuroimaging by synthetic aperture magnetometry (SAM). In *Recent advances in biomagnetism*, 302–305. Sendai, Japan: Tohoku University Press.

Sarvas, J. (1987). Basic mathematical and electromagnetic concepts of the bioelectromagnetic inverse problem. *Phys. Med. Biol.*, *32*, 11–22.

Scherg, M., and von Cramon, D. (1985). Two bilateral sources of the late AEP as identified by a spatio-temporal dipole model. *Electroencephalography and Clinical Neurophysiology*, *62*, 32–44.

Singh, K. D., Barnes, G. R., Hillebrand, A., Forde, E. M. E, and Williams, A. L. (2002). Task-related changes in cortical synchronisation are Spatially coincident with the haemodynamic response. *NeuroImage*, *16*, 103–114.

Singh, K. D., Barnes, G. R., and Hillebrand, A. (2003). Group imaging of task-related changes in cortical synchronisation using non-parametric permutation testing. *NeuroImage*, *19*(4), 1589–1601.

Singh, K. D., Holliday, I. E., Furlong, P. L., and Harding, G. F. A. (1997). Evaluation of MRI-MEG/EEG co-registration strategies using Monte Carlo simulation. *Electroencephalography and Clinical Neurophysiology*, *102*, 81–85.

Sporns, O., Tononi, G., and Edelman, G. M. (2000). Connectivity and complexity: The relationship between neuroanatomy and brain dynamics. *Neural Networks*, *13*, 909–922.

Tesche, C. D., and Karhu, J. (2000). Theta oscillations index human hippocampal activation during a working memory task. *Proceedings of the National Academy Sciences, USA*, *97*(2), 919–924.

van Drongelen, W., Yuchtman, M., Van Veen, B. D., and van Huffelen, A. C. (1996). A spatial filtering technique to detect and localize multiple sources in the brain. *Brain Topography*, *9*(1), 39–49.

Van Veen, B. D., van Drongelen, W., Yuchtman, M., and Suzuki, A. (1997). Localization of brain electrical activity via linearly constrained minimum variance spatial filtering. *IEEE Transactions on Biomedical Engineering*, *44*(9), 867–880.

Vrba, J., and Robinson, S. E. (2001). Signal processing in magnetoencephalography. *Methods*, *25*(2), 249–271.

Wood, C. C. (1982). Application of dipole localization methods to source identification in human evoked potentials. *Annals of the New York Academy of Sciences*, *388*, 139–155.

13 The Chemistry of Cognition

Stephen D. Hall and Peyman Adjamian

As a research concept, the chemistry of cognition is informed by many diverse disciplines, both directly and indirectly, and encompasses a broad spectrum of research methods: animal and human, in vivo and in vitro, postmortem and genetic, psychophysical and pharmacological, to name but a few. This chapter focuses on the application of human functional neuroimaging modalities to the investigation of the underlying chemical mechanisms of cognition.

The functional modalities and methodologies available for investigating neurological and cognitive function, some extensively described in previous chapters, form a formidable arsenal for the willing neuroscientist. It is the aim of this chapter to provide readers with a brief overview of the prominent functional modalities that can be applied to and give some insight into cognitive chemistry research.

At the end of the "decade of the brain" and at the beginning of a new millennium, it is apparent that no single technique holds the key to understanding the human mind. Rather, it is increasingly clear that only through multimodal integration will the most intricate workings of the human brain be revealed.

There are, as with any approach, a series of limitations to the methods discussed. We will elaborate on some of the difficulties faced by each of the neuroimaging methods used in the investigation of cognitive chemistry and will discuss how these can be overcome or minimized. Integrating the methods discussed is an intricate, and in itself, error-prone task. As we adopt increasingly integrative approaches, minimizing the technical difficulties associated with integration becomes a crucial point of interest (Adjamian et al., 2004a). We discuss the technical difficulties associated with cognitive chemistry research and explore current and developing methods for addressing these.

Development

The neurochemicals of primary interest to us in this chapter are roughly divided into neurotransmitters and energy metabolites, although the two groups are not mutually exclusive, a factor of principal importance in the discussions relating to magnetic resonance spectroscopy (MRS) methods (Danielsen and Ross, 1999). The origins of neurochemical study can be traced back to the work of Otto Loewi in 1921 and his discovery of the release of a substance, now known as acetylcholine (Valenstein, 2002). It was Loewi who forged the concept that neurons communicate with adjoining neurons or target organs using chemical messengers. Research over subsequent decades has revealed there to be many diverse neurotransmitters, all with varying functional mechanisms and physiological consequences. In this chapter, we touch on those which are better understood and hence more technically viable in functional research.

Our knowledge of metabolic processes and our understanding of the importance of energy metabolism stem from the work of the cell biologists, biochemists, and molecular biologists of the past century. The work of people such as Gustav Embden and Otto Meyerhof (see Kresge, Simoni and Hill, 2005) and Hans Krebs (see Buchanan, 2005) in the 1930s and 1940s, discovering metabolic pathways such as glycolysis and the tricarboxylic acid (TCA) cycle, provides the basis for our understanding of the substrates necessary for the functioning of cells of the nervous system. Similarly, the work of Alan Hodgkin and Andrew Huxley in the 1950s in determining the ionic mechanisms of neuronal signal conduction (see Häusser, 2000) provides the basis for our understanding of the central nervous system and forms the physiological basis of modern techniques.

These fundamental principles have been exploited by ever-evolving fields of research, to expand our understanding of neurochemistry to the point we have reached today. Biochemists have identified a vast array of neurotransmitters and metabolites of intricate neuronal significance; pharmacologists have elucidated the target receptors and their physiological consequences; and molecular biologists have established the structure of these receptors and their mechanisms of action. Using all of this information and a modicum of serendipity, pharmaceutical drug designers have created therapeutic agents of cognitive significance (Lestage, 2000).

What, then, can functional neuroimaging contribute to our already considerable understanding of the effects of these chemicals on various cells and target molecules and to our more limited understanding of the interactions within tissues of interest? As we will see in the following sections, functional neuroimaging picks up where the above-mentioned disciplines leave off. Functional neuroimaging reveals information regarding the physiological and chemical environments of the human brain in vitro, without the need for invasive surgical techniques. Moreover, it allows us to investigate the intrinsic chemical and physiological environment as a global entity, rather than as disparate units. For example, magnetoencephalography (MEG) allows us to look at function in a population or network of more than 100,000 neurons and to observe modulations in response to cognitive task, neurological impairment, or pharmacological intervention (Hillebrand et al., 2005).

Through the use of chemical and functional neuroimaging modalities, we can perform what amounts to a "virtual biopsy," taking a snapshot of the chemical environment at a spatially specific location, without the need for an actual biopsy (Danielsen and Ross, 1999). Finally, integrating chemical and functional neuroimaging modalities with one another, as well as applying information gathered from other research methods, enables us to obtain complete physiological and chemical profiles with spatial resolution on the order of millimeters, and temporal resolution on the order of milliseconds (see Singh, chapter 12, this volume).

Principles

In this chapter, we define the term *chemistry of cognition*, as the study of the chemical factors that underlie the physiological processes of cognition. Our focus is on functional neuroimaging aspects of this study, some of which are introduced and extensively explained in previous chapters (see, for example, Bandettini, chapter 9, this volume, on functional magnetic resonance imagining). Other modalities are described for the first time here, and we apologize in advance for the brevity of our technical discussion.

We divide functional neuroimaging modalities into two groups, chemical and physiological, based on their focus, although the boundaries between the groups are, of course, flexible and not exclusive. Functional neuroimaging in the field of neuropharmacological research is used to observe three fundamental features: cognitive function, physiological response, and underlying chemical mechanism. A central premise of cognitive chemistry is that, if we can fully establish the chemical mechanisms that mediate the physiological processes underlying cognition, then we will have all of the necessary information to understand how these systems operate. It is this premise which we will pursue in the present chapter.

Positron-Emission Tomography

An imaging modality designed to determine the spatial distribution of chemical constituents of the brain, PET makes use of a radioactive emitter, a chemical whose molecules are labeled with a radioisotope, also referred to as a "radionuclide." Depending on the nature of the radionuclide, it can be either inhaled or ingested by the subject, but, typically, it is administered through intravenous injection. In recent years, PET has been most often and most widely deployed in the observation of task-related increases in brain activity, represented by elevated metabolic activity, as indicated either by increased regional cerebral blood flow (rCBF), measured using water labeled with ^{15}O, or by increased glucose metabolism, measured using deoxyglucose labeled with ^{18}F, called ^{18}F-fluoro-deoxy-glucose (^{18}F-FDG). Both measurement methods are based on the assumption that elevated levels of tracer will accumulate in regions of the brain that are more active and therefore demand more energy substrates (van Heertum et al., 2004).

Although cerebral blood flow is more sensitive to neuronal activity than glucose metabolism and, as such, provides a more accurate indication of brain function, because of its physical properties, ^{18}F is a more detectable, and thus more accurate tracer than ^{15}O. This is possibly why ^{18}F-FDG is the most widely used tracer in PET studies. (Interested readers may find details of PET methods and clinical applications in Cunningham, Gunn, and Matthews, 2004.)

The principal success of PET lies in its advantage over other radio-tracer techniques, such as single-positron-emission-computed tomography (SPECT), in offering the quantitative measurements of biochemical and physiological processes in vivo, which can be particularly useful for detecting the neuropathology of disease states such as dementia (Frackowiak, 1989). By mathematically modeling the kinetics of the radionuclide in vivo as it participates in a given biological process, researchers can calculate the rate of the process and quantify the regional cerebral blood flow. Moreover, improvements in spatial accuracy of PET have facilitated direct comparison of human with animal results (see Jacobs et al., 2003).

Among the clinical applications of PET is cancer detection. Through the quantitative measurement of ^{18}F-FDG uptake in tumors, which reflects tissue metabolism, PET can detect the presence or absence of malignancy at the earliest stages, whereas anatomical imaging methods such as functional magnetic resonance imaging (MRI) are dependent on the physical manifestation of lesions to determine the existence and extent of disease. This factor makes the approach potentially invaluable as a tool for evaluating pharmacodynamics which is integral to drug development (Cunningham, Gunn, and Matthews, 2004).

On the other hand, progress made in hemodynamic observations using fMRI has forced simple metabolic measures using PET to take a back seat. As a consequence, recent PET studies have focused on more complex and specific chemical substrates, opening up new avenues of investigation. These more recent applications of the technique demonstrate that PET is once again coming into its own with respect to identifying the neurochemical features of the brain in health and pathology.

Based on the principle that the spread of a given substance throughout the brain is dependent on local neurochemistry, which typically relies on the activity of specific neuronal populations, there are two general methods of applying PET as a neurochemical and cognitive tool.

First, simple radiotracers are used to observe changes in regional cerebral blood flow or glucose metabolism (figure 13.1a, plate 17) in response to cognitive tasks or to cognitive impairment. For example, using PET, Liddle (2000) observed the dynamic imbalance in rCBF that may underlie cognitive impairments in patients with social dysfunction. This first method, though informative by itself, is often combined with the use of specific pharmacological agents to chemically manipulate neuronal systems in specific, observable ways. Thus, using PET, Dolan et al. (1995) observed increased cognitive activation of the anterior cingulate of schizophrenic patients treated with the dopamine agonist apomorphine, demonstrating the dopaminergic involvement in schizophrenia.

Second, specific radioligands are used to bind with distinct chemical targets (receptors). For example, in their PET studies, Toczek et al. (2003) used [18F]FCWAY, a selective 5HT-1A receptor antagonist, to determine that there is reduced serotonin receptor binding in temporal lobe epilepsy (TLE) foci; Simpson et al. (2003) used the serotonin transporter ligand [11C]McN5652 to rule out serotonin transport abnormalities in obsessive-compulsive disorder. PET has been applied with particular success in determining underlying chemical features of dementia through the use of labeled pharmacological substrates (for a review, see Herholz, 2003). Moreover, this second method enables researchers to regionally identify, and then quantify, chemical substrates. It may also be combined with a cognitive investigative approach, allowing researchers, in the case of competitive binding, to observe intrinsic chemical composition and ongoing neuronal activity. Both general methods may be used to observe the conditions of pathology and how they differ from the control population. For example, Aalto et al. (2005) used the dopamine D_2 receptor tracer [11C]FLB457

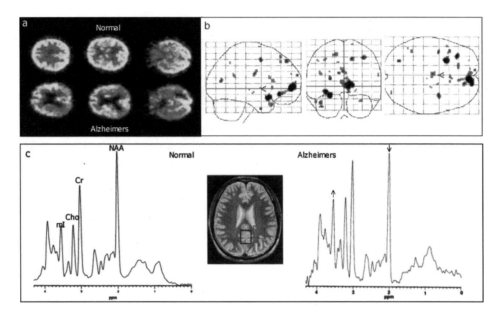

Figure 13.1
PET, fMRI, and MRS in cognitive chemistry. (*a*) Use of FDG-PET to show glucose
metabolism in the healthy population (top) and patients with Alzheimer's disease
(bottom) to reflect reduced regional energy demand (modified from Jagust, 2004).
(*b*) Use of fMRI to show regions of increased blood supply during the Stroop task,
under conditions of serotonin depletion in the brain (modified from Horacek et al.,
2005). (*c*) Use of MRS to determine the difference in grey matter spectrum metabolite ratio in Alzheimer's disease (*right*) compared to normal (*left*), showing reduced
NAA and increase mI. The center brain image shows a typical voxel for gray matter
(red) and white matter (green) acquisition (adapted from Danielsen and Ross, 1999).
See plate 17 for color version.

during cognitive tasks to demonstrate reduced receptor occupancy,
implicating frontotemporal dopaminergic networks in working memory
performance.

A third general method of applying PET combines the first two in
order to identify both regionally specific modulations in neuronal metabolism and additionally to identify the interaction of specifically designed
radioligands with molecules of interest, thus providing complementary
information about neuronal populations and chemical mediators. Mielke
et al. (1998) demonstrated a linkage between longitudinal loss of benzodiazepine binding and global metabolic decline, on the one hand, and progressive cognitive decline in patients with cerebellar ataxia, on the other.

Magnetic Resonance Spectroscopy

As with many of the other modalities, MRS has faced concerns about its reliability and accuracy (Lenkinski, 1989). In recent years, however, magnetic resonance hardware and methods have made enormous advances in range and sensitivity to chemical substrates, the significance of the brain's metabolites has become better understood, and the reliability of the technique has been proven to the point of widespread acceptance. Indeed, MRS is now recognized as an invaluable and indispensable tool in neurological diagnosis (Danielsen and Ross, 1999). As its efficacy has become apparent, MRS has emerged as a promising modality that offers numerous approaches to pathology and health research (Lenkinski, 2001).

Although complex, the theory behind the practice of magnetic resonance spectroscopy is based on the fact that, when surrounded by a magnetic field, atomic nuclei may be disrupted by radio frequency waves at specific frequencies, which cause the nuclei to generate signals that can be detected by a radio receiver. These signals can then be converted into meaningful information in the form of spectra, which can subsequently be interpreted to gain information concerning the chemical composition at the region of interest (ROI). Central to the theory behind MRS is the concept of atomic spin, which designates a physical property of subatomic particles. The overall spin of a nucleus is determined by its mass number, the total number of protons and neutrons it contains: an even mass number results in no net spin, whereas an uneven mass number results in a net spin. To be "visible" to MRS, a molecule must contain a nucleus with a net spin, consequently MRS observes molecules having isotopes whose mass numbers are uneven, such as hydrogen (^{1}H), phosphorus (^{31}P), lithium (^{7}Li), fluorine (^{19}F), and sodium (^{23}Na). Moreover, to be detected, the molecule must exist in natural abundance. (For a comprehensive review of the complex physics underlying MRS, see Keshavan, Kapur, and Pettegrew, 1991.)

When struck by radio waves, the spinning nuclei move to a higher energy state and tilt further from their spin angle. When the radio waves stop, the nuclei "relax," that is, they return to a lower energy state and resume their usual spin angle. It is at the point of *relaxation* that the nuclei emit an electromagnetic signal, which can be detected by an RF receiver. Because the signal generated by an atom such as ^{1}H is affected by its neighboring atomic environment, each molecule has a different resonant frequency, referred to as its "chemical shift."

The mathematical transformation provides a graphical representation of chemical shift (figure 13.1c), with the horizontal axis indicating the chemical shift in parts per million (ppm), and the vertical axis, the quantity of the metabolite. Each metabolite has a specific chemical shift frequency. For magnetic resonance spectroscopy using ^{1}H, the principal metabolites are closely linked and reside near to the tricarboxylic acid (TCA) cycle stage of the metabolic pathway. Although there are overlaps in the shift frequency, the position along the horizontal axis defines the metabolite.

In short, the ^{1}H MRS spectral profile of the "normal" brain reflects a number of metabolites at various points in the trace, of which N-acetylaspartate (NAA), creatine (Cr), choline (Cho), and Myoinositol (mI) constitute the four highest peaks. These metabolites are of such a robust nature that they (particularly in white matter) are aligned at approximately a 45-degree angle, often referred to as "Hunter's angle," with respect to one another (see figure 13.1c; Danielsen and Ross, 1999). NAA is a marker of neuronal viability and density; creatine, a marker of normal cerebral metabolism; choline, a cellular membrane marker; and myoinositol, an astrocyte marker and product of demyelination. In addition to these principal metabolites, glutamine and glutamate (referred to by their common designator "glx"), gamma-aminobutyric acid (GABA), and several other metabolites are observed, although not easily or reliably resolved without the aid of modeling software.

Furthermore, ^{1}H MRS allows us to observe a range of metabolites whose presence or whose variance from normal metabolite ratios is specifically indicative of an abnormal or pathological condition. Thus lactate is a product of failed oxidation, and lipid reflects a multitude of abnormalities such as necrosis or interruption of the myelin sheath. Using ^{1}H MRS, clinicians can diagnose numerous neurological conditions (for details on neuropathology diagnoses, see Danielsen and Ross, 1999; Brandao, 2004).

Software packages typically use either frequency or time-frequency domain modeling to quantify the chemical concentrations of the MRS spectra. The quantification is determined with respect to standardized phantom recordings containing accurately preprepared chemical concentrations of the relevant brain metabolites.

There are essentially three main approaches to the use of magnetic resonance spectroscopy for investigating the chemistry of cognition: (1) baseline MRS; (2) pharmaco-MRS; and (3) functional MRS. Baseline MRS distinguishes a particular patient group from a control population based on the variance of its local or global spectra from the baseline chemical spectra of the control population. Essentially a neurological diagnosis approach, it relies on the proven robustness of MRS spectra of gray and white matter in various regions of the brain. Even though these spectra demonstrate some variation between locations such as frontal lobe, occipital lobe, and cerebellum, they are reliable across subjects to the degree that disease may be diagnosed in an individual based upon a specific deviation from mean ratios (Danielsen and Ross, 1999). When investigating conditions in which cognitive impairments are evident through behavioral, functional, genetic, or other assessment, baseline MRS is used to ascertain a corresponding variation in metabolite ratio/concentration from the control group. The location identified as the region of interest (ROI) is in some cases taken from specific theories of the disease; in other cases, from preceding functional imaging studies; and in some "globally affective" cases, from the representative regions of gray and white matter in the occipital and parietal regions (figure 13.1c), respectively (Danielsen and Ross, 1999).

A method of increasing interest, pharmaco-MRS measures metabolites or the modulation of concentrations of endogenous substrates following the administration of a drug or the systemic introduction of a metabolite. This, of course, has important implications for understanding the mechanism and site of action of particular agents and additionally for informing pharmacokinetic models (Port and Wolf, 2003).

Functional MRS, sometimes called the "holy grail of research" as far as magnetic resonance spectroscopy is concerned, observes changes in the chemical composition of a specific brain region in response to cognitive demand. As we have noted, during the neural processing of cognition, neuronal populations are activated at all levels, from simple sensory input to complex, higher levels of processing. And, at all levels, this involves increased energy demand and therefore increased metabolic demand as well, resulting in changes in the concentrations of energy substrates and metabolic products, such as glucose and lactic acid.

More important and perhaps more informative are changes in the concentrations of the units of neuronal function, the neurotransmitters, insofar as these relate to various neuronal networks in cognitive processes of interest. Difficulties arise, however, in the measurement of these neurochemicals because of limitations imposed both by spectral resonance and by natural abundance. The concentrations of even the most abundant neurotransmitters, glutamate and GABA, are only 1–10 millimoles at most, and these concentrations are hundreds of times greater than those of most other neurotransmitters.

Baseline MRS

Across the field of cognitive research, conditions with cognitive deficits have been compared to matched controls using magnetic resonance spectroscopy. The principal focus of these studies has been the ratio between concentrations of N-acetylaspartate (NAA) and creatine. Because the concentration of creatine is known to be comparatively constant, a reduction in the ratio of NAA to creatine is assumed to reliably reflect reduced or lower neuronal density or viability (Brandao, 2004).

Baseline MRS has been used to provide chemical evidence of a physiological mechanism of cognitive decline or deficit. For example, frontal lobe NAA was found to vary with direct measures of verbal intelligence (Pfliederer et al., 2004); decreased NAA concentrations in frontal and occipital lobe were found to correlate with cognitive impairment following stroke (Ross et al., 2005); NAA-to-creatine ratios were found to be predictive of accompanying attention deficit disorder (Sun et al., forthcoming). Children with autism were found to have reduced NAA and increased lactate ratios in the frontal lobe compared to controls, consistent with a hypothesis of reduced neuronal viability and abnormal metabolism (Chugani et al., 1999). Patients with clinical depression exhibited reduced anterior cingulate glutamate, in comparison to age-matched controls (Auer et al., 2000). Patients suffering from schizophrenia demonstrated reduced NAA in medial temporal structures (Fukazo et al., 1999). Migraine with aura patients showed reduced choline concentration in the cerebellum (Macri et al., 2003), and patients with developmental dyslexia, showed lateralized differences between choline to NAA ratios that were absent in the control population (Rae et al., 1998). These studies, among numerous others, demonstrate the ability of MRS to distinguish cognitive deficits based on variations in physiologically significant metabolite ratios.

Pharmaco-MRS

When used to observe the kinetics and dynamics of pharmacological agents in vivo as indicated by the presence of the drug carrier propylene glycol in the spectrum (Danielsen and Ross, 1999), pharmaco-MRS has been tested and shown to be a feasible investigative approach. It has demonstrated increases in gamma-aminobutyric acid (GABA) concentrations following administration of the GABA tranaminase inhibitor vigabatrin (Weber et al., 1999), as well as changes in glutamate concentrations following transferral of epilepsy patients from one medication to another (Goff et al., 2002). In their study of the uptake profile of exogenous chemicals, Pietz et al. (2003) established that MRS concentration measures of phenylalanine following peripheral administration are accurate enough to monitor brain pharmacokinetics in vivo.

Functional MRS

This third method has restrictions to its application that relate directly to the need for reliably quantifiable measurements of change in metabolites. As discussed previously, many metabolites are present in such small quantities that their measurement per se is difficult enough. Thus, depending on the metabolite, a relatively large change in concentration is required in order to provide a reliable measure. As such, previous research has used paradigms with rather intense stimulus properties and has restricted its metabolic focus to higher-concentration substrates. Nonetheless, successful functional MRS experiments of the visual system have been performed where photic stimulation was demonstrated to produce significant changes in the relative concentration of lactate in the visual cortex (Prichard et al., 1991; Sappey-Marinier et al., 1992). Perhaps versions of the method using the more precise modeling software will expand the range of metabolite detection to incorporate more informative molecules such as glutamate and GABA, although this remains to be seen.

In the studies discussed above almost or all the researchers used proton ^1H magnetic resonance spectroscopy, most of them operating 1.5- or 3-tesla systems. Recent and ongoing advances in magnetic resonance technology have given rise to other spectroscopy species (previously alluded to), such as ^{31}P MRS, which are now commonly used and often integrated with ^1H hardware (Murphy-Boesch, 1994). Moreover, MRS systems of 4 tesla and greater are increasingly available, although the potential risk factors and unknowns of these more powerful systems generally restrict their use to animal studies. Nevertheless, the greater signal resolution of these evolving systems may prove to be the future of the field.

Innovation

Magnetoencephalography

A reflection of ionic flux in the signaling units of the brain that are intricately linked to various neurotransmitters of the central nervous system, MEG is a physiological measurement technique; as such, it provides no direct information regarding the actual pharmacological mediators of the electrical activity it observes. (For a comprehensive discussion of MEG, see Singh, chapter 12, this volume.) The technique has lent itself, however, to three distinct, innovative approaches to investigating the chemistry of cognition: (1) neuromodeling; (2) pharmaco-MEG; and (3) pharmaco-cognitive MEG.

With information from in vitro and in vivo animal research on cellular contributions to network signaling, neuromodeling employs the detailed mathematics of neural network modeling, typically based on the Hodgkin-Huxley models previously discussed. Its parameters identified in specific cell signaling, a neurotransmitter-specific network can be linked with the observed changes in electrical signals observed under specific conditions (Jensen et al., 2002, 2005).

Pharmaco-MEG uses specific pharmacological agents, typically of known mechanistic properties, to inform the spatial and temporal profile of changes in electrical activity. These agents act on known intrinsic neuronal targets; for example, neurotransmitter receptor agonists or antagonists are used to identify changes in oscillatory activity that occur as a result of neuronal excitation or inhibition. This approach has been recently developed and expanded to provide information concerning the effect of a specific agent over an extended window, enabling researchers to observe changes in cortical oscillations throughout the duration of drug uptake. Thus pharmaco-MEG provides information regarding the pharmacokinetics and pharmacodynamics of cognition in terms of neuronal population interactions.

An extension of pharmaco-MEG into the cognitive function domain, pharmaco-cognitive MEG uses particular pharmacological substrates to modulate known task-related cortical activity. Cognitive paradigms can be used to identify the spatial and temporal structure of evoked and induced changes that occur in response to a specific cognitive function. As we have noted, much like the BOLD response of fMRI, MEG can identify the modulation of neuronal activity in response to auditory, visual, or somatosensory stimulation in terms of its spatial and temporal profile (for a review, see Hillebrand et al., 2005). Pharmaco-cognitive MEG observes the changes in these dimensions in response to the substrates in question, thus providing information about the chemical constituents underlying a particular cognitive function.

Neuromodeling

This MEG approach to the chemistry of cognition requires some introduction regarding the chemical, physiological, and perceptual significance of current findings (see also Rippon, chapter 10, and Singh, chapter 12, this volume). Here we focus on a current subject of some debate: the observation of gamma frequency (30–70 Hz) activity in the visual cortex in response to visual stimulation.

Initially observed by electrode recordings in the cat visual cortex (Eckhorn et al., 1988; Gray et al., 1989), "visual gamma" oscillations were found in response to simplistic visual stimuli, such as achromatic moving bars. These were found to be robust findings across animal species and using more complex recording methods (Gray and McCormick, 1996; Kreiter and Singer, 1996; Logothetis et al., 2001). The findings were replicated in the human using duplicate paradigms and EEG recordings (Lutzenberger et al., 1995; Muller et al., 1996, 1997) and have more recently been explored using MEG (Jensen, Hari, and Kaila, 2002; Adjamian et al., 2004b; Hall et al., 2005). Recent studies using magnetoencephalography demonstrate the sensitivity of gamma oscillatory power to simple stimulus parameters such as spatial frequency (Adjamian et al., 2004b) and stimulus contrast (Hall et al., 2005). These findings have given a further twist to the ongoing debate concerning the complexity of the cognitive significance of gamma activity. All the more so because visual gamma oscillations have been implicated in the mediation of intricate cognitive mechanisms, such as object recognition (Tallon-Baudry and Bertrand, 1999), selective attention (Fell et al., 2003) and memory (Burgess and Ali, 2002).

More important, however, gamma oscillations are widely recognized as a likely mechanism for temporally integrating the numerous and varied features of a visual scene, a conundrum commonly referred to as "the binding problem" (Singer and Gray, 1995). The emergence of gamma synchrony as an integral component of perceptual binding has promising implications for understanding cognitive mechanisms and, in particular, for understanding the neuropathology of disorders with perceptual bases such as migraine visual aura and photosensitive epilepsy (PSE).

Gamma oscillatory power in the visual cortex is maximal in response to stimulus parameters that are conducive to paroxysmal responses from the visual cortex. For example, spatial frequencies around 3 cycles per degree (cpd) induce the highest gamma oscillatory power (figure 13.2a; Adjamian et al., 2004b) and are also found to be most effective in inducing visual illusions, headaches, and EEG abnormalities (Wilkins, 1995). Furthermore, the finding that high stimulus contrast at 3 cpd induces highest gamma oscillatory power (figure 13.2b; Hall et al., 2005) is consistent with the characteristics of stimuli most likely to provoke attacks of photosensitive epilepsy (Wilkins, 1995; Harding and Jeavons, 1994) (see plate 18).

The relationship between gamma and cortical hyperexcitability is further supported by the findings that changes in gamma activity coincide in duration with visual disturbance in migraine visual aura (Hall et al., 2004). Further support for the linkage between gamma and GABA has been

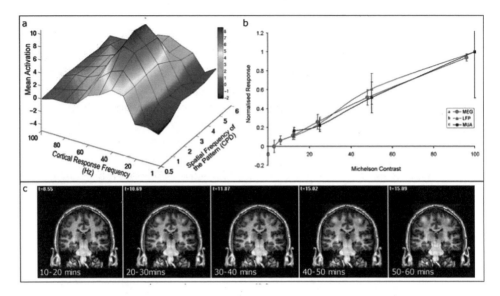

Figure 13.2
Visual gamma and pharmaco-MEG. Modulation of gamma oscillatory activity in the human visual cortex in response to visual stimulation, showing that peak oscillatory power is observed at 3 cpd (*a*) and 100 percent contrast (*b*) (Adjamian et al., 2004b, and Hall et al., 2005). Use of the pharmaco-MEG (*c*) to observe changes in beta (15–25 Hz) activity in the motor cortex over a 60-minute period following administration of diazepam. See plate 18 for color version.

provided by intracranial observations of gamma activity at the onset of epileptic seizure (Traub et al., 2001).

This hyperexcitability of neuronal activity is thought to be controlled by the GABAergic inhibitory mechanism (Meldrum and Wilkins, 1984). Indeed, the treatment of epilepsy is based on the premise that too much excitation through glutamergic systems, too little inhibition through GABAergic systems, or both are responsible for epileptic seizures. It is hypothesized that in patients with intact GABAergic systems, gamma activity may lead to visual abnormalities without clinical manifestation whereas in patients with a GABAergic defect gamma activity is a precursor to photoparoxysmal responses (Parra et al., 2003; Adjamian et al., 2004b).

Let us turn now to the neuromodeling approach, which has been used to artificially link neuronal networks of known properties to the oscillatory activity observed in magnetoencephalography. For example, Jensen, Hari, and Kaila, (2002) constructed a model network of 100 Hodgkin-Huxley type neurons to simulate the electrical activity of a visual cortex inhibitory network during stimulation; thereby demonstrating a link between the visual gamma oscillations previously discussed and GABAergic systems. In similar work, Jensen et al. (2005) used GABAergic benzodiazepine diazepam to modulate beta activity in the motor cortex and used a similar modeling approach, in which excitatory and inhibitory units were included. They discuss the relationship between real pharmacological modulation of the MEG signal and a simulated GABAergic motor cortex network. This approach demonstrates a crossover between the modeling and pharmaco-MEG approaches. A similar approach using beamformer based analysis (described in Singh, chapter 12, this volume) expands on the effect of diazepam on motor cortex beta activity.

Pharmaco-MEG

This emerging methodology affords observation of changes in intrinsic electrical activity, such as ongoing oscillations following administration of a drug. As previously discussed, Jensen et al. (2005) demonstrated a change in the oscillatory power of the beta (15–30 Hz) band in the motor cortex following administration of diazepam. A novel beamformer-based pharmaco-MEG approach called "synthetic aperture magnetometry" (SAM; see Hillebrand et al., 2005) was used to temporally define the changes in beta activity in the motor cortex following diazepam administration over a 1-hour period (figure 13.2c). Pharmaco-MEG provides the basis for a pharmacokinetic model of cortical chemistry through observed changes in intrinsic oscillatory activity Hall et al's. unpublished results demonstrate increases in beta synchronous power commensurate with the profile of diazepam, which reaches maximal availability at 45 minutes to 1 hour after administration.

Pharmaco-Cognitive MEG

An extension of pharmaco-MEG, this innovative approach takes an established cognitive task–related change in electrical activity and observes the modulation of this activity by altering the neurochemical environment, typically through administration of a neuroactive substrate, although modulation of the normal environment can be just as informative. For example, Kasai et al. (2002) used MEG to examine the effects of anxiolytics and hypnotics on the mismatch negativity (MMN) response in schizophrenics. Although they found no significant effects, their study represents yet another application of pharmaco-cognitive MEG to well-established cognitive experiments and cognitive deficits. Ahveninen et al. (2002) used a method of depleting the amino acid tryptophan, which results in a reduction in brain serotonin (5 HT) levels. They used MEG to determine the effects of reduced serotonin (a neurotransmitter) levels on specific forms of attention. Finally, related to the described neuromodeling and pharmaco-MEG research (Jensen et al., 2005; Hall et al, unpublished data), Haueisen et al. (2000), using MEG and the benzodiazepine lorazepam to investigate the somatosensory evoked response, demonstrated increased source strengths in both early evoked and high-frequency components following lorazepam uptake.

Pharmaco-fMRI

As observed using fMRI, the blood oxygenation level–dependent (BOLD) response is, per se, a reflection of intrinsic metabolic and therefore low-level chemical changes in the brain (For a more detailed description of the BOLD response, see Bandettini, chapter 9, this volume.) Unlike magnetoencephalography, however, functional magnetic resonance imaging infers a physiological change due to electrophysiological (neuronal) activity; as such, affords no direct information regarding the specific neurochemical mechanisms.

On the other hand, by using established observations of spatially discrete, task-dependent changes in cortical activity of cognitive significance, pharmaco-fMRI examines the effect of specific pharmacological agents on this activity (figure 13.1b). This innovative approach can be extended to conditions of neurological or cognitive deficit to examine the effects specific medications or to determine underlying chemical mediators of disease. Although, as discussed under " Limitations," the approach has its drawbacks, pharmaco-fMRI has been used with some degree of success in cognitive investigations. For example, Del Ben et al. (forthcoming), used fMRI and the selective serotonin reuptake inhibitor (SSRI) citalopram to examine the involvement of serotonin in neurological disorders such as depression and anxiety, found evidence of task-specific serotonergic modulation of psychiatric processes. When Horacek et al. (2005) monitored the hemodynamic response in individuals to the Stroop task and then modulated serum concentrations of tryptophan (the precursor to serononin), they observed subsequent modulations in the BOLD response to the same task. Finding that depletion increased activation in bilateral mediofrontal cortex, they have postulated that serotonergic medial forebrain pathways play a role in the activity of cortical structures involved in Stroop-type processing.

Multimodal Investigation

As discussed at the beginning of this chapter, the technological advances in functional imaging, particularly over the past decade, have resulted in a complement of neuroinvestigative modalities with greater range and accuracy than could be previously contemplated. As attested by the studies described in the previous sections, these modalities have been applied to the extent of their abilities in the pursuit of neuroscientific gain. As a consequence, it is now apparent that the way forward is to integrate these modalities to exploit their collective gain. Therefore, without intending to diminish the importance of the innovative approaches discussed above, we consider multimodal investigation, whose emerging importance in elucidating the larger picture of cognition is already abundantly clear, to be the most promising innovative approach to the chemistry of cognition.

The integration of various modalities has already been instigated in a number of pharmacoimaging studies. Because the modalities are themselves constantly evolving, however, the potential for scientific gain from multimodal approaches to the chemistry of cognition appears limitless. The principal obstacles to realizing this potential lie in the need to combine the data from modalities into a comprehensive framework and to create a spatially accurate method of transfer between modalities, discussed briefly under "Integration" (for a review of the issues on integrating various data, see Horwitz and Poeppel, 2002).

These obstacles can be overcome and, indeed, various studies have done so, at least in part. Thus, when Northoff et al. (2002) combined fMRI and MEG to investigate the role of lorazepam in emotional processing, they found that $GABA_A$ receptors modulate negative emotional processing in the orbitofrontal cortex independently of the effects on cortical motor function. When Nishitani (2003) combined MEG and MRS in a study that used pleasant and unpleasant stimuli to investigate the corresponding electrophysiological and chemical changes, compared to the baseline, he found clear evidence of event-related synchronization (ERS) and modulation of creatine and choline ratios when compared to the control. In his discussion of the potential gains of physiological and chemical integrative strategies, Morris (2002) explores the view that integration of fMRI, MRS, and MEG provides an ultimate picture of the associated changes in electrophysiological response in the brain, enabling researchers both to observe relative changes in blood supply and glucose metabolism with fine temporal accuracy and to achieve a relative quantification of the neurotransmitter concentrations.

In a clinical application of multimodal pharmacoimaging, Shih et al. (2004) found lower N-acetyl aspartate (NAA) and choline ratios in the MEG-localized "spike zone," when compared to contralateral regions in a cohort of patients with temporal lobe epilepsy. We may expect further progress in this type of work as pharmaco-MEG measures are integrated with MRS chemical measures in the exploration of oscillatory change, effectively combining the "virtual electrode" (Hillebrand et al., 2005) with the "virtual biopsy."

These multimodal studies represent just some of the steps taken toward a fully integrated strategy for examining brain function. They have paved the way for integrating PET, MRS, MEG, and fMRI with other modalities and disciplines such as transcranial magnetic stimulatior electroencephalography, psychophysics, and genetics, facilitating the exchange of information between human and animal studies.

Limitations

There are a number of factors that limit the ability of researchers using the neuroimaging techniques discussed in this chapter to reveal the neurochemistry of the underlying cortex. Two principal limitations shared by all the techniques are (1) they are expensive to acquire; and (2) they require a high level of aptitude to operate, particularly in the practices described.

Positron Emission Tomography

Because it typically involves the intravenous injection of a radioactive tracer, PET is considered to be a relatively invasive and risky functional imaging technique. Its use in healthy participants thus requires greater consideration than most other imaging modalities. Furthermore, due to the radioactive nature of the tracer, PET experimenters face restrictions on dosage and repetition frequency. And because typical PET tracers have relatively short half-lives, PET experiments must also be of short duration, with the sequence of tracer administration and acquisition being a crucial factor.

The creation of specific PET ligands requires special facilities and expertise, as do the administration and disposal of the PET tracer. Consequently, the cost per subject of PET experiments is relatively high. Moreover, the technique's relatively low spatial resolution gives rise to blurry images, with precise areas of activity difficult to determine. Nevertheless, these limitations are more than offset by PET's neurochemical mapping specificity.

Magnetic Resonance Spectroscopy

Limitations of this technique revolve around its ability to detect specific metabolites, with each receiver coil having its own range of detectable chemicals. This applies not only to ^{1}H MRS, discussed in this chapter, but to all other types of MRS as well. As we have noted, metabolites must be present in sufficient concentrations in order to be detected above the neurochemical noise level, a particular concern for functional MRS. Irrespective of their concentration, however, the chemical structure of some compounds, for example, choline compounds inside cell membranes, makes them invisible to MRS. Moreover, the MRS signal is affected by physical factors such as the echo time, repetition time, number of averages, voxel size, and field homogeneity (referred to as the "shim"). The medium itself also affects MRS spectra: gray matter and white matter have different metabolite ratios. More important, certain MRS voxels exclude skull or cerebrospinal fluid because these contain lipid and lactate, respectively (for details on these limitations, see Danielsen and Ross, 1999).

Magnetoencephalography

As noted above, pharmaco-MEG observes neurochemical changes following administration of a particular drug and makes inferences about the underlying changes in neuronal function and activity. (For a thorough discussion of MEG's technical considerations, see Singh, chapter 12, this volume.) The technique's limitations revolve around a central assumption, that the observed activity is a direct result of the agonistic or antagonistic properties of the administered drug. This appears to be a reasonably solid assumption, particularly, for drugs in which the receptor interaction is known. Because of the complex network interactions involved in brain function, however, the proportion of the response that arises from a primary target neuronal population is ambiguous. Essentially, although we can be sure that the primary target is a contributing factor, we cannot be sure of the effect of this change on other neuronal populations. Furthermore, although pharmaco-MEG shows great promise for drug development and investigation, the application of a novel drug entails a wide range of unknowns, specifically, with regard to the drug's effect on the primary target and on any secondary messengers involved. These limitations can be overcome to a great degree, however, by observing concurrent changes in chemical composition or effect with the integrative approaches discussed above.

The limitations of neuromodeling using MEG revolve around the nature of the neuronal populations being modeled. The proportions of neurons mediated by various neurotransmitters in the brain are vastly uneven. Although all types and subtypes of neurons play an undoubtedly important and integral role in brain function, the proportions of some neurons (e.g., glutamergic) are far greater than others (e.g., serotonergic). Moreover, because the brain works on the basis of neuronal network communication, even though we may safely assume that a network of neurons gives rise to an observed magnetic field, it is highly unlikely that any single neuronal type within that network gives rise to an observed signal.

Functional Magnetic Resonance Imaging

A principal limitation of pharmaco-fMRI is the unknown effect of a drug on a neuronal network, given the lack of temporal or spectral information. Although most networks are gathered within reasonably small areas, the technique assumes, without clear justification, that any observed regional effect is the result of a single network. For a magnetic resonance signal to be observed within a given neuronal population, a significant number of neurons must be activated; likewise, for a specific drug effect to be observed, a significant number of the same target neuron type within that population must be located within a particular cortical density. Although this is unlikely to present a problem for networks of GABAergic neurons, say, for neurons of lesser abundance, it limits the observable effect. The greatest problem facing pharmaco-fMRI, however, is that fMRI measures vasculature-related changes and that many of the drugs of interest have secondary vasoactive effects, often potent such effects, for example, serotonergic agonists and antagonists. Indeed, such interference with the central measurement mechanism of fMRI makes the interpretation of pharmaco-fMRI data studies rather difficult, to say the least (Salmeron and Stein, 2002). This problem is compounded by the fact that receptor densities in the vasculature show high regional variability.

Integration

It is clear from this and previous chapters on various neuroimaging modalities that each modality offers a different type of information regarding brain function. It is therefore clearly advantageous to combine these modalities in any research or clinical neuroimaging study. As previously mentioned, such integration requires a localization strategy whereby the two (or more) sets of data are transformed into a single coordinate system, a procedure referred to as "coregistration." The integration of fMRI and MRS is a relatively trivial matter because both modalities rely on a structural MRI volume, which can be obtained with little difficulty using the same hardware. On the other hand, the integration of fMRI or MRS with non-MR modalities is anything but trivial, particularly in clinical applications, such as presurgical mapping. A number of coregistration methods have been proposed using fixed markers (Fitzpatrick, West, and Maurer, 1998) and fiducial points based on anatomical landmarks that are first identified in both modalities and then aligned (George et al., 1989). Other methods are based on matching a set of head points obtained from the segmented scalp of a subject's MRI to another set of points obtained by running a digitizing pen to obtain the subject's head shape in the MEG coordinate system (Pelizzari et al., 1989). For integration of MEG and MRI, a successful method is based on anatomical fiducial markers identified in the MEG coordinate system, which are then coregistered with the MR image using a surface-matching procedure (Singh et al., 1997; Adjamian et al., 2004a).

Integration also requires that the different data types be converted into a coherent and informative format. Because the actual combination of data types and information often proves difficult, if not problematic, and because there are no standard approaches, this task is, in general, tackled by each institution individually (see Horwitz and Poeppel, 2002).

Conclusion

This chapter has provided an overview of some of the neuroimaging modalities that can be used to investigate the chemistry of cognition. We have discussed a corner of the broad field of neuroimaging and -recording approaches, the functional imaging domain, summarizing the experimental approaches illustrated by selected studies. Furthermore, we have discussed the integration of these and other modalities, which we believe hold the key to better understanding brain function in both health and disease. In overcoming the obstacles posed by integration, we can capitalize on the fact that multimodal imaging yields more than the sum of its parts.

Acknowledgments

We would like to thank the Dr Hadwen Trust and Lord Dowding Fund for supporting the MEG and MRI Laboratory work shown in figure 13.2.

References

Aalto, S., Bruck, A., Laine, M., Nagren, K., and Rinne, J. O. (2005). Frontal and temporal dopamine release during working memory and attention tasks in healthy humans: A positron emission tomography study using the high-affinity dopamine D2 receptor ligand [11C]FLB 457. *Journal of Neuroscience, 25,* 2471–2477.

Adjamian, P., Barnes, G. R., Hillebrand, A., Holliday, I. E., Singh, K. D., Furlong, P. L., Harrington, E., Barclay, C. W., and Route, P. J. (2004a). Co-registration of magnetoencephalography with magnetic resonance imaging using bite-bar-based fiducials and surface-matching. *Clinical Neurophysiology, 115,* 691–698.

Adjamian, P., Holliday, I. E., Barnes, G. R., Hillebrand, A., Hadjipapas, A., and Singh, K. D. (2004b). Induced visual illusions and gamma oscillations in human primary visual cortex. *European Journal of Neuroscience, 20,* 587–592.

Ahveninen, J., Kuhkonen, S., Pennanen, S., Liesivuori, J., Ilmoncemi, R. J., and Jaaskelainen, I. P. (2002). Tryptophan depletion effects on EEG and MEG responses suggest seroterrogic modulation of auditory involuntary attention in humans. *Neuroimage, 16,* 1052–1061.

Auer, D. P., Putz, B., Kraft, E., Lipinski, B., Schill, J., and Holsboer, F. (2000). Reduced glutamate in the anterior cingulate cortex in depression: An in-vivo proton magnetic resonance spectroscopy study. *Biological Psychiatry, 47,* 305–313.

Brandao, L. (2004). *MR spectroscopy of the brain.* Philadelphia: Lippincott Williams and Wilkins.

Buchanan, J. M. (2002). Biochemistry during the life and times of Hans Krebs and Fritz Lipmann. *Journal of Biological Chemistry, 277,* 33531–33536.

Burgess, A. P., and Ali, L. (2002). Functional connectivity of gamma EEG activity is modulated at low frequency during conscious recollection. *International Journal of Psychophysiology, 46,* 91–100.

Chugani, D. C., Sundram, B. S., Behen, M., Lee, M. L., and Moore, G. J. (1999). Evidence of altered energy metabolism in autistic children. *Progress in Neuropsychopharmacology and Biological Psychiatry, 23,* 635–641.

Cunningham, V. J., Gunn, R. N., and Matthews, J. C. (2004). Quantification in positron emission tomography for research in pharmacology and drug development. *Nuclear Medicine Communications, 25,* 643–646.

Danielsen, E. R., and Ross, B. (1999). *Magnetic resonance spectroscopy diagnosis of neurological diseases.* New York: Marcel Dekker.

Del-Ben, C. M., Deakin, J. F., McKie, S., Delvai, N. A., Williams, S. R., Elliott, R., Dolan, M., and Anderson, I. M. (forthcoming). The effect of citalopram pretreatment on neuronal responses to neuropsychological tasks in normal volunteers: An fMRI study. *Neuropsychopharmacology.*

Dolan, R. J., Fletcher, P., Frith, C. D., Friston, K. J., Frackowiak, R. S., and Grasby, P. M. (1995). Dopaminergic modulation of impaired cognitive activation in the anterior cingulate cortex in schizophrenia. *Nature, 378,* 180–182.

Eckhorn, R., Bauer, R., Jordan, W., Brosch, M., Kruse, W., Munk, M., and Reitboeck, H. J. (1988). Coherent oscillations: A mechanism of feature linking in the visual cortex? Multiple electrode and correlation analyses in the cat. *Biological Cybernetics*, *60*, 121–130.

Fell, J., Fernandez, G., Klaver, P., Elger, C. E., and Fries, P. (2003). Is synchronized neuronal gamma activity relevant for selective attention? *Brain Research: Brain Research Reviews*, *42*, 265–272.

Fitzpatrick, J. M., West, J. B., and Maurer, C. R. (1998). Predicting error in rigid-body point-based registration. *IEEE Transactions on Medical Imaging*, *17*, 694–702.

Frackowiak, R. S. (1989). PET: Studies in dementia. *Psychiatry Research*, *29*, 353–355.

Fukuzako, H., Kodama, S., Fukuzako, T., Yamada, K., Doi, W., Sato, D., and Takigawa, M. (1999). Subtype-associated metabolite differences in the temporal lobe in schizophrenia detected by proton magnetic resonance spectroscopy. *Psychiatry Research*, *92*, 45–56.

George, J. S., Jackson, P. S., Ranken, D. M., and Flynn, E. R. (1989). Three-dimensional volumetric reconstruction for neuromagnetic source localization. In S. J. Williamson, M. Hoke, G. Stroink, and M. Kotani (Eds.), *Advances in biomagnetism*. New York: Plenum Press.

Goff, D. C., Hennen, J., Lyoo, I. K., Tsai, G., Wald, L. L., Evins, A. E., Yurgelun-Todd, D. A., and Renshaw, P. F. (2002). Modulation of brain and serum glutamatergic concentrations following a switch from conventional neuroleptics to olanzapine. *Biological Psychiatry*, *51*, 493–497.

Gray, C. M., König, P., Engel, A. K., and Singer, W. (1989). Oscillatory responses in cat visual cortex exhibit intercolumnar synchronization which reflects global stimulus properties. *Nature*, *338*, 334–337.

Gray, C. M., and McCormick D. A. (1996). Chattering cells: Superficial pyramidal neurons contributing to the generation of synchronous oscillations in the visual cortex. *Science*, *274*, 109–113.

Hall, S. D., Barnes, G. R., Hillebrand, A., Furlong, P. L., Singh, K. D., and Holliday, I. E. (2004). Spatio-temporal imaging of cortical desynchronization in migraine visual aura: a magnetoencephalography case study. *Headache*, *44*, 204–208.

Hall, S. D., Holliday, I. E., Hillebrand, A., Singh, K. D., Furlong, P. L., Hadjipapas, A., and Barnes, G. R. (2005). The missing link: Analogous human and primate cortical gamma oscillations. *NeuroImage*, *26*, 13–17.

Harding, F. A., and Jeavons, P. M. (1994). *Photosensitive epilepsy*. New ed. Suffolk, England: Lavenham Press.

Haueisen, J., Heuer, T., Nowak, H., Liepert, J., Weiller, C., Okada, Y., and Curio, G. (2000). The influence of lorazepam on somatosensory-evoked fast frequency (600 Hz) activity in MEG. *Brain Research*, *874*, 10–14.

Häusser, M. (2000). The Hodgkin-Huxley theory of the action potential. *Nature Neuroscience*, *3*, Suppl. 1165.

Herholz, K. (2003). PET studies in dementia. *Annals of Nuclear Medicine*, *17*, 79–89.

Hillebrand, A., Singh, K. D., Holliday, I. E., Furlong, P. L., and Barnes, G. R. (2005). A new approach to neuroimaging with magnetoencephalography. *Human Brain Mapping*, *25*, 199–211.

Horacek, J., Zavesicka, L., Tintera, J., Dockery, C., Platilova, V., Kopecek, M., Spaniel, F., Bubenikova, V., and Hoschl, C. (2005). The effect of tryptophan depletion on brain activation measured by functional magnetic resonance imaging during the Stroop test in healthy subjects. *Physiological Research*, *54*, 235–244.

Horwitz, B., and Poeppel, D. (2002). How can EEG/MEG and fMRI/PET data be combined? *Human Brain Mapping*, *17*, 1–3.

Jacobs, A. H., Li, H., Winkeler, A., Hilker, R., Knoess, C., Ruger, A., Galldiks, N., Schaller, B., Sobesky, J., Kracht, L., Monfared, P., Klein, M., Vollmar, S., Bauer, B., Wagner, R., Graf, R., Wienhard, K., Herholz, K., and Heiss, W. D. (2003). PET-based molecular imaging in neuroscience. *European Journal of Nuclear Medicine and Molecular Imaging*, *30*, 1051–1065.

Jagust, W. (2004). Molecular neuroimaging in Alzheimer's disease. *NeuroRx*, *1*, 206–212.

Jensen, O., Hari, R., and Kaila, K. (2002). Visually evoked gamma responses in the human brain are enhanced during voluntary hyperventilation, *NeuroImage*, *15*, 575–586.

Jensen, O., Goel, O., Kopell, N., Pohja, M., Hari, R., and Ermentrout, B. (2005). On the human sensorimotor-cortex rhythm: Sources and modeling, *NeuroImage*, *26*, 347–355.

Kasai, K., Nakagome, K., Hoh, K., Koshida, I., Hata, A., Iwanami, A., Fokuda, M., and Kato, N. (2002). Impaired Cortical network for preattentive detection of change in speech sounds in schizophrenia: A high resolution event-related potential study. *American Journal of Psychiatry*, *159*, 546–553.

Keshavan, M. S., Kapur, S., and Pettegrew, J. W. (1991). Magnetic resonance spectroscopy in psychiatry: Potential, pitfalls, and promise. *American Journal of Psychiatry*, *148*, 976–985.

Kreiter, A. K., and Singer, W. (1996). Stimulus-dependent synchronization of neuronal responses in the visual cortex of the awake macaque monkey. *Journal of Neuroscience*, *16*, 2381–2396.

Kresge, N., Simoni, R. D., and Hill, R. L. (2005). Otto Fritz Meyerhof and the elucidation of the glycolytic pathway. *Journal of Biological Chemistry*, *28*, 280.

Lenkinski, R. E. (1989). Clinical magnetic resonance spectroscopy: A critical evaluation. *Investigative Radiology*, *24*, 1034–1038.

Lenkinski, R. E. (2001). MR spectroscopy: Clinical tool or research probe? (revisited). *Academic Radiology*, *8*, 567–570.

Lestage, P. (2000). Pharmacologic treatment for cognitive disorders: An update. *Thérapie*, *55*, 507–512.

Liddle, P. F. (2000). Cognitive impairment in schizophrenia: Its impact on social functioning. *Acta Psychiatrica Scandinavica*, *400*, 11–16.

Logothetis, N. K., Pauls, J., Augath, M., Trinath, T., and Oeltermann, A. (2001). Neurophysiological investigation of the basis of the fMRI signal. *Nature*, *412*, 150–157.

Lutzenberger, W., Pulvermuller, F., Elbert, T., and Birbaumer, N. (1995). Visual stimulation alters local 40-Hz responses in humans: An EEG study. *Neuroscience Letters*, *183*, 39–42.

Macri, M. A., Garreffa, G., Giove, F., Ambrosini, A., Guardati, M., Pierelli, F., Schoenen, J., Colonnese, C., and Maraviglia, B. (2003). Cerebellar metabolite alterations detected in-vivo by proton MR spectroscopy. *Magnetic Resonance Imaging*, *21*, 1201–1206.

Meldrum, B. S., and Wilkins, A. J. (1984). Photosensitive epilepsy: Integration of pharmacological and psychophysical evidence. In P. Schwatzkroin and H. V. Wheal (Eds.), *Electrophysiology of epilepsy*. London: Academic Press.

Mielke, R., Hilker, R., Weber-Luxenburger, G., Kessler, J., and Heiss, W. D. (1998). Early-onset cerebellar ataxia (EOCA) with retained reflexes: Reduced cerebellar benzodiazepine-receptor binding, progressive metabolic and cognitive impairment. *Movement Disorders*, *13*, 739–745.

Morris, P. G. (2002). Synaptic and cellular events: The last frontier? *European Neuropsychopharmacology*, *12*, 601–607.

Muller, M. M., Bosch, J., Elbert, T., Kreiter, A., Sosa, M. V., Sosa, P. V., and Rockstroh, B. (1996). Visually induced gamma-band responses in human electroencephalographic activity: A link to animal studies. *Experimental Brain Research*, *112*, 96–102.

Muller, M. M., Junghofer, M., Elbert, T., and Rochstroh, B. (1997). Visually induced gamma-band responses to coherent and incoherent motion: A replication study. *NeuroReport*, *8*, 2575–2579.

Murphy-Boesch, J., Srinivasan, R., Carvajal, L., and Brown, T. R. (1994). Two configurations of the four-ring birdcage coil for 1H imaging and 1H-decoupled 31P spectroscopy of the human head. *Journal of Magnetic Resonance*, *B103*, 103–114.

Nishitani, N. (2003). Dynamics of cognitive processing in the human hippocampus by neuromagnetic and neurochemical assessments. *NeuroImage*, *20*, 561–571.

Northoff, G., Witzel, T., Richter, A., Gessner, M., Schlagenhauf, F., Fell, J., Baumgart, F., Kaulisch, T., Tempelmann, C., Heinzel, A., Kotter, R., Hagner, T., Bargel, B., Hinrichs, H., Bogerts, B., Scheich, H., and Heinze, H. J. (2002). GABA-ergic modulation of prefrontal spatio-temporal activation pattern during emotional processing: A combined fMRI/MEG study with placebo and lorazepam. *Journal of Cognitive Neuroscience, 14*, 348–370.

Parra, J., Kalitzin, S. N., Iriarte, J., Blanes, W., Velis, D. N., and Lopes da Silva, F. H. (2003). Gamma-band phase clustering and photosensitivity: Is there an underlying mechanism common to photosensitive epilepsy and visual perception? *Brain, 126*, 1164–1172.

Pelizzari, C. A., Chen, G. T., Spelbring, D. R., Weichselbaum, R. R., and Chen, C. T. (1989). Accurate three-dimensional registration of CT, PET, and/or MMR images of the brain. *Journal of Computer Assisted Tomography, 13*, 20–26.

Perkins, A. C., and Frier, M. (2004). Radionuclide imaging in drug development. *Current Pharmaceutical Design, 10*, 2907–2921.

Pfleiderer, B., Ohrmann, P., Suslow, T., Wolgast, M., Gerlach, A. L., Heindel, W., and Michael, N. (2004). N-acetylaspartate levels of left frontal cortex are associated with verbal intelligence in women but not in men: A proton magnetic resonance spectroscopy study. *Neuroscience, 123*, 1053–1058.

Pietz, J., Lutz, T., Zwygart, K., Hoffmann, G. F., Ebinger, F., Boesch, C., and Kreis, R. (2003). Phenylalanine can be detected in brain tissue of healthy subjects by ^{1}H magnetic resonance spectroscopy. *Journal of Inherited Metabolic Disease, 26*, 683–692.

Port, R. E., and Wolf, W. (2003). Noninvasive methods to study drug distribution. *Investigational New Drugs, 21*, 157–168.

Prichard, J., Rothman, D., Novotny, E., Petroff, O., Kuwabara, T., Avison, M., Howseman, A., Hanstock, C., and Shulman, R. (1991). Lactate rise detected by ^{1}H NMR in human visual cortex during physiologic stimulation. *Proceedings of the National Academy of Sciences, USA, 88*, 5829–5831.

Rae, C., Lee, M. A., Dixon, R. M., Blamire, A. M., Thompson, C. H., Styles, P., Talcott, J., Richardson, A. J., and Stein, J. F. (1998). Metabolic abnormalities in developmental dyslexia detected by 1H magnetic resonance spectroscopy. *Lancet, 351*, 1849–1852.

Ross, A. J., Sachdev, P. S., Wen, W., Valenzuela, M. J., and Brodaty, H. (2005). 1H MRS in stroke patients with and without cognitive impairment. *Neurobiolical Aging, 26*, 873–882.

Salmeron, B. J., and Stein, E. A. (2002). Pharmacological applications of magnetic resonance imaging. *Psychopharmacology Bulletin, 36*, 102–129.

Sappey-Marinier, D., Calabrese, G., Fein, G., Hugg, J. W., Biggins, C., and Weiner, M. W. (1992). Effect of photic stimulation on human visual cortex lactate and phosphates using 1H and 31P magnetic resonance spectroscopy. *Journal of Cerebral Blood Flow and Metabolism, 12*, 584–592.

Shih, J. J., Weisend, M. P., Lewine, J., Sanders, J., Dermon, J., and Lee, R. (2004). Areas of interictal spiking are associated with metabolic dysfunction in MRI-negative temporal lobe epilepsy. *Epilepsia, 45*, 223–229.

e

Simpson, H. B., Lombardo, I., Slifstein, M., Huang, H. Y., Hwang, D. R., Abi-Dargham, A., Liebowitz, M. R., and Laruelle, M. (2003). Serotonin transporters in obsessive-compulsive disorder: A positron emission tomography study with [(11)C]McN 5652. *Biological Psychiatry*, 54, 1414–1421.

Singer, W., and Gray, C. M. (1995). Visual feature integration and the temporal correlation hypothesis. *Annual Review of Neuroscience*, 18, 555–586.

Singh, K. D., Holliday, I. E., Furlong, P. L., and Harding, G. F. (1997). Evaluation of MRI-MEG/EEG coregistration strategies using Monte-Carlo simulation. *Electroencephalography and Clinical Neurophysiology*, 102, 81–85.

Sun, L., Jin, Z., Zhang, Y., Zeng, Y., Liu, G., Li, Y., Seidman, L., Faraone, S. V., and Wang, Y. (forthcoming). Differences between attention-deficit disorder with and without hyperactivity: A 1H-magnetic resonance spectroscopy study. *Brain and Development*.

Tallon-Baudry, C., and Bertrand, O. (1999). Oscillatory gamma activity in humans and its role in object representation. *Trends in Cognitive Sciences*, 3, 151–162.

Toczek, M. T., Carson, R. E., Lang, L., Ma, Y., Spanaki, M. V., Der, M. G., Fazilat, S., Kopylev, L., Herscovitch, P., Eckelman, W. C., and Theodore, W. H. (2003). PET imaging of 5-HT1A receptor binding in patients with temporal lobe epilepsy. *Neurology*, 60, 749–756.

Traub, R. D., Whittington, M. A., Buhl, E. H., LeBeau, F. E., Bibbig, A., Boyd, S., Cross, H., and Baldeweg, T. (2001). A possible role for gap junctions in generation of very fast EEG oscillations preceding the onset of, and perhaps initiating, seizures. *Epilepsia*, 42, 153–170.

Valeustein, E. S. (2002). The discovery of chemical neurotransmitters. *Brain and Cognition*, 49, 79–95.

Van Heertum, R. L., Greenstein, E. A., and Tikofsky, R. S. (2004). 2-deoxy-fluorglucose-positron emission tomography imaging of the brain: Current clinical applications with emphasis on the dementias. *Seminars in Nuclear Medicine*, 34, 300–312.

Weber, O. M., Verhagen, A., Duc, C. O., Meier, D., Leenders, K. L., and Boesiger, P. (1999). Effects of vigabatrin intake on brain GABA activity as monitored by spectrally edited magnetic resonance spectroscopy and positron emission tomography. *Magnetic Resonance Imaging*, 17, 417–425.

Wilkins, A. J. (1995). *Visual stress*. Oxford: Oxford University Press.

Contributors

Peyman Adjamian
Neurosciences Research Institute, Aston University, Birmingham, UK

Peter A. Bandettini
Laboratory of Brain and Cognition and Functional Magnetic Resonance Imaging Core Facility, National Institutes of Mental Health, NIH, USA

Mark Baxter
Department of Experimental Psychology, Oxford University, UK

Antoine Bechara
Department of Neuroscience, University of Iowa, USA

Anthony S. David
Institute of Psychiatry and Guy's, Kings, and St. Thomas' School of Medicine, London

James Dobson
The fMRI Data Center, Dartmouth College, USA

Ian Foster
Distributed Systems Laboratory, University of Chicago and Argonne National Laboratory, USA

Michael Gazzaniga
Dartmouth Center for Cognitive Neuroscience, Dartmouth College, USA

Stephen D. Hall
Neurosciences Research Institute, Aston University, Birmingham, UK

Dietmar G. Heinke
Behavioural Brain Sciences, University of Birmingham, UK

John M. Henderson
Department of Psychology and Cognitive Science Program Michigan State University, USA

Glyn W. Humphreys
Behavioural Brain Sciences, University of Birmingham, UK

Venkata Mattay
Genes, Cognition and Psychosis Program, National Institute of Mental Health, NIH, USA

Andreas Meyer-Lindenberg
Genes, Cognition and Psychosis Program, National Institute of Mental Health, NIH, USA

Elisabeth A. Murray
Laboratory of Neuropsychology, National Institute of Mental Health, NIH, USA

Nasir H. Naqvi
Department of Neuroscience, University of Iowa, USA

Gina Rippon
Neurosciences Research Institute, Aston University, Birmingham, UK

Tamara Russell
Neurosciences Institute for Research in Schizophrenia and Allied Disorders and Macquarie Center for Cognitive Science, Sydney

Carl Senior
Neurosciences Research Institute, Aston University, Birmingham, UK

Philip Shaw
Genes, Cognition and Psychosis Program, National Institute of Mental Health, NIH, USA

Krish D. Singh
Neurosciences Research Institute, Aston University, Birmingham, UK

Marc A. Sommer
Department of Neuroscience and Center for the Neural Basis of Cognition, University of Pittsburgh, USA

Lauren Stewart
Institute of Cognitive Neuroscience, University College London, UK

John D. Van Horn
The fMRI Data Center, Dartmouth College, USA

Jens Voeckler
Distributed Systems Laboratory, University of Chicago, USA

Vincent Walsh
Institute of Cognitive Neuroscience, University College London, UK

Daniel R. Weinberger
Genes, Cognition and Psychosis Program, National Institute of Mental Health, NIH, USA

Michael Wilde
Distributed Systems Laboratory, University of Chicago and Argonne National Laboratory, USA

Jeffrey Woodward
The fMRI Data Center, Dartmouth College, USA

Robert H. Wurtz
Laboratory of Sensorimotor Research, National Eye Institute, NIH, USA

Eun Young Yoon
Behavioural Brain Sciences, University of Birmingham, UK

Yong Zhao
Distributed Systems Laboratory, University of Chicago, USA

Index